Uprootings/Regroundings

Uprootings/Regroundings

Questions of Home and Migration

Edited by
**Sara Ahmed, Claudia Castañeda,
Anne-Marie Fortier and Mimi Sheller**

Oxford • New York

First published in 2003 by
Berg
Editorial offices:
1st Floor, Angel Court, 81 St Clements St, Oxford OX4 1AW, UK
838 Broadway, Third Floor, New York, NY 10003–4812, USA

Berg is the imprint of Oxford International Publishers Ltd.

Library of Congress Cataloging-in-Publication Data

A catalogue record for this book is available from the Library of Congress.

British Library Cataloguing-in-Publication Data

A catalogue record for this book is available from the British Library.

ISBN 1 85973 624 6 (Cloth)
1 85973 629 7 (Paper)

Typeset by JS Typesetting Ltd, Wellingborough, Northants.
Printed in the United Kingdom by Biddles Ltd, Guildford and King's Lynn.

www.bergpublishers.com

Contents

Contents

List of Figures

Acknowledgements

We would like to thank all of the speakers and participants in the Uprootings/Regroundings Seminar Series and Dayschool held at Lancaster University in 2000, with funding from the Faculty of Social Sciences. We also extend special thanks to all of our colleagues and students in the Institute for Women's Studies and the Department of Sociology at Lancaster University, who have supported our work and created the environment in which our collaboration has been possible.

All photographs are reproduced courtesy of the artists, to whom we are very grateful. The following articles are reproduced by permission of the publishers:

Gayatri Gopinath (1997), 'Nostalgia, Desire, Diaspora: South Asian Sexualities in Motion', in *Positions*, 5(2): 467–89. Copyright, 1997, Duke University Press. All rights reserved. Used by permission of the publisher.

Kaplan, C. (2002), 'Transporting the Subject: Technologies of Mobility and Location in an Era of Globalization'. Reprinted by permission of the Modern Language Association of America from *PMLA* (January 2002).

Verstraete, G. (2001), 'Technological Frontiers and the Politics of Mobilities', from the *Mobilities* issue, *New Formations*, 43. Copyright Lawrence and Wishart, London, Spring 2001. Used by permission of the publisher.

Notes on Contributors

Sara Ahmed is a Reader in Women's Studies at Lancaster University and was Director of the Institute for Women's Studies between 2000 and 2003. Her research interests include feminist and post-colonial theory, and her recent publications include: *Differences that matter: Feminist Theory and Postmodernism* (1998); *Strange Encounters: Embodied Others in Post-Coloniality* (2000); *Transformations: Thinking Through Feminism* (2000) and *Thinking Through the Skin* (2001). She is currently working on a book entitled *The Cultural Politics of Emotion* (Edinburgh University Press, forthcoming).

Rutvica Andrijasevic is a PhD candidate at Netherlands Research School of Women's Studies at Utrecht University, where she is currently completing her doctoral thesis on the topic of 'trafficking' in women in Europe. After studying African American Literature at Trieste and Bologna Universities, she completed with honours her second MA in Gender Studies at the Central European University in Budapest. The key issues of migration, gender, race and borders are common threads throughout her work. She has published in Italian journals *Leggendaria* (2000) and *Derive Approdi* (2002), and the French journal *Multitudes* (2003). She is a member of the NextGENDERation network.

Gannit Ankori is a lecturer at the department of art history, Hebrew University, Jerusalem. She has published several articles and a book – *Imaging Her Selves: Frida Kahlo's Poetics of Identity and Fragmentation* (Greenwood Press 2002) – on the art of Frida Kahlo, and is guest curator of a Kahlo exhibition at the Jewish Museum in New York (September 2003–January 2004). Her recently completed book *Dis-Orientalism: Palestinian Artists Between East and West* is scheduled for publication next year. Dr Ankori has published numerous articles in English, Hebrew, Arabic, German and French on a wide variety of topics related to visual manifestations of individual and collective aspects of identity, emphasizing gender, hybridity and nationalism in contemporary art. She is currently engaged in two major research projects: 'The Poetics and Politics of the Body in Art' and 'Trauma and the Visual Arts'.

Claudia Castañeda is lecturer in Women's Studies at Lancaster University. She is the author of *Figurations: Child, Bodies, Worlds* (Duke University Press 2002). Her work is situated at the junction of feminist, postcolonial, cultural and science and technology studies; it has appeared in journals – including *Feminist Theory* and *Science as Culture* – and anthologies – including Van Loon (ed.), *Positioning Risk* (Sage 2000), and Ahmed and Stacey (eds), *Thinking Through the Skin* (Routledge 2001).

Anne-Marie Fortier is lecturer in the Sociology department at Lancaster University. She is the author of *Migrant Belongings: Memory, Space, Identity* (Berg 2000). Her work on migrant belongings, home and the intersections of gender/sexuality/ethnicity has appeared in several anthologies and journals, including *Theory, Culture & Society*, *Diaspora* and the *European Journal of Cultural Studies*. She is co-editor (with Sara Ahmed) of a forthcoming issue on 'Re-Imagining Communities' of the *International Journal of Cultural Studies*. Her current project is called *Multicultural Horizons: Community, Diversity and the 'New Britain'*.

Irene Gedalof is senior lecturer in Women's Studies at London Metropolitan University. She is the author of *Against Purity: Rethinking Identity with Indian and Western Feminisms* (Routledge 1999) and has published articles in the *European Journal of Women's Studies*, *Women's Philosophy Review* and *Women: A Cultural Review*. Her current research interests include Foucauldian feminist approaches to politics and questions of home and belonging in relation to refugee women.

Gayatri Gopinath is Assistant Professor of Women and Gender Studies at the University of California, Davis. Her work on gender and sexuality in the South Asian diaspora has appeared in numerous anthologies and journals, including *GLQ, Positions* and *Diaspora*. She is currently completing a book manuscript entitled *Impossible Subjects: Queer Diasporas and South Asian Public Cultures*, forthcoming from Duke University Press.

Breda Gray is Senior Lecturer, Women's Studies in the Department of Sociology, University of Limerick, Ireland. Prior to that she was Head of Research at the Irish Centre for Migration Studies, National University of Ireland, Cork. Her publications are in the areas of Irish women, migration and diaspora and include *Women and the Irish Diaspora* (Routledge 2003).

Sneja Gunew has taught in England, Australia and Canada. She has published widely on multicultural, postcolonial and feminist critical theory. She is professor of English and Women's Studies at the University of British Columbia, Canada and Director of the Centre for Research in Women's Studies and Gender Relations (July 2002–07). She has edited (with Anna Yeatman) *Feminism and the Politics of Difference* and (with Fazal Rizvi) *Culture, Difference and the Arts*. Her most recent book is *Framing Marginality: Multicultural Literary Studies*, and *Haunted Nations: The Colonial Dimensions of Multiculturalism* is forthcoming from Routledge. Her current work is in comparative multiculturalism and in diasporic literatures and their intersections with national and global cultural formations using theoretical frameworks deriving from feminist, postcolonial, and critical multicultural theory. She has recently become a Fellow of the Royal Society of Canada.

Caren Kaplan is an Associate Professor in the Department of Women's Studies at the University of California at Berkeley. She is the author of *Questions of Travel: Postmodern Discourses of Displacement* (Duke UP 1996) and the co-editor with Inderpal Grewal of *Scattered Hegemonies: Postmodernity and Transnational Feminist Practices* (Minnesota UP 1994) and *Introduction to Women's Studies: Gender in a Transnational World* (McGraw-Hill 2001), as well as *Between Woman and Nation: Nationalisms, Transnational Feminisms, and the State* (Duke UP 1999) with Norma Alarcón and Minoo Moallem.

Aileen Moreton-Robinson is a postdoctoral fellow located in the Australian Studies Centre, University of Queensland. Previously she was convenor of Indigenous Studies at the School of Humanities, Griffith University and taught women's studies at Flinders University. Dr Moreton-Robinson has been involved in the struggle for Indigenous rights at local, state and national levels, and has worked for a number of Indigenous organizations. She is the author of *Talkin' Up to the White Woman: Indigenous Women and Feminism* (University of Queensland Press 2000). Her publications in the area of native title, whiteness, race and feminism have appeared in anthologies and journals in Australia and internationally.

Catherine Nash is Reader in Human Geography in the Department of Geography, Queen Mary, University of London. Her research interests are in the postcolonial politics and geographies of identity. Her most recent research has addressed diasporic and local negotiations of belonging in two twinned projects: one exploring popular genealogy, ethnicity and

Irishness, and the other focused on local history in Northern Ireland. She is currently extending this work by addressing themes of ancestry, inheritance and descent in popular genealogy and population genetics. Her work has been funded by the British Academy, the Leverhulme Trust, and the Arts and Humanities Research Board and appeared in journals such as *Feminist Review; Gender, Place and Culture; Transactions of the Institute of British Geographers; Society and Space*, and *History Workshop Journal*.

Mimi Sheller is Senior Lecturer in Sociology at Lancaster University, Co-director of the Centre for Mobilities Research and Vice-Chair of the Society for Caribbean Studies. She is the author of *Consuming the Caribbean: From Arawaks to Zombies* (Routledge 2003) and *Democracy After Slavery: Black Publics and Peasant Radicalism in Haiti and Jamaica* (Macmillan 2000). Her work on publics, mobility and democracy has appeared in *Theory and Society; International Journal of Urban and Regional Research; Theory, Culture & Society*; and *Environment and Planning: Society and Space*. She is currently completing a book on colonial and postcolonial formations of gender, race, ethnicity and citizenship in the post-slavery Caribbean.

Ginette Verstraete holds the Simone de Beauvoir Chair in Contemporary Intellectual History at the University of Amsterdam. She is also the Director of the MPhil Programme in Cultural Analysis and member of the Amsterdam School for Cultural Analysis. She is the author of, among others, *Fragments of the Feminine Sublime in Friedrich Schlegel and James Joyce* (State University of New York Press 1998). She is currently finishing a book on cultural practices of travel, migration and globalization in the United States and Europe, provisionally entitled *Tracking the Nation: Travel, Technology and the Politics of Location*.

Introduction: Uprootings/Regroundings: Questions of Home and Migration

Sara Ahmed, Claudia Castañeda, Anne-Marie Fortier, Mimi Sheller

Uprootings/Regroundings is concerned with the ways in which different bodies and communities inhabit and move across familial, national and diasporic locations. The chapters in this collection examine both how migration is experienced in relation to home and belonging, and how home and belonging are formed in relationship to individual and collective migration. We begin from the premise that the forms and conditions of movement are not only highly divergent – consider the difference between tourism and exile – but also necessarily exist in relation to similarly divergent configurations of placement, or being 'at home'. Who moves, who stays, under what conditions? What is the relationship between those who stay and those who arrive and leave? What forces entrench migration, or propel staying 'at home'?

Each contribution to this collection brings to the fore in its own particular way the work of migration and the work of inhabitance, including that which goes into making and unmaking familial, communal, national and transnational borders, kinships and identities. Highlighting the laborious effort that goes into uprooting and regrounding homes, and the energy that is expended in enabling or prohibiting migrations, allows us to challenge the presumptions that movement involves freedom from grounds, or that grounded homes are not sites of change, relocation or uprooting. *Being grounded is not necessarily about being fixed; being mobile is not necessarily about being detached.* Thus the overall project of this collection is to call into question the naturalization of homes as origins, and the romanticization of mobility as travel, transcendence and transformation.

The concept of 'uprootings/regroundings' provides a framework for rethinking home and migration in ways that open out the discussion beyond oppositions such as stasis versus transformation, or presence versus absence. Rather than thinking of home and migration as constituted through processes that neatly map onto 'migrating' and 'homing', uprootings/regroundings makes it possible to consider home and migration in terms of a plurality of experiences, histories and constituencies, and of the workings of institutional structures. The task is therefore not to categorize 'home' as a condition distinct from 'migration', or to order them in terms of their relative value or cultural salience, but to ask how uprootings and regroundings are enacted – affectively, materially and symbolically – in relation to one another. It is not possible, from this point of view, to even define or describe the nature of homing and migrating as either separate or combined processes through which homes are made, lost, rejected or revisited, or migrations are undertaken, forced or forbidden. Rather, this volume brings together scholarship on home and migration that pays close attention to specific processes, modes and materialities of uprootings and regroundings, in different contexts and on different scales.

Integrating a diversity of approaches and subject matters (detailed below), this collection elucidates the intricate and variegated processes of uprootings and regroundings, from the micro-politics of embodied inhabitance and migration, to the macro-politics of transnationalism and global capital. The chapters in this volume attend to the histories, geographies, practices, forms of experience and relations of power that mark processes of uprootings and regroundings. They address a range of arenas in which issues of home and migration are negotiated, from art, the law and language to collections of objects, popular culture and the internet. And they consider differential identities, affects, cultural investments and political struggles at work in uprootings and regroundings, at both individual and collective levels. Uprootings and regroundings emerge from this collective work as simultaneously affective, embodied, cultural and political processes whose effects are not simply given. For example, regroundings – of identity, culture, nation, diaspora – can both resist and reproduce hegemonic forms of home and belonging.

This reflection on mobility and placement as interdependent is timely, given that much recent theorizing privileges movement as the dominant form of social life and individual experience of the contemporary 'global' world of 'flows' and 'liquidity' (e.g. Castells 1996; Bauman 2000; Robertson et al. 1994; Urry 2000). Much of this research suggests that mobility and migrancy destabilize identities and communities precisely insofar as they detach identity from place (Chambers 1994), enable the creation of new 'nomadic' identities (Braidotti 1994), or lead to the 'creolization' of 'global culture' (Hannerz 1996; Featherstone 1995). While recognizing that the transnational movements of bodies, objects and images have transformed concepts and experiences of home and belonging (defined as locality and community as well as nation), we question the presumptions that rootless mobility is the defining feature of contemporary experience and that it stands against any form of 'rooted belonging'. With others across a range of disciplinary and interdisciplinary locations who call these universalizing and over-generalized characterizations of 'the global' into question (Brah 1996; Cresswell 1996; Grewal and Kaplan 1994; Kaplan 1996; Massey 1999; Pels 1999), we seek to address the variegated texture of habitation and migration in transnational circuits of exchange and power.

We take as a model those feminist studies that have been concerned with the intersectionality of race, class, gender and sexuality in the making and theorizing of transnational domains (Ahmed 2000; Alexander and Mohanty 1997; Castañeda 2002; Enloe 1989; Franklin et al. 2000; Kaplan et al. 1999; Mohanty et al. 1991; Ong 1999). These approaches have laid the groundwork for our own thinking about feminist and post-colonial interventions in the realm of the transnational and global, suggesting both that the nature of uprootings and regroundings are linked to such differences and that a focus on these differences requires new ways of theorizing home and migration. *Uprootings/Regroundings* therefore contributes to rethinking what home and migration mean – and how these meanings are being reimagined – by reconsidering long-standing categories of difference addressed in feminism through the framework of uprootings and regroundings.

Uprootings/Regroundings also converses with the recently established field of investigation around transnationalism, widely understood as referring to the multiple activities – economic, political, cultural, personal – that require sustained contacts and travel across national borders (Portes et al. 1999; Basch et al. 1994). Studies in transnationalism problematize conventional understandings of homes and communities as stable, spatially fixed locations, from which migrants depart and in which they relocate 'new' homes, even while attending to the continuing importance of the nation-state in migrants' lives, thus questioning the assumption that we live in a post-national world (Westwood and Phizacklea 2000; Rouse 1991; Basch et al. 1994). Ethnographies of 'transnational migrant circuits' and of 'the conjunctural and situated character of globalization' (Inda and Rosaldo 2002: 27) suggest some of the ways in which bodies, families, communities and nations are together reprocessed within transnational connections. They reveal the fluidity and diversity of these exchanges, and complicate the unilateral relationship between belonging and location by investigating the ways in which new forms of political and cultural belonging are anchored in multi-local ties (Levitt 2001) and in deterritorialized notions of a person's rights and responsibilities (Soysal 1994).

Cosmopolitanism, crucially, is theorized as a set of predispositions and practices predicated on extensive mobility, including corporeal, imaginative and virtual travel, which allow for a comprehension of local specificity while fostering an openness to the 'globalising world' (Szerszynski and Urry 2002: 470–1, cf. Tomlinson 1999). However, the emergence of seemingly open and flexible cosmopolitan cultures or civil societies still depends on the constraints of particular articulations of power, hierarchy, inequality and positioning. Aihwa Ong, for example, has shown how the border-crossing activities and 'flexible citizenship' of Chinese transnational subjects depend on 'different modalities of governmentality – as practiced by the nation-state, by the family, by capital – that intersect and have effects on each other, variously encoding and constraining flexibility in global (re)positioning' (Ong 1999: 113). Thus a Chinese-diasporan (post)colonial habitus based on *guanxi* (interpersonal relations) entails particular family regimes, biopolitics, and post-nationalist cosmopolitan affiliations. It is precisely these collisions of the corporeal, the familial and the (post)national that create the densely conjoined (and often traumatic) struggles over identity, belonging and longing within uprootings and regroundings.

With the focus on migration and its effects on accepted understandings of what constitutes communities (local and national), 'location' often remains a primary concern in studies of transnationalism, where movement is largely conceived as operating between two distinct national formations, 'here' and 'there' (one notable exception is Castañeda 2002). Though we recognize the importance of the task of specifying experiences of migration themselves, we also seek to escape the immediacy of location as a discrete entity, and to blur the distinction between here and there. Where or what is 'there'? Is it necessarily *not* 'here'? How long is 'there' a significant site of connection? And for whom? How far away is 'there'? Such questions have been raised in the literature on borderlands, perhaps most notably in the work of Gloria Anzaldúa (1987). Conceived against the homogenizing tendencies of the (US) nation-state, the concept of borderlands has largely contributed to opening up discussions of belonging and identity to new mappings of space. Anzaldúa shows how Chicano/a culture is constituted in and through the border between Mexico and the United States, whose exact location is itself a matter of debate. Who inhabits whose land? Which culture borrows from which other? As cultural and spatial boundaries are reconfigured in this contested borderzone, new 'homes' and 'migrations' also become intelligible in the form of hybridized cultures without 'pure' origins. Anzaldúa's regrounding of Chicano/a in the borderzone simultaneously uproots the apparently fixed boundaries of the US nation-state. As Laura Perez puts it, 'Chicana/o cultural practices have operated in disordering, profoundly disturbing ways with respect to dominant social and cultural, spatial and ideological topographies of the "proper" in the United States' (Perez 1999: 19).

As this work on borderzones suggests, uprootings and regroundings are constituted through the reconfiguration of space, just as the redrawing of boundaries can generate new processes of uprooting and regrounding. Postcolonial feminist theorists have led the way in theorizing 'border-zones' and *mestizo* identities in relation to the work of migration and inhabitance (Anzaldúa 1987; Ifekwunigwe 1999; Kaplan et al. 1999; Lorde 1982; Moraga 1983). They have made us aware that the greatest movements often occur within the self, within the home or within the family, while the phantasm of limitless mobility often rests on the power of border controls and policing of who does and does not belong. And they have shown us that long-standing categories of difference addressed in feminist work become important in new ways when addressed in relation to uprootings/regroundings.

We can also draw from critical geography the insight that both staying put and moving can take place out of necessity or force as well as 'choice', and thus depend on specific enabling or disenabling relations of power (Cresswell 1996; Massey 1999; Miles 1999; May 2000). How are the materialities, affects and politics of diverse uprootings and regroundings simultaneously played out upon bodies, families and nations, within the constraints imposed by violences and disciplines of many kinds? More specifically, feminist geographers have taught us that it is crucial to pay attention not only to the gendering of spaces of domesticity and move-ments in public space (Wolff 1993; Massey 1994), but also to the domesti-cated gender, racial, sexual and class dynamics of both national and transnational relations and borders (Enloe 1989; Parker et al. 1992). For example, much work goes into the making of homes, national and other-wise, and the labour of re-producing them is often designated as 'women's work' (see Gedalof, Chapter 4 in this volume). From this point of view, how women negotiate such genderings of space and labour become part of the story of home and migration. Processes of homing and migration take shape through the imbrication of affective and bodily experience in broader social processes and institutions where unequal differences of race, class, gender and sexuality, among many other relevant categories, are generated. We can ask: how are uprootings and regroundings embod-ied and imagined in relation to immigration laws, border police, socio-economic inequalities and prejudice (racism, sexism, homophobia, xenophobia and so on)? How can movement or staying put be a form of privilege that 'extends' the reach of some bodies, for example when the movement of some takes place through 'fixing the bodies of others' (Ahmed 2000), or when staying put takes place through displacing others?

Home and migration cannot be adequately theorized outside of these spatialized relations of power. Mobility can be foisted upon bodies through homelessness, exile and forced migration just as the purported comforts of the familial 'home' may be sites of alienation and violence (for women, children, queers). The founding of homelands and places of belonging can entail the displacement of others from their homes. It can also involve the spoliation of the homes of those who nevertheless remain 'in place', as is so evident in the migration of European settlers that has historically entailed the desecration of indigenous peoples' homelands (see Moreton-Robinson, Chapter 1 in this volume).

Just as we draw on feminist research in framing this collection, we also recognize that feminism itself is both located and shaped by the specificities of its location, whilst also 'on the move' or affected by transnational movements of bodies, knowledges and capital. As Alexander and Mohanty argue

> to talk about feminist praxis in global contexts would involve shifting the unit of analysis from local, regional and national culture to relations and processes across cultures . . . we also need to understand the local in relation to other cross-national processes. This would require a corresponding shift in the conception of political organising and mobilization across borders (1997: xix; see also Lowe and Lloyd 1997: 15; Kang 2002).

We would suggest that the challenge for transnational feminism is both critical and affirmative. First, it remains crucial to critique the gendered dimension of the international division of labour, which places women in highly differentiated and unequal positions in the global economy (Grewal and Kaplan 1994: 19). As feminist critics have shown, capital accumulation relies on traditional and gendered notions of work in order to constitute subjects who can meet the needs of transnational capital (Freeman 2000; Mies 1986; Mitter 1986; Ong 1987; Tinker 1990). Second, transnational feminism has an affirmative dimension in the desire to create ethical forms of solidarity with others. Such solidarities must involve respect for differences that cannot be translated, and for situated attachments to land and place (Spivak 1995). Political and ethical solidarity does not require giving up the local or transnational but finding ways of working politically with both dimensions, and with what moves between them.

Feminist theorists have also related the question of movement more broadly to questions of privilege and marginality. In particular, as said earlier, we are concerned with the privileging of movement over 'staying put'. With others who have addressed transnational issues in these terms (Brah 1996; Grewal 1996; Kaplan 1996; Lowe 1996), we suggest that the question of *who can travel* has to be supplemented by the question of *who can stay at home*? These privileges are negotiated precisely in relationship to the inhabiting of spaces and to the 'passports' that are required not only to move between places, but also to stay 'at home' in them. Some contributions to this volume show how technologies of travel (Kaplan, in Chapter 9) or the geopolitics of mobility (Andrijasevic in Chapter 11, Verstraete in Chapter 10) require the sedentariness of some labourers, or limit the movement of others. The restrictions on movement for some (in relations of force and violence) ensure the extended freedom of movement for subjects who remain 'firmly located' (Verstraete) in specific territories and identities – they own the 'right' passports. Other contributors discuss under what conditions – of violence, hatred, war, alienation – homes become sites of estrangement, and for whom (Ankori in Chapter 3, Gedalof in Chapter 4, Gunew in Chapter 2, Moreton-Robinson in Chapter 1). For even individuals who have not left the nation, region or town in which they were born, have not necessarily stayed at home, and if they have stayed at home, it is not necessarily the case that they have not moved.

Histories of colonization and decolonization are critical here, for as Caren Kaplan has written, 'the emergence of terms of travel and displacement (as well as their oppositional counterparts, home and location) must be linked to the history of the production of colonial discourses' (1996: 2). This question draws attention to how the differentiated histories of movement that were central to the imperial process are still lived and negotiated in the forming of spaces of inhabitance understood in terms of 'home' (e.g. nation or homeland). If the circulation of bodies, objects and images in globality is dependent upon, and re-enacts, the colonization of some peoples and cultures by others, then how do contemporary concepts and experiences of home and belonging relate to such histories?

Drawing on earlier postcolonial theorists (Bhabha 1994; Gilroy 1987, 1993; Hall 1990, 1991), we might ask how the presence and experiences of migrants put any normative notion of culture, identity and citizenship in question by their very location 'outside' of the time-space of the nation. Within postcolonial studies and critical cultural theory, the concept of 'diaspora' has developed as an emblem of multi-locality, 'post-nationality' and non-linearity of *both* movement and time. Thus diaspora questions the language of integration, assimilation or inclusion assumed within national frames, which takes for granted a linear narrative of migration as disconnected from colonial, postcolonial and neo-colonial relations of power. The notion of diaspora opens up 'a historical and experiential rift between the locations of residence and the locations of belonging' (Gilroy 2000: 124), and compels us to rethink the problematic of 'home' and 'homeland', and migrants' relations to them. Though much of the literature and debates on diaspora have centred on the homeland as a primary site of identification for diasporic subjects, we retain from some key interventions on diaspora (Gilroy 1993, 2000; Brah 1996; Clifford 1994) the need to rethink the assumption that 'home', in migration, is simply something we 'leave behind'. Several chapters in this volume revisit the concept of diaspora in light of specific migrations. Fortier, in Chapter 5, considers different narratives of queer migration, including some where home is destination, rather than origin, or others that suggest that the 'diasporic home' itself makes it possible to 'queer' established conceptions of home in ways that are perhaps not accessible to all. Other contributors to this volume point to the limitations of celebrations of the diaspora as a sign of diversity and tenacious cultural transmission. In Chapter 7, Breda Gray questions the implications of diaspora as a source for rebranding the Irish nation, which sits uneasily with gendered conceptions of 'home', genealogy and cultural continuity. Gayatri Gopinath, in Chapter 6, critiques hegemonic constructions of both nation and diaspora from the vantage point of the 'impossible' queer South Asian diasporic subject.

Through the important task of specifying experiences of migration in themselves, then, it becomes possible to re-form or re-animate our perceptions of home, without then assuming home is fixed prior to the experiences of migration. While insisting on the interdependence of home and migration, this book is perhaps especially attentive to processes of *homing* as a feature of this relation. What, for example, is the relationship between leaving home and the imagining of home? How are homes made in the context of migration? And what, having left home, might it mean to return? Much of the literature on 'home' has sought to account for how homes come to be lived, felt and made (Allan and Crow 1989; Davidoff and Hall 1987; Chapman and Hockey 1999), including how it is lived in migration (Rapport and Dawson 1998; Hage 1997). We join them in this project, while we also insist that we can only do this if we avoid assuming that home has an essential meaning, in advance of its making. Black feminists have long since alerted us to the contradictions of family life for black women and to the ways in which intersections of race, family and nation crystallize within ideas of 'home' (Amos and Parmar 1984; Carby

1982; Dill 1988; Coontz 1992; Webster 1998; Collins 2000). These interventions have challenged universal definitions of home defined in terms of the white middle-class patriarchal family. We seek to take this challenge forward by questioning the very *terms* of home which delimit it as an accomplished site of belonging and governance. Homes are always made and remade as grounds and conditions (of work, of family, of political climate, etc.) change.

'Homing' entails processes of home-building (Hage 1997), whether 'at home' or in migration. Making home is about the (re)creation of what Eva Hoffman would call 'soils of significance' (1989: 278), in which the affective qualities of home, and the work of memory in their making cannot be divorced from the more concrete materialities of rooms, objects, rituals, borders and forms of transport that are bound up in so many processes of uprooting and regrounding. Homing, then, depends on the reclaiming and reprocessing of habits, objects, names and histories that have been uprooted – in migration, displacement or colonization. Inherent to the project of home-building *here and now*, is the gathering of 'intimations' of home, 'fragments which are *imagined* to be traces of an equally imagined homely whole, the imagined past "home" of another time and another space' (Hage 1997: 106; emphasis added). In this respect, being at home and the work of home-building is intimately bound up with the *idea* of home: the idea of a place (or places) in the past, and of *this* place in the future. Making home is about *creating* both pasts and futures through inhabiting the grounds of the present (see Sheller's Chapter 12 in this volume). And indeed, both uprooting and regrounding can entail forms of mourning, nostalgia and remembrance as well as physical sickness and experiences of trauma (see Ankori's Chapter 3 and Gunew's Chapter 2 in this volume).

The affectivity of home is bound up with the temporality of home, with the past, the present and the future. It takes time to feel at home. For those who have left their homes, a nostalgic relation to both the past and home might become part of the lived reality in the present. As many of the contributors show, nostalgia plays a crucial part in the imagining of 'cultures of relatedness' (Nash, Chapter 8 in this volume), whether direct kinship or wider circles of ethnic and national belonging. Several of the chapters explore forms of nationalist nostalgia in popular culture such as the nostalgic representations of Irish migrancy (Gray, Chapter 7) or of white Australian belonging to a land of migrants (Moreton-Robinson, in Chapter 1). But nostalgia and memory can also take what Gopinath calls 'a generative or enabling' form when it is used for the reinterpretation of homes and homelands, or in the case of colonized lands when it is used by indigenous or uprooted people to hold on to their ties to places from which they have been dispossessed, as Aileen Moreton-Robinson and Gannit Ankori suggest.

Thus the work of making home, affective and physical, is an ongoing process. Against the assumption that movement takes place 'away from home' only when one leaves home, this book crucially stresses that 'staying put' is not without movement. Both Fortier and Gedalof refuse the idea that home is about stasis, suggesting instead that homes involve 'a continuous act of production and reproduction that is never fully complete' (Gedalof in Chapter 4 of this volume). For Fortier, 'homing desires' (Brah 1996) are not only the effect of migration, but are part and parcel of the daily practices of making home. Such 'home work' is affective work, but the nature of that work must be specified: it may be a labour of love, or hatred; it may involve conservative nationalist desires or claims to homelands as historical reparation; it may be haunted by fear of loss or filled with hope for different, more peaceful and equitable futures.

Uprooting Homes, Grounding Migration

Each of the chapters that make up this book addresses questions of home and migration through a particular configuration of methods, materials and definitions. This range of approaches – from the reading of autobiographical accounts, fictional narratives and popular media through the analysis of rules of law, government policies and theoretical texts – exemplifies precisely the as yet under-examined richness and complexity of home and migration. In addition, each of the chapters calls into question the privileging of mobility over dwelling in different ways, including: how the mobilities of some subjects and the immobilities of others are co-produced; theorizing home as a site of movement; unsettling linear narratives of origin and migration; and rethinking the relation between embodied subjectivity, place and belonging. While the lines of connection between the chapters might have been drawn in a number of ways, we have chosen to divide them according to three themes: the dwelling and movement of bodies (Part I), moving into and out of 'homes' understood as forms of relatedness (Part II), and trans/national border crossings (Part III). However, the apparent distinction between these apparent 'levels' (the micropolitics of the body, the domestic politics of the familial and the transnational politics of border crossing) should be understood as a product of the interdependence between these realms. As the chapters will demonstrate, borders are biopolitical, bodies are affected by border policies and feelings of kinship or estrangement and familial genealogies depend on systems of travel that recognize different kinds of relatedness.

In the first section, 'Bodies at Home and Away', contributors investigate ways in which home and migration are embodied. To be sure, embodiment is crucial to any investigation of the effects of migrations, exiles and displacements on identity and community. Experiences of exile, for example, are experiences of being out of place in one's body (Ankori), while experiences of migration may be felt as sickness and discomfort (Gunew). So too, experiences of being-at-home can involve bodily trauma, when one's home is invaded by others (Moreton-Robinson). The chapters in this section rethink the relationship between bodies, places and mobility by regrounding these concepts in specific histories, locations and forms of displacement and emplacement.

In the first chapter of this section, Aileen Moreton-Robinson articulates Australian indigenous peoples' relationship to home as one that depends on the indivisible relation between the collective body and the land. She contrasts this relation to white Australian sentimental narratives of belonging to a land of migrants. She shows that unlike other narratives of the postcolonial as always diasporic, for Australian Indigenous peoples, the experience of dispossession did not arise out of physical migration, but was instead one of 'staying put' while being in exile from the homeland. Claims to a home there also depend on contesting the specific terms of displacement and dispossession, namely the declaration that Australia was an uninhabited land prior to European settlement.

For Sneja Gunew in Chapter 2, reading canonical Australia through the 'lens of "immigrant" nostalgia', 'not feeling at home' is a kind of homecoming that is lived through the migrant body. Gunew asks what happens to the mother/land when the referent is somewhere else. She suggests that feelings of out-of-place-ness for migrant subjects can involve an uncanny relation to home: the once-familiar home becomes strange, and this alienation takes form through language as well as the body. For Gunew this bodily discomfort may be productive: the 'stammer' of the migratory subject may enable new bodies and new homes to come into being. That is, the struggle with another tongue – a tongue that is not the mother tongue – may create a bodily nausea, from which a different bodily relation to an adopted home becomes possible.

Gannit Ankori in Chapter 3 also addresses the way in which alienation from the 'homeland' is experienced viscerally within the body. Ankori addresses a different configuration of dispossession and reclamation through a reading of the work of three Palestinian artists, displaced from their homeland in different ways, whether by exile or by occupation. She suggests that the three artists represent loss of a Palestinian home as a kind of disorientation, which they configure materially in the form of vulnerable carnal bodies and objects that bear bodily traces. Ankori's careful descriptions of this embodied art, especially through the rendering of skin, suggests how losing one's home can be embodied as the loss of embodiment itself, in this case the loss of a relationship to the skin. Regrounding becomes a process of finding new skins, new ways of inhabiting bodies and worlds.

In the final chapter of this section, Irene Gedalof links the theme of 'bodies at home and away' to the question of community. She focuses specifically on women's bodies and their role in the regrounding of communities in the contexts of war, violence and displacement. Gedalof details how 'women' in these contexts are required to reproduce the community through the reproductive work they do within the family. With specific reference to experiences of ethnic conflict, violence and instability, Gedalof shows us precisely that 'home' is never just there, as a place that subjects simply inhabit. Instead, homes are continually being remade by – in this and many other cases – women's bodies and agencies. This suggests in turn that women's work of reproducing domestic *and* broader cultural or national homes can take different shapes across successive generations. For Gedalof, women's bodies cannot be held in place as ground, or as matter that instantiates home, but are about the creative remaking and reimagining of inhabitance.

Like Gedalof, the authors in the second section, 'Family Ties', offer critical perspectives on how family, genealogy and kinship are implicated in the uprooting and regrounding of homes. While not all formations of home are grounded in concepts of family, this seemingly indivisible association is a dominant feature in considerations of home as a site of relatedness. The chapters in this section question discourses of familial homes and home-as-familiarity as necessary sites of seamless belonging, continuity and affinity.

The section opens with Anne-Marie Fortier's reading of narratives of queer migrations, in Britain and in the United States. In this chapter, Fortier contrasts the ways queer migrant subjects have reimagined their childhood homes and their places of origin against established, seemingly more progressive narratives of 'coming out'. Reflecting on the way in which 'coming out' is conventionally narrated as 'moving out' of the family home, Fortier argues that narratives by queer migrant subjects refigure coming out in ways that do not necessarily require the wholesale rejection, or loss, of the familial home. By tracing the movements of queers outside, between and within the homespace, she explores the possibility of rethinking the familial home in ways that open it up to 'queer belongings'. Fortier's reassessment of the ideal of home-as-familiarity through queer lenses decentres the heterosexual, familial 'home' as the emblematic model of comfort, care and belonging, and questions the actions undertaken in the name of 'home' or 'hominess' within wider sites of domesticity and national culture.

Gayatri Gopinath in Chapter 6 also examines the relationship between queer sexuality and discourses of family and home, but this time in relation to Indian nationalism. She considers how queer South Asian diasporic subjects negotiate their elision from national memory as well as the 'threat' they pose to the linked sites of family, home and nation. In particular, she examines how a queer South Asian diasporic imaginary, featuring 'a queer boy in a sari' as well as narratives of female homo-eroticism within 'traditional' domestic spaces, disrupts heteronormative accounts of the mother/national home. Using close readings of two South Asian texts, she further argues that narratives of same-sex desire for diasporic subjects do not necessarily follow the trajectory of 'coming out' into the public sphere, but instead may work to reinhabit and re-eroticize domestic and private spaces differently. Gopinath's analysis shows us how the remaking of the middle-class and bourgeois family in this way also opens up ways of 'homing' non-normative diasporic sexualities.

In the third chapter of this section, Breda Gray addresses the narration of the Irish diaspora as a gendered and global epic. Through a close examination of the television series *The Irish Empire* (1999), she shows how memories of Irish diasporization mobilize a romantic and nostalgic story of family separations. In particular, she considers the centrality of heterosexual love crucial for the fantasy of national Irish identity and consolidation. Gray's analysis focuses on the ways in which this televisual narrative relies on the family as a site of continuity, and simultaneously produces profound gaps and discontinuities, since family memories are never fully reshaped into either national, diasporic or global Irish belonging.

Catherine Nash in Chapter 8 also asks us to think more about what home can mean by rethinking 'the familial' in the specific transnational practice of 'doing family trees'. Nash's study of 'genealogical tourists' who trace their genealogical 'roots' to Ireland – through the internet or travel to Ireland – shows how the construction of family trees is achieved by making selective links between identity, culture, geography and location. While some connections to places and between people are made to matter, other connections are erased, forgotten or kept in the possession of particular family members. The practice of genealogical tourism is much more about evoking delimited pathways into the present (e.g.

patrilineal, 'white', European, upwardly mobile) than it is about simply finding an existing but as yet undiscovered 'home' of Irish relations. Finally, Nash argues that the complexity of genealogical relatedness depends upon the making of homes *as* blood relations – with the expectations of mutuality that come with them – while also 'uprooting' their significance as the basis of home.

In the third section of the book, 'Trans/Nations and Border Crossings', contributors examine how the movement of some bodies across national borders works to both enforce and challenge ideas of community and belonging. The chapters highlight the ways in which categorical inequalities such as class, race, ethnicity, gender and sexuality continue to operate as exclusionary devices for sorting who can be mobile and who cannot. In the first chapter in this section, Caren Kaplan reflects on the making of transnational subjects through locatedness as well as movement. Her discussion concerns the ways in which the apparent freedoms of privileged 'travel' rest on the labour of located – or 'local' – workers. More specifically, she suggests that the appearance of mobility, flux and 'disembodied subjects' in cyberspace cannot be detached from the necessary locatedness of those of the new proletariat who service the global economy. From phone-sex workers to the workers making computer microchips, she asks us to consider those whose subjectivities lie outside the privileged space of flows.

In the second chapter in the section, Ginnette Verstraete demonstrates how the production of a 'borderless' Europe actually depends on the co-constitution of national borders at the edges of 'Schengen space' with 'illegal bodies' at the border crossings. The mobilities of capital and of white propertied nationals across the apparently frontierless new Europe are matched by the immobilization of illegal aliens who are sent back (again and again) to their places of origin. But Verstraete pointedly shows how the repeated removal of migrants 'can only exist by way of a state sanctioned traffic of illegal "aliens"', where illegality is a marketable commodity. 'Aliens' can try again, travelling as packages in trailers, as long as the 'borderless world' is paid for.

It is the very experiences of 'trafficking' across EU borders that Rutvica Andrijasevic investigates in the following chapter. Analysing testimonies of Eastern European women formerly involved in prostitution in Italy, Andrijasevic considers the relationship between crime and victimhood. Typical narratives of trafficking – political, popular and theoretical – turn EU borders into scenes of crime, where women are positioned as victims of criminal networks. For Andrijasevic, these models cannot account for the lived experiences of crossing borders. She thus shows that while border crossings are certainly shaped by policing, this does not simply produce victimization or the loss of agency in non-privileged subjects, but entails much more complex and varied negotiations with equally multiple outcomes.

In the final chapter, Mimi Sheller examines how the concept of creolization has been adopted into theories of 'global culture'. Describing this adoption as a form of 'piracy', Sheller shows how the transnational traffic in theories from the Caribbean to hegemonic anglophone academia repeats the 'theft' and appropriation of others that was crucial to the colonization process out of which theories of creolization arose in the first place. Here, the 'unmarking' of postmodern theory (and theorists) occurs through the erasure of specificities fundamental to the theories of creolization that they 'uproot'. Indeed, Sheller's analysis reminds us that questions of home and migration are relevant not only as subjects of academic discourse, but in the practice of that discourse itself. That is, questions of 'uprootings' and 'regroundings' in transnational relations of power are fundamental with regard to how we use and produce knowledge *about* home and migration.

Together, the chapters in this volume bring to the fore the work of 'uprooting' and 'regrounding' in both local and global fields of affect, embodiment and power. In gathering this work together, we seek to trouble simplified claims concerning the nature of home and migration in contemporary lives and worlds. Though the common grounding that we present in this introduction is by no means inhabited in the same way by each of us, it is the result of our own work of moving through and settling in the process of writing a collective introduction. More importantly still, while the collection itself is grounded – it has its location, for sure – the chapters housed within it also inhabit and disrupt the overall theme of home and migration in ways that cannot be contained within our introduction. Indeed, for us the strength of the collection lies in the particularity of each chapter, in the ways in which each one takes up questions of home or migration and moves both within and beyond the terms we have had the capacity to imagine.

References

Ahmed, S. (2000), *Strange Encounters: Embodied Others in Post-coloniality*, London and New York: Routledge.
Alexander, M.J. and Mohanty, C.T. (1997), 'Introduction: Genealogies, Legacies and Movements', in M.J. Alexander and C.T. Mohanty (eds),

Feminist Genealogies, Colonial Legacies, Democratic Futures, London: Routledge.

—— (eds) (1997), *Feminist Genealogies, Colonial Legacies, Democratic Futures*, London: Routledge.

Allan, G. and Crow, G. (eds) (1989), *Home and Family: Creating the Domestic Space*, Basingstoke: Macmillan.

Amos, V. and Parmar, P. (1984), 'Challenging imperial feminism', *Feminist Review*, 17 (Autumn): 3–19.

Anzaldúa, G. (1987), *Borderlands/La Frontera: The New Mestiza*, San Francisco: Aunt Lute.

Basch, L., Glick Shiller, N. and Szanton Blanc, C. (1994), *Nations Unbound: Transnational Projects, Postcolonial Predicaments, and Deterritorialized Nation-States*, Amsterdam: Gordon and Breach.

Bauman, Z. (2000), *Liquid Modernity*, Cambridge: Polity.

Bhabha, H.K. (1994), *The Location of Culture*, London and New York: Routledge.

Brah, A. (1996), *Cartographies of Diaspora: Contesting Identities*, London and New York: Routledge.

—— Hickman, M. and Mac an Ghaill, M. (eds) (1999), *Global Futures: Migration, Environment and Globalization*, Basingstoke: Macmillan.

Braidotti, R. (1994), *Nomadic Subjects. Embodiment and Sexual Difference in Feminist Theory*, New York: Columbia University Press.

Carby, H. (1982), 'White Woman Listen! Black Feminism and the Boundaries of Sisterhood', in Centre for Contemporary Cultural Studies, *The Empire Strikes Back*, London: Hutchinson.

Castañeda, C. (2002), *Figurations: Child, Bodies, Worlds*, Durham, NC and London: Duke University Press.

Castells, M. (1996), *The Rise of the Network Society*, Oxford and New York: Blackwell.

Chambers, I. (1994), *Migrancy, Culture, Identity*, London: Routledge.

Chapman, T. and Hockey, J. (eds) (1999), *Ideal Homes? Social Change and Domestic Life*, London and New York: Routledge.

Clifford, J. (1994), 'Diasporas', *Cultural Anthropology*, 9(3): 302–38.

Collins, P. H. (2000), 'It's All in the Family: Intersections of Gender, Race and Nation', in U. Narayan and S. Harding (eds), *Decentering the Center: Philosophy for a Multicultural, Postcolonial, and Feminist World*, Bloomington and Indianapolis, Indiana University Press.

Coontz, S. (1992), *The Way We Never Were: American Families and the Nostalgia Trap*, New York: Basic.

Cresswell, T. (1996), *In Place/Out of Place: Geography, Identity and Transgression*, Minneapolis: University of Minnesota Press.

Davidoff, L. and Hall, C. (1987), *Family Fortunes: Men and Women of the English Middle Class, 1780–1850*, Chicago: University of Chicago Press.

Dill, B.T. (1988), 'Our Mothers' Grief: Racial Ethnic Women and the Maintenance of Families,' *Journal of Family History*, 13: 415–31.

Enloe, C. (1989), *Bananas, Beaches and Bases: Making Feminist Sense of International Politics*, London: Pandora.

Featherstone, M. (1995), *Undoing Culture: Globalization, Postmodernism and Identity*, London: Sage.

Franklin, S., Lury C. and Stacey, J. (2000), *Global Nature, Global Culture*, London: Sage.

Freeman, C. (2000), *High Tech and High Heels in the Global Economy*, Durham, NC and London: Duke University Press.

Gilroy, P. (1987), *There Ain't no Black in the Union Jack*, London: Unwin Hyman.

—— (1993), *The Black Atlantic: Modernity and Double Consciousness*, London and New York: Verso.

—— (2000), *Between Camps: Nations, Cultures and the Allure of Race*, London and New York: Penguin.

Grewal, I. (1996), *Home and Harem: Nation, Gender, Empire, and the Cultures of Travel*, Durham, NC and London: Duke University Press.

—— and Kaplan, C. (eds) (1994*), Scattered Hegemonies: Postmodernity and Transnational Feminist Practices*, Minneapolis: University of Minnesota Press.

Hage, G. (1997), 'At Home in the Entrails of the West: Multiculturalism, Ethnic Food and Migrant Home-building', in H. Grace, G. Hage, L. Johnson, J. Langsworth and M. Symonds, *Home/World: Space, Community and Marginality in Sydney's West*, Sydney: Pluto.

Hall, S. (1990), 'Cultural Identity and Diaspora', in J. Rutherford (ed.), *Identity: Community, Culture, Difference*, London: Lawrence & Wishart.

—— (1991), 'Old and New Identities, Old and New Ethnicities', in A.D. King (ed.), *Culture, Globalization and the World-System*, London: Macmillan.

Hannerz, U. (1996), *Transnational Connections: Culture, People, Places*, London: Routledge.

Hoffman, E. (1989), *Lost in Translation: A Life in a New Language*, London: Minerva.

Ifekwunigwe, J. (1999), *Scattered Belongings: Cultural Paradoxes of 'Race', Nation and Gender*, London and New York: Routledge.

Inda, J. and Rosaldo, R. (eds) (2002), *The Anthropology of Globalization: A Reader*, Malden, MA and Oxford: Blackwell.

Kang, L. Hyun Yi (2002), *Compositional Subjects: Enfiguring Asian/American Women*, Durham, NC: Duke University Press.

Kaplan, C. (1996), *Questions of Travel: Postmodern Discourses of Displacement*, Durham, NC: Duke University Press.

—— Alarcón, N. and Moallem, M. (eds) (1999), *Between Woman and Nation: Nationalisms, Transnational Feminisms, and the State*, Durham, NC and London: Duke University Press.

Levitt, P. (2001), *The Transnational Villagers*, Berkeley: University of California Press.

Lorde, A. (1982), *Zami: A New Spelling of My Name*, New York: The Crossing Press.

Lowe, L. (1996), *Immigrant Acts: On Asian American Cultural Politics*, Durham, NC: Duke University Press.

Lowe, L. and Lloyd, D. (1997), 'Introduction', in L. Lowe and D. Lloyd (eds), *The Politics of Culture in the Shadow of Capital*, Durham, NC: Duke University Press.

Massey, D. (1994), *Space, Place and Gender*, Cambridge: Polity.

—— (1999), 'Imagining Globalization: Power-Geometries of Time-Space', in A. Brah, M. Hickman and M. Mac an Ghaill (eds), *Global Futures: Migration, Environment and Globalization*, Houndmills: Macmillan.

May, J. (2000), 'Of Nomads and Vagrants: Single Homelessness and Narratives of Home as Place', *Environment and Planning D: Society and Space*, 18: 737–59.

Mies, M. (1986), *Patriarchy and Accumulation on a World Scale: Women in the International Division of Labour*, London: Zed.

Miles, R. (1999), 'Analysing the Political Economy of Migration: the Airport as an "Effective" Institution of Control', in A. Brah, M. Hickman and M. Mac an Ghaill (eds), *Global Futures: Migration, Environment and Globalization*, Basingstoke: Macmillan.

Mitter, S. (1986), *Common Fate, Common Bond: Women in the Global Economy*, London: Pluto.

Mohanty, C.T., Russo, A. and Torres, L. (eds) (1991), *Third World Women and the Politics of Feminism*, Bloomington: Indiana University Press.

Moraga, C. (1983), *Loving in the War Years: Lo Que Nunca Pasó Por Mis Labios*, Boston: South End Press.

Ong, A. (1987), *Spirits of Resistance and Capitalist Discipline*, Albany: State University of New York Press.

—— (1999) *Flexible Citizenship: The Cultural Logics of Transnationality*, Durham, NC: Duke University Press.

Parker, A., Russo, M., Sommer, D. and Yaeger, P. (eds) (1992), *National-isms and Sexualities*, New York and London: Routledge.

Pels, D. (1999), 'Privileged Nomads: On the Strangeness of Intellectuals and the Intellectuality of Strangers', *Theory, Culture & Society*, 16,(1): 63–86.

Pérez, L. (1999) 'El desorden, Nationalism, and Chicana/o Aesthetics', in C. Kaplan, N. Alarcón, M. Moallem (eds), *Between Woman and Nation: Nationalisms, Transnational Feminisms, and the State*, Durham, NC and London: Duke University Press.

Portes, A., Guarnizo, L.E. and Landolt, P. (eds) (1999), 'Transnational Communities', special issue of *Ethnic and Racial Studies*, 22(2): 217–37.

Rapport, N. and Dawson, A. (eds) (1998), *Migrants of Identity: Percep-tions of Home in a World of Movement*, Oxford: Berg.

Robertson, G., Tickner, L., Curtis, B. and Putnam, T. (eds) (1994), *Travel-lers' Tales: Narratives of Home and Displacement*, London: Routledge.

Rouse, R. (1991), 'Mexican Migration and the Social Space of Post-modernism', *Diaspora*, 1(1) (Spring 1991): 8–23.

Soysal, Y.N. (1994), *Limits of Citizenship. Migrants and Postnational Membership in Europe*, Chicago and London: University of Chicago Press.

Spivak, G.C. (1995), Translator's Preface and Afterword in *Imaginary Maps*, London: Routledge.

Szerszynski, B. and Urry, J. (2002), 'Cultures of Cosmopolitanism', *The Sociological Review*, 50:(4): 461–81.

Tinker, I. (ed.) (1990), *Persistent Inequalities: Women and World Devel-opment*, New York and Oxford: Oxford University Press.

Tomlinson, J. (1999), *Globalization and Culture*, Cambridge: Polity.

Urry, J. (2000), *Sociology Beyond Societies: Mobilities for the Twenty-first Century*, London: Routledge.

Webster, W. (1998), *Imagining Home: Gender, 'Race' and National Identity, 1945–64*, London: UCL Press.

Westwood, S. and Phizacklea, A. (2000), *Trans-nationalism and the Politics of Belonging*, London and New York: Routledge.

Wolff, J. (1993), 'On the Road Again: Metaphors of Travel in Cultural Criticism', *Cultural Studies*, 7: 224–39.

Part I
Bodies at Home and Away

I Still Call Australia Home: Indigenous Belonging and Place in a White Postcolonizing Society

Aileen Moreton-Robinson

> Our story is in the land . . . it is written in those sacred places. My children will look after those places, that's the law. Dreaming place . . . you can't change it no matter who you are. No matter you rich man, no matter you King. You can't change it . . . Rock stays, earth stays. I die and put my bones in cave or earth. Soon my bones become earth . . . all the same. My spirit has gone back to my country . . . my mother. (Big Bill Neidjie, in *Kakadu Man* [1985: 47, 62]).

> I've been to cities that never close down, from New York to Rio to old London town but no matter how far or how wide I roam, I still call Australia home. I'm always trav'lin, I love being free and so I keep leaving the sun and the sea, but my heart lies waiting – over the foam. I still call Australia home. (Extract from the song *I Still Call Australia Home* written by Australian international entertainer Peter Allen.)

Migrancy and dispossession indelibly mark configurations of belonging, home and place in the postcolonizing nation-state.[1] In the Australian context, the sense of belonging, home and place enjoyed by the non-Indigenous subject – colonizer/migrant – is based on the dispossession of the original owners of the land and the denial of our rights under international customary law. It is a sense of belonging derived from ownership as understood within the logic of capital; and it mobilizes the legend of the pioneer, 'the battler', in its self-legitimization. Against this stands the Indigenous sense of belonging, home and place in its incommensurable difference. It is these differences in conceptions and experiences of belonging that I address in this chapter. I do this through a reconsideration of the discourses on British migrancy and a critique of the ways that migrancy is mobilized in postcolonial theory. My focus on white British migrancy is because of its role in colonization and the dominant and privileged location of white people and institutions, which remain at the centre of Australian society. I then discuss some of the ways in which Indigenous people configure home, place and belonging and the social, political and legal impositions that define us, the original owners, as not belonging, but as homeless and out of place. I argue that Indigenous belonging challenges the assumption that Australia is postcolonial because our relation to land, what I call an ontological belonging, is omnipresent, and continues to unsettle non-Indigenous belonging based on illegal dispossession.

British Migrancy and the Sentiment of Belonging

The words of Bill Neidjie and Peter Allen carry the marks of these differences in relations of belonging. Bill Neidjie is of the *Bunitj* clan, *Gagudju* language group, a traditional owner of the world heritage-listed Kakadu National Park in the Northern Territory. The late Peter Allen was a white Australian entertainer and songwriter who mostly lived out of Australia. His song 'I still call Australia home' is used by Australia's international airline to promote travel. It is a song that has wide appeal among many non-Indigenous white Australians because it captures the experience of 'awayness' and 'belonging'. It points to the current of movement and migrancy, which runs through conceptions of belonging among non-Indigenous white Australians and is at the heart of Australian colonial history. This sense of belonging is often expressed as a profound feeling of attachment. It is derived from ownership and achievement and is inextricably tied to a racialized social status that confers certain privileges: a social status that is enhanced by a version of Australian history that privileges the exploits of white Australians by representing them as the people who made this country what it is today.

The British Empire established itself through colonization and the concomitant waves of migrants from British shores to colonized ones. This was not a passive enterprise but was bound inextricably with the dispossession of the original owners of the land. Under international customary law colonies were established usually under the doctrines of conquest or cession. Possession of Australia was taken on a different basis. The first wave of invading white British immigrants landed on our shores in 1788. They claimed the land under the legal fiction of Terra Nullius – land belonging to no one – and systematically dispossessed, murdered, raped and incarcerated the original owners on cattle stations, missions and reserves. In all these contexts the lives of Indigenous people were controlled by white people sanctioned by the same system of law that enabled dispossession. Indigenous people were denied their customary proprietary rights under international law and their rights as British subjects of the crown. Indigenous people only attained Australian citizenship in the late 1960s and continue to be the most socio-economically impoverished group in Australian society today. The non-Indigenous sense of belonging is inextricably tied to this original theft: through the fiction of Terra Nullius the migrant has been able to claim the right to live in our land. This right is one of the fundamental benefits white British migrants derived from dispossession.

This fiction is constitutive of discourses on British migrancy. Recent studies of British migrants who came to Australia in the 1880s show that their sense of belonging was to Britain, and their relationship to Australia was a resource for the Empire. Migrants envisaged their task as being the establishment of a new colony for Britain. They were her 'pioneers', with all the associations that term has with notions of the new and previously unexplored, the unknown. They saw themselves as the first to take control of and manage the land; according to these discourses, it was the hard work and determination of these early migrants that developed the nation (Nettelbeck 2001: 100). Through their achievement, usually understood as being individual in nature, singular and independent, these British migrants brought us 'civilization'; they 'gave' us democracy and the market economy.

These migrants represented the newly emerging national identity. Belonging to this new nation, therefore, was racialized, and inextricably tied to the accumulation of capital, and the social worth, authority and ownership which this conferred. The Indigenous was excluded from this condition of belonging. The right to determine who was allowed into the country and therefore who could belong was exercised by a white British constituency at the heart of the nation. They legally ensured their social reproduction through the *Immigration Restriction Act, 1901* and the white Australia policy, which until the 1950s gave preference to white British, Canadian, American or New Zealand migrants (Markus 1995). The white body was the norm and measure for identifying who could belong. The white Australia policy despite being revoked in 1973 continued in practice for many years as Cavan Hogue, a former Australian ambassador to the Philippines in the 1970s, discloses:

Mixed race applicants could be approved if they were 75 percent European in appearance. We had some guidance on what to look for but measurement was difficult. You had to measure their noses, check the skin colour, gaze into their eyes and try to calculate the percentage of European appearance . . . In 1981 I went to work for Ian MacPhee (minister) and John Menadue (secretary) in Immigration. They wanted someone with Asian experience to help cope with the refugee influx and also to participate in a review of policies and practices. We found many leftovers of White Australia . . . For example, staffing patterns still reflected the good old days so processing was quicker and easier in the 'traditional' countries. We had some anomalies such as the British Boys Scheme where the taxpayer paid to send to Australia people who wouldn't make it if they applied in the normal way (Hogue 1998: 17).

The need to reproduce socially whiteness saw the continued migration of British after the Second World War, and the pioneer legend continued well into the mid-twentieth century. It is evident in the accounts of post-war British migrants and their representations of themselves as 'battlers', people who struggled to overcome adversity, worked hard and achieved a better life in the new society (Hammerton and Coleborne 2001; Thomson 2001). Their achievements were perceived as positive contributions to and investments in the nation and reinforced their social status. Their 'right to be here' attached particular capacities, opportunities and privileges to them, including a sense of ownership and authority, by virtue of their legal and social status as white immigrants. This notion of rights and the sense of belonging it engendered were reinforced institutionally and socially.

Australia is less white than it used to be due to the global shift to decolonization and economic necessity. Multiculturalism was adopted as the charter for the nation in 1970s by the Commonwealth government. In his book *Belonging: Australians, Place and Aboriginal Ownership*, Peter Read analyses a cross-section of migrant Australians of different ethnicities about their sense of belonging, in particular with reference to Indigenous ownership and the history of dispossession. Many of the non-white migrants' responses echoed a familiar theme. They felt that they belonged to Australia because they had chosen to live here and had contributed to the nation through their hard work. However, many believed that other Australians questioned their right to belong. They can belong but they cannot possess. Non-white migrants' sense of belonging is tied to the fiction of Terra Nullius and the logic of capital because their legal right to belong is sanctioned by the law that enabled dispossession. However, whiteness is the invisible measure of who can hold possession. The majority of voices in this book were troubled by the history of dispossession and Indigenous ownership but this did not erase their sense of belonging. Read himself feels similarly, and in this book tries to apprehend his own sense of belonging and its groundings. As a white Anglo middle-class male who considers himself 'native-born', he writes that for him, his profound attachments derive from many sources: from literature, awe, fear and fascination, respect for spirituality. They derive from listening rather than speaking, sharing rather than competing, the self flowing into and part of the whole, a sadness at the violation of what we first encountered. And belonging derives partly from law. (Read 2000: 217).

Then later he goes on to say:

I have no right to claim on behalf of non-Aboriginal Australia that all the non-Indigenous are now part of Australia's deep past, nor do I wish to. Belonging ultimately is personal. There are as many routes to belonging as there are non-Aboriginal Australians to find them. My sense of the native-born has come – is coming. It comes through listening but with discernment; through thinking but not asserting; through good times with my Aboriginal friends but not through wanting to be the same as them; through understanding our history but being enriched by the sites of past evil as well as good. It comes from believing that belonging means sharing and that sharing demands equal partnership (ibid.: 223).

For Read and others belonging is experienced as a profound attachment, one figured as *personal*. Personal sentiment is privileged in Read's account. This is problematic for a number of reasons, notably for its denial of the racialized structural power relations that have produced the legal conditions in which this sentiment is possible, enabled and inscribed. In the context of Australian postcolonizing relations, these power relations are themselves based on the denial of original dispossession.[2] It is the foundation of the nation and its structures. Likewise it is the denial of original (and continuing) dispossession that forms the foundation for Read's belief that his personal sense of belonging is based on an equal partnership with Indigenous people. There can be no equal partnership while there is illegal dispossession.

Who calls Australia home is inextricably connected to who has possession, and possession is jealously guarded by white Australians. Australia's migration patterns are less white than they used to be in part out of economic necessity, including the perceived imperative that Australia has increased influence in the Asia-Pacific region. However, the dominant institutions such as law and government, and their epistemologies, remain anglicized. The current Australian government, under the leadership of Prime Minister John Howard, ran its 2001 election campaign along race lines. The campaign played on the fears held widely among white Australians that the country is under threat of invasion from 'queue jumpers' and terrorists among the refugees from Iran, Iraq and Afghanistan. Since arriving on our shores, they have been placed in detention centres, under conditions many have argued are in breach of international law. In this move, the Government asserted white sovereignty. It asserted its right to choose who enters Australia – that is, who will be granted the status of migrant and who will be deemed 'illegal' trespasser – and to choose along race lines. This occurred despite its avowed policies of 'multiculturalism' and the ostensible breakdown of hegemonic whiteness.

Postcolonial Theory and the Metaphor of Migrancy

Postcolonial theorists provide us with useful concepts such as diaspora and hybridity to explain the experience of migration by coercion and choice (Ashcroft et al. 1995; Gandhi 1998; Bhabha 1994; Chambers and Curti 1996). In particular there is an interest in exploring the ways in which, under conditions of diaspora, multiple and hybrid identities and cultures emerge. According to these postcolonial theorists, in this hybridity lie possibilities for counter-hegemonic discourses. Diasporas are seen to produce conditions in which the cultural traditions of an imagined homeland are infused with structures of subordination and oppression in the new country, producing hybridity. Experiences of dislocation are disruptive of the migrant's sense of belonging to a particular place and provide the conditions for multiple identities.

In the process of theorizing the postcolonial, the narrative of colonization is significantly restaged. As Stuart Hall writes, it has come to signify 'the whole process of expansion, exploration, conquest, colonisation and imperial hegemonisation which constituted the "outer face", the constitutive outside, of European and then Western Capitalist modernity after 1492' (Hall 1996: 249). Postcolonial theory examines the effects of colonization and reconfigures the colonizer/colonized axis in different ways. The utility of postcolonialism lies in its ability to reveal the operations of counter-hegemonic discourses as produced by the dispersed, or diasporic, subject. However, for many it does so through a metaphor of migrancy that privileges the positionalities, multiplicities and specificities of migration. In doing so it can say very little about the effects, or the positionalities, multiplicities and specificities of Indigenous subjects. As Huggan eloquently summarizes:

> What is noticeable in much of this work, which might be loosely bracketed under the fashionable heading of 'travelling theory', is the *metaphorisation* of migration as a composite figure for a series of metaphysical, as well as physical, displacements. The metaphor of migration serves a variety of

different purposes: to illustrate the increasing fragmentation of subjecthood and subjectivity under (post)modernity; to reflect on the semantic instability underlying all constructions of (personal/cultural/national) identity; to insist on the homology between experiences of dislocation and the destablisation of essentialist ideologies and 'fixed' paradigms and patterns of thought. Migration has become a useful code-word for the different kinds of conceptual slippage that are characteristic of postmodern/poststructuralist approaches toward linguistic and cultural systems; in addition, migration functions as a catalysing metaphor of the exploration of cultural change and the apprehension of new, mobile cultural subjects in the nominally postnational era . . . migration and other patterns of human movement in the modern era tend to carry an imperial legacy that is often mystified in the voguish academic categories of nomadism, migrancy and displacement (Huggan 2001: 119).

In the work of Homi Bhabha (1996) and Iain Chambers (1990) for example, what is often overlooked is the particular situatedness of different migrants in relation to power and the legal context in which their hybridity has been and is manufactured. Social constructions of home, place and belonging depend not just on ethnicity and ties to an imagined homeland. They are conditional upon a legal and social status as well as upon the economic and political relations in the new country and its imperial legacy. What is often emphasized is the emergence of hybridity in the new country. This forecloses considerations of, for instance, the specificities of Irish, Scottish and English migrants' situatedness because it refuses the hybridity that has already resulted from the Irish and Scottish diasporas in England. That is, all British migrants are not positioned in the same way in relation to British imperialism because of their ethnicity. But in the Australian context whiteness confers certain privileges to those whose skin colour represents sameness. Irish, English and Scottish post-war migrants to Australia are differently positioned in relation to British imperialism than, say, Italian, Greek and Vietnamese migrants, and different conceptions of home, place and belonging are therefore produced. The elision of certain kinds of migration denies the way in which whiteness as a possession will mark migrants' differing implications in a colonizing relationship between themselves and Indigenous people.

This is also evident where post-colonial critics have recognized the ambivalent relationship of Australia to her colonial past through the terms 'settler' and 'settler culture'. There is a tendency for analyses to equate the empirical and substantive with the semantic and the metaphorical, which has the effect of reducing racialized power relations to the symbolic through the figurative possibility of language. In *Uncanny Australia, Sacredness and Identity in a Postcolonial Nation*, Ken Gelder and Jane

Jacobs (1998) argue that Australia is postcolonial because the Indigenous population are now inserted into the national imaginary through the symbolic rendering of 'the sacred'. They argue that this is an outcome of land rights struggles and the recognition of sacred sites. What they fail to acknowledge is that the majority of Indigenous people in Australia do not have land-rights nor do they have legal ownership of their sacred sites. This representation of postcolonial Australia offers the symbolic appropriation of the sacred as a way that white Australia can seek to achieve the unattainable imperative of becoming Indigenous in order to erase its unbelonging. A sentiment of belonging is furthered through white possession of the 'Indigenous sacred' as well as Indigenous lands. This is a problematic view of postcolonialism for it rests on the premise that the Indigenous population and white Australia have equal access to symbolic and material power (Schech and Haggis 2001: 145).

Against this and other representations of Australia as postcolonial, I argue that it is not postcolonial in the same way as India, Malaysia and Algeria can be said to be. These nations do not have a dominant white setter population. In Australia the colonials did not go home and 'post-colonial' remains based on whiteness.[3] This must be theorized in a way which allows for incommensurable difference between the situatedness of the Indigenous people in a colonizing settler society such as Australia and those who have come here. Indigenous and non-Indigenous peoples are situated in relation to (post)colonization in radically different ways – ways that cannot be made into sameness. There may well be spaces in Australia that could be described as postcolonial but these are not spaces inhabited by Indigenous people. It may be more useful, therefore, to conceptualize the current condition not as postcolonial but as *postcolonizing* with the associations of ongoing process which that implies. Through my use of the term 'postcolonizing' I seek to distinguish between the specificities of Indigenous/white settler societies such as Australia and those countries such as India and Algeria where the different specificities of historical experience are theorized within postcolonial studies. For the majority of the population in Australia belonging, home and place are inextricably linked to dispossession because

> [t]he resonance of migrancy is compounded . . . by the twinning of the always having arrived with the wilful forgetting of the nature of that arrival – of colonial conquest and racism – such that a sense of belonging and being at home was always reliant on a tension between awareness of arrival and skating over the nature of that arrival and its consequences (Schech and Haggis 2001: 148).

In postcolonizing settler societies Indigenous people cannot forget the nature of migrancy and we position all non-Indigenous people as migrants and diasporic. Our ontological relationship to land, the ways that country is constitutive of us, and therefore the inalienable nature of our relation to land, marks a radical, indeed incommensurable, difference between us and the non-Indigenous. This ontological relation to land constitutes a subject position that we do not share, and which cannot be shared, with the post-colonial subject whose sense of belonging in this place is tied to migrancy. Indigenous people may have been incorporated in and seduced by the cultural forms of the colonizer but this has not diminished the ontological relationship to land. Rather, it has produced a doubleness whereby Indigenous subjects can 'perform' whiteness while being Indigenous. In this sense, we are not 'other' or 'non-other' as Fanon describes the colonized subject in the Algerian context. There is always a subject position that can be thought of as fixed in its inalienable relation to land. This subject position cannot be erased by colonizing processes which seek to position the Indigenous as object, inferior, other, and its origins are not tied to migration. It is an incommensurate subject position evident in the work of Indigenous scholars such as Gunn Allen (1992), Huggins (1998), Monture-Angus (2000), Churchill (1994; 1995) but under-theorized within postcolonial theory.

Indigenous Belonging

Australia was a multicultural society long before migrants arrived. It is estimated that over 500 language groups held title to land prior to colonization. Indigenous people owned, lived on, were taught to know and belonged to particular tracts of 'country' which is the term used to refer to one's territory/land of origin or a person connected to the same piece of land. Indigenous people's sense of belonging is derived from an ontological relationship to country derived from the Dreaming, which provides the precedents for what is believed to have occurred in the beginning in the original form of social living created by ancestral beings (Moreton-Robinson 2000). During the Dreaming, ancestral beings created the land and life and they are tied to particular tracks of country. Knowledge and beliefs tied to the Dreaming inform the present and future. Within this system of beliefs there is scope for interpretation and change by individuals through dreams and their lived experiences.

The ancestral beings created animals, plants, humans and the physiographic features of the country associated with them. They also established the Aboriginal ways of life: a moral code for its social institutions and patterns of activity. Ancestral beings provided the rules for what can and cannot be done through both good and bad behaviour. Ancestral beings are immortal. They are creatures of the Dreaming who moved across country leaving behind possessions which designate specific sites of significance. They met others of their kind; they created and left the world of humans through being metamorphosed as stone or some other form, disappearing into the territory of another group or into the sky, ground or water. In doing so they leave behind tangible evidence of their presence on earth.

Ancestral beings also changed form and gender and in many cases are associated with elements or natural species. For example an ancestral being who is in one form an owl is in the mundane world associated with all owls today, thus the spirit character of the ancestral being continues today. Because the ancestral spirits gave birth to humans, they share a common life force, which emphasizes the unity of humans with the earth rather than their separation. The ontological relationship occurs through the inter-substantiation of ancestral beings, humans and land; it is a form of embodiment. As the descendants and reincarnation of these ancestral beings, Indigenous people derive their sense of belonging to country through and from them. Thus for example Warlpiri, Kaurna and Quandamooka people belong to Warlpiri, Kaurna and Quandamooka countries. This ontological relationship to country was not destroyed by colonization.

It may be argued that to suggest an ontological relationship to describe Indigenous belonging is essentialist or is a form of strategic essentialism because I am imputing an essence to belonging. From an Indigenous epistemology, what is essentialist is the premise upon which such criticism depends: the Western definition of the self as not unitary nor fixed. This is a form of strategic essentialism that can silence and dismiss non-Western constructions, which do not define the self in the same way. The politics of such silencing is enabled by the power of Western knowledge and its ability to be the definitive measure of what it means to be human and what does and what does not constitute knowledge. Questioning the integrity and legitimacy of Indigenous ways of knowing and being has more to do with who has the power to be a knower and whether their knowledge is commensurate with the West's 'rational' belief system. The anti-essentialist critique is commendable but it is premised on a contradiction embedded within the Western construction of essentialism; it is applied as a universal despite its epistemological recognition of difference.

Home and Place

The premise of colonization that Australia *belonged to no one* informed the relationship between Indigenous people and the nation state from its very inception and continues to do so. Legislation and state policies served to exclude Indigenous people from participation as citizens through their removal to reserves, missions and cattle stations where their everyday lives were lived under regimes of surveillance. Many people were removed from their traditional countries but carried with them knowledges of those countries, while others were not removed. Some reserves and missions were set up on other people's traditional country where the incarcerated traditional owners retained close links and ties to that country. Similarly, cattle stations usually had traditional owners of that country attached to them and hunting and gathering subsidized their de facto indentured labour. Other Indigenous people were stolen from their families and placed in institutions or adopted by white families. In effect colonization produced multiple contexts that shaped the construction of Indigenous subjectivities, which were and are positioned within discursive formations of history relative to a particular space, country and time. These subjectivities are tied to our ontological relationship to the land and serve to ground our political as well as our cultural identities.

We are not migrants in the sense that we have moved from one nation state to another, but the policies of removal transferred different indigenous peoples from their specific country to another's. This dislocation in effect means that Indigenous people can be out of place in another's country but through cultural protocols and the commonality of our ontological relationship to country we can be in place but away from our home country. This is a different experience of migrancy to that of the postcolonial subject. It is not a hybridity derived from a third space; a kind of menagerie of fluid diasporic subjects. Instead there is an incommensurate doubleness superimposed by marginality and centring. Marginality is the result of colonization and the proximity to whiteness, while centring is achieved through the continuity of ontology and cultural protocols between and among Indigenous people. This suggests that Indigenous subjectivity represents a dialectical unity between humans and the earth consisting of subject positions whose integration requires a degree of mimetic performativity.

The effects of removal and dislocation have resulted in different constructions of subjectivity that link people to place in multiple ways. In the last two decades of the twentieth century, Indigenous women wrote their life histories. All these women were removed from their families and country of origin. Indigenous women's life histories are based on the collective memories of inter-generational relationships between predominantly Indigenous women, extended families and communities. These relationships are underpinned by connections with one's country and the spirit world. In all of the life histories, Indigenous people are related either by descent, country, place or shared experiences.

Social relationships are important in all cultural domains, but their nature differs and the moral universe, which informs these relationships in Indigenous cultural domains, is outside the experience of migrants. Relationality is one dimension of this moral universe that is spiritually interconnected. Indigenous women perceive the world as organic and populated by spirits which connect places and people. In *My Place*, Sally Morgan's grandmother and mother hear the corroboree in the swamp when Sally's father is ill and understand this as the spirit's recognition of the father's mental turmoil (Morgan 1987). After his death the corroboree is no longer heard. When Daisy Corunna dies, it is the call of the bird that tells Sally about the end of her grandmother's life. In *Wandering Girl*, Glenyse Ward learns from the older girls of the spiritual beings, the *mumaries*, in the caves near Wandering mission. The older girls tell her that if she and the other children are naughty the *mumaries* will come and take them away (Ward 1988). And in *When the Pelican Laughs*, Alice Nannup returns to make peace with her country by performing a water-based ritual to appease the snake that lives in the waterhole at Mallina (Nannup et al. 1992). In *Ruby Don't Take Your Love to Town*, Ruby Langford receives a sign of bad news when late at night there are three knocks at her door but no one is in sight (Langford 1988). The next morning Ruby's friend Harold Leslie is told his father has died.

These experiences illustrate the way in which the spiritual nature of the world is incorporated into one's connection to place, home and country (Moreton-Robinson 2000: 19). The spiritual world is immediately experienced because it is synonymous with the physiography of the land. In the life histories the reality of spirituality is a physical fact because it is experienced as part of one's life. Indigenous women perceive themselves as being an extension of the earth, which is alive and unpredictable. Hence their understandings of themselves, their place and country also reflect this view. In their life histories Indigenous women perceive their experiences and others' experiences as extensions of themselves. This is a construction of subjectivity that extends beyond the immediate family. As Barry Morris points out

The interconnectedness of self to others is related to those with whom one is familiar: those with whom one is related, one grows up with or, more specifically, those with whom one engages in relations of mutuality . . . where notions of generalised reciprocity shape and inform daily interactions (Morris 1989: 215).

The life histories of Indigenous women show a moral ordering of sociality that emphasizes mutual support and concern for those with whom they are interconnected. Their ontological relationship to home and place facilitates this connectedness and belonging. While this ontology is omnipresent it is rarely visible, often elusive and most often unrecognizable for many non-indigenous people in their inter-subjective relations with Indigenous people.

Homelessness

This ontological relationship to land is one that the nation state has sought to diminish through its social, legal and cultural practices. The nation state's land-rights regime is still premised on the legal fiction of Terra Nullius. After a sustained effort over a number of years by Koiki Mabo and others, the existence of indigenous proprietary rights in land was recognized by the High Court of Australia in *Mabo & Ors vs Queensland (NO 2) (1992)*. However, Professor Kent McNeil argues that the rule of extinguishment used by the High Court in the Mabo (2) decision is inconsistent with the broad rule of common law. The High Court's interpretation, that at Common law, native title can be extinguished by the nation state if it is inconsistent with its sovereign power, transgresses the common law rule that the Crown cannot derogate from the vested interests of its subjects (McNeil 1995: 36). This rule is encapsulated in the Privy Council decision in *Attorney General of the Isle of Man v MyIchreest* (1879) 4 AC 294 (McNeil 1995: 39). McNeil argues that 'it doesn't matter whether those rights were derived from Crown grant or adverse possession or customary law. That is a fundamental limitation on the executive power' (1995: 41). Effectively what the High Court did in the Mabo (2) decision was to invent a rule of extinguishment that did not exist under common law, to allow for inconsistent grants to extinguish native title prior to the Racial Discrimination Act (1975). That is, it invented a rule of extinguishment that allowed the Crown to derogate retrospectively from the vested rights of its Indigenous subjects. In doing so the High Court judges made a decision based on politics and economics rather than on the rule of the law. The decision affirms the nation state's sovereignty by creating in law a hybrid of settlement that diminishes but does not erase Terra Nullius.

Pursuant to the Mabo decision and the subsequent *Native Title Act (1993)*, Indigenous people have in effect become trespassers in our own land until we prove our native title. Tragically and ironically, even though we were dispossessed of our lands by White people, the burden of proof for repossession of our lands is now placed on us, and it must be demonstrated in accordance with the White legal structure in courts controlled predominantly by white men (Moreton-Robinson 1998). As the written word is generally regarded as more reliable by courts, all claimants must be able to substantiate their oral histories with documents written by white people such as explorers, public servants, historians, lawyers, anthropologists and police. These documents often distort and misrepresent events through misinterpretation as they are racially and culturally biased. In the process of preparing a native title claim, this often results in the generation of conflicting reports, which lawyers usually seek to resolve by introducing the words or texts of yet another white expert. Confirmation of the Indigenous belonging to country is dependent on the words of white people.

The legal regime of the nation state places Indigenous people in a state of homelessness because our ontological relationship to the land, which is the way we hold title, is incommensurable with its own exclusive claims of sovereignty. The legal regime has reproduced the doctrine of Terra Nullius in order to give place and a sense of belonging to itself and its citizens. According to this regime it is Indigenous people who belong nowhere unless they can prove their title according to the criteria established by the state. Those who are unable to demonstrate ritual, ceremonial and the exercising of continuous rights in land do not belong anywhere other than to be positioned within a discourse of citizenship that seeks to erase dispossession through privileging white sameness over Indigenous difference.

Conclusion

Our ontological relationship to land is a condition of our embodied subjectivity. The Indigenous body signifies our title to land and our death reintegrates our body with that of our mother the earth. However, the state's legal regime privileges other practices and signs over our bodies. This is because underpinning this legal regime is the Western ontology in which the body is theorized as being separate from the earth and it has no bearing on the way subjectivities, identities and bodies are constituted. In Australia, Indigenous subjectivity operates through a doubling of marginality and centring, which produces an incommensurate subject that negotiates and manages disruption, dislocation and proximity to whiteness. This process does not erase Indigenous ontology; this suggests that Indigenous subjectivity is processual because it represents a dialectical unity between humans and the earth. It is a state of embodiment that continues to unsettle white Australia.

The subsequent legal regimes we all live under are outcomes of postcolonizing conditions. Indigenous people's circumstances are tied to non-Indigenous migration and our dislocation is the result of our land being acquired for the new immigrants. We share this common experience as Indigenous people just as all migrants share the benefits of our dispossession. In most postcolonial theory the postcolonial is positioned in relation to the dominant culture in the country of arrival and the one they left. In this sense postcolonialism or, as Ahmed (2000) argues, post-coloniality exists in Australia but it too is shaped by white possession. What requires further theorizing is how the white and non-white postcolonial subject is positioned in relation to the original owners not through migrancy but possession in countries such as Australia.

As I have argued, Indigenous people's sense of home and place are configured differently to that of migrants. There is no other homeland that provides a point of origin, or place for multiple identities. Instead our rendering of place, home and country through our ontological relation to country is the basis of our ownership. It informs a counter-hegemonic discourse to that of citizenship and migrancy. Gelder and Jacobs's (1998) assertion that Australia is postcolonial due to the symbolic incorporation of the Indigenous Sacred into the nation belies the kind of discourses whereby we are symbolically placed outside the nation.

Under Australia's white anglicized legal regime Indigenous people are homeless and out of place because the hybrid of settlement, which now exists in common law, continues the legal fiction of Terra Nullius through positioning us as trespassers. Who belongs, and the degree of that belonging, is inextricably tied to white possession. The right to be here and the sense of belonging it creates are reinforced institutionally and socially; personal profound sentiment is enabled by structural conditions. The colonizer/colonized axis continues to be configured within this postcolonizing society through power relations that are premised on our dispossession and resisted through our ontological relationship to land. Indigenous people's position within the nation state is not one where colonizing power relations have been discontinued. Instead, these power relations are at the very heart of white nationhood and belonging; they are postcolonizing.

Acknowledgements

I am indebted to Jane Haggis, Alison Ravenscroft and Fiona Nicoll for their invaluable comments on this chapter.

Notes

1. I use the verb *postcolonizing* to signify the active, the current and the continuing nature of the colonising relationship that positions us as belonging but not belonging.
2. My point here is that the law shapes our behaviour but our consciousness of it usually occurs through breaking it. We do not walk around contemplating what piece of legislation governs our ability to function and perform in any context on a daily basis second by second, minute by minute, hour by hour.
3. I use whiteness in accordance with Frankenberg's (1993) definition: a position from which white people view the world, as a privileged structural location and a set of cultural practices.

References

Achebe, C. (1995), 'Named for Victoria, Queen of England', in B. Ashcroft, G. Griffiths and H. Tiffin (eds), *The Post-colonial Studies Reader*, London: Routledge.

Ahmed, S. (2000), *Strange Encounters: Embodied Others in Post-coloniality*, London and New York, Routledge.

Allen, P. (date?) *I still call Australia home*, http://www.gigglepotz.com/f_songs8.htm (accessed 2 September 2001).

Ashcroft, B., Griffiths, G. and Tiffin, H. (eds) (1995), *The Post-colonial Studies Reader*, London: Routledge.

Bhabha, H.K. (1994), *The Location of Culture*, London and New York: Routledge.

—— (1996), ' Unpacking My Library . . . Again', in I. Chambers and L. Curti (eds), *The Post-colonial Question: Common Skies, Divided Horizons*, London: Routledge.

Chambers, I. (1990), *Border Dialogues: Journeys in Postmodernity*, London: Routledge.

—— and Curti, L. (1996), *The Post-colonial Question: Common Skies, Divided Horizons*, London: Routledge.

Chun, A. (2001), 'Diasporas of Mind, or Why There Ain't no Black Atlantic in Cultural China', in *Communal Plural, Journal of Transnational and Crosscultural Studies*, 9(1) (April): 95–110.

Churchill, W. (1994), *Indians are Us? Culture and Genocide in Native North America*, Monroe, ME: Common Courage Press.

—— (1995), *Since Predator Came: Notes on the Struggle for American Indian Liberation*, Littleton, CO: Aigis Press.

Frankenberg, R. (1993), *White Women, Race Matters: The Social Construction of Whiteness*, Minneapolis: University of Minnesota Press.

Gandhi, L. (1998), *Postcolonial Theory: A Critical Introduction*, St. Leonards: Allen & Unwin.

Gelder, K. and Jacobs, J. (1998), *Uncanny Australia, Sacredness and Identity in a Postcolonial Nation*, Carlton: Melbourne University Press.

Goldie, T. (1995), 'Representation of the Indigene', in B. Ashcroft, G. Griffiths and H. Tiffin (eds), *The Post-colonial Studies Reader*, London: Routledge.

Gunn Allen, P. (1992), *The Sacred Hoop: Recovering the Feminine in American Indian Traditions*, Boston: Beacon.

Hall, S. (1992), 'New Ethnicities', in J. Donald and A. Rattansi (eds), *Race, Culture and Difference*, London: Sage.

—— (1996), 'When was "the post-colonial?" Thinking at the Limit', in I. Chambers and L. Curti (eds), *The Post-colonial Question: Common Skies, Divided Horizons*, London: Routledge.

Hall, S. and du Gay, P. (1996), *Questions of Cultural Identity*, London: Sage.

Hammerton, J.A. and Coleborne, C. (2001), 'Ten-pound Poms Revisited: Battlers' Tales and British Migration to Australia, 1947–1971', in *Journal of Australian Studies*, 68: 86–96.

Hogue, G. (1998), Letter to the editor, *Courier Mail*, Tuesday, 17 February 1998, p. 17.

Huggan, G. (2001), 'Unsettled Settlers, Postcolonialism, Travelling Theory and the New Migrant Aesthetics', in *Journal of Australian Studies*, 68: 117–27.

Huggins, J. (1998), *Sister Girl*, St Lucia: Queensland University Press.

Langford, R. (1988), *Don't Take your Love to Town*, Ringwood: Penguin.

Mabo & Ors vs Queensland (NO2) (1992) Australian Commonwealth Law Report No. 1, Canberra: Australian Government Publishers.

Markus, A. (1995), 'Legislating White Australia', in D. Kirkby (ed.), *Sex, Power and Justice: Historical Perspectives on Law in Australia*, Melbourne: Oxford University Press.

McNeil, K. (1995), 'Native Title and Extinguishment', in *FAIRA Native Title Conference Papers*, Brisbane: Foundation for Aboriginal and Islander Research Action Ltd.

Monture-Angus, P. (2000), *Journeying Forward: Dreaming Aboriginal Peoples' Independence*, Annadale: Pluto.

Moreton-Robinson, A. (1998), 'Witnessing Whiteness in the Wake of Wik', in *Social Alternatives*, 17(2): 11–14.

—— (2000), *Talkin' up to the White Woman: Indigenous Women and Feminism*, St Lucia: Queensland University Press.

—— (2001), 'A Possessive Investment in Patriarchal Whiteness: Nullifying Native Title', in C. Bacchi and P. Nursey-Bray (eds), *Left Directions: The Third Way*, Perth: University of Western Australia Press.

Morgan, S. (1987), *My Place*, South Freemantle: Freemantle Arts Centre Press.

Morley, D. and Kuan-Hsing, C. (1996), *Stuart Hall: Critical Dialogues in Cultural Studies*, London: Routledge.

Morris, B. (1989), *Domesticating Resistance: the Dhan-Gadi and the Australian State*, Oxford: Berg.

Nannup, A., Marsh, L. and Kinnane, S. (1992), *When the Pelican Laughed*, South Freemantle: Freemantle Arts Centre Press.

Native Title Act (1993), 'Legislation with Commentary by the Attorney-General's Legal Practice', Canberra: Australian Government Publishing Service.

Neidjie, B., Davis, S. and Fox, A. (1985), *Kakadu Man: Bill Neidjie*, New South Wales: Mybrood.

Nettelbeck, A. (2001), 'South Australian Settler Memoirs', *Journal of Australian Studies*, 68: 97–104.

Read, P. (2000), *Belonging: Australians, Place and Aboriginal Ownership*, Cambridge: Cambridge University Press.

Schech, S. and Haggis, J. (2001), 'Migrancy, Multiculturalism and Whiteness: Re-charting Core Identities in Australia', in *Communal Plural, Journal of Transnational and Crosscultural Studies*, 9(2) (October): 143–61.

Thomson, A. (2001), 'Recording British Migration: Place, Meaning and Identity in Audio Letters from Australia, 1963–1965', *Journal of Australian Studies*, 68: 105–16.

Ward, G. (1988), *Wandering Girl*, Broome: Magabala Books.

–2–

The Home of Language:
A Pedagogy of the Stammer
Sneja Gunew

'Do not shoot . . . I am a B-b-british object!'

David Malouf: *Remembering Babylon*

'the detours and blockages of the stutter with its rejection of familiar endings'

Sandra Buckley: 'An Aesthetics of the Stutter'

The first register on the sensory grid is acoustic, a soundscape of the accents, before arrival and touching ground. Then the smell – the gum trees perhaps. Tullamarine airport on the outskirts of Melbourne. And then, finally, the light, usually in winter since that is the summer break in the northern hemisphere, occasions I can get away. The horizon has expanded, flooded by the sun that now punctures my skin almost instantaneously. Australia makes me sick – a sickness for and of the home.[1] I pay for each visit with months of antibiotics and salves. What has happened to my immune defenses in these intervening years? The skin barrier is now more porous than ever, a foreign body open to invasion by Australia.

A stammering and unsettling pedagogy may well be the only ethical possibility for a serial immigrant critic and teacher such as myself. This chapter attempts to locate a home within language (which language and within it what kind of register?), a language which is not one's first language complicated further by having to fashion it into a pedagogical tool and having to do this in a displaced context, that is, one in which one did not 'grow up' like a tendril or vine clinging to the certainties of particular social and physical structures. Yet in a different sense, language remains the most portable of accessories, one which has carved out a corporeal space; and when there are several languages the body sometimes transits from one to the other less than gracefully.[2] As well, one needs to recall Derrida's distinction between writing and speech[3] and the characteristics of the textual and spatial dimensions within which each operates. Nonetheless languages, with their inflections and rhythms, as much as their overt signification, invariably function to remind one of home in palpable ways. It is the meanings we first encounter in a specific language that structure our later lives psychically and physically and at the same time provide a prophylactic against the universalist claims of other linguistic meaning structures. Displaced from home, we are thus unable to feel at home because we are too aware of the alternatives.

The texts of the Australian writer David Malouf, of British and Lebanese descent, often deal with that sense of being strangers at home or dwellers within an estranged home. Malouf's *Remembering Babylon* explores early white settlement in Australia, where the darkness stereotypically associated with the 'primitive' Indigeneous peoples is ultimately shown to resonate *within* the white settler invaders. Meanwhile, the Aboriginal presences weave in and out of these textual spaces mediated by the fragmented subjectivity of Gemmy, a character who was left to die by his white shipmates and who is taken in and raised by an Aboriginal tribe. Gemmy is a Lacanian '(h)ommelette' if ever there was one,[4] and it is his line: 'Do not shoot . . . I am a B-b-british object!' which forms a kind of epigraph for the text (Malouf 1995: 3). Indeed, why bother to shoot when the constitution of 'objecthood' had already done its damage? When we first encounter him, even his humanity is in doubt:

> But it wasn't a raid, there was just one of them; and the thing, as far as he could make it out through the sweat in his eyes and its flamelike flickering, was not even, maybe, human. The stick-like legs, all knobbed at the joints, suggested a wounded waterbird, a brolga, or a human . . . that had been changed into a bird, but only halfway, and now, neither one thing nor the other, was hopping and flapping towards them out of a world over there, beyond the no-man's-land of the swamp, that was the abode of everything savage and fearsome . . . that belonged to the Absolute Dark (Malouf 1995: 2–3).

Gemmy's spastic body and abject stutter could be seen as performing the provisional location of the colonizers in a charged liminal contact zone (Pratt 1992). As Kristevan 'speaking subject', a subject-in-process, Gemmy's encounters with orality are subsequently confounded by the 'white writing' (the transcription of his tale), which he believes to have appropriated his soul. In the inner speech (third-person intimate or free indirect discourse) Malouf assigns to him, he is unstammeringly eloquent and complex:

And in fact a good deal of what they were after he could not have told, even if he had wanted to, for the simple reason that there were no words for it in their tongue; yet when, as sometimes happened, he fell back on his native word, the only one that could express it, their eyes went hard, *as if the mere existence of another language they did not know was a provocation*, a way of making them helpless . . . There was no way of existing in this land, or of making your way through it, unless you took it into yourself, discovered on your breath, the sound that linked up all the various parts of it and made them one. Without that you were blind, you were deaf, as he had been, at first, in their world (Malouf 1995: 65, my emphasis).

Gemmy appears to stammer only when he is interpellated as a British object, reattached to a place that barely impinges on his memory, one where he was abused and tortured, the equivalent of an unhoused nineteenth-century 'street kid' in an unhomely environment. He is also ultimately a pedagogue, teaching each group about the other in ways that destabilize their stereotypic anxieties about each other. He does not, of course, appear to be a pedagogue and it is often his very corporeality, its unexpected and awkward gestures, which conveys his didactic purpose. And in ways not unlike the subaltern example in Gayatri Spivak's famous essay, the suicide of Bhuvaneswari Bhaduri (Spivak 1988: 307–8), it is ultimately his corpse (or what remains of it) which offers a final message, a kind of resolution. Lachlan, the character who had elicited that first comment from Gemmy, comes upon the remains of a massacre many years later:

He looked at one dry bundle, then another – they were not distinguishable – and felt nothing more for one than for any of them . . . He sorrowed quietly for all, in the hope that it might also cover his bones, if they were here, and decided, without proof, out of a need to free himself at last of a duty he had undertaken, a promise made, and a weight on his heart, that this was the place and that one of these parcels, which could not be disturbed, contained the bones of a man with a jawbone different from the rest, enlarged joints, the mark of an old break on the left leg, whose wanderings had at least come to an end . . . (Malouf 1995: 197).

But what more could one say about this stammer? Kristeva notes that for classical Greek culture the barbarians are the ones identified by their clumsy and improper speech (Kristeva 1991: 51). Gilles Deleuze conceptualizes the stammer, or stutter, in ways reminiscent of his and Guattari's early work on Kafka and minority languages. In their influential essay, 'What is a Minor Literature?' they state: 'A minor literature doesn't come from a minor language; it is rather that which a minority constructs within a major language' (Deleuze and Guattari 1986: 16). Their analogies are telling: 'Prague German is a deterritorialized language, appropriate for strange and minor uses. (This can be compared in another context to what blacks in America today are able to do with the English language.)' (Deleuze and Guattari 1986: 17). Analogously, the stutter in language is carefully differentiated from the stutter in speech. In the former, language itself begins to 'vibrate and stutter' (Deleuze 1997: 108) and the writer 'makes the language as such stutter: an affective and intensive language, and no longer an affectation of the one who speaks' (Deleuze 1997: 107). As in the Kafka essay Deleuze describes the process as inventing a '*minor* use of the major language' (109) as 'minorizing' the major language. In sum, it renders the native language foreign or discovers the foreignness within it, 'he carves out a non-preexistent foreign language *within* his own language' (Deleuze 1997: 110). The further result is to conjure the limits of language and to situate it primarily in relation to silence. It is also important to note the distinction between speech and writing, something Deleuze and Guattari touch upon but don't pursue at this stage: 'Since articulated sound was a deterritorialized noise but one that will be reterritorialized in a sense, it is now sound itself that will be deterritorialized irrevocably, absolutely. The sound or the word that traverses this new deterritorializion no longer belongs to a language of sense, even though it derives from it' (Deleuze and Guattari 1986: 21). After Derrida, we are accustomed to thinking about speech as the privileged location of an authorizing presence and thus to stutter in speech is to destabilize this privileged zone from the outset but, traditionally, it is not perceived as such but rather as having a disabled access to speech. To stutter in writing provides other complexities, conjuring simultaneously a subaltern 'dysfunctional' access or imminent silencing and the skilled theoretical reflexivity associated with the postcolonially informed subaltern who, in Spivak's terms, can no longer claim a subaltern location (Spivak 1988).

In an essay on Freda Guttman's opera *Cassandra: An Opera in Four Acts,* Sandra Buckley traces an 'aesthetics of the stutter' as a way of destabilizing and deterritorializing meaning structures. Attempting to turn the stammer into a pedagogical model, as I am trying to do, means that one reveals to North American students, for example, the 'foreignness' of another culture at the same time as one destabilizes their own cultural assumptions and certainties in producing 'relays of meaning' (Buckley 1989). But perhaps even more interesting, in ways that link this process to my own earlier pedagogical efforts in Australia, it reveals the foreign within Australian culture itself – once again. My general argument in that former life had been that canonical Australian Literature, as a particular manifestation of the dominant culture, could productively be reread by means of nostalgia (the liberation of the uncanny) from positions currently outside that canon, that is, those constructed in non-Anglo-Celtic Australian writings (Gunew 1994).

These musings began for me some decades ago when I tried to think about what the mother tongue meant to me. What happens to the subject-in-process when it passes from one language system to another? What form of repression takes place when the subject is forced to enter a new symbolic order? What happens to the other and prior language attached to a specific culture (Kristeva 1980)? Is the first language subsequently rendered alien, shameful, transgressive, particularly if it is outside the acceptable repertoire of 'foreign languages'? But why refer to psychoanalytical models and discourses when psychoanalysis as institution and practice has been deeply implicated within colonialism and ethnography? One answer would be to say that from the outset I realized that the veneer of the rational would always impede attempts to analyse the nature of the dominant culture's resistance to attempts at questioning its orthodoxies. Psychoanalysis offered a persuasive account of subjectivity that allowed for the irrational, for the influence of sub-rational forces. At the same time, by that stage the historical work identifying the importance of Freud's own cultural marginality had prepared the way for being alert to the minoritarian status of other psychoanalytical practitioners, including Kristeva (Kristeva 1996). My project attempted to continue one associated with Fanon's intervention in psychoanalysis: 'Fanon's contribution as psychiatrist in the colony was to insist on the importance of the cultural context in which symptoms appear' (Vergès 1996: 85), and I would extend this to say that cultural contexts are always a dimension in any psychoanalytical encounter though this is not always acknowledged. What I would reinforce now is that within psychoananlysis, language is both symptom and 'cure' and that language as much as 'skin', or Spivak's 'chromatism' (Spivak 1999: 164–6), functions as constitutive element in the creation of the 'outsider'.

In the new order that immigrants enter in Australia, the forces of assimilation (in all its meanings) affect the status to which their former subjectivity is relegated, especially when the father's proper name is often repudiated as illegitimate. This takes place not only in terms of the classic formulations of Lacanian psychoanalysis, where the symbolic order is governed by the name of the father, but also in a cruder sense where the loss of the family patronymic (too hard, too foreign) is repetitively staged in immigrant narratives, often in conjunction with the injunction to repress a whole language:

We were so big there and could do everything. When you have lots you know it. Lucky and lucky and money. My father was the tallest man in the world. Here we were nothing. There vet in the district and respect. The head of the returned soldiers and medals. Here washed floors in the serum laboratory. Shrinking man. I grow smaller every day (Walwicz 1982).

What happens when the subjectivity acquired within one symbolic order is lost in another: are we left with an empty space and a vacated subjectivity, a type of aphanisis or fading of the subject (Lacan 1979)? This loss of self is eloquently expressed by the Polish American writer Eva Hoffman:

> For a while, like so many immigrants, I was in effect without language, and from the bleakness of that condition, I understood how much of our inner existence, our sense of self, depends on having a living speech within us. To lose an internal language is to subside into an inarticulate darkness in which we become alien to ourselves (Hoffman 1999: 48).

Is it not of significance that the subject enters the symbolic order through a *particular* language?[5] It would appear that this first subjectivity, by necessity, is repressed – but where then is its locus? It has been noted that the development of language takes place at the same time as learning to walk and thus involves 'the acquisition of a whole spatial organization regarding separation from the primary object, experiments in detachment, and the possibility of verbal conjunction with the distant object' (Amati-Mehler et al. 1993: 126). Does it make sense to locate the first subject-in-language in the pre-symbolic which Kristeva, for example, characterizes as the domain of the semiotic and the maternal? Does the disowned father become the mother? Does it make sense to refer to a 'first' symbolic order and to relocate it in the Lacanian Imaginary where the subject experiences illusory totality with a phallic mother? What is both seductive and perverse about psychoanalytical discourse is that terms such as 'mother' and 'father' function as both *langue* and *parole* in the Saussurian (1959) sense. That is, they are *parole* in that each of us fills these terms with specific content and *langue* in that they function as abstract zones of affect which transform our *paroles* into phantasmatic projections, not unlike the process that occurs with pedagogues as well.

In trying to understand Australia's settler-colonial culture I identified a process of repression, with immigrants functioning as the irruption of the repressed in unpredictable ways – a rhythmic babble, perhaps, for those who inhabit the established cultural order. Is this how immigrant languages are heard within an Anglophone context? Was the delegitimized name and law of the father reattached to the maternal, the female custodians of these multi-cultures: customs, cooking, costumes and the old tongues, elements in an apparently benignly conceived nostalgia where 'they' could keep their ghetto existences so long as they remained within boundaries and were not too noisy? My contention at that time was that the machinery of nostalgia was not simply benign but released the uncanny, as we find when we scrutinize the process of memory and its legitimations. Presumably, this nostalgia comprised the desire for access through language to direct and unmediated experience, outside a representation that is always a misrepresentation. The term 'nostalgia' derives from the Greek, combining 'a return home' and 'pain'; a prolonged absence from home, homesickness. In the index to Freud's collected works the closest term to nostalgia is *Heimweh* a pregnant term containing the home, the mother, sickness *for* but also *of* the home. The term also relates to adjectives *heimlich,* secret, and *unheimlich,* uncanny, whose etymology may be traced in Freud's essay on that theme as a cluster of terms variously defining a mechanism of repression.

The most significant features of Freud's essay developing this relay of terms, 'The Uncanny', can be summarized as follows: 'for this uncanny is in reality nothing new or alien, but something which is familiar and old-established in the mind and which has become alienated from it only through the process of repression' (Freud 1985 [1919]: 363–4). Toward the beginning of the essay, Freud traces the etymology of the word in various languages beyond the limited equation, 'uncanny' equals 'unfamiliar'. Indeed, his analysis eventually links the home, the family and the secret, within both; secret and uncanny (*heimlich* and *unheimlich*) have their roots in the home (*Heim*). The erasure of this distinction embraces many others – for example, that between inside and outside – in respect of which Freud cites illustrations of death-in-life, life-in-death. Since the framework of the analysis is Hoffmann's story, 'The Sandman', automata, that nineteenth-century obsession, exemplify something dead that appears to live and, conversely, those living who imitate the dead when they indulge in mechanistic behaviour. Here sight becomes the privileged sense and, when threatened, signifies castration. The figure of the double is insurance against, but also a harbinger of, the death of the unique and sovereign subject. Finally, there is the important insight that the main symptom of the uncanny is repetition – the compulsion itself, rather than its content, is linked in turn to animism and the omnipotence and logic of thought which, like the compulsion to repeat, testifies to the need to control, 'animism, magic and sorcery, the omnipotence of thoughts, man's attitudes to death, involuntary repetition and the castration complex comprise practically all the factors which turn something frightening into something uncanny' (Freud 1985 [1919]: 365). In her influential book *Strangers to Ourselves*, Kristeva situates her further musings on Freud's uncanny at the heart of her text. The uncanny is located precisely within the subject's unconscious, 'The other is my . . . unconscious' (ibid.: 183), such that 'when we flee from our struggle against the foreigner, we are fighting our unconscious' (Kristeva 1991: 191). Thus immigrants in these settler-cultures often (along with others such as the Indigenous peoples) become representatives of the unconscious.

Rereading canonical Australian Literature through the lens of 'immigrant' nostalgia (the recognition of the workings of the uncanny), as exemplified in non-Anglo-Celtic Australian writings, would render uncanny traditional versions of home/mother/land, in which the referent is an Australia always mediated by somewhere else (most often, the shadow of England and Ireland). Indeed, secrets might be revealed, akin to the parcel of bones, which may or may not be those of a white Aboriginal[6] called Gemmy. In the writings of those who adopt the cultural positions of Anglo-Celts, Australia is situated paternally, as the father or third term that disrupts the mother-child dyad. The suggestion I made during that period was that 'Australia' is never located in the pre-symbolic for the descendants of the settler-colonizers, in contrast with a critical tradition that has always been quick to construct an organic (and maternal) link between writing and land (for example, the work of P.R. Stephensen).[7] In actuality, it is always refracted by particular cultural prisms from elsewhere. In itself, this is hardly challenging or new – how could any writing not be mediated or exist anywhere but in the mediatory symbolic order? But what has still not been analysed in any detail is the nature of these mediations in relation to a 'home' culture and land or place. That the referent for an Australian home/mother/land need not inevitably be England or Ireland is the working assumption of all my work.[8]

In addition, what might 'Australia' look like when these *other* motherlands and tongues are acknowledged as spaces of origin? Australia is the mother who is not mother, the uncanny place that will never give birth: the still-born. For white Australians, the country is the dead centre, the mother who ingests life. As Kristeva states: 'Freud noted that the archaic, narcissistic self, not yet demarcated by the outside world, projects out of itself what it experiences as dangerous or unpleasant in itself, making of it an alien *double*, uncanny and demoniacal' (Kristeva 1991: 183). For the descendants of the settler-colonizers, life in Australia traditionally exists in the cities, on the edge, where the land is covered over, pressed under, and where the subject is lost in the automatic, automaniac maze:

life-in-death, death-in-life. The maternal space is always elsewhere, though repressed; in other cultures, though disavowed. Paradise, the illusion of language devoid of the figurative, the nostalgia for utopia, are always an element in the uncanny which functions in its contradictions as a sickness for and of the home.

My pedagogical efforts in Australia over twenty-five years took several forms and are documented elsewhere (Gunew 1994). In short, they used what was then the fledgling terrain of poststructuralist critical terms and debates to argue a case against the canonical culture, including its literature. It involved setting up the first courses in non Anglo-Celtic Australian writing and orature (Gunew and Longley 1992), immigrant histories, library collections and bibliographies (Gunew et al. 1992) and framing the first (multi)cultural arts policies (Gunew and Rizvi 1994).This was at a time when Australian mainstream culture was busily attempting to cut its ties with England and construct itself as a republic (Hudson and Carter 1993) and as postcolonial. Destabilizing that model using poststructuralist and (increasingly) postcolonial criticism comprised a frustrating pedagogical agenda (Gunew 1999). Within university structures the descendants of the post-war immigrants were not as yet a substantial presence and those few who surfaced in the universities were quickly corralled into the study of canonical versions of the culture. Many left. My flight to another settler-colony, Canada, served to unsettle my own pedagogy. In the first instance what had been perceived as not quite white in Australia and heard as an 'accent' no longer registered as the same kind of 'foreignness'. If anything, ironically, the speech was heard as 'British'. The institutional agenda thrust upon me was to teach 'Commonwealth' or 'World' literature and a new unease descended. The task now was to destabilize the models of postcolonialism that were already congealing into orthodoxies and to discover those who continued to be marginalized in those 'authentic' postcolonial cultures, those settler-colonies, the Americas. The communities of those who 'broke' English (Fusco 1995) beckoned, as did the politics of language, including transnational English (Talib 2002).These explorations are unfinished (Gunew 2002; Gunew forthcoming) but in the remainder of the chapter are some speculations around texts assembled to represent an insertion of the stammer in 'Commonwealth' and 'post-colonial' literatures.[9]

When language as a natural extension of acquired corporeality is unsettled the consequences can be both painful and deadly. In Maori writer Patricia Grace's novel *Baby No- Eyes*, one of the characters is killed by the war between her first language and the imposition of colonial English:

For a while she was happy and we played together, then when it was time to go to school again she became sick and couldn't eat. Her throat closed and wouldn't let any food go down. Her skin was moist all the time and she couldn't get out of bed.
Not long after that she died.
Killed by school.
Dead of fear. (Grace 1999: 38)

Stories of Indigenous children being punished for speaking their first language have, sadly, become a trope within Indigenous literatures across the world and indeed the pragmatic results are that many of these languages have now disappeared. But there are also many other accounts of the actual physical pain involved in the internal clash of languages – the dis-ease they create within the individual body. In a poem tracing the history of English for the descendants of slaves, Canadian Caribbean writer Marlene NourbeSe Philip declares succinctly, 'english/is a foreign anguish' (Philip 1989: 58).

Meena Alexander's story of acquiring English (several times over) at the cost of Malayalam and Hindi, illustrates this contention. While English had been relatively benevolently embedded in the flow of her Indian languages, in Khartoum the disciplinary protocols were differently imposed in ways that secured an undisputed dominance for English. The tutor 'made me repeat the words she felt I should learn till their sharpness overwhelmed me, made my mouth hurt' (Alexander 1993: 112). Later in the essay she acknowledges that 'I realized the forked power in the language I had acquired: English alienated me from what I was born to' (ibid.: 116). In a type of ultimate betrayal by her body, English becomes associated with an abjective state, which is manifested when she retreats to the toilet to write in that most private of genres – poetry: 'I had to be secretive about the writing that came out of my own body . . . Little did I know that years later that hot unease I had first felt as a small child learning to repeat English words . . . that dense tissue of feeling (. . . a shame, finally, of being improper, not quite right, never quite right) would return sharply, enveloping me. Once again I felt the hot scent: forcing me back onto myself, onto a border existence . . . female, Indian, Other' (ibid.: 114). At an even later stage, she experiences the pressure to translate her mother tongue into English as equivalent to being dismembered (ibid.: 121). Writing poetry in English becomes a refuge once again, although this time it represents a liberation from the body, or at least from that body which wanted to retain its place within the mother tongue.

The betrayals of language are registered as well in Japanese Canadian poet Roy Kiyooka's account of 'growing up yellow in a white world', a betrayal that reached its most treacherous expression in the internment of Japanese Canadians during the Second World War. The various alienations Kiyooka experienced meant that 'whatever my true colours, I am to all intents and purposes, a white anglo saxon protestant, with a cleft tongue' (Kiyooka 1997: 182).The idea of the bifurcated, forked tongue returns in a number of these accounts of struggling with the imposition of a colonizing language forced onto a mother tongue, split in the process. 'We speak a patois, a forked tongue, a variant of two languages' (Anzaldúa 1987: 55), Gloria Anzaldúa states in her passionately argued plea for the recognition of Chicano/a difference from both Mexican Spanish and US English. For those who speak Chicano, descendants of those displaced or annexed when the United States took over vast portions of Mexico, language remains the only home. It is only within this 'dialect' with its many inflections and particularities that the history of this unhoused group is retained. Anzaldúa's account is punctuated by terms from her linguistic legacy, daring her readers to acknowledge their ignorance, to be frustrated into doing the painstaking work of translation. The border consciousness explored in her work has produced a whole cultural field that extends this perspective (Fusco 1995). Thus we have a different notion of those 'song lines' associated with the work of Aborigines carrying their custodial responsibilities toward their particular 'countries' with them in their songs. In the case of the Chicana, the song of the language actually becomes the home, such as it is, and when used signals the presence of compatriots.

Alexander's reference to the movement between public and private, in which the private is signalled by the written rather than the spoken, is transposed in Richard Rodriguez's well-known memoirs about learning to speak and 'become' English out of Mexican roots. Rodriguez's account is usually cited in support of those who argue against bi- or multi-lingual education, in other words as a plea for assimilation to English. However, what one discovers in his memoirs is a very painful account of a child who becomes alienated from his family, particularly his parents – unhoused from his own past. The family, as with many immigrants, fiercely guards its secrets from the outside world. In writing, which draws upon his individual life, Rodriguez's first-person narrator is perceived by his family as betraying their secrets. In their daily dealings with the outside world, the mother, for example, has a particular 'visitor's voice', an oral register of inhibition, of retaining an acoustic mask for the benefit of shielding their meanings, their familial idiolect, from the ear of the other. In writing, 'There seemed to me something intrinsically public about written words' (Rodriguez 1982: 180), the narrator is perceived as betraying these protocols. Caught between these opposing ways of moving through the world, the narrator comes to realize that 'By finding public words to describe one's feelings, one can describe oneself to oneself. One names what was previously only darkly felt' (ibid.: 187). However, there is the inescapable sense that in acquiring this plenitude the narrator is giving up at least one version of home. That difference between (public) writing and (private) speech functions to draw us back to the distinction Deleuze makes between the stutter in speech and that in language itself (its stammerings within).

Japanese American writer Garrett Hongo, on the other hand, finds himself suddenly transported to a home he had almost forgotten by encountering the unexpected cadences of a taxi-driver in Los Angeles. Agonizing about his life, moreover the life of his sons, growing up in 'blond'-dominated Oregon, Hongo encounters the familiar 'torque and torsion' of the taxi-driver's hybrid speech (Hongo 1998: 8). Its music and rhythm evoke that impure mixture of peoples and tongues, which had evolved over several generations in those diasporic catchment areas of Hawaii and Los Angeles.[10] It registers once again that the sense of belonging is most specifically caught in those webs of dialect or patois, those ephemeral but surprisingly resilient minor languages that carry with them the abrasions of specific and troubled histories, poignantly caught in that moment before they disappear. Their particularities have evolved in relation to the momentary and completely serendipitous juxtaposition of diasporic groups – never to be repeated and doomed to change even more rapidly than the transformations that are always part of any language. Those who aspire to the cultural capital of the dominant language, to the kind of assimilation supposedly celebrated in Rodriguez's memoirs, are doomed to hear these first languages as disabled tongues, as lingual impediments, a stammering spasm in the midst of sleek, global rhythms. Kristeva notes that the new language is akin to a prosthesis detached from the unconscious so that the speaker can 'say anything', reproduce the other language, but never be innovative in it for 'his unconscious shelters itself on the other side of the border' (1991: 32).

In an earlier era these different rhythms were perceived in terms of a battle between the maternal semiotic and the paternal symbolic, witness my attempts to argue for a particular kind of pedagogy, as described above. In the decade when feminist theorists were attempting to argue for an *écriture féminine* writers such as Daphne Marlatt spoke eloquently about being caught in the acoustic register of the maternal body which imposes its rhythms before we acquire language, 'we learn the sounds before we learn what they say' (Marlatt 1998: 10). It is a rhythmic perception that comes into being before the conscious sense of linguistic meaning and is retained in poetry or reaccessed in poetry. In more recent theorizing it is associated with the 'chora', derived from Plato and reinterpreted by Kristeva, which represents that maternal space of possibilities:

> Discrete quantities of energy move through the body of the subject who is not yet constituted as such and, in the course of his development, they are arranged according to the various constraints imposed on this body – always already involved in a semiotic process – by family and social structures. In this way the drives, which are 'energy' charges as well as 'psychical' marks, articulate what is called the *chora*: a nonexpressive totality formed by the drives and their stases in a motility that is as full of movement as it is regulated. We borrow the term *chora* from Plato's *Timaeus* to denote an essentially mobile and extremely provisional articulation constituted by movements and their ephemeral stases (Kristeva 1984: 25).

The initial problem with this line of argument for some feminists is that it restricts the 'feminine' to the sphere of the chaotic and the always-deferred future – pregnant with possibilities but never actually articulating or communicating sense in a more hard-edged notion of language and the social. This ensures that the 'feminine' always remains at the edges of power: the power of language and the language of power. On the other hand, there is now perhaps more of a search for and an understanding of those dynamics and rhythms which function beneath the surface, whether of consciousness, corporations or corporeality. What we see, or even hear, is not necessarily the sum of what we are getting.

Cassandra, the prophet doomed never to be believed, has been represented as speaking in tongues, as stammering and hysterical (Wolf 1984), but was of course vindicated by history. One likes to imagine those Delphic female prophets being licked by the forked tongues of their serpentine familiars, whose split languages communicated more than surface meanings. The notion of a stammering pedagogy does not offer such grandiose claims. It is an attempt to suggest a model for teaching that does not claim to have answers, indeed, which is sceptical of the discourse of answers, the position of 'those who know'. Such a pedagogy is attuned to the ghostly dimension of other meanings in any pursuit of a definitive meaning. Like Henry Giroux's 'border pedagogies' (Giroux 1992; Giroux and McLaren 1994), it is a matter not only of constantly crossing borders but of drawing attention to their presence – the ways in which their barbed-wire fences, their cells of solitary confinement, suddenly appear in the heart of the homeland, the metropolitan centre. *Cut along the dotted lines!* It is tuned in to the stammerings and dislocations that see beneath the surfaces, whether these be of globalization or nationalisms. It hears the unbearable sadness lurking beneath the acclaimed fable of assimilation Rodriguez presents to the world. As in the case of Malouf's character Gemmy, it notes the darkness the settler invaders carry within themselves and project recklessly as they intrude their deadly veneers on their chosen 'homes'. It registers as much in footnotes as in the main body of an academic text.

The post-war immigrants who entered Australia as displaced persons from all over the world harboured within their bodies the viruses and noisy parasites (Attali 1977; Serres 1982) of languages other than English. They were feared as bearers of contamination whose linguistic pluralities registered the welts of their visible difference on the skin, even of those who looked 'white'. Their stammering apologies haunt the presence of those desperate contemporary refugees cast into desert camps in apparent perpetuity who have sewn up their own lips and those of their children (Refugees).[11]

Notes

1. I explain this phrasing with reference to an essay I wrote some years ago (Gunew 1988), some of which weaves its way through this chapter in a different articulation.
2. I look at some of the ways in which languages carve a corporeal space in Gunew 2002. I consider a number of examples in which usage of a particular language creates an 'affect' that registers corporeally and, inevitably, has a lot to say about the post- or neo-colonial dimensions within which this operates.
3. In a series of books in the late 1960s Jacques Derrida explored the implications of Western metaphysics which he described as being predicated on what he termed a 'logocentrism' in which 'writing' (indicating the absence of an authorizing presence) was placed in opposition to 'speech'. (Derrida 1976; 1978).
4. The term represents Lacan's play on the 'little man' in his attempt to find images to suggest a fragmented subjectivity in relation to language and the symbolic. See Lacan 1977.
5. These questions are discussed more now than they were 10 years ago. See for example Amati-Mehler et al. 1993.

6. For discussions of 'white Aboriginality' see McLean, who traces the rise of Australian nativism in conjunction with the Modernist movement in the Arts. A Canadian critic who examines white indigeneity is Terry Goldie.

7. Stephensen (1969) is often perceived as the father of Australian literary and cultural studies and his essay coined the famous term 'cultural cringe'. He argued that Australians had transcended their colonial origins through their organic relationship with the land – a classic myth of autochthonous origins.

8. While *Uncanny Australia* (Gelder and Jacobs 1998) has since appeared and been influential in Australian cultural studies, their analysis is restricted to the 'uncanny' in relation to Aboriginality, in all its forms.

9. In a twin to this chapter, I use the case study of teaching Australian literature to a group of graduate students and it is here that I first broach the notion of the stammering nature of my pedagogy. See Gunew forthcoming.

10. I have written about Hongo's attempts to recover his Japanese past in Hawaii (Gunew 2002).

11. The reference is to the following report: 'More than 200 people at the bleak desert centre began a hunger strike eight days ago. Immigration Minister Philip Ruddock ordered five children removed from the camp to protect them from having their lips sewn together like those of other children in the protest' (Refugees).

References

Alexander, M.J. (1993), 'Language and Shame', *Fault Lines*, New York: Feminist Press, pp. 111–131.

Amati-Mehler, J., Argentieri, S. and Canestri, J. (1993), *The Babel of the Unconscious: Mother Tongue and Foreign Languages in the Psychoanalytic Dimension*, trans. J. Whitelaw-Cucco, Madison, CT: International Universities Press.

Anzaldúa, G. (1987), 'How To Tame a Wild Tongue', in *Borderland/La Frontera: The New Mestiza*, San Francisco: Aunt Lute.

Attali, J. (1977), *Noise: The Political Economy of Music*, Minneapolis: University of Minnesota Press.

Buckley, S. (1989), 'An Aesthetics of the Stutter', in *Cassandra: Voix Intérieures/Voices from the Inside*, Montréal: Oboro.

Deleuze, G. (1997), 'He Stuttered', in *Gilles Deleuze: Essays Critical and Clinical,* trans. D.W. Smith and M.A. Greco, Minneapolis: University of Illinois Press.

—— and Guattari, F. (1986), *Kafka: Toward a Minor Literature*, trans. D. Polan, Minneapolis: University of Minnesota Press.

Derrida, J. (1976), *Of Grammatology*, trans. G.C. Spivak, Baltimore: Johns Hopkins University Press.

—— (1978), *Writing and Difference*, trans. A. Bass, Chicago: University of Chicago Press.

Freud, S. (1985 [1919]), 'The Uncanny', in A. Dickson (ed.), *Art and Literature, Vol. 14. The Penguin Freud Library*, trans. J. Strachey, London: Penguin.

Fusco, C. (1995), *English is Broken Here: Notes on Cultural Fusion in the Americas*, New York: New York University Press.

Gelder, K. and Jacobs, J.M. (1998), *Uncanny Australia: Sacredness and Identity in a Postcolonial Nation*, Carlton: Melbourne University Press.

Giroux, H.A. (1992), *Border Crossing: Cultural Workers and the Politics of Education*, New York : Routledge.

—— and McLaren, P. (eds) (1994), *Between Borders: Pedagogy and the Politics of Cultural Studies*, New York: Routledge.

Goldie, T. (1989), *Fear and Temptation: The Image of the Indigene in Canadian, Australian and New Zealand Literature*, Kingston, ON: McGill-Queen's University Press.

Grace, P. (1999), 'Kura', in *Baby No-Eyes*, London: Women's Press.

Gunew, S. (1988), 'Home and Away', in P. Foss (ed.), *Island in the Stream: Myths of Place in Australian Culture*, Leichhardt: Pluto.

—— (1994), *Framing Marginality: Multicultural Literary Criticism*, Melbourne: Melbourne University Press.

—— (1999), 'The Dilemmas of a Multicultural Nomad Caught up in (Post)Colonialism', *Postcolonial Studies*, 1(3): 321–31.

—— (2002), 'Technologies of the Self: Corporeal Affects of English', *South Atlantic Quarterly* (February), 727–45.

—— (forthcoming) 'Stammering "Country" Pedagogies: Sickness for and of the Home', in L. Dale and M. Henderson (eds), *Terra Re-cognition: New Essays in Australian Studies*, St Lucia: University of Queensland Press.

——, Houbein, L., Karakostas-Seda, A. and Mahyuddin, J. (eds) (1992), *A Bibliography of Australian Multicultural Writers,* Geelong: Deakin University Press.

—— and Longley, K.O. (eds) (1992), *Striking Chords: Multicultural Literary Interpretations*, Sydney: Allen & Unwin.

—— and Rizvi, F. (eds) (1994), *Culture, Difference and the Arts*, Sydney: Allen & Unwin.

Hoffman, E. (1999), 'The New Nomads', in A. Aciman (ed.), *Letters of Transit: Reflections on Exile, Identity, Language, and Loss*, New York: New Press and New York Public Library.

Hongo, G. (1998), 'Lost in Place', in C.C. O'Hearn (ed.) *Half and Half: Writers Growing Up Biracial and Bicultural*, New York: Pantheon.

Hudson, W. and Carter, D. (eds) (1993), *The Republicanism Debate*, Kensington: University of NSW Press.

Kiyooka, R. (1997), *Mothertalk: Life Stories of Mary Kiyoshi Kiyooka*, ed. Daphne Marlatt, Edmonton: NeWest Press.

Kristeva, J. (1980), *Desire in Language: A Semiotic Approach to Literature and Art*, Oxford: Blackwell.

—— (1982), *Powers of Horror: An Essay on Abjection*, New York: Columbia University Press.

—— (1984), *Revolution in Poetic Language*, trans. M.Waller, New York: Columbia University Press.

—— (1991), *Strangers to Ourselves*, trans. L. Roudiez, New York: Columbia University Press.

—— (1996), *Julia Kristeva Interviews*, ed. R.M. Guberman, New York: Columbia University Press.

Lacan, J. (1977), *Écrits: A Selection*, trans. A. Sheridan, London: Tavistock.

—— (1979), *The Four Fundamentals of Psycho-Analysis*, ed. J.-A. Miller, trans. A. Sheridan, Harmondsworth: Penguin.

McLean, I. (1998), *White Aborigines: Identity Politics in Australian Art*, Cambridge: Cambridge University Press.

Malouf, D. (1995), *Remembering Babylon*, Milsons Point, New South Wales: Random House Australia (Chatto & Windus).

Marlatt, D. (1998), 'Musing with Mothertongue (1982–1983)', in S. Kamboureli (ed.), *Readings from the Labyrinth: The Writer as Critic:IV*, Edmonton: NeWest Press.

Philip, M.N. (1989), 'Discourse on the Logic of Language', in *She Tries Her Tongue, Her Silence Softly Breaks*, Charlottetown, PEI: Ragweed Press.

Pratt, M.L. (1992), *Imperial Eyes: Travel Writing and Transculturation*, New York: Routledge.

'Refugees drink detergent as Australian protest grows', *Globe and Mail*, 24 January, A 14.

Rodriguez, R. (1982), 'Mr. Secrets', *Hunger of Memory*, New York: Bantam.

Saussure, F. (1959), *Course in General Linguistics*, New York: Philosophical Library.

Serres, M. (1982), *The Parasite*, Baltimore: Johns Hopkins University Press.

Spivak, G.C. (1988), 'Can the Subaltern Speak?', in C. Nelson and L. Grossberg (eds), *Marxism and the Interpretation of Culture*, London: Macmillan.

—— (1999), *A Critique of Postcolonial Reason: Toward a History of the Vanishing Present*, Cambridge, MA: Harvard University Press.

Stephensen, P.R. (1969), 'The Foundations of Culture in Australia', in J. Barnes (ed.), *The Writer in Australia*, Melbourne: Oxford University Press.

Talib, I.S. (2002), *The Language of Postcolonial Literatures: An Introduction*, London: Routledge.

Vergès, F. (1996), 'To Cure and to Free: The Fanonian Project of "Decolonized Psychiatry"' in . L.R. Gordon, T.D. Sharpley-Whiting and R.T. White (eds), *Fanon: A Critical Reader*, Oxford: Blackwell.

Walwicz, A. (1982), 'So little', *Mattoid*, 13, Geelong: Deakin University Press, 19.

Wolf, C. (1984), *Cassandra: A Novel and Four Essays*, trans. J. van Heurck, New York: Farrar, Strauss, Giroux.

–3–

'Dis-Orientalisms': Displaced Bodies/ Embodied Displacements in Contemporary Palestinian Art

Gannit Ankori

It is an oft-cited fact that Palestinian art and literature – like other national cultures – is replete with images that conjure up the body of the mother as a metaphor for the homeland.[1] In contrast to the ubiquitous references to the maternal metaphor, little scholarly attention has been devoted to the fact that Palestinian artists also equate the carnal Self with the native place. *'Our country is flesh of our flesh, bone of our bone'* proclaims Mahmoud Darwish, one of Palestine's most prominent authors (quoted in Jayyusi 1992: 51). By intentionally alluding to Genesis, Darwish generates a multi-layered metaphor, in which the homeland is identified as the poet's 'flesh and bone' (an individual and collective body); as the beloved first Woman, divinely created of and for Man; and as the primal Maternal being, all in one. Given this set of compounded identifications, it becomes clear why post-1948 experiences of loss, displacement and exile are imaged by Palestinian artists not only as a traumatic separation from the mother, but also as the visceral and excruciatingly brutal rupture between the Self and one's very own body.

Sliman Mansour's mud relief titled *Hagar* (1996) (see cover) preserves aspects of the archetypal mother-earth/homeland metaphor while, at the same time, challenging conventional representations that sentimentalize Palestine as an ideal, fertile mother. Parched desert-like earth composes Hagar's fragmented and cracked visage (Figure 3.1). Thus, her physical and emotional experiences of thirst and destitution are etched upon her very skin. Thematically, the biblical protagonist's role as the mother of Ishmael and the Arabs, her continual oppression by Sarah, ancestor of the Jewish people (Genesis 16), and her expulsion into exile (Genesis 21) transform her into a symbolic figure, representing the plight of Palestinians both under occupation and in exile.[2]

Figure 3.1 Sliman Mansour, *Hagar*, 1996. Mud on wood. 90 × 60 cm. Detail. Photo: Gannit Ankori.

Following the creation of *Hagar*, Mansour produced numerous self-portrait mud reliefs, as well as three-dimensional sculptures, that merge his entire body or dismembered vital organs with the earth itself.[3] One iconic object presents an abstract image of a heart fashioned of cracked mud (*Heart,* 2000) (Figure 3.2). This image recalls Frantz Fanon's post-colonial discourse that links the act of liberation with invasive, visceral self-knowledge as it equates the body of the individual with the collective body of his people: 'The native intellectual . . . who is willing to strip himself naked to study the history of his body, is obliged to dissect the heart of his people', Fanon wrote (1963: 44).[4] Mansour's image of a cracked (dissected?) heart, however, seems critically double-edged: on the one hand, it conveys the artist's desire to unite with his native soil. On the other hand, this heart – a lifeless lump of clay – evokes a sense of tragedy and death that undermines any simplistic heroic or 'romantic' reading.

Figure 3.2 Sliman Mansour, *Heart*, 2000. Mud. 17 cm height. Photo: Noel Jabbour.

Sliman Mansour was born in Bir-Zeit in 1947.[5] His artmaking is linked to his rural place of birth and closely relates – both thematically and technically – to the manual labour of the *fellah* (peasant farmer) who tills the soil, builds his mud hut and digs his grave. Since 1967, Mansour has been living under Israeli occupation. Through the use of desiccated and fractured images of Mother, Body and Heart submerged in mud, his art reflects a central dialectic that defines contemporary Palestinian identity, the oscillation between rootedness and displacement.[6]

In her critique of contemporary theories that metaphorize and essential-ize rootedness and displacement, Sara Ahmed asserts that experiences of migration and exile materialize within specific corporeal, temporal and spatial co-ordinates. 'The movements of selves between places . . . involve the discontinuities of personal biographies and wrinkles in the skin', she states (1999: 343). The discussion that follows not only con-firms this statement, but also attempts to illustrate how these mechanisms, that involve sites, bodies and lives within concrete political and social contexts, find embodiment in the work of individual Palestinian artists. In this chapter, I will analyse selected artworks by Mona Hatoum and Khalil Rabah, two Palestinian artists who radically reconfigure the relationship between their own body, the real or symbolic body of the mother and the native place.

Mona Hatoum's 'Dis-Orientalism'

Mona Hatoum's entire oeuvre, spanning more than two decades – from her earliest performance pieces, through her video works, installations and sculptural objects – is marked by a deep sense of dislocation and disorientation. These feelings are often expressed through the body – the body of the artist, the body of her mother, the body of the spectator, and surrogate objects that represent the absent human body. The acute sensation of 'unsettledness' (to use the artist's own terminology, Hatoum 1996: 134) that emanates from Hatoum's art and viscerally affects the viewers, is composed of two interconnected ingredients, both related to the artist's biography.

Mona Hatoum was born in Beirut in 1952, the youngest daughter of Palestinian exiles from the coastal town of Haifa. Four years before her birth, the Hatoum family was forced to flee their home, along with most of Haifa's Arab population.[7] Although the artist did not experience the Palestinian *Nakba* [catastrophe] first-hand, her family's violent uprooting affected her profoundly.[8] Before discussing its artistic manifestations, an extract from a letter written by the artist's mother (incorporated into Hatoum's 1988 video work *Measures of Distance*), poignantly exposes the underlying biographical foundations of this 'second-generation' trauma. The text is a portion of a letter in which the mother explains why she had seemed withdrawn and distant when Mona was a child. In the video, which will be discussed in detail later in this chapter, the mother's words, softly read in translation by the daughter, unravel a tale of traumatic rupture and shattered lives, transmitted from mother to daughter, from generation to generation:

> You say you can't remember that I was around when you were a child. Yes, things were different for your sisters, because before we ended up in Lebanon we were living on our own land . . . with our family and friends around us always ready to lend us a hand. We felt happy and secure and it was paradise compared to where we are now. So if I seemed to be always irritable and impatient, it was because life was very hard when we first left Palestine. Can you imagine us having to separate from all our loved ones, leaving everything behind and starting again from scratch, our family scattered all over the world, some of our relatives we never saw again to this day? I personally felt as if I had been stripped naked of my very soul. I'm not just talking about the land and property we left behind, but with that, our identity and sense of pride in who we are went out the window. Yes, of course, I suppose this must have affected you as well, because being born in exile, in a country that does not want you, is not fun at all. And now, that you and your sisters have left

Lebanon, you are again living in another exile and in a culture that is totally different to your own. So, when you talk about a feeling of fragmentation and not knowing where you really belong, well, that has been the painful reality of all our people.

The first component of Hatoum's 'unsettledness,' then, relates to the experiences of her early years, of being born to displaced and dispossessed parents, who were abruptly transformed into isolated members of a scattered and shattered community. These profoundly destabilizing formative sensations are expressed in Hatoum's art through various devices. For example, by modifying domestic objects 'of the home' into *unheimlich* or threatening objects; by creating ambiguous spaces that incarcerate the viewer; by transforming the very ground we walk upon into an unstable surface – as in her carpets of pins or marbles; by placing dangerous electric wires or heating elements in close and seemingly dangerous proximity to the viewers; by manipulating the size of objects, so that we are dwarfed by them, Alice in Wonderland style.

The second facet of Hatoum's 'unsettledness' relates to her literal 'loss of the Orient' as a result of the artist's double exile, first in Lebanon, later in the West. As a Palestinian in Beirut, Hatoum was – from the very start – an outsider. She spoke Arabic with a Palestinian accent that differed from the Lebanese accent which dominated the region. Her schooling was in French. In 1975, when she was in London for what was initially planned as a brief visit, the Lebanese civil war broke out. Stranded in England, she became an 'Arab' exile. Later she enrolled in art school, where English was the language of discourse.[9] Negotiating between three countries (Palestine, Lebanon, England) none of them her 'real' home, and between three languages (Arabic, French, English), Hatoum struggled to 'reorient' herself.[10] Displaced and distant from her mother tongue, she espoused a self-created 'dialect' composed as an amalgam of body language and the language of art. In this 'language' she became masterfully fluent.

Hence, the dis-orientation embedded within the art of Mona Hatoum is not merely *physical* and *spatial*, but also *geographical* and *cultural*. I coin the term 'Dis-Orientalism' here, in order to suggest a hybrid concept which merges Edward Said's term 'Orientalism' – expounded in his seminal treatise that critically examines the Western construction of the Orient – with Hatoum's own visual vocabulary of dislocated positions between East and West, shifting grounds and non-belonging. This neologism also stresses an essential, intellectual bond between Hatoum and Said: both are exiled Palestinian Arabs who operate (with great success) within the English-speaking West. Simultaneously inside and outside both cultures, they are hybrids of extreme talent, whose creativity is nurtured by the cultural treasures of both East and West. Their mutual respect for one another is also evident: Hatoum chose Said's article 'Reflections on Exile' as her favourite text to be excerpted in a 1998 monograph devoted to her work (Said 1998: 110–13); Said composed an illuminating and appreciative catalogue essay about the artist's exhibition at the Tate Gallery (Said 2000).[11]

The Displaced Body

Under Siege, performed in London in 1982, was a gruelling performance, in which Hatoum placed her own naked body literally and figuratively 'under siege' within a plastic cell. Significantly, though, the artist described this physical ordeal in a detached, self-estranged manner, referring to herself in the third person:

> A human figure reduced to a form covered in clay, trapped, confined within a small structure, struggling to stand up again and again . . . slipping and falling again and again . . . The live action was repeated over a duration of seven hours and was accompanied by three different sound tapes repeatedly blasting the space from different directions creating a collage of sounds: revolutionary songs, news reports and statements in English, French and Arabic (Hatoum 1983: 122).

Clearly, this quote reflects Hatoum's sense of alienation and instability, as well as her awareness of the trilingual context of her existence. In a later interview, Hatoum explained: 'Thinking about this work in retrospect, I feel it marked a phase of transition and acted as *rite de passage*' (Hatoum 1983: 122). Traditionally, a 'rite of passage' involves a ritual whereby the individual must undergo a trying physical ordeal before he or she is accepted as part of the collective or community. Hatoum's performance was explicitly related to her Palestinian identity: 'As a Palestinian woman this work was my first attempt at making a statement about a persistent struggle to survive in a continuous state of siege . . .' (Hatoum 1983: 122).

The powerful impact of *Under Siege* may still be experienced, as filmed sections of this performance were incorporated into Hatoum's 1984 video work, entitled *Changing Parts* (Figure 3.3). In the video piece, the images from *Under Siege* were juxtaposed with black-and-white photographs of the bathroom of Hatoum's childhood home in Beirut.[12] The latter were taken by the artist during a 1981 visit to Lebanon, in a manner that reveals her predilection for geometric patterns and formal, modernist

Displaced Bodies/Embodied Displacements

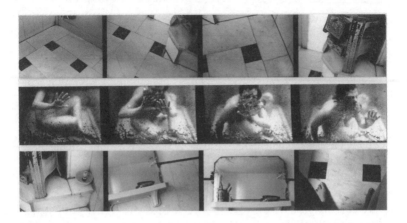

Figure 3.3 Mona Hatoum, from *Changing Parts*, 1984. 24-minute video, a Western Front Video Production.

structures. Bach's Cello Suite no. 4 accompanies the images as they appear and reappear slowly in various sequences, as if following the scrutinizing gaze of the artist who examines, in an alienating, objectifying manner, details of what once was a familiar, intimate site. After almost thirteen minutes in which every corner, niche and pipe of the bathroom is subjected to a scrutinizing gaze, Bach's sombre cello music is interrupted by harsh noise and an incoherent, blurry image that fills the screen. The association of running water is created through the sound track and the shower images, only to be undermined by the consequent sights and sounds. It is here that segments from Hatoum's *Under Siege* performance appear, accompanied by the deafening noise of radio static and barely audible reports about the war in Lebanon. Hatoum's naked body is seen, trapped within the transparent plastic cubicle that evokes a shower stall. However, as her body slowly becomes smeared with mud (dirtied rather than cleansed), and as she falls into various positions of vulnerability, the true nature of her predicament becomes apparent. The images of her body evoke a lifeless corpse, slowly falling down; a foetus or a cadaver in a foetal position; a caged wild animal, struggling to break out of its confining cell. The soft mud often looks like blood, making the image even more expressive.

Interspersed among these images of the artist's vulnerable body, photographs from the Beirut home return to the screen. This time, the tiled floor quivers, as if shattered by an earthquake that disrupts its geometric purity and threatens the stability of life itself. The image of the bathroom window appears to become dark and ominous. In this video piece, Hatoum, who was seemingly safe in London, inflicted the torment and pain of being under siege upon her very own body. Although (or perhaps because) she was in exile, she felt compelled to 'change parts' (change roles, change places, change body parts), with members of her family, who were actually living under siege in their Beirut home. Listening to the extreme sorrow of the cello music chosen by Hatoum for this piece, it becomes clear that one may leave home, but 'home' never leaves the body. Exile, Said tells us, 'is the unhealable rift forced between a human being and a native place, between the self and its true home: its essential sadness can never be surmounted' (Said 1990: 357).

Other performances enacted by Hatoum during the war years similarly placed the dis-placed body of the exiled artist as an agent of participation in the tragic events 'back home.' The artist laconically described her 1983 tableau vivant *The Negotiating Table* (Figure 3.4) thus:

> I was lying on a table, my body covered with entrails, bandages and blood and wrapped up in a body bag. There were chairs around the table and sound tapes of speeches of Western leaders talking about peace (Hatoum 1987: 127).

The artist explicitly linked this work with the September 1982 massacres in the Palestinian refugee camps Sabra and Shatila: 'This piece was the most direct reference I had ever made to the war in Lebanon. I made this work right after the Israeli invasion and the massacres in the camps, which for me was the most shattering experience of my life' (Hatoum 1987: 127).

Close-up photographs that document Hatoum's performance (Figure 3.5) and verbal descriptions of the work relate the fact that, as the artist was lying inside the body bag, 'sanguineous entrails bulged from her abdomen' (Boullata 2001: 172). I suggest that this potent and visceral image harks back to the events that triggered the Hatoum family's traumatic expulsion from home: '*I heard my mother say: they were disembowelling pregnant women, that's why we had to leave!!!*' Mona Hatoum recalled a haunting nightmare/memory decades later (Hatoum 1983: 122). The harrowing image of disembowelled pregnant women relates to one of the cruelest episodes associated with the *Nakba*, the Dir Yasin massacre: On 9 April 1948, members of an extreme right-wing group of Jewish militants (*Irgun*) slaughtered 245 men, women and children in Dir Yasin, a peaceful village near Jerusalem, and, according to eyewitnesses, slashed open the belly of at least one pregnant woman. Reports of these atrocities spread like wildfire throughout Palestine. On 21 April 1948, just twelve days after the Dir Yasin massacre, as Jewish forces began to bombard

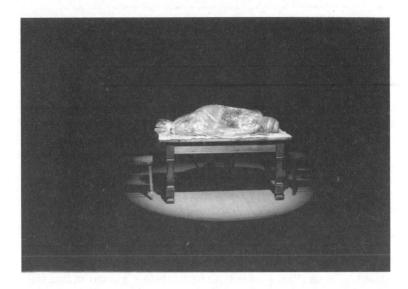

Figure 3.4 Mona Hatoum, from *The Negotiating Table*, 1983. 3-hour performance. Photo: Eric Metcalfe.

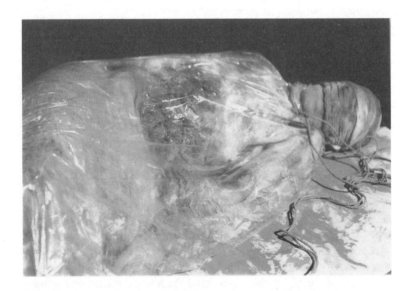

Figure 3.5 Mona Hatoum, from *The Negotiating Table*, 1983. 3-hour performance. Detail. Photo: Eric Metcalfe.

Haifa's Arab neighbourhoods, fear triggered by the horrors of Dir Yasin compelled the Hatoum family to run for their lives, leaving everything behind. In her 1983 work, Hatoum *re-placed* the disembowelled Palestinian victims with her very own (exiled or *dis-placed*) body, merging traumatic images of Dir Yasin with contemporary images from the Sabra and Shatila camps.

A decade later, in 1993, Hatoum produced a monumental black cube entitled *Socle du Monde,* paying homage to Piero Manzoni's 1961 upside down cube, that served as an ironic 'base' for the world. Undermining the minimalist purity of the cube, Hatoum composed her own cube of black iron filings that were organized by magnets in the shape of entrails (see illustrations, Archer et al. 1998: 108–9). Two years later, the artist constructed a floor piece made of silicone rubber fashioned like meandering entrails and appropriately titled *Entrails Carpet* (1995) (Archer et al. 1998: 19). Thus far, these works have been discussed in formal terms, or as they relate to the attraction–repulsion sensations experienced by viewers (Archer 1998: 17–18). I believe that both works reflect Hatoum's aforementioned preoccupation with entrails that stems from her early traumatic exposure to reports of the disembowelled women of Dir Yasin. Viewed from this perspective, both the 'base of the world' and the 'carpet of entrails' may be interpreted as the literal and metaphoric foundations upon which Hatoum's imagery is based.

Hatoum's *Corps étranger* (1994) (Figure 3.6) provides a radical expression of the estrangement caused by displacement and its impact upon the bodies of both artist and viewers. In this video installation, the artist forces the viewers into a claustrophobic cylinder-shaped space. Within this cell, enlarged images taken from endoscopic and colonoscopic footage of the artist's body are projected onto the floor. As the audience stands precariously upon the ever-changing images of viscera, the ground is transformed into an unstable abyss, while sounds of the artist's breathing and pulse echo inside the tight, confining and disorienting space.

Equipped with technological devices and espousing the invasive medical gaze, Hatoum images her own naked body in a way that diverges dramatically from traditional artistic depictions of the female nude. Lynda Nead's analysis of the conventions that govern the representation of the female body in Western art stresses the fact that certain aspects of the body – its juices, orifices and internal organs – are deemed unworthy of representation. External contours, on the other hand, are emphasized as they define and seemingly control and contain the 'unruly' (hence threatening) aspects of the body (Nead 1992). Throughout her career, Hatoum consistently focused on the 'unsightly' and taboo aspects of the body, using

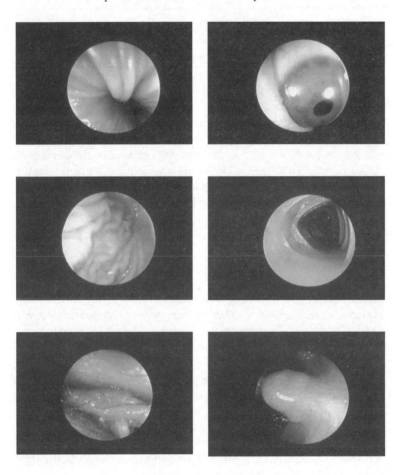

Figure 3.6 Mona Hatoum, details from *Corps étranger*, 1994. Video installation with cylindrical wooden structure. 350 × 300 × 300 cm. Photo: Philippe Migeat.

materials such as urine and hair to create art. In this work, she deliberately confounded two disparate modes of visuality vis-à-vis the body – the conventions of art and the conventions of medical science.

Ironically, Hatoum's exposure of the most intimate aspects of her own body – close-ups of skin, pores, body hair, membranes, orifices and internal spaces – produces an affect that is the very opposite of intimacy. The strange and defamiliarized body-scapes provoke a blend of scopophilia and aversion, embarrassment and nausea in the viewers. The medical gaze fragments the body in a way that depersonalizes it and virtually annihilates the Self. A strong sense of *self*-estrangement also pervades Hatoum's work. Hatoum, the 'native daughter', to use Fanon's terminology, 'is willing to strip [herself] naked to study the history of [her] body'. When she does so, she exposes herself as a 'foreign body' (literally: *corps étranger*), the exilic daughter of exiles, somebody (a body) who is forever displaced.

Finally, as Hatoum forces the viewers to trespass upon her body and to experience a disturbing 'voyage' through her entrails, the memory of the disembowelled women of Dir Yasin comes to mind. Perhaps what the artist forces into our range of vision are repressed images of corporal cruelty, traumata imprinted upon her body and soul, even before she was born.

The Maternal Body

In the aforementioned *Measures of Distance* (1988) (Figure 3.7), Hatoum explores her relationship with her mother – who is represented textually and audio-visually – as woman and as matrix. The fifteen-minute video is composed of two overlapping visual images and two overlapping sound tracks. The visual images, both of which are fragmented, relate to the artist's mother. They are grainy photographs of sections of her naked body and fragments of her letters, written in Arabic upon grid-like graph paper. The letters form a link between mother and daughter on a semantic level, yet visually they create a barrier between the daughter's gaze and the body of the mother, which is never completely or clearly visible. Sections of the maternal body are seen from differing perspectives, as though the daughter seeks (but never finds) the 'whole' maternal body.

The work also consists of two overlapping soundtracks. A lively, intimate, mother-daughter conversation is heard in the background. Spoken in Arabic, it is inaccessible to most Western viewers. Yet its intonations and the sporadic laughter that punctuates the chatter convey a sense of intimacy and joy. In the superimposed sound track the artist sombrely reads translations of her mother's letters. Thus, the audio and visual images overlap, as the letters are both text and image, both sight and sound. Hatoum's voice is distant and subdued. The sense of distance is amplified by other means as well: it is implied by the very function of the letters; it is expressed semantically, as the letters speak of geographical distance and the desire for emotional closeness; visually, the letters form a barrier that veils the mother; finally, in terms of syntax, the literal English

Figure 3.7 Mona Hatoum, from *Measures of Distance*, 1988. 15-minute video. Photo: the artist.

translation of the original idiomatic Arabic forms an estranged, third, foreign language that reinforces the feeling of distance, displacement and alienation.

In showing her mother in the shower, Hatoum brings to life the empty bathroom of *Changing Parts*. She also breaks deep-seated stereotypes that pervade both Arab and Western cultures. In lieu of an abstract (often mute and passive) image of Motherhood, she presents the voice, the texts and the naked body of an ageing Arab woman, endowing her protagonist with vital sexuality and a complex personality. As she revisions the mythical mother-son dyad as a concrete mother-daughter relationship, Hatoum breaks both oriental and occidental conventions and taboos.

Measures of Distance both delineates a compelling portrait of the artist's mother and represents the complex mother-and-daughter relationship, through the mediation of the daughter's voice and vision. The work also deals with the construction of Hatoum's own identity, against a backdrop of a dislocated family and a disintegrating traditional society. It relates to her initial confrontation with menstruation and sexuality, with her feelings of loneliness as a child, and with the conflict between the paternal domain in which the father views his wife's body as 'his property' and the newly created 'open space' inhabited by mother and daughter that undermines the patriarchal order. Hatoum's video – with its double imagery, double soundtrack and direct references to her double exile – exposes an inner schism that permeates the artist's being. Although it exposes an inherent and essential fragmentation, it also expresses the artist's desire to heal or mend the 'broken narratives' of her life and fractured pieces of her mother's body – her literal and metaphoric 'place of origin' – through the creation of a coherent work of art.[13]

An analogous process of reconstruction may be detected in Hatoum's obsessive attempt to collate and revive the physical residue produced by her own body. Linking the 're-collecting' of the body with 'recollected' memories, she wrote:

> I used to collect all my nail parings, pubic hair, bits of skin and mix them with pulp and bodily fluids to make paper: a kind of recollecting of the body's dispersals, if you like. Pubic hair I had collected all these years ago ended up in a much later work I called *Jardin Public*. A wrought iron garden chair with a triangle of pubic hair that looks like it is growing out of the holes in the seat. Incidentally, this work was the result of discovering that the words 'public' and 'pubic' come from the same etymological source (Hatoum quoted by Archer 1998: 25).

Jardin Public (1993) is one of many works in which an inanimate quotidian object – such as a piece of furniture, a domestic object or a kitchen utensil – becomes anthropomorphized and stands in for the absent human body.[14]

Since a full analysis of all these objects is beyond the scope of this chapter, I wish to focus on four sculptures, based on cribs, that Hatoum produced in the mid-1990s. *Incommunicado* is an infant's hospital crib made of steel (1993) (Figure 3.8). In lieu of a mattress, the artist placed sixteen razor-sharp wires, that offer danger rather than comfort, bodily harm rather than rest. The crib bears wheels, indicating its unstable and temporary position. In this extremely distressing work, what should be the safest place for a helpless newborn is transformed into a mobile, cagelike trap. The title of the work expresses the infant's inability to articulate fear and also evokes the notion of solitary confinement and extreme isolation and loneliness. Psychologically, Hatoum's images imply a return to infancy, when a primal and visceral knowledge that nowhere is safe was imbibed by the artist with her mother's milk.

In 1994 Hatoum produced a second crib, this one of glass tubes (Figure 3.9). The work projects extreme fragility as well as a painful beauty. Its transparency transforms it into an almost non-existent object, amplifying

Figure 3.8 Mona Hatoum, *Incommunicado*, 1993. Mild steel, wire, rubber. 127 × 49.5 × 95.5 cm. Photo: Edward Woodman.

its vulnerability. Its title – *Silence* – reinforces the feeling of helplessness and inability to express one's pain, one's fear, one's self.[15] In contrast to the angular and hard-edged cribs discussed above, *Marrow* (1996) (Figure 3.10) is a soft crib made of honey-coloured marrow-like rubber. Janine Antoni compared the work with a collapsed body (Antoni 1998: 59). Hatoum's last crib to date, titled *First Step*, was made during a 1996 residency in the Shaker community in Sabbathday Lake, Maine. The work is composed of a wooden, mattressless crib that was placed on wheels. An

Figure 3.9 Mona Hatoum, *Silence*, 1994. Laboratory glass tubes. 127 × 93 × 59 cm. Photo: D. James Dee.

imprint of the crib's metal springs, re-produced on the floor with sprinkled icing sugar, was exposed after the crib was moved slightly to the side (took a first step). Thus, both the cot and its ghostlike, temporary trace may be seen. Hatoum's crib sculptures are substitutes for the absent body. The imprint of the crib indicates that the human body is even further removed,

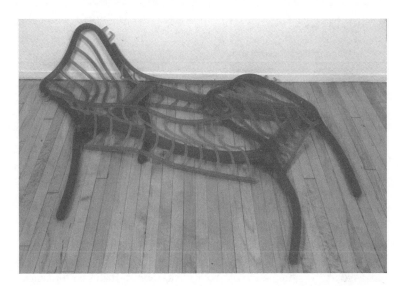

Figure 3.10 Mona Hatoum, *Marrow*, 1996. Rubber, dimensions variable. Photo: Bill Orcutt.

amplifying our awareness of the absence of the infant's body. The ironic use of sweet sugar and the reference in the title to the normal development of babies, who take their 'first step' as they naturally grow from infants to toddlers, exacerbates our sense of loss.[16]

Hatoum's cribs forcefully confront the viewers with their own mortality and fragility. Our instinctive need to protect newborns compounded by our own extreme vulnerability threaten us, in much the same way as the disorienting, imprisoning spaces of Hatoum's installations or the uncanny kitchen utensils that she produces tend to do.

Parallel to the creation of *First Step*, Hatoum made a series of works in which imprints of kitchen utensils were embedded in Japanese wax paper. Extremely subtle and virtually transparent, these works address the desire to embody absent objects that speak of absent bodies. Indeed, within Hatoum's oeuvre, a prevailing sense of ephemerality and fragility puts into question the very existence of the artist and her viewers. In 1994, the artist placed a mirror on the wall. Upon it she etched the words 'You Are Still Here'. In Hatoum's 'Dis-Orientalized' world, in which the self is forever uprooted, dislocated and negated, embodying absence is not merely related to the praxis of art, it is an act of survival.

Khalil Rabah's In-between

The cloud of migrations is in his eyes

Waleed Khazindar (quoted in Jayyusi 1992: 199)

Khalil Rabah was born in Jerusalem in 1961 to a prominent family from Ramallah. As a young man he left Ramallah, occupied by Israel since 1967, in order to pursue his studies. He majored in Fine Art and Architecture at the University of Texas at Arlington, and resided in the United States for over a decade.

During the Israeli invasion of Lebanon, Rabah was still in the United States, far away from the battleground. Yet, in his work from this period, he subjected his body – much as did Hatoum in her contemporaneous performances – to distressing ritualistic suffering. The title of his 1982 performance, *Self-Invasion*, indicates that the artist deliberately intended to symbolically participate in the events 'back home'. In this performance, Rabah went through a *via dolorosa* of his own construction. He placed his body in a position of humiliation and subjugation and crawled upon shards of glass, allowing acute physical pain to invade his body. The artist's *Kaffiye* headgear and *Kaffiye* loincloth emphasized his Arab – specifically Palestinian – identity.

In the early 1990s Rabah returned to Ramallah, where he worked as an architect for several years until he decided to close his practice and devote his time solely to art. Rabah's life and work as an artist diverge radically from the traditions of Palestinian society. His videos, installations and contemporary artforms are considered incomprehensible by many members of his community. Although he has shown his work in local venues, he often exhibits abroad, where opportunities are more readily available. A gentle and soft-spoken man, endowed with originality of thought and vision, he seems to be an outsider both at home and abroad.

In 1995 Rabah took part in the exhibition 'Dialogues of Peace' at the Palais des Nations in Geneva, where he exhibited an installation entitled *Grafting* (Figure 3.11). In this work, uprooted olive trees from Palestine were literally 'regrounded' by the artist in the grassy lawns of Geneva's Ariana Park. Using the most basic metaphor, *Grafting* explored the experience of exile, migration and hybridity with great clarity and force.

The ring of brown soil that separated the newly planted trees from the green terrain – their new 'home' – speaks volumes about the displacement and separateness of the newcomer and the difference between belonging and being set apart. Simone Weil's statement, *'To be rooted is perhaps the*

Figure 3.11 Khalil Rabah, *Grafting*, 1995. Olive trees, cotton threads, earth.

most important/and least recognized need of the human soul' comes to mind (quoted in Said 1990: 364).

Another aspect of *Grafting* was the multicoloured embroidery threads that the artist wrapped around the limbs of his transplanted trees. Alluding to Palestinian culture, epitomized by its traditional embroidery, the migrant trees were bestowed with the hybrid identity of immigrants, who retain elements of their national heritage even when they relocate. Rabah's manner of wrapping the branches with threads evoked an image of bandages that imply the presence of a hidden wound. The title of the work –

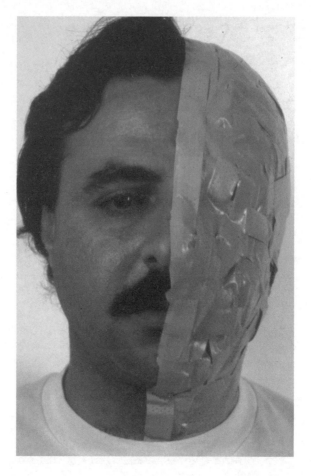

Figure 3.12 Khalil Rabah, *Half-Self-Portrait*, 1997. Photographs of live work. Plaster band-aids. 60 × 40 cm. Photo: Issa Freij.

Grafting – points to the nature of the wound. A graft, the Webster dictionary tell us, is 'a small shoot or bud of a tree or plant inserted into another tree or plant where it continues to grow, becoming a permanent part . . . In surgery, [it is] a piece of living tissue joined to any part or member of a person or animal where it grows and becomes a permanent part'. Thus, in trees, in human beings, indeed in all living creatures, grafting implies the creation of a hybrid being, that is both self and other, both here and there. Rabah's own position – oscillating between 'home' and 'away'– is clearly analogous to that of his uprooted/regrounded trees.

Black Skin/White Masks

The deep, wounding schism caused by dislocation, applied to olive trees in *Grafting*, was internalized and embodied by Rabah in his 1997 series of *Half-Self-Portraits* (Figure 3.12). These live works show the artist from diverse angles, with half of his face completely covered with adhesive band-aids.

Rabah's split Self projects acute physical discomfort onto the viewers. These sensations are followed by inescapable metaphoric interpretations of the work. The initial sense of distress is caused by the band-aids, which signify the existence of a painful wound. Moreover, the brutality of the vertical line that cuts the human face in half, and the sight (and tactile sense) of eyes, skin and facial hair covered with adhesive band-aids, cause unpleasant physical sensations. The ambiguous function of the band-aids compounds the viewers' anguish: Do these medical elements hold the fragments of the halved face together? Do they protect and heal the concealed wound? Or, conversely, do they simply brutally block the eye, the nostril, the ear and part of the mouth, rendering the 'half-Self' helpless, unable to use its sensory organs, disempowered?

Another important aspect of the work relates to the stark, visually perceived contrast between the 'black' skin and the pinkish 'white' mask formed by the band-aids. Rabah is a dark-skinned man with black hair and a full moustache. Band-aids are supposed to hide or camouflage a wound and, as a surrogate skin, they are meant to blend in with one's skin colour. This happens, of course, only if one is of the 'right' – i.e. white – colour. The juxtaposition between black and white recalls the title of Frantz Fanon's autobiographical volume, *Black Skin, White Masks*, and relates to Fanon's personal and theoretical discussion of 'racial epidermal schema' as a factor that determines the construction of identity. In the chapter 'The Fact of Blackness', Fanon stresses the conflict between his inner, human sense of Self, and the external identity that was bestowed upon him by those who set up 'white' skin as the attribute of normative humanity, and 'black' skin as a signifier of inherent racial inferiority: 'the Negro is an animal, the Negro is bad, the Negro is mean, the Negro is ugly . . .'. Fanon lists prevailing stereotypes that dispossess his humanity with merciless bluntness (Fanon 1967: 113). A seemingly trivial experience of being pointed out by a white child, who said: 'Mama, see the Negro! I'm frightened', is recounted by Fanon as a shattering experience: 'I came into the world imbued with the will to find a meaning in things, my spirit filled with the desire to attain to the source of the world, and then I found that I was an object in the midst of other objects . . . I burst apart. Now the fragments have been put together again by another self' (ibid.: 109).

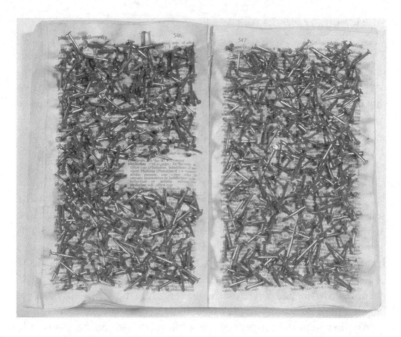

Figure 3.13 Khalil Rabah, *Dictionary Work*, 1997. Paperback book, nails. Photo: Issa Freij.

A similar sense of fragmentation, founded on a dichotomy between black and white and between internal and external constructions of selfhood, permeates Rabah's work. The halved self-portraits expose a painful rift between the artist's human, vulnerable self, and the external definition of him as dark, Arab, non-white, other.

The same year that he imaged himself in this series of *Half-Self-Portraits*, Rabah also explored the collective identity that was bestowed upon him from the outside. *Dictionary Work* (1997) (Figure 3.13) presents – quite literally – a definition of the 'Palestinian' articulated by the English-speaking West. The work is constructed from an English–English pocket dictionary that is nailed open on the page that includes the entry 'Philistine'. The meaning of the word in English is based on 'historical' racist notions, regarding the inhabitants of ancient Palestine. The pronunciation of the word is related to the contemporary Arab word designating a Palestinian. The open dictionary's double spread of pages is completely covered with nails upon twisted nails, with only a single definition left exposed. It reads:

Philistine: n. often cap (Philistine inhabitant of ancient Philitia {Palestine}):
a materialistic person, esp: one who is smugly insensitive or indifferent to
intellectual or artistic values.

From afar, the nails that penetrate the dictionary seem jewel-like, as they
glisten with deceiving sheen. Only upon closer inspection do the sharp
pain that they imply and the damage that they inflict become obvious to
the viewer. Upon reading the definition, one understands that it was the
wound that was inflicted upon the artist that caused him to redirect his pain
by hammering nails into the book. The sharp, puncturing nails seem less
painful, in fact, than the realization that Rabah is identified and defined
in a way that precludes his ability to be an artist, to pursue intellectual
values, to be human.

Rabah's wound is manifested in his art through the use of band-aids
and nails. Related to religion and medicine, nails and bandages are applied
to objects that stand in for the human body, usually substituting for the
artist himself. Although the artist has used his grandmother's embroidered
dress, a jacket, pieces of furniture, a *Kaffiye* and various other tools and
utensils as anthropomorphic substitutes in his art, he most frequently uses
shoes.

Unlike other garments, shoes acquire the shape and form of the body
part that they protect. Thus, composed of leather 'skins', they closely
resemble the individual's feet. In his monumental work *On What Ground*
(1997) (Figure 3.14), for example, Rabah dug out a large square area of
the tiled floor of Gallery Anadiel.[17] Literally removing the ground by
digging it up, he destabilized the very foundation upon which both artist
and audience stand. Within the newly formed square 'crater' he placed
hundreds of slim, white church candles in grid-like form. Upon the
candles, Rabah precariously balanced forty-eight shoes. Twenty-three
pairs were hammered brutally with nails that rendered them completely
dysfunctional and gave them the painful appearance of pierced and
wounded feet.[18] The allusion to Christ's nailed limbs exacerbated the
visceral sense of pain that was projected onto the viewers.[19] The use of
worn-out shoes as anthropomorphic stand-ins for the human body also
recalled Van Gogh's images of the twisted shoes of peasants. Yet, in spite
of the religious props (candles) and symbols (nails), Rabah's work is
secular rather than religious, expressing human rather than divine pain.

In another installation entitled *Strip* (1996), single (rather than paired)
shoes covered with adhesive band-aids were scattered upon a narrow path
that was also coated with bandages. The pinkish flesh colour of both the
path and the shoes transformed the quotidian inanimate footwear into

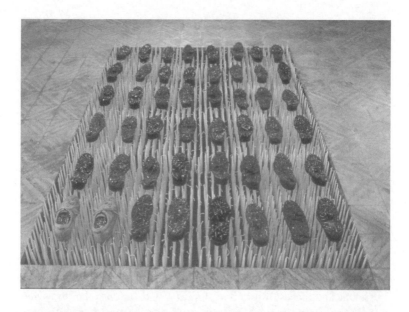

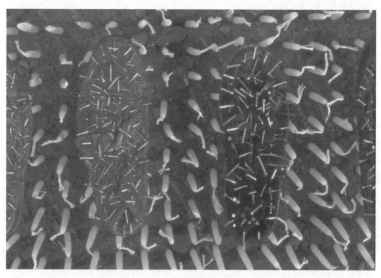

Figure 3.14 Khalil Rabah, detail from *On What Ground*, 1997. Shoes, nails, candles. 160 × 240 × 60 cm. Photo: Issa Freij.

anthropomorphic and fetishized objects that obliquely evoke René Magritte's feet-cum-shoes. Pointing in various different directions, the humanized shoes appeared like dismembered feet or like three-dimensional ghostlike footprints, displaced on their way to an unknown destination. The title of the work, *Strip*, alludes to two separate meanings: to the act of undressing, referring to the nakedness of the shoes that appear as bare feet; and to the narrow 'strip', that is, the skin-like path upon which the shoes tread. Hence, in this work, as in numerous other projects by Rabah that focus on shoes and paths, the exposed body is inseparably linked to the road of migration.

Rabah's 8-minute video piece, ironically titled *My Body and Sole* (1996), links body and shoe even more explicitly, as it shows the artist interacting in various ways with a shoe. Rabah begins by trying to put on a shoe that is too small to fit his foot. As he attempts this over and over again, he wounds his finger in the process. Metaphorically, the individual's attempt, and consequent failure, to fit into roles or places that do not suit him are shown to be wounding experiences. The allusion to Cinderella introduces gender ambiguities that appear in other works by Rabah as well. In another sequence of the video, the artist places the shoe on his crotch, fetishizing it, creating an equivocal image of erotic suggestiveness. Finally, Rabah tries to eat the sole of his shoe, an act that bruises his sensitive lips. The latter section, that vaguely recalls the poverty-stricken Charlie Chaplin's attempt to eat his shoes in *The Gold Rush*, exposes the existential desperation that motivates Rabah's actions, as well as his use of humour and the absurd to protest a condition of human suffering.

'*The wound in our suitcases bears our features*' wrote the Palestinian poet Suhair Abu Shayib (quoted in Jayyusi 1992: 99). In 1997, Rabah coated a large suitcase with band-aids and titled the work *Womb* (Figure 3.15). This hybrid-looking, skin-covered container is empty save for an ordinary chair that is also coated with a surrogate skin of band-aids. Emphasizing the 'void' inside the suitcase and the chair's inability to fit comfortably within it, Rabah seems to undermine traditional Palestinian representations of the homeland as a positive, nurturing Mother (Sherwell 2001: 161). This empty, wounded womb appears to be related to Hatoum's threatening and fragile cribs: they, too, are barren 'vessels' that fail to offer warmth or protection to helpless newborns.

In her interpretation of Rabah's work, Danielle Knafo suggested a link between the name of the innermost layer of the skin, *pia mater*, and Rabah's *Womb*, which she views as a reference to the mother as container that the artist 'continues to carry with him'. She also related the work to

Figure 3.15 Khalil Rabah, *Womb*, 1997. Suitcase, chair, adhesive bandages (band-aids). 50 × 90 × 70 cm. Photo: Issa Freij.

Otto Rank's thesis, which posits that art is a way for the artist to restore the lost unity with the mother (Knafo 1999: 15–16).

It may be possible, however, to read the work in yet another way. The chair that Rabah places within his suitcase is, literally, a 'seat' or a 'place'. Thus, the artist attempts to 'give birth' and to carry with him – wherever he goes – a place for himself. If so, then Rabah's suitcase that doubles as a wounded womb may contain an ambiguous reference to Darwish's oft-recited verses, which variously link the homeland with the suitcase: 'My homeland is a suitcase/and my suitcase is a homeland', Darwish wrote. And elsewhere, he declared:

> *Ah my intractable wound!*
> *My country is not a suitcase*
> *I am not a traveler*
> *I am the lover and the land is the beloved.*

Indeed, for the nomad, the suitcase *is* a substitute for the motherland, a portable womb or container that produces and re-produces his unsettled identity. In this case, Rabah's suitcase must also be seen within a broader context. As Sarit Shapira noted in her essay on nomadism in Israeli art:

'The suitcase is a distinctive characterization of the contemporary nomad, a figure who carries all his belongings with him, perhaps as a result of his non-belonging to a fixed environment' (Shapira 1991: 192). More recently, Irit Rogoff observed: 'Those who have visited contemporary art exhibitions over the past decade have become accustomed to seeing a plethora of suitcases . . . the suitcase has become the signifier of mobility, displacement, duality and the overwrought emotional climates in which these circulate' (Rogoff 2000: 36).

Khalil Rabah's images of the split self and his wounded, anthropo-morphic objects articulate a poetics of non-belonging that is both personal and political, both Palestinian and universal. Moreover, his art poignantly expresses the desire to heal the visceral torment of being neither here nor there, of being perpetually 'out of place.'[20]

Conclusion

The artworks discussed in this chapter present the maternal body, the carnal Self and the native place as interconnected sites (and sights) that exist within an elusive, interstitial gap between familiarity and estrange-ment, between longing and belonging. Sliman Mansour's *Hagar* and *Heart* were introduced as transitional works, which merge a traditional approach with a more innovative interpretation of the metaphoric cluster: mother/body/land. The main portion of the text was devoted to the more radical images produced by Hatoum and Rabah. As we have seen, Hatoum breaks taboos as she presents the Maternal as the fragmented naked body of her own mother, who seems alternately distant and close. The artist's empty, fragile or threatening crib sculptures also evoke an unrequited desire for a nurturing maternal presence and the absence – (literally, the absent bodies) – of both mother and child. Rabah ironically replaces the paradigmatic mother-earth figure with a suitcase that is constructed as a wounded, sterile surrogate womb.

Frantz Fanon's imperative which instructs the native intellectual to conduct visceral self-analysis – 'to strip himself naked to study the history of his body' – was linked to Hatoum's *Under Siege, The Negotiating Table, Corps étranger* and to Rabah's *Self-Invasion* and *Half-Self-Portraits*. In these works, as we have seen, the burden of displacement is physically imprinted upon the carnal Self that is imaged as wounded, invaded, fragmented or dismembered. The dismembered body parts – Mansour's *Heart*, Hatoum's obsessively re-created entrails, and Rabah's endless procession of tortured, surrogate feet, for example – clearly reflect how individual memory threads and collective narratives interlace in art. Finally, it was shown how experiences of uprootings and regroundings are embodied through epidermal images: in Mansour's *Hagar* with her cracked earth-skin; in Hatoum's medically examined close-ups of skin, pores and internal membranes; and in Rabah's band-aids – literally a second layer of skin.

The skin is the external contour of the carnal Self, delineating the border between the body and the place it inhabits. Displacements, as Ahmed writes, imprint themselves upon the body and inevitably rupture its defining skin-contour. Hence, regroundings require a reconstruction of the skin, a redefinition and repositioning of the body, of the Self. Often, as in the case of contemporary Palestinian art, it is precisely at the painful juncture where bruised skins, dislocated bodies and lost homes intersect that works of Art come into being.

Acknowledgements

This chapter is based on sections of my forthcoming book titled: *Dis-Orientalism: Palestinian Artists between East and West.* I thank Kamal Boullata, Larry Abramson, Yosefa Loshitzky and Shlomit Shaked for their constructive critique of an earlier version of this text. I thank the artists Sliman Mansour, Mona Hatoum and Khalil Rabah for allowing me to reproduce their works.

Notes

1. For a discussion of the homeland/mother metaphor, see Ankori 1988: 87; Tamari and Johnson 1995; and Sherwell 2001.
2. Since the 1950s Hagar and Ishmael have appeared in both Israeli and Palestinian literature and art as emblematic figures representing Palestinian refugees. See for example Z. Amishai-Maisels 1977.
3. Mansour's self-portraits are entitled *I Ishmael,* continuing the biblical allusion (see Ankori 1997). For colour reproductions, see al-Wasiti Arts Center 2000.
4. Kamal Boullata (1971, 1977) based his pioneering analysis of Arab and Palestinian art on Fanon's chapter 'On National Culture' (1963: 206–48). Although this chapter deals with other aspects of Fanon's

text, I gratefully acknowledge my indebtedness to Boullata's seminal contributions to the study of Palestinian culture.

5. Unless otherwise indicated, all biographical information is based on my own interviews with the artists.

6. For a Palestinian perspective on this dialectic, articulated as the tension between the 'interior' and the 'exterior', see Said 1986: 51–84. On the related concept *Sumud* (steadfastness), see Shehadeh 1982. Certain poems by Mahmoud Darwish and by Tawfik Zayyad parallel Mansour's 'poetics of *Sumud*' in verse (see Jayyusi 1992: 146, 327–8).

7. A full discussion of the abrupt and panic-stricken flight of most of Haifa's 70,000 Arab inhabitants is, of course, beyond the scope of this chapter. For a contemporary eyewitness report by Zionist leader Ben-Gurion, see Ben-Gurion 1982: 378, 381 [in Hebrew]. Also see Morris 1986: 109–34 [in Hebrew]. For a literary account by a Palestinian writer, see Kanafani 2000: 149–96.

8. The 1948 Arab-Israeli conflict, war and their aftermath (named *The War of Independence* by Israelis), is called *al-Nakba* – the catastrophe – by the Palestinians.

9. For a chronology of Hatoum's development, see Archer et al. 1998: 146–57. For a comprehensive overview of her work, see Brett 1998.

10. Hatoum's use of homing devices in her art – e.g. compasses – relates to her desire for reorientation.

11. The name of Hatoum's exhibition 'The Entire World as a Foreign Land' is taken from Said's (1990) 'Reflections on Exile'.

12. For an illuminating analysis see Philippi 1990.

13. For another interpretation, see Ross 1996: 55–61.

14. The *unheimlich* aspect of Hatoum's objects and their threatening, unsettling impact have been discussed in other contexts. An exhibition curated by the author with Jack Persekian at Gallery Anadiel in 1997, titled *Home,* included several works by Hatoum that stressed the transformation of familiar domestic objects into *unheimlich* objects (see Ankori and Persekian 1997; and see also Ankori 1997/1998; Cottingham 1999; Steward Heon 2001: 11–17).

15. The painful feeling of being unable to express oneself (perhaps as a result of losing a 'mother tongue') is forcefully expressed in Hatoum's first video work *So Much I Want to Say* (1983) (see Ankori 1997/1998: 581–2).

16. A student in one of my seminars, Maha al-Nakib, suggested that Hatoum's cribs may allude to stories about Palestinians who lost their infants while fleeing their homes in 1948. For a well-known literary account relating to Haifa, see Kanafani 2000.

17. Gallery Anadiel, a private Palestinian venue devoted to the exhibition of contemporary and experimental art, was founded in 1991 by Jack Persekian, who also curated many of Rabah's exhibitions.
18. One pair of sports shoes served as containers for nails.
19. On the image of the Palestinian poet as Christ see Ashrawi 1976.
20. Significantly, these conflicting sentiments continue in Rabah's most recent work. His one-man exhibition in Cairo's *Townhouse Gallery* (2001) was entitled: 'Feeling a(part)' thus verbally accentuating the oscillations between belonging and non-belonging.

References

Ahmed, S. (1999), 'Home and Away: Narratives of Migration and Estrangement', *International Journal of Cultural Studies*, 2(3): 329–47.

Amishai-Maisels, Z. (1977), 'Steinhardt's Call for Peace', *Journal for Jewish Art*, 3/4: 90–102.

Ankori, G. (1988), 'The Other Jerusalem: Images of the Holy City in Contemporary Palestinian Painting', *Jewish Art*, 14: 74–92.

—— (1997), 'Voies choisies: l'art de Sliman Mansour', *Artistes palestiniens contemporains*, Paris: Institut du Monde Arabe.

—— (1997/1998), 'Behind the Walls: The Real and Ideal Jerusalem in Contemporary Palestinian Art', in B. Kühnel (ed.), *The Real and Ideal Jerusalem in Jewish, Christian and Islamic Art*, Jerusalem: Hebrew University of Jerusalem, special issue, *Jewish Art*.

—— and Persekian, J. (1997), 'Home', in A. Badran, D. Golan and J. Persekian (eds), *Sharing Jerusalem*, Jerusalem: the Jerusalem Link.

Antoni, J. (1998), 'Mona Hatoum', *Bomb*, 63, Spring: 54–61.

Archer, M. (1998), 'Interview: in Conversation with Mona Hatoum', in M. Archer, G. Brett and C. de Zegher (eds), *Mona Hatoum*, London: Phaidon.

——, Brett, G. and de Zegher, C. (eds) (1998), *Mona Hatoum*, London: Phaidon.

Ashrawi, H.M. (1976), *Contemporary Palestinian Literature under Occupation*, Birzeit: Birzeit University.

Ben-Gurion, D. (1982), *The War of Independence, Ben-Gurion's Diary*, Tel Aviv: Ministry of Defense Publishers, vol. 1 [in Hebrew].

Boullata, K. (1971), 'Toward a Revolutionary Arab Art', in N. Aruri (ed.), *Palestinian Resistance to Israeli Occupation*, Wilmette, IL: Medina University Press.

—— (1977), 'Modern Arab Art: The Quest and the Ordeal,' *Mundus Artium*, (10)1: 106–133.

—— (2001), 'The World, the Self, and the Body: Pioneering Women in Palestinian Art', in T. Ben Zvi and Y. Lerer (eds), *Self Portrait: Palestinian Women's Art*, Tel Aviv: Andalus.

Brett, G. (1998), 'Itinerary,' in M. Archer, G. Brett, and C. de Zegher (eds), *Mona Hatoum*, London: Phaidon.

Cottingham, L. (1999), 'Mona Hatoum', in L. Cottingham, *Mona Hatoum 99.2*, San Antonio: ArtPace.

Fanon, F. (1963), *Wretched of the Earth*, New York: Grove.

—— (1967), *Black Skin, White Masks*, New York: Grove.

Hatoum, M. (1983), 'Under Siege', in M. Archer, G. Brett, and C. de Zegher (eds), *Mona Hatoum*, London: Phaidon.

—— (1987), 'Interview with Sara Diamond', in M. Archer, G. Brett, and C. de Zegher (eds), *Mona Hatoum*, London: Phaidon.

—— (1996) 'Interview with Claudia Spinelli', in M. Archer, G. Brett, and C. de Zegher (eds), *Mona Hatoum*, London: Phaidon.

Jayyusi, S.K. (1992), *An Anthology of Modern Palestinian Literature*, New York: Columbia University Press.

Kanafani, G. (2000), *Returning to Haifa*, in K.E. Riley (trans.), *Palestine's Children*, Boulder and London: Lynne Rienner.

Knafo, D. (1999), 'Skin and Psyche: From Womb to Tomb', in Suzanne Landau (ed.), *Skin-Deep: Surface and Appearance in Contemporary Art*, Jerusalem: Israel Museum.

Morris, B. (1986), *The Birth of the Palestinian Refugee Problem 1947– 1949*, Tel Aviv: Am Oved Publishers [in Hebrew].

Nead, L. (1992), *The Female Nude: Art, Obsenity and Sexuality*, London: Routledge.

Philippi, D. (1990), 'Mona Hatoum: The Witness Beside Herself', *Parachute*, 58, April/June: 11–15.

Rogoff, I. (2000), *Terra Infirma*, London: Routledge.

Ross, C. (1996), 'To Touch the Other: A Story of Corpo-electric Surfaces', in *Touch in Contemporary Art*, Toronto: Public Access.

Said, E. (1986), *After the Last Sky: Palestinian Lives*, New York: Pantheon.

—— (1990), 'Reflections on Exile', in R. Ferguson, M. Gever, T.T. Minh-ha and C. West (eds), *Out There: Marginalization and Contemporary Cultures*, New York and Cambridge, MA: New Museum of Contemporary Art and MIT Press.

—— (1998), 'Reflections on Exile (extract)', in M. Archer, G. Brett and C. de Zegher (eds), *Mona Hatoum*, London: Phaidon.

—— (2000), 'The Art of Displacement: Mona Hatoum's Logic of Irreconcilables', in M. Hatoum, E. Said and S. Wagstaff, *Mona Hatoum: the Entire World as a Foreign Land*, London: Tate Gallery.

Shapira, S. (1991), *Routes of Wandering: Nomadism, Journeys and Transitions in Contemporary Israeli Art*, Jerusalem, Israel Museum.

Shehadeh, R. (1982), *The Third Way*, New York: Quarter.

Sherwell, T.M. (2001), 'Imaging Palestine as the Motherland', in T. Ben Zvi and Y. Lerer (eds), *Self Portrait: Palestinian Women's Art*, Tel Aviv: Andalus.

Steward Heon, L. (ed.) (2001), *Mona Hatoum: Domestic Disturbance*, North Adams, MA: Mass MoCa.

Tamari, V. and Johnson, P. (1995), 'Loss and Vision: Representations of Women in Palestinian Art under Occupation', in A. Moor, T. van Teffelen, S. Kanaana and I. Abu Ghazaleh (eds), *Discourse, Power, Text and Content*, Amsterdam: Het Spinhuis.

al-Wasiti Arts Center (2000), *Sliman Mansour: Ten Years in Mud*, Jerusalem: al-Wasiti Arts Center.

de Zegher, C. (1998), 'Hatoum's *Recollections:* About Losing and Being Lost', in M. Archer, G. Brett, and C. de Zegher (eds), *Mona Hatoum*, London: Phaidon.

Taking (a) Place: Female Embodiment and the Re-grounding of Community
Irene Gedalof

From moral panics about immigration and asylum seekers in Western Europe to violent confrontations in the Middle East, India and Eastern Europe, we live in a world in which conflict organized along national, ethnic and racialized lines occurs daily. The communities that are 'imagined' in these contexts of conflict are grounded in absolutist and exclusionary definitions of belonging, of strict dividing lines between self and other. For many feminists, a key problem with these definitions of national, ethnic and racialized communities has been the ways in which women are positioned as a resource or ground for the politics of collective reproduction.[1] This is exacerbated in contexts of aggravated conflict, where 'resources' can become the target of violent appropriation, and where the stability of the grounds of collective identity is shaken. How should this positioning of women in the ethnic politics of community be conceptualized, and what alternatives can feminist theories of identity propose for a more promising regrounding of community belonging?

Feminist scholarship has already made important contributions to exposing the many ways in which the female body, symbolic representations of Woman, and women's activities are repeatedly appropriated as markers of national, racial, religious and ethnic communities in dominant discourses of identity.[2] It has demonstrated the deeply constraining, always problematic and sometimes deadly effects on women of their symbolic and strategic positioning as resources for the reproduction of particular versions of community belonging. Feminist theorists of identity who draw on postmodern and post-structuralist challenges to old ontological, epistemological and normative certainties have worked to destabilize the dualistic self-other paradigms that underpin such definitions of collective belonging. Others have resisted these deconstructive moves, but have developed a variety of theoretical arguments that draw on concepts of citizenship, gender interests or universal human rights to refuse the place offered to women in these exclusionary narratives of ethnic identity and conflict. Despite their different theoretical starting points, both these perspectives contribute to a crucial clearing of the ground, in which definitions of the category 'women' are being uprooted from their place in dominant identity narratives. What emerges is a kind of consensus that the 'homes' being offered women in these identity narratives, that are in important ways constituted through women, are not homes we want to stay in. Rather, there is an insistence on women's 'right to travel', to refuse to settle down in/as the place upon which oppressive forms of social cohesion and social identities are wrought.

But at the same time, another insight, which emerges especially from the work of black, postcolonial and diasporic feminisms, argues that problems occur when feminist theories of identity take too lightly women's attachment to, and investment in, their specific positioning within particular communities. When women of a given community are targeted by racism, ethnic absolutism, religious hatred or other forms of intolerance or violence because of their membership in that community, it makes no sense to claim that these women's sense of themselves as women is not intimately bound up with their sense of belonging to that community. Nor should this only be seen as a reactive response to processes of 'othering', for this would leave unexamined the ways in which the identities of women belonging to dominant racialized or ethnic groups are also marked by their specific positioning. Rather, we need to be able to theorize the ways in which gender, race, ethnicity, nation, etc. are mutually constitutive. So, is it possible to think both these moves together? Is it possible *both* to take into account and value the work that women do to reproduce a sense of 'home' and community belonging *and* to challenge the constraining effects of prevailing models of identity that tie women to a particular model of community? In this chapter I argue that such a double move is possible; however, it is necessary to rethink the terms within which notions of female embodiment, women's reproductive activities, 'home' and 'community' are defined, in order that a more promising 'regrounding' might begin to take place. In order to do this, I draw on a Foucauldian understanding of power, embodiment and identity politics and put this together with an Irigarayan attention to the specifically female body. I argue that the exclusionary and absolutist models of community belonging that fuel ethnic and racialized conflict are underpinned by a notion of reproduction-as-stasis that ties female embodiment and women's reproductive activities to a logic of sameness. What is needed is a different kind of feminist refusal – not of women's relationship to the reproduction of national, ethnic and racialized communities or embeddedness in these specific spaces, but of the underlying definition of reproduction that has been associated with women and that has been drawn on as a resource for exclusionary definitions of community.

My starting point is Foucault's conceptualizing of power as productive of bodies and subjects, and more specifically, Foucault's argument that modern disciplinary power works by making bodies 'knowable' and 'useful' as power is exercised through them (Foucault 1977a). In a Foucauldian view, power 'needs' to be able to make bodies useful in specific ways, to enable subjects of a particular kind, in order to be articulated. Related to this view of productive power is Foucault's 'politics of refusal', his claim that the target of a critical politics of social change is 'not to discover what we are, but to refuse what we are . . . to promote new forms of subjectivity through the refusal of [the] kind of individuality which has been imposed on us for several centuries' (Foucault 1982: 216). In 'What is Enlightenment', Foucault framed this as a challenge:

> to separate out, from the contingency that has made us what we are, the possibility of no longer being, doing or thinking what we are, do, think. It is not seeking to make possible a metaphysics that has finally become a science; it is seeking to give new impetus, as far and wide as possible, to the undefined work of freedom (Foucault 1997: 315–16).

One of the things that needs to be refused, according to Foucault, is the notion that the 'we' of collective identities, or of political unity or action, has to be assumed in advance, or posited as a fixed precondition of those identities or actions:

> The problem is . . . to decide if it is actually suitable to place oneself within a 'we' in order to assert the principles one recognises and the values one accepts; or if it is not, rather, necessary, to make the future formation of a 'we' possible by elaborating the question. Because it seems to me that the 'we' must not be previous to the question; it can only be the result – the necessarily temporary result – of the question as it is posed in the new terms in which one formulates it (Foucault 1984: 385).

When these three moves are put together, we get the following line of argument. Power works by producing useful bodies and subjects. Resistance involves revisiting those useful bodies and subjects in order to refuse the ways in which their usefulness has been managed and constrained within prevailing deployments of power; it is from that refusal that new forms of subjectivity can emerge. But this is not only a question of the way power works to produce the individual self. Challenging the terms within which these useful bodies and subjects are associated with a particular 'we' – including national, ethnic or racialized communities – can also create the possibility for new forms of collective belonging to emerge.[3]

What needs to be added to this argument is an attention to women and the specifically female body, which is why my title, 'Taking (a) Place', refers not to Foucault, but to the work of Luce Irigaray. Irigaray argues that, within prevailing relations of power, woman is positioned as the 'still silent ground' upon which identities are constituted. In *Speculum of the Other Woman* (1974), she writes that Woman is called upon to *be* place, to serve that symbolic function as place, rather than to either take a place of her own, or even to take place, that is, to occur, to exist, to define identities on her own terms. Irigaray's focus, particularly in her early work, has been to expose the ways in which Western philosophy is founded on an 'original crime of matricide' (Whitford 1991: 34) that places female embodiment, birth and women outside its frame of reference. But she has combined that critical move with an insistence that we begin to imagine a different frame of reference in which female embodiment, female genealogies, and another kind of 'woman' might be able to be symbolized. Feminist philosophers have drawn on Irigaray's work to begin to rethink models of the self (Battersby 1998) and of individual subjectivity (Walker 1998). Here, I draw on Irigaray's work to reconsider models of collective identities and women's place in them. While recognizing that they work from quite radically different starting points, I think that Foucault's politics of refusal and Irigaray's politics of sexual difference can be made to converse fruitfully in this specific context.

Useful Bodies

The work of black, diasporic and postcolonial feminisms over more than 20 years has meant that, by now, it is a fairly common insight that, both symbolically and strategically, the female body is repeatedly appropriated as a marker of national, racial, religious and ethnic communities.[4] In recent years, we have seen this in the ways in which racial or ethnic terror has been exercised on women's bodies, in the form of sexual violence, in the former Yugoslavia, in Rwanda, in Indonesia and in communal conflict in India. It seems clear that at least part of what is at stake here is the female capacity for birth, and the access to origins that birth represents. Whenever group or community identities are 'imagined' (Anderson 1991) to be wholly or partly birth-based – and this remains largely the case wherever nations, races and many other forms of community are imagined

– then exercising the power to define those identities involves taking women's bodies as both a symbolic and material target of conflict and contestation. By associating the female body with community origins, many identity narratives position 'Woman' as 'place', as the pure space of 'home' in which tradition is preserved from outside contamination (Rose 1993; Sarkar 1987; Yuval-Davis 1997). Hence, we have the heightened salience of the forcible displacement of women in the context of ethnic conflict. As Maja Korac, writing about the situation of refugee women in Serbia puts it:

> uprooted women become symbolically and strategically important in the destruction of opposed ethnic-national collectivities . . . a forced migration of women in wars expressing ethnic-national oppositions is both practically and symbolically the most effective way to (re)shape the boundaries of an ethnic-national collectivity (Korac 1999: 194–5).

So, what can a Foucauldian-inflected feminism add to the insights that have already emerged about women's problematic positioning in relation to ethnic or racialized community identities? What changes in our analysis of the ways in which female bodies are targeted in contexts of ethnic conflict when we think about those bodies as 'useful' in the Foucauldian sense? For me, one of the problems with many feminist discussions of the relationship between women and ethnic identities is that they seem to set up a too-clear opposition between on the one hand, 'women's interests', usually understood as gendered identity and interests, and on the other hand the identity and interests of the community in question. The processes through which ethnic identity is constituted are seen as something that happens *to* women, is imposed *on* women, on their bodies, from somewhere outside. They appropriate women's bodies, control them – in terms of how power is understood in these analyses, it is a model of power that violates, dominates, forces a submission, binds the female body to, and marks it with, an externally imposed allegiance. These terms are all ones that Foucault uses to describe the older forms of repressive power (1977a: 137), and I would not want to deny that these forms of repressive power continue to be directed at women, particularly, if not exclusively, in contexts of violent conflict. And yet, if we only stay within the terms of such a model of power, we leave too much unsaid about women's relationship to community identities, and we propose theoretical and political alternatives that have a number of problematic consequences.

Politically, it can lead to strategies that aim to separate gender out from national, racial, ethnic identities, with the result that key aspects of their complex interrelationship is lost from view. For example, it has become quite common, in the recent feminist scholarship on the issue of women and national/ethnic differences or conflict, to counterpose national or ethnic identities with ideas of citizenship. The prospects for promoting women's solidarity and gendered interests are allied to a forward-looking notion of citizenship and cross-border solidarities.[5] While I agree that this is an important move, and have made a related argument for thinking about women as citizens elsewhere (Gedalof 1999), I think that there are some limitations in the way that this is sometimes articulated. Fixed notions of ethnic or community belonging won't yield to a more mobile model of citizenship unless the very gendered definition of the citizen is also challenged. The notion of citizen as a public individual negotiating civil society needs to be de-linked from its conceptual association with, and opposition to, a private sphere in which the work of kinship, affective ties and belonging continues to be done. It is this conceptualization of the opposition between public citizen and private senses of belonging that also is at work in binding women to a particular version of 'home' and 'place', which in turn makes their access to the status of citizen problematic. The problem, therefore, is not only the association of women with fixed notions of community belonging, but also the definition of community belonging in terms of fixity. There is a binary logic at work here which defines fixed notions of belonging, together with 'woman', 'home' and the reproductive sphere – as the realm of 'being' – in opposition to the mobile, fluid space of citizenship, rights, justice and political 'desire' or becoming. That underlying binary logic also needs to be refused, rather than only arguing that women should have access to the more mobile space of citizenship or becoming. I will return to this question in more detail in the next section, but here want to focus on how this is related to the model of power at work.

As long as we think that racialized, ethnic or national identities are only imposed on women from the outside in order to keep them 'in their place,' then we are likely to look for political solutions that come from some other space that is untainted by these constraints. This can lead to the dangerous illusion that there is some pure, power-free zone from which women can defend their interests 'as women'; in Foucault's terms, 'there are no "margins" for those who break with the system to gambol in' (1977b: 141). Or it can lead to the kind of untenable political strategies that ask women to choose between their identities and interests 'as women' and as members of a particular community. What needs to be added to the story is some consideration of the ways in which women's identities are actually embedded in, and produced in the context of, the reproductive work they do to constitute a sense of community belonging. We need to have a way of recognizing and valuing the work that women do to produce a sense of home, place and community, while simultaneously challenging the constraining effects of prevailing models of identity that tie women to a particular, fixed version of place. Community identities are not just something that happen to women, and neither the 'community' nor the 'women' in question should be seen as fixed, pre-given entities that then confront each other. Rather, women are produced as women of a particular kind, as they help to produce those collective identities through the discursive representations of 'woman' with which women must negotiate, and through the embodied practices in which women engage. For me, this is much more like Foucault's model of disciplinary power that enables as it constrains, which makes bodies more obedient to prevailing power relations as it makes them more useful, and more useful as they are made more obedient (1977a: 138). The female body, its capacity for birth, needs to be made discursively and materially useful in particular ways, in order for these collective identities to be produced and re-produced within the terms of community belonging that currently prevail. This is a body that is not (or at least not only) abjected, objectified, repressed or dominated; it is (also) an enabled body and, while power has been invested in that body in order to constrain it, there is always the possibility of unintended effects, in Foucault's terms, of 'power, after investing itself in the body, find[ing] itself exposed to a counter-attack in that same body' (1975: 56).

Such a view of power working in and through female bodies allows us to revisit the issue of women's positioning in communities, and in contexts of violent conflict, from a different direction on at least two levels. It suggests, first of all, that gender and community identities are not so easily disaggregated as the presence of these two separate concepts might lead us to pretend. What turns female embodied persons into 'women' is intimately bound up with the work of producing specific collective identities. Strategies which aim at separating gender interests out from their location within specific communities cannot address this interconnectedness. To illustrate what I mean, I want to discuss the following statement made by Mirjana Morokvasic in her powerful analysis of the politics of rape in the Yugoslav wars of the 1990s:

> rape becomes a political concern only when it ceases to be a crime against women and becomes exclusively a crime against the group to which a woman is assumed to belong (Morakvasic 1998: 81).

Bodies at Home and Away

I find much to agree with here – if women are discursively and strategically positioned as the ground upon which competing identity claims are
contested, then there is no doubt that, in contexts of ethnic conflict they
can and will be 'used' by both their attackers and their self-proclaimed
defenders. We can see this logic at work in the following statement by one
prosecutor at an International War Crimes Tribunal trial of three Bosnian
Serb soldiers:

> This is not just a rape case like those in national jurisdictions. These crimes
> were committed during an armed conflict and were widespread and systematic.
> What happened to the Muslim women of Foca occurred *purely because of their
> ethnicity or religion,* and because they were women' (*Guardian*, 21 March
> 2000, p. 3, emphasis added).

On the same page on which these words were reported, another article
records the complaints of the international organization Human Rights
Watch, taking issue with British and American government claims that the
Serbs had set up 'rape camps' in Kosovo. While insisting that rape was
indeed being used as an instrument of war against Kosovo Albanian
women, Human Rights Watch noted that the rape-camp allegations had
come the day after NATO's attack on a train in Serbia in which 20 civilians
were killed:

> we are concerned that Nato's use of rape to bolster support for the war relied
> on unconfirmed accounts. Offering such accusations . . . suggests that those
> invoking the abuses may have been more concerned with pursuing certain
> political goals (ibid.).

These examples would seem to confirm Morokvasic's view. Where I
stumble, however, is over Morokvasic's phrase 'the group to which a
woman is assumed to belong'. To me, this is part of an underlying strand
in Morokvasic's argument that conceptualizes gender as distinct from, and
primary to, other aspects of women's identity, and sees community
belonging as something that is imposed on women as symbols, tools,
victims, and only very rarely as actors. Elsewhere in her article, Morokvasic writes passionately about the broader appropriation of women in
nationalist discourse. Their discursive positioning as 'either a protector
and regenerator of the collective or a possession of that collective' means
that woman's identity as an 'individual self' is subsumed within the
collective identities of family, nation, Church (Morokvasic 1998: 75). It
is only within the context of the dominant nationalist discourse, as fighters
for the nation – to kill or be killed, another kind of sacrifice of the self to

– 98 –

the collective – that a language of equal agency is permitted to women (Morokvasic 1998: 83). While some women had 'fallen into the nationalist trap' in this way, she argues that the more characteristic responses of women were either to oppose actively or to disengage from this kind of ethnic absolutism (Morokvasic 1998: 84–6). My disagreement with this line of reasoning is not a simple or straightforward one, so let me try to be clear. I am not arguing that dominant nationalist or ethnic absolutist discourses do not work in this way in relation to women. The moves to restrict women's agency to the act of self-sacrifice, and to obliterate the individual self within an all-consuming collective identity have also been explored in Indian feminist discussions of Hindu–Muslim communal conflict (Butalia 1993; Sarkar 1991, 1995). The imagining of national, ethnic and racialized communities in these absolutist terms positions women both symbolically and strategically in deeply problematic ways, and it has been tremendously important that feminists expose the devices through which this occurs. It is with the question of where we take the analysis once the exposure of the imagined status of these communities has been accomplished that my problems begin. Does recognizing that these communities are imagined mean that they have no 'truth effects' for women, in terms of how they position themselves or experience their own sense of belonging? Can we separate women's individual sense of self out from all senses of collective identity? Is an unspecified 'gender' the only collective category to which women, as individual selves, can be acknowledged to belong? Is women's only possible mode of engagement with national, ethnic or racialized communities to 'fall into the nationalist [or ethnocentric, or racist] trap'? If we want to be consistent with the insight that has proved so important to feminism, and that Morokvasic shares, that 'gender relations cross-cut other social and political relations and gender identities are constitutive elements of other identities' (1998: 81), then I think we have to answer 'no' to these questions. This is where a Foucauldian model of power producing 'useful' bodies and subjects, which are simultaneously enabled and constrained, can make a difference. It allows us to recognize the problematic, and sometimes disastrous, ways in which women are positioned as the useful embodied ground for models of ethnic community belonging. But it also requires us to acknowledge that resistance to that positioning only emerges from those same useful bodies and subjects, who continue to be embedded in the discourses and practices of reproducing specific communities, and whose sense of themselves 'as women' is always inflected by those specific community locations. It is only there, 'from the contingency that has made us what we are', that something different might emerge. Appeals to women's solidarity across community divisions are not irrelevant; indeed, as I will discuss in the next section, they are part of the resources for refusing prevailing power relations and identity models. But they need not be articulated in ways that suggest that women have no stake in any form of community identity. Nor, importantly, should they be articulated in ways that suggest that women themselves are never active perpetrators of ethnocentrism, narrow nationalism or racism. As some of the feminist scholarship on women's coalition work across ethnic divides has begun to suggest, the most promising alliances hold on to a double move of acknowledging women's 'rootedness' in different identities while working to shift the terms within which those differences are currently defined (see Yuval-Davis 1997 and Cockburn 1998).

A Foucauldian view of power as productive also suggests that we should look at the ways in which women's bodies have been made 'useful' to prevailing identity models and power relations, in order to locate the potential points of refusal, resistance and change that can emerge, which might turn power back on itself. Such a view of power invites us to revisit the reproductive female body, and women's reproductive work, to find the points of dissonance that contest the constraining effects of the dominant identity models in which they are currently enmeshed. It means revisiting the 'homes' that women stand for and work to reproduce and finding there 'from the contingency that has made us what we are, the possibility of no longer being, doing or thinking what we are, do, think'. I think what we can find there are ways to refuse what we are that undo the logic of dualisms that associates 'home', community and belonging with notions of fixity, and that positions women as resources in the reproduction of that version of community. And I think it is this kind of undoing that Foucault had in mind when he cast his politics of refusal in terms of 'promoting new forms of subjectivity' or 'the undefined work of freedom'.

Refusing Who/What 'we' are

Theoretical work by postcolonial and diasporic feminists and empirical work on migrant women[6] already suggest some of the resources we can draw on to develop such a politics of refusal. Sara Ahmed, in her book *Strange Encounters* (2000), challenges the association of 'home' with notions of fixity. She takes issue with the conceptual model that has our sense of home being produced once and for all through the drawing of an exclusionary border. Rather, she argues, there is an ongoing process of rehearsal and reconstitution of a sense of home/community that is worked through encounters with 'the stranger within', and, drawing on Avtar Brah's (1996) notion of 'diaspora space', through a never-ending series of encounters between staying put, arriving and leaving. 'Home' is produced through a constant process of adjustment, transformation, negotiation, redefinition – a never-ending, ongoing work to reproduce the appearance of stability and fixity that is part of the imagined community, whether that community is being thought about in terms of nation, ethnicity, race, religion, etc. And when I think about this in connection with women's 'useful bodies' and 'useful' embodied practices, I can't help but think of the never-ending reproductive work that is done (mainly) by women. The daily rituals of caring, cleaning, feeding as well as the culturally specific emotional kinwork that is always to be redone, necessary but never complete, serve to provide the appearance of sameness and stability in ever-changing contexts.

What this means is that part of the process of refusing what we are can be to challenge the ways in which reproductive work is associated with 'the stasis of being' (Ahmed 2000: 89) and is set up in opposition to the productive work of becoming. Instead we might argue that the 'home' that is produced through discursive constructs of 'Woman' and by the embodied practices of women is one in which being and becoming are always entangled. Women's bodies are made useful to a particular version of community belonging, one that positions them within a dominant discourse of stasis and fixity. But in order to be useful in this way, to reproduce that sense of fixity, women have to work through that constant process of adjustment, transformation, negotiation and redefinition. They have to manage that never-ending series of encounters between staying put, arriving and leaving. We can see this work of producing 'home', therefore, as a site or space of dissonance, where a counter-discourse might emerge that refuses the equivalence of belonging with stasis.

In contexts of ethnic conflict, violence and social instability, this space of dissonance is heightened. Here the myth of home as source of stable origins clashes against the reality of being called upon to reproduce that 'home' in the context of forced displacement. I've written elsewhere about some of the complexities women face in refugee camps, where the burden of reproducing a household where there is no physical household to work with falls primarily on them (see Gedalof 2000). Much of the recent feminist work on the conflicts in the former Yugoslavia provides other examples. Women displaced by violent conflict are being asked to reproduce home – to create a bit of familiar physical and emotional space – in the unfamiliar and overcrowded households of relations and friends

(Mladjenovic and Matijasevic 1999). Korac catalogues a variety of dilemmas about what home means and how to reproduce it facing women in these conflicts. Bosnian Muslim women displaced to Serbia are asked to rebuild home in what has been defined by the conflict as enemy territory. Bosnian Serb or Croatian Serb women displaced to Serbia, or forcibly returned to 'liberated' areas in Croatia and Bosnia in order to repopulate local Serb communities are told that they have been returned 'home', but it doesn't feel that way to them. Korac (1999) writes as well about the ambiguous positioning of women and girls in families of mixed ethnicity, caught between two mutually exclusive narratives of belonging and home. To these examples we can add the ways in which memories of ethnic conflict might eliminate the possibility of 'home' ever again being thought of as somewhere familiar and unchanging. Accounts of women in Croatia, Bosnia, Kosovo, from all sides of the ethnic divides (Korac 1999), or of Hindu, Muslim and Sikh women who experienced communal rioting in Delhi (Mankekar 1999), all echo a sense that 'home' is not the same place it once was. And this sense of the 'unhomeliness' of home must be particularly pertinent for the women who are expected nevertheless to reproduce it.

The notion that 'mothering' is simply about preserving a space of the same is also challenged by these contexts. In her classic anthropological study of everyday violence in shanty-town life in Brazil, *Death Without Weeping*, Nancy Scheper-Hughes (1992) writes of women obliged to participate in the community's 'space of death' by making innumerable little 'selections' that have life-and-death consequences. What quality and quantity of food to give to younger and older, weaker and stronger children? Who gets access to filtered or boiled water? Who gets taken for emergency medical care? Who gets new shoes? The particular reproductive burden that is placed on women is to carry on living and making these decisions in this space of death (Scheper-Hughes, 1992: 407–8). Although she was writing about a community facing a different kind of violence, I think that her reflections have a wider resonance for how we think about the reproductive work of communities in contexts of violence and dislocation. In contexts of relative peace and economic development, where communities might reasonably expect their children to survive and their homes to remain intact, a discourse of motherhood that casts reproduction in terms of continuous nurturing, of repetition, of preserving the same, might continue to stand as a norm that women can take up as 'truth'. War, violence, dislocation and poverty make clear(er) the fragility or impossibility of those terms; here, reproduction involves unbearable choices that still need to be borne – of letting go and holding on, of deciding what can be preserved and what has to change, which parts of disassembled homes can be reassembled, and in what form.

Scheper-Hughes, of course, was not writing about a community facing violent conflict defined along ethnic lines as in the examples given above from the former Yugoslavia or India. It might appear, then, that the kinds of decision she discusses, and the practices of mothering of which they are a part, have more to do with survival of the self and the family than of specific communities defined in terms of race, ethnicity, religion or 'culture'. But this distinction is difficult to sustain if we think about mothering as a 'matrix of ideas, meanings, sentiments and practices that are everywhere socially and culturally produced' (Scheper-Hughes 1992: 341). The material and emotional resources women draw on to make these survival decisions are always culturally specific: without our cultures 'we simply would not know how to feel' (ibid.: 431). The 'meanings' of love, attachment, mourning and grief that inform such reproduction decisions are embedded in and emerge from culturally specific relations of power (ibid.: 412), which are in turn reconstituted and (potentially) reconfigured through those reproductive decisions. What these examples suggest, then, is a view of the work of reproduction necessarily opening out to difference. Yet in contexts of ethnic conflict, this view is covered over by a dominant discourse of community belonging that ties women to the preservation of pure, authentic origins and sameness.

One response to all this might be to refuse any sense of belonging at all, but a potentially more subversive refusal might be to refuse the narrow terms of belonging being offered, while insisting on the 'right' to belong in more than one way. Cockburn suggests some of the ways in which this might be happening, in her study of women's organizing in the context of the Serbian, Irish and Israeli-Palestinian conflicts. These include women's accounts of trying to create and sustain new, hybrid cultural rituals and activities that can link their families to some broader sense of belonging that draws from, but is not bound to, a single religion or ethnicity. They also include women's attempts to refuse the polarized terms of the conflicts in which they find themselves, not by denying difference but rather by bringing in and acknowledging other differences, including those which don't fit on either side of the polarization (Cockburn 1998). Cockburn sees in these women's strategies the need to give up the comfortable but dangerous illusion that community must equal consensus; rather, she argues, they suggest the need to settle for the difficult reality of unavoidable, unending, careful and respectful struggle (ibid.: 216). The most successful alliances of women across their differences, Cockburn believes, are good at 'non-closure on identity'. They don't predict what might emerge, they are willing to wait to see if there might be different ways of living a particular community identity which, when articulated with 'woman', might be given a different meaning (ibid.: 225).

What all this suggests is a space of emerging discourses and practices from which to refuse the positioning of women as the ground of one form of imagined community, and to begin to ask questions about a reimagined 'we' that proceeds on a different basis. Reimagining 'home', reimagining the reproductive work that women do there, and also reimagining the useful, reproductive female body can potentially yield a model of belonging that refuses to be a resource for the exclusionary politics of ethnic absolutism, narrow nationalism or racism. What this requires, though, is a wrenching away of our understanding of reproduction from its long-standing conceptual association with stasis, being, with repetition of the same, and this is where I think we can usefully turn to Irigaray. In Irigaray's view, the history of Western philosophy can be read as one in which 'any theory of the "subject" has always been appropriated by the "masculine"' (1974: 133). Crucial to this appropriation has been an active denial of the maternal body, of any space for 'woman' and women within the realm of what counts as meaning, truth, action, desire, becoming, etc. Mother, matter, the female capacity for physical birth – for Irigaray, these need to be conceptualized as an inert ground upon which the masculine dream of self-birth is erected within prevailing systems of signification and relations of power. At the level of theorizing the individual subject or self, this means that the only available option is a self defined by exclusion of the (m)other. At the level of theorizing social or political structures, this means a recurring tendency to erect the realms of culture, the *polis*, civil society and production upon the necessary-but-inert ground of nature, the private, the reproductive sphere.[7]

For Irigaray, as long as the 'woman as ground' logic stays in place, then there can be no place to symbolize reproduction within what she calls a female genealogy. I understand this to mean, among other things, a way of thinking about the connections between individual selves, and therefore about differences, which is not premised on a cut between self and other. In Irigaray's account, it is the exclusion of the (m)other, the wilful 'forgetting' of the maternal body that initiates and sustains 'the hardening of all dichotomies, categorical differences, clear-cut distinctions, absolute discontinuities, all the confrontations of irreconcilable representations' (1974: 246). This is the legacy of a genealogical line drawn according to the Law of the Father. As Michelle Boulous Walker argues in her reading of Irigaray, within this patriarchal law, reproduction – the realm of the silenced mother – is equated with repetition-as-same (1998: 163). But in a different, still unsymbolized genealogy of mothers and daughters, there might be the possibility of repetition opening out towards difference (ibid.: 170). In the figures of mother and daughter – who are both same in their sex/gender and different in their individual and generational positionings – Irigaray is gesturing toward a way of thinking identity that refuses both the dichotomies and categorical distinctions of binary logic and the association of repetition/reproduction with sameness. It is a model of identity that insists on the space between selves while refusing to define that space of difference in oppositional terms. And it is one that insists that change, flux, movement can be understood in ways that don't conform to that oppositional logic (ibid.: 172–3).

In Irigaray's project, what is at stake is mainly the question of the individual subject or self. One problem with this is that it can lead to a focus on an undifferentiated or unspecified woman/mother/daughter. But if we use these insights in relation to questions of collective identities, then the woman/mother/daughter in question can be more specifically located. What this gives us is a way of imagining, or of symbolizing, the reproduction of collective identities in which change, exchange (i.e. negotiation, interaction), difference and movement are bound up with the persistence of identities. Writing about the processes that go into producing the notions of family, home and belonging that prevail in contexts of ethnic conflict, Cynthia Cockburn uses the image of a family tree, in which all the messy connections, of 'every wife, cousin and sister-in-law' have to be left out in order to clearly trace the (male) line of descent (1998: 229). The family tree – and the model of 'proper' community belonging it represents – only works by removing from the frame all that in real life complicates it. Irigaray's gesture toward an alternative genealogy suggests that we need to find ways to belong to altogether messier family trees.

What Irigaray also gives us is a sense of just how difficult this is. As long as this alternative way of thinking genealogies remains outside the symbolic or outside the terms of dominant discourses of collective identity, then the mother-daughter relation, or any relationship between women, remains one that is highly problematic. The options available to women are limited: in Irigaray's terms, simply privileging an all-powerful but necessarily silenced mother within patriarchal law can only lead to the fusion and death of the daughter as desiring subject. At the same time, the 'woman-ness' of the mother is also being denied (Walker 1998: 170–2). Such a view certainly has a resonance with the situation women often confront in relation to specific ethnic community identities. Mothers are invested with great authority and importance within the family so long as they can be seen as reproducers of 'authentic' community traditions and values that, in turn, bind both them and their daughters to positions of subordination. As long as reproduction is defined through a logic of repetition-as-same, women's reproductive work in relation to community identities will continue to constrain the possibilities for both mothers and daughters, and make the inter-generational relationship between mothers and daughters a site fraught with conflict. But if we attend to the ways in which women's specific, embodied practices actually exceed that logic, then we might go some way toward the possibility of communities that trace their genealogies differently.

That genealogy might dislodge the 're-membering [of] shared belongings' (Fortier 2000: 173) that is so often women's work from an association with a notion of an 'original, pristine culture' (ibid.: 63). Rather, it might see the work of re-membering as the reworking of always-messy origin stories told to and by ever-changing selves, which allows for a persistence of a sense of community without recourse to a story that says: 'this is how it has always been, you must do things this way so that we know who we are'. It might recognize that mothers of different generations are always restaging the meanings of origins, that the work of cultural reproduction is never a simple repetition or replication but is always a creation of something new (Tsolidis 2001: 193). Community belonging and survival might be premised, then, not on the timeless permanence and stasis of repetition, but on the endless daily decisions about what to hold on to and what to let go. Home might be refigured, not as a fixed ground of identity from which to act, but as itself a continuous act of production and reproduction that is never fully complete. Such a view of home, belonging and community as a kind of work-in-progress cuts the discursive ground out from under the feet of those who would justify inter-ethnic violence on the basis of fixed certainties.

In conclusion, then, what is needed is a feminist reclaiming of the ground of community belonging, that works from a reimagining of the specifically female body. I propose this, in the spirit of Foucault's politics of refusal, not in order to 'discover' what women 'really are' or to erect a new metaphysics that will become a science, but because women will not be able to refuse effectively their positioning as the useful embodied ground of oppressive forms of community belonging until communities can be imagined on a different basis. And because the beginnings of those different forms of belonging might be found in the ways that women are reworking a sense of place in the unhomely homes they find themselves in. The still more common feminist response to this dilemma has been to challenge the association of women with 'place', to argue for women's 'right to travel', as nomads, as citizens, as women. And yet to abandon the ground of belonging is to leave intact the opposition between being/ belonging and becoming, and to foreclose on the possibility of the future formation of a different kind of 'we' that is not bound by the logic of narrow identity politics.

Breda Gray (1996), writing about the situation of migrant Irish women in London, suggests that the migrant woman is forced to construct an identity in the imaginary, as no territory is possible for her. But, she goes on to ask, if women are identified in nationalist discourse with the territory of the nation, as the ground of identity, can territory ever be part of any women's self-representation, whether migrant or not, except as allegory? I understand Gray to be using this point of dissonance to unsettle or dislodge that association of women with any kind of territorial belonging, but I think it can also be turned to more positive effect. Could this not be a space for a reimagining of belonging that is more aware of its imaginary, always-to-be-re-created status, and that therefore refuses to settle down within the familiar terms of stasis and sameness? As Irigaray wrote in another context, but which I believe takes on new meaning here:

> once imagine that woman imagines and the object loses its fixed, obsessional character . . . If the earth turned, and more especially turned upon herself, what would there be (for the subject) to rise up from and exercise his power over? (1974: 133).

It may seem unfair to end with a series of questions, but what I am hoping is that these are the kinds of differently formulated question that, in Foucault's terms, might make the future formation of a 'we' possible. If the ground of community belonging that is 'woman' turns, and turns to reimagine herself, then we might also be clearing the ground for radically new forms of belonging.

Acknowledgements

Thanks to Sara Ahmed, Anne-Marie Fortier, and the staff and students of the School of Women's Studies, York University, Canada, for their helpful comments on earlier drafts of this chapter.

Notes

1. See for example Anthias and Yuval-Davis 1989, Chhachhi 1991, Mani 1990, Morokvasic 1998, Sarkar and Butalia 1995, Sunder Rajan 1993.
2. See among many others Brah 1996, Charles and Hintjens 1998, Hasan 1994, Kandiyoti 1993, Yuval-Davis 1997.
3. In taking up this move, I differ from those feminist commentators on Foucault who see his approach as one that might be useful to feminism in a 'deconstructive' or critical mode, but who argue that Foucault has little to offer in the way of positive political or normative alternatives (see for example Fraser 1989 and McNay 1992). Rather, I share the view of Lloyd (1996), Grimshaw (1993) and Sawicki (1991, 1996) that Foucault's politics of refusal can more positively open up the boundaries of the political (Lloyd 1996: 242). To date, though, most of these claims for a Foucauldian feminist politics have remained quite general, if intriguing, suggestions for future work. While I don't claim to go very much further in what follows, I hope to begin to flesh out what this might mean more specifically in relation to the question of women and the politics of ethnic community reproduction.
4. See Gedalof (1999 and 2000) for more detailed discussions of these issues.
5. The possibilities for women of reclaiming a notion of citizenship that opens up toward broader solidarities are explored particularly in Yuval-Davis and Werbner (1999), but related discussions can also be found in Charles and Hintjens (1998), Corrin (1996) and some of the contributors to Maynard and Purvis (1999), in particular Pettman.
6. See for example Alund 1999, Fortier 2000, Ganguly 1992, Gray 1999, Huang et al. 2000, Tsolidis 2001, Walter 2001 and Webster 1998.
7. In *Speculum*, Irigaray tracks these moves through the work of Plato, Descartes, Kant, Hegel and, of course, Freud, among others. Michelle Boulous Walker draws on Irigaray's insights to further uncover the workings of this masculine dream of self-birth in Freud's elaboration of the unconscious and the conscious self to which it gives birth. She also presents a powerful analysis of the active denial of the maternal body in the work of Althusser, whose concern for identifying self-generating systems (which include Freud's theory of the unconscious and his own theory of Ideological State Apparatuses) betrays, according to Walker, a desire for a kind of reproduction that is not dependent on the female body or women (1998: 33–49). Walker identifies other recurring moves to associate female reproduction with stasis, or

'repetition-as-same' in Marx, de Beauvoir and, to some extent, Deleuze (Walter 1998: 85–89, 165–6, 168).

Bibliography

Ahmed, Sara (2000), *Strange Encounters: Embodied Others in Post-coloniality*, London and New York: Routledge.

Alund, Aleksandra (1999), 'Feminism, Multiculturalism, Essentialism', in N. Yuval-Davis and P. Werbner (eds) *Women, Citizenship and Difference*, London and New York: Zed.

Anderson, Benedict (1991), *Imagined Communities*, London: Verso.

Anthias, Floya and Yuval-Davis, Nira (eds) (1989), *Woman-Nation-State*, London: Macmillan.

Battersby, Christine (1998), *The Phenomenal Woman*, Cambridge: Polity.

Brah, Avtar (1996), *Cartographies of Diaspora: Contesting Identities*, London and New York: Routledge.

Butalia, Urvashi (1993), 'Community, State and Gender: On Women's Agency during Partition', *Economic and Political Weekly*, 24 April: WS12–24.

Charles, Nickie and Hintjens, H. (eds) (1998), *Gender, Ethnicity and Political Ideologies*, London and New York: Routledge.

Chhachhi, Amrita (1991), 'Forced Identities: The State, Communalism, Fundamentalism and Women in India', in D. Kandiyoti (ed.) *Women, Islam and the State*, London: Macmillan.

Cockburn, Cynthia (1998), *The Space Between Us: Negotiating Gender and National Identities in Conflict*, London: Zed.

Corrin, Chris (ed.) (1996), *Women in a Violent World: Feminist Analyses and Resistance across Europe*, Edinburgh: Edinburgh University Press.

Fortier, Anne-Marie (2000), *Migrant Belongings: Memory, Space, Identity*, Oxford and New York: Berg.

Foucault, Michel (1980 [1975]), 'Body/Power', in M. Foucault, *Power/Knowledge*, ed. C. Gordon, London: Harvester Wheatsheaf.

—— (1977a), *Discipline and Punish: The Birth of the Prison*, New York: Vintage.

—— (1977b), 'Power and Strategies', in M. Foucault, *Power/Knowledge*, ed. C. Gordon, London: Harvester Wheatsheaf (1980).

—— (1982), 'The Subject and Power', Afterword in H. Dreyfus and P. Rabinow, *Michel Foucault: Beyond Structuralism and Hermeneutics*, London: Harvester Wheatsheaf.

—— (1984), 'Polemics, Politics and Problematizations: An Interview with Michel Foucault', in P. Rabinow (ed.), *The Foucault Reader*, London: Penguin.

—— (1997), 'What is Enlightenment?', in M. Foucault, *Ethics*, ed. P. Rabinow, London: Penguin.

Fraser, Nancy (1989), *Unruly Practices: Power, Discourse and Gender in Contemporary Social Theory*, London: Polity.

Ganguly, Keya (1992), 'Migrant Identities: Personal Memory and the Construction of Selfhood', *Cultural Studies*, 6(1), January: 27–50.

Gedalof, Irene (1999), *Against Purity: Rethinking Identity with Indian and Western Feminisms*, London and New York: Routledge.

—— (2000), 'Identity in Transit: Nomads, Cyborgs and Women', *European Journal of Women's Studies*, 7: 325–42.

Gray, Breda (1996), 'Irish Women in London: National or Hybrid Diasporic Identities?', *NWSA Journal*, 8(1), Spring.

—— (1999), '"The Home of our Mothers and our Birthright for Ages"? Nation, Diaspora and Irish Women', in M. Maynard and J. Purvis (eds), *New Frontiers in Women's Studies: Knowledge, Identity and Nationalism*, London: Taylor and Francis.

Grimshaw, Jean (1993), 'Practices of Freedom', in C. Ramazanoglu (ed.), *Up Against Foucault*, London and New York: Routledge.

Guardian, The (2000), 'Serbs "Enslaved Muslim Women at Rape Camps"', 21 March: 13.

—— (2000), 'Pattern of violent assaults revealed in Kosovo', 21 March: 13.

Hasan, Zoya (ed.) (1994), *Forging Identities: Gender, Communities and the State*, Delhi: Kali for Women.

Huang, Shirlena, Teo, P. and Yeoh, B. (2000), 'Diasporic Subjects and Identity Negotiations: Women in and from Asia', *Women's Studies International Forum*, 23(4) 391–8.

Irigaray, Luce (1985 [1974]), *Speculum of the Other Woman*, trans. Gillian C. Gill, Ithaca, New York: Cornell University Press.

Kandiyoti, Deniz (1994), 'Identity and its Discontents: Women and the Nation', in P. Williams and L. Chrisman (eds), *Colonial Discourse and Post-Colonial Theory*, London: Harvester Wheatsheaf.

Korac, Maja (1999), 'Refugee Women in Serbia: Their Experiences of War, Nationalism and State Building', in N. Yuval Davis and P. Werbner (eds), *Women, Citizenship and Difference*, London and New York: Zed.

Lloyd, Moya (1996), 'A Feminist Mapping of Foucauldian Politics', in S. Hekman (ed.), *Feminist Interpretations of Michel Foucault*, University Park: Pennsylvania State University Press.

Mani, Lata (1990), 'Contentious Traditions: The Debate on *Sati* in Colonial India', in Kumkum Sangari and Sudesh Vaid (eds), *Recasting Women: Essays in Indian Colonial History*, Delhi: Kali for Women Press.

Mankekar, Purnima (1999), *Screening Culture, Viewing Politics: An Ethnography of Television, Womanhood and Nation in Postcolonial India*, Durham, NC and London: Duke University Press.

Maynard, Mary and Purvis, J . (eds) (1999), *New Frontiers in Women's Studies: Knowledge, Identity and Nationalism*, London: Taylor and Francis.

McNay, Lois (1992), *Foucault and Feminism*, Cambridge: Polity.

Mladjenovic, Lepa and Matijasevic, D. (1996), 'SOS Belgrade July 1993–1995: Dirty Streets', in C. Corrin (ed.), *Women in a Violent World*, Edinburgh: Edinburgh University Press.

Morokvasic, Mirjana (1998), 'The Logics of Exclusion: Nationalism, Sexism and the Yugoslav War', in N. Charles and H. Hintjens (eds), *Gender, Ethnicity and Political Ideologies*, London and New York: Routledge.

Pettman, Jan Jindy (1999), 'Boundary Politics: Women, Nationalism and Danger', in M. Maynard and Purvis, J. (eds) *New Frontiers in Women's Studies: Knowledge, Identity and Nationalism*, London: Taylor and Francis.

Rose, Gillian (1993), *Feminism and Geography*, Cambridge: Polity.

Sarkar, Tanika (1987), 'Nationalist Iconography', *Economic and Political Weekly*, 21 November: 2011–15.

—— (1991), 'The Woman as Communal Subject', *Economic and Political Weekly*, 31 August: 2057–62.

—— (1995), 'Heroic Women, Mother Goddesses: Family and Organization in Hindutva Politics', in Tanika Sarkar and Urvashi Butalia (eds), *Women and the Hindu Right*, Delhi: Kali for Women.

—— and Urvashi Butalia (eds) (1995), *Women and the Hindu Right*, Delhi: Kali for Women.

Sawicki, Jana (1991), *Disciplining Foucault*, London and New York: Routledge.

—— (1996), 'Feminism, Foucault and "Subjects" of Power and Freedom', in S. Hekman (ed.), *Feminist Interpretations of Michel Foucault*, University Park: Pennsylvania State University Press.

Scheper-Hughes, Nancy (1992), *Death Without Weeping: The Violence of Everyday Life in Brazil*, Berkeley and London: University of California Press.

Sunder Rajan, Rajeswari (1993), *Real and Imagined Women*, New York and London: Routledge.

Tsolidis, Georgina (2001), 'The Role of the Maternal in Diasporic Cultural Reproduction – Australia, Canada and Greece', *Social Semiotics*, 11(2): 193–208.

Walker, Michelle Boulous (1998), *Philosophy and the Maternal Body: reading silence*, London and New York: Routledge.

Walter, Bronwyn (2001), *Outsiders Inside: Whiteness, Place and Irish Women*, London and New York: Routledge.

Webster, Wendy (1998), *Imagining Home: Gender, 'Race' and National Identity, 1945–64*, London: UCL Press.

Whitford, Margaret (1991), *Luce Irigaray: Philosophy in the Feminine*, London and New York: Routledge.

Yuval-Davis, Nira (1997), *Gender and Nation*, London: Sage.

—— and Werbner, P. (eds) (1999), *Women, Citizenship and Difference*, London and New York: Zed.

Part II
Family Ties

–5–

Making Home: Queer Migrations and Motions of Attachment

Anne-Marie Fortier

Within predominantly gay, but also lesbian, literatures of the Euro-American world, the 'coming out' story has become an established genre of self-narrative and self-identification (Plummer 1995). A recurring theme in these stories is the association of migration with the fulfilment of the 'true' homosexual self *outside* of the family home of one's child-hood: 'coming out' means 'moving out' of the childhood 'home' and relocating oneself elsewhere, in another 'home' (Brown 2000: 50 *inter alia*). This chapter is about evocations of the 'original' family home in narratives of queer[1] migrations, and how this 'home' is differently figured and refigured in relation to different movements: leaving home, returning home and homing. I discuss how narratives of queer migrations constitute different versions of what Avtar Brah (1996: 180) calls 'homing desires': desires to feel at home achieved by physically or symbolically (re)consti-tuting spaces which provide some kind of ontological security in the context of migration (Fortier 2000: 163). For as David Eng states, 'despite frequent and trenchant queer dismissals of home and its discontents, it would be a mistake to underestimate enduring queer affiliations to this concept' (1997: 32).

What interests me here is not *why* gay and lesbian affiliations to home endure, but *how* 'home' is deployed in gay and lesbian migration narra-tives. More specifically, I shall examine how the familial home figures in textual renditions of queer migrations. Rather than seeing the childhood home as simply left behind, displaced or replaced by something new in the process of migration, I propose to explore how it is produced differ-ently through different movements of the 'queer' outside or inside the homespace. A central aim of this chapter is to decentre the heterosexual, familial 'home' as the emblematic model of comfort, care and belonging. I thus offer a re-reading of the trope of 'coming out' of the childhood home, on the one hand (in the first section), which I cast against narratives of returning to that home, on the other (second and third sections). Through this review of different ways of negotiating the childhood home, I seek out how 'home' may be more effectively theorized as a space that is not foundational, nor determining, indeed a conception that refuses an ontology of 'home' as a necessary function of heterosexuality. Would it be possible to think of the familial home differently, in ways that open it up to 'queer belongings'?

It seems to me that the assumption that one has to move out in order to come out is largely connected to particular ideas about the *inherent qualities* of 'home', and related ideas of hominess. When I began reading the texts discussed below, I was struck by the widespread assumptions about 'home' as a necessary space of comfort and familiarity. This model of 'home as familiarity' attributes inherent qualities to home which, in turn, becomes the cause of its refusal when one no longer feels 'familiar' in the childhood home. 'Home-as-familiarity' entails stasis – it is a site where things and subjects stand still, and it is there to be left behind or desired. While some authors have sought to unfix home from its static position, and suggested that 'movement can be one's very own home' (Rapport and Dawson 1998: 27; see also Chambers 1990), few have questioned the very attributes projected onto 'home' in narratives of migration (one notable exception being Ahmed 2000). Hence in what follows, I unpack the attributes given to 'home' and question the tendency to oppose queerness and the childhood home, where the latter is a space where queerness does not fit. In short, I argue that queer migrations are not merely *against* the childhood home but, rather, that they *reprocess* the childhood home differently. By viewing home as 'reprocessed', I suggest, following Alison James (1998: 144), that home is a 'spatial context where identities are worked on'. This means that the identities of 'home' as well as those who inhabit it are never fixed, but are continuously reimagined and redefined. In addition, I seek to unveil how home remains widely conceived as an imagined, isolated space that is rarely connected to wider social contexts.[2] Moreover, there is something about how home is posited not only an *enclosed* space, but, as Jennie Germann Molz points out, 'as a site of [heterosexualized] *familial* relations . . . [that] reproduce home *as* home'[3] that is worth pursuing. How is the re-imagining of home also about the re-imagining of the family?

The chapter contains three sections: leaving home/moving home, returning home, and homing. The sections all feed into each other in a kind of 'motion' of thought, insofar as the analysis of each type of narrative leads to questions that I consider in the subsequent part.[4] In the first section, I discuss theoretical narratives of queer migration as homecoming, where 'home' is both origin and destination. Second, I consider the movement back home and how home is reimagined or reconstituted through memories that challenge the ideal of home-as-familiarity. Drawing on autobiographical renditions of queer migrations and remembrances of home, I examine the effect of returning home on the very conception of the childhood home. Third, against a conception of home as *engendering* a movement *elsewhere*, toward (becoming) queer, I ask, paraphrasing Ahmed (2000: 88), how does being at home already *encounter* movement and queerness? Thus in the third section, I offer a different version of 'returning home' – homing – and wonder how memories of home can relocate queerness resolutely within the home. Finally in the concluding section, and in light of the narratives discussed here, I propose to extend Brah's definition of 'homing desire' to include its embeddedness within what I call 'motions of attachment'.

Leaving Home, Moving Home: Migration-as-homecoming

For some, queer migrations constitute migration as emancipation. Described as a 'traumatic displacement from the lost heterosexual "origin"' by David Eng (1997: 32), queer migration is conceived, by others, as a movement toward another site to be called 'home'. Thus Alan Sinfield writes:

> most of us are born and/or socialized into (presumably) heterosexual families. We have to move away from them, at least to some degree; and *into*, if we are lucky, the culture of a minority community. 'Home is the place you get to, not the place you came from', it says at the end of Paul Monette's novel, *Half-way Home*. In fact, for lesbians and gay men the diasporic sense of separation and loss, so far from affording a principle of coherence for our subcultures, may actually attach to aspects of the (heterosexual) culture of our childhood, where we are no longer 'at home'. Instead of dispersing, we assemble. (2000: 103; italics original)

Sinfield's intervention inserts itself within a wider discussion, in queer studies, about the fruitfulness of the term 'diaspora' to think about the transnational and multicultural network of connections of queer cultures and 'communities' dispersed worldwide. For Sinfield, queers and diasporas share similar experiences of exile and forced migration outside of an original home. He draws attention to how the 'diasporic sense of separation and loss' experienced by lesbians and gay men results from being cut off from the 'heterosexual culture' of their childhood, which becomes the site of impossible return, the site of impossible memories. This story is about the absence, or loss, *in* childhood, of 'hominess'. To put it simply, the absence/loss of home, here, is located in the familial home, not as a result of leaving home.

In contrast to diaspora, then, Sinfield argues that lesbians and gays do not disperse from a shared home but, rather, 'assemble' in the new home. In a noteworthy reversal of the diasporization narrative, 'home', here, is not an origin, but rather a destination; there is no return, only arrival.[5] This ties in with the idealization of migration as necessary to the fulfilment of the true homosexual self. Such narratives establish an equation between leaving and becoming, and create distinctively queer migrant subjects: those who are forced to get out in order to come out. Books such as Paul Monette's *Half-Way Home*, where 'home' is a destination, or John Preston's *Hometowns: Gay Men Write about Where they Belong*, conjure up stories of exile, abandonment, and loss of the childhood home where the queer is a stranger that does not fit in. 'I had to leave my family in order to be gay', writes Preston in *A Member of the Family* (cited in Brown 2000: 48). The assumption is that one has to leave 'home' in order to realize oneself in *another* place, outside of the 'original' home. 'Once the journey is complete, the self can be completed' (Brown 2000: 49).

More broadly, this testifies to the enduring power of the model of home-as-familiarity, a place where one seamlessly fits in, thus leaving little room for feelings of estrangement. When such feelings emerge, the story suggests, one has to leave. Sinfield is implying that the condition of joining the gay and lesbian subculture is determined by the estrangement from the childhood home. By the same token, the 'homey' gay and lesbian subculture is defined by the estrangement from the 'original' home. But this estrangement is not the result of leaving home, of leaving a space that was, or felt like, home – which is how migration is widely conceived – but, rather, leaving the childhood home is triggered by *becoming* a stranger *at* home; we leave, Sinfield suggests, when 'we are no longer "at home"' in the childhood home (2000: 103). Narratives of queer migration-as-homecoming thus locate estrangement in the original home. The movement, here, is a movement away from being estranged, which has triggered the migration in the first place.

For Sinfield the resolution to estrangement is not a return 'home', or a return to the past, but the movement into a new 'home'. His migration narrative maintains a linear trajectory that posits homecoming as a desirable destination. For Sinfield, people move away from 'home' and '*into, if we are lucky*' (ibid., second emphasis added), a gay or lesbian subculture.[6] But can the journey ever be completed? Is there a final arrival? For

Sinfield, arrival is always deferred. Lesbians and gay men are 'stuck at the moment of emergence. For coming out is not once-and-for-all' (ibid.). Within the hegemonic heteronormative worlds we live in, lesbians and gay men are often misrecognized as straight. Hence insofar as the queer diasporic journey is one of 'envisioning ourselves *beyond* the framework of normative heterosexism' (ibid., my emphasis), the final completion of this movement, the final arrival 'home', is never achieved. As David Eng suggests, 'suspended between an 'in' and an 'out' . . . – between origin and destination, and between private and public – queer entitlements to home . . . remain doubtful' (Eng 1997: 32). Not only are queers forced to leave, but their entitlement to 'home' is questioned because of the irreconcilability of being queer and being 'home', insofar as 'home' is a function of heterosexuality.

Within such narratives of queer migration as homecoming, the lesbian and gay 'subcultures' – or other spaces people are said to move toward to 'feel at home' – acquire a quasi-mythical status. Lawrence Schimel's comment on queer 'cultural homelands' (for example San Francisco's Castro, or Provincetown and Northampton in Massachusetts) within US lesbian and gay culture is apposite in this respect: 'our visits feel like a return home, even if we've never set foot there before' (1997: 167). The lesbian and gay 'homes' are conceived as the locations par excellence for queer subjects to inhabit. The mythification of these homes infuses them with a life and a will of their own, and with the power to *draw* us there because they offer the promise of hominess.[7] While the fantasy of 'home' and belonging is projected onto these 'imaginary homelands' (Rushdie 1991), the material conditions that determine their existence are concealed. A striking feature of the discourse of migration-as-homecoming is how 'home' is devoid of individual bodies or, rather, how it is assumed that *any* (gay and lesbian) body will feel at home in its hub. Likewise, the very materiality of 'making home' is obscured: the economic capital, the laws of consumer capitalism, the daily labour of maintenance and of 'servicing' the clientele, the struggles to create and maintain 'safe' spaces in the face of adversity, and so on. In this respect, 'home' becomes a fetish by virtue of this double process of concealment and projection.[8] 'Home' remains widely sentimentalized as a space of comfort and seamless belonging, indeed fetishized through the movement away from the familial home toward an imagined other space to be called 'home'.

The movement away from home-as-origins becomes a vector for producing 'queerness' as an original stranger, who is always already not-at-home in the childhood home; becoming a 'stranger' is not a result of leaving home but, rather, was the cause of leaving home. This conception suggests a double-life model, where being queer and being 'at home with the family' are kept separate. The point I wish to make here is twofold. First, as stated earlier, the queer 'home', defined in terms of community, is idealized as a space of comfort and sameness that is inherently different to, and separate from, the '(heterosexual) culture of our childhood' (Sinfield 2000: 103). Indeed, Sinfield's 'subcultures' and Schimel's 'cultural homelands' are very different from the 'homes' we 'make' for ourselves, in our everyday lives; they are very different to the domestic 'home', which remains associated with the estranged childhood home. Both 'homes' – the 'community' home and the childhood home – remain untouched by one another, isolated in their respective boundaries. The childhood home is isolated in the past – home as not-home – while the queer home is isolated in the future – home as desirable destination.

Second, the familial home remains unproblematically heterosexualized and defined exclusively in terms of normative 'family values'. By locating the origins of migration, and the subsequent divided life, *within* the heteronormative family, the heterosexual modus vivendi is fatalistically inscribing, and inscribed within, the family. The childhood home is fixed as unbearably heterosexual and inherently 'gay unfriendly', if not homophobic. The family becomes the original cause of the displacement, and a site of impossible emancipation. What would it mean to 'reassess' the childhood home? Would it open it up to 'queer belongings'?

Returning Home: Migration as Re-membering

In his introduction to *Invented Identities? Lesbians and Gays Talk About Migration*, Bob Cant suggests that migration brings opportunities for individuals to 'reassess their childhoods' (1997: 6). More broadly, Cant uses diaspora to capture the 'complex set of loyalties' and multiple attachments that many gays and lesbians feel (ibid.: 14). In a manner akin to Paul Gilroy's borrowing of W.E. Dubois' notion of double consciousness (Gilroy 1993), Cant writes of the 'two-mindedness' of lesbians and gay men, which differs radically from the 'double life' model. For Cant, two-mindedness is about the everyday work of translation, and the opportunities of greater insight into the seemingly opposed worlds lesbian/gay migrants inhabit. It signals an openness, however fraught, about the multiple belongings that one negotiates in one's life, rather than the concealment of one against the privileging of another in the 'double life' model. Such refusals to deny sexuality and origins pave the way, for Cant, to the possibility of new forms of belonging that are not predicated on single, unitary identities.

Within this conceptual context, Cant's childhood is not lost, or kept as distant site of impossible return.

> It was only when I had been in London for some years as an openly gay man that I was able to re-examine my childhood and youth in a farming community in the East of Scotland. On some level I had behaved for years as if the gay man I became in London was a totally new invention with no past. It took some time before I could acknowledge the enforced isolation of my youth and the impact which it had upon my whole personal development. Eventually I was able to look at the culture of normality which affirmed that 'everyone' lived in families and 'everyone' subscribed to values of the Church of Scotland. It was a culture which made me feel like an outsider; it was only after I left that area that I realized I was not the only outsider. (1997: 7)

Although Cant still conjures up a childhood home that forced him out, his return breaks away from a linear conception of migration. His reassessment opens up the possibility that the childhood home can be lived differently in its re-membering. Cant's reassessment uncovers how childhood, and the idea of 'home' that it is enmeshed with, 'cannot simply be something that proceeds chronologically' (Agamben in Probyn 1996: 101), but rather that it is continually reprocessed, redeployed in narratives of beginnings. Cant reassesses his childhood through the double process of recognition and reconnaissance (Probyn 1996: 110): surveying his childhood locale for other instances of estrangement, sighting moments of recognition with other 'outsiders'. While his remembrance relocates his 'child' as an outsider, it also displaces him by bringing into play his lonely 'I' with a collective 'we' in the creation of new terrains of belonging where multiple 'strangers' co-existed. The act of reconnoitring reconciles Cant with his 'home' by finding in the wider community the effects of social forces of exclusion that unite him, retrospectively, with other outsiders.

In *Invented Identities?*, story after story tells of multiple movement between homes – of flights, detours, returns – and of multiple encounters with estrangement and familiarity experienced in different locales. Within these narratives, 'home' oscillates between different modes of articulation: 'as originary, as nostalgic, as quintessential, as anecdotal, as fiction, as fact' (Probyn 1996: 96). For some, 'home' and family are deeply enmeshed into one another, and become a site to which one regularly returns. For Chris Corrin, for example, the Isle of Man she left when a student will remain a place called home as long as her mother is there. 'Home' is attached to place and to a particular body or, more pointedly, to a particular *relationship*: the mother-daughter relationship. But when her mother dies, Corrin writes, she could 'be faced with the need to find a "real" home', a space where she can feel at home, such as the 'family of lesbians and one or two gay men who live mostly on these islands but also in some other further-flung places' (1997: 114). The death of her mother, she anticipates, will engender a detachment that will force her to re-create home through other attachments, other relationships. A 'home' that is not necessarily place-based but that is grounded in the sense of 'family' and belonging provided by her dispersed friends. The Isle of Man is 'home' by way of familial ties, and it becomes un-homey under the spectre of death, which in turn triggers the desire for a home, the movement forward, *into* the quest for home.

For others, home is a place one returns to after multiple migrations, and rekindles with the sense of safety and comfort 'home' provides. Jean Clitheroe: 'I'm kind of resting now. I'm not sure who I am but it's quiet and I feel safe' (1997: 27). Her return comes with new friendships, new workmates. 'Home' is *not* what it used to be; it is not better, nor worse, but different simply because differently inhabited. Significantly, home is not resolving the undecidability of her present self-identity – 'I'm not sure who I am' – and in this sense, Clitheroe has not 'fully arrived' in the terms of the previous narrative of migration-as-homecoming. Nonetheless, she 'feels safe'. Finally, other contributors, like Tom Shakespeare (1997) or Spike Pittsberg (1997), barely mention the childhood home. Instead, their accounts move from home to home, as if between sites of momentary dwelling dotted along a network of connections.

The striking feature of these autobiographical texts of migration is that overall, childhood homes do not acquire any definitional, foundational status. It is not a necessary site of estrangement, nor of comfort nor of identity affirmation. The childhood homes, here, are not simply left behind, nor are they isolated and detached from present lives, wherever those may be. Surfacing from these narratives is a succession of stories of (re)settlement, encounters, emotional ties, work, love, sweat and tears (to use a worn-out cliché): 'the lived experience of locality' (Brah 1996: 192). Rather than isolated sites of (un)belonging, 'homes' are locations criss-crossed by a variety of forces the authors had to negotiate again and again. Though all the texts begin with a story about the 'original' home, it soon becomes one among many other places that could be called 'home', even temporarily. Each is inhabited by different people – friends, colleagues, family, lovers – who touched the authors differently – in caring, friendly or even, but to a lesser extent, antagonistic encounters. In these stories, remembrances of home at once empty it of any definitional and absolute status, while they continuously *attach* the ideal of home to places that acquire meaning in the process. Hence if, as Paul Gilroy argues (1993,

2000), memory becomes a primary ground of identity formation in the context of migration, where 'space' is decentred and exploded into multiple settings, it is nonetheless tied to the creation of the identity of places (Fortier 2000; Khan 1996). The authors in *Invented Identities?* ruminate on their geographical movements through remembering events in their lives, thus giving 'place' a special significance as a result of its association with events in their life course (Espin 1996: 82). Their narratives relate to the living memory of place without, however, reducing identity to that place.

In contrast to the narrative of 'leaving home', which maintains the ideal of the childhood home as necessarily excluding queerness, these texts suggest what might happen when queer migrants *return* home. Elspeth Probyn writes that 'you can never go home. Or rather, once returned, you realize the cliché that home is never what it was' (1996: 114). If 'home' is no longer what it was, the stories in Cant's anthology suggest what it would look like if it were deployed as such, that is, if it were to be turned into a question of 'it ain't what it's cut out to be'; a question of 'so what' or 'whatever', as Probyn suggests (1996: 97).

Probyn argues against a foundationalist account of childhood as origin by looking at childhood as 'event'. Rather than taking 'home' as some point toward which, or away from which, we might unhesitatingly move, I take from Probyn's insights on childhood memories the challenge to experiment with memories of 'home' within an 'empty dimension', as 'suspended beginnings', that is, 'beginnings that are constantly wiped out, forcing me to begin again and again' (ibid.: 101). This would mean to stop where Sinfield cannot: at the moment of suspension between beginning and his anticipated ending and resolution. It suggests that we accept that 'home' is not a unitary, coherent origin fixed in the distant past, a place that was simply left behind. Furthermore, Probyn's project is to refuse a chronological ground, to refuse the appropriation of the past by way of explaining the present. She proposes to resist looking for signs in my childhood or family that will 'explain' my queerness, and, I would add, that will explain my migration. Following on from this, I consider the childhood home as repeatedly reprocessed through multiple returns to the past – physical or mnemonic. How, then, does returning home rework 'home' in different ways?

The narratives examined here are autobiographical accounts of migrations and of different returns home. They are forms of remembering home through migrations, where memory plays a significant role in 'returning home'. If memory may be seen, following Bergson (1993 [1939]: 31), as an act of duration where different states and moments have no beginning nor ending but rather extend into one another, it also includes discrete 'moments' that combine forces of movement and attachment at once (Fortier 2000: 173–4). As Andrew Quick (2001) suggests, if lived experience can be seen as filmic, memory can be seen as photographic: it 'stills' moments, reprocesses them in different sequences. Hence memories of home conjure up images of places, people, houses, events, all of which attach 'home' to physical locations, things and bodies. Home as attachment, then, is also a site which is attached, fixed into place, in acts of remembering 'what it was like', so that I can move on, into another place, another becoming. For if returns home lead to the realization that it is not what it used to be, it is also a space that must stay in place, even momentarily, if one is to return again and again.

Remembering home, then, is more than simply retrieving memories of homes past; it is about defining and naming 'places', and calling them 'home'. In addition, if, as stated earlier, we are to consider 'home' as a space inhabited by people, a 'spatial context where identities are worked on' (James 1998: 144), we also need to ask how home is differently *re-membered*. In the stories collected in *Invented Identities?*, re-membering 'home' is about the processes through which spaces of hominess – imagined or physical – are inhabited, in the literal sense of dwelling, in the sense of 'membering' spaces with ghosts revived from the past or presences envisaged in an imagined future, and in the sense of manufacturing subjects.[9]

Still, while the narratives in *Invented Identities?* offer a good example of how 'home' is continually reprocessed, this reprocessing is conceived by Cant, in his introduction, as only possible through migration. In other words, migration offers the possibility of reassessing, and reconciling with, the childhood home. Leaving home, in this respect, remains the necessary condition for emancipation, for some kind of liberation from the constraints of the childhood home, which will be 'loosened' at a distance, *outside* the childhood home. Only after this initial distancing can the possibility of return be considered. Within this conception, the fantasy of home, the 'myth' of home (Chambers 1990), acquires a special significance as a result of the movement away from an originary home which, in the case that concerns me here, is the 'childhood home'. Homing desires, here, are determined by leaving home. In contrast, is it possible to conceive of homing desires as already engendered at home (Ahmed 2000: 88)? Can the desire to 'feel at home' be engendered and lived *at* home?

Homing: Home as Queer

In her remarkable memoirs, *Night Bloom*, US-Italian lesbian author Mary Cappello (1998) writes poignantly of her and her immigrant family's 'lived experience of locality' (Brah 1996: 192) by firmly locating her story in working-class South Philadelphia. She relates her grandparents' and parents' struggle to 'integrate' not in terms of simple adaptation to the culture of the country of immigration (the United States) but, rather, in terms of the difficult negotiation of injunctions stemming from both Italy and the United States.

Cappello refuses fixed definitions of ethnicity and sexuality and finds in the broader sense of 'queer' an appropriate description of the Italian/American contexts within which she grew up.

> However well I try to place it, 'my lesbianism' insists on returning to the unarticulated space between my maternal and paternal legacies. Rather than having emerged, in true Oedipal fashion, out of an identification with one parent and disavowal of the other, my willingness to inhabit a space of transgressive pleasure found its impetus in the unresolved area of desire/lack that was the space between Anglo ideals and Italian realities. In 'becoming queer', I was becoming what my Italian/American forebears denied about themselves even as they provided the example. In becoming queer I see myself as having made something wonderful out of an Italian/American fabric, the Italian/American weavers of which were too ready and willing to discard. (1998: 181)

In her own version of reassessing her childhood, Cappello finds queerness *within* the very space of 'betweenness' typically attributed to the 'diasporic space' located between 'here' and 'there' (Brah 1996; Clifford 1994). Drawing on 'queer' as a conceptual tool that disrupts binary oppositions, Cappello expands the 'betweenness' of diaspora to unmoor fixed-gender roles and identifications. Cappello is suggesting that the diasporic home is already queer because it is always somehow located in a space of betweenness: that it is a site of struggle with multiple injunctions of being and 'fitting in' that come from 'here' and 'there'. In this respect, *'home' is intensely queer, and queer, utterly familiar.*

But there is more to her account than queering the diasporic home. Cappello presents a complex fabric of queerness that exceeds sexuality, and of Italianità that exceeds ethnicity. Indeed, it is often assumed that 'ethnicity' and homosexuality are incompatible, and that lesbian/gay people from ethnic minorities will necessarily lead a double life. Giovanna (Janet) Capone expresses this division very clearly:

instead of feeling like one integrated person, I often feel torn in half. It feels like I'm Italian in New York, and a lesbian in California . . . I feel constantly divided. I think my dilemma is one faced by many gay and lesbian people, whose *unpopular* sexual orientation means they end up needing a certain distance from their families. I think this semi-estrangement is especially painful for those of us raised in close knit, ethnic families. (Capone 1996: 36, italics original)

For Capone, the impossibility of reconciling her lesbianism with her Italianness is located in what she identifies as her *Italian* family ethos. Ethnicity is an obstacle in her queer becoming, and reconciling her homosexuality and ethnic identity is an issue that she does not resolve.[10] In contrast, Cappello resolves this problem by drawing a family portrait where ethnicity and sexuality are rather 'mutually articulated through other discursive conditions like religious practice and class' (1996: 91). In other words, Cappello refuses to situate her queer Italianness either inside an essentialized conception of sexuality *as* identity – that's who I am – or within an essentialized US-Italian ethnicity that is relentlessly heterosexual, staunchly patriarchal, and deeply homophobic.

What I could never fail to notice about the men and women in my Italian/ American family . . . was [how] the men failed miserably and with varying degrees of unhappiness in conforming to the mask of white, middle-class masculinity, and the women wielded word, story, their own bodies, in ways that could never pass for demure. By Anglo-American standards, to put it crudely, the male members of my family were soft and the females were hard. Mightn't the fraternal demolition parties that Hollywood cinema has invented for Italian/ American subjectivity be indicative of precisely the fear that those dark, curly-haired, music-loving, flower-tending Italian/Americans are queer? (1996: 96)

Exploring the intersections of immigration, ethnicity and sexuality, Cappello interrogates the very construction of Italian patriarchal culture, epitomized and celebrated in *The Godfather* sequels. The Anglo-US construction of Italian sex-gender norms, she argues, circumscribe the confines of US-Italian belonging. Cappello thus reveals the intricate web of connections between ethnicity and homophobia, and suggests that *queer* is a US construct that *keeps the non-conforming Italian immigrant at a distance, 'out of place'*.

Now I try to understand the pathological sense of loss (in the form of depression) and fear (in the form of phobia) that characterizes my ethnic heritage . . . I can locate the source of disjunction in the immigrant status, the initial anomie of being out of place; but that sense of separation may have only expanded in proportion to my grandfather's un-macho ways and my mother's unladylike tendency to tell it like it is. (1998: 73)

Cappello writes about the longing to belong, and of the painful difficulties that emerge when this longing is caught up with and defined against the wider social and cultural norms of intelligibility. Within this context, exceeding these norms can only be understood as queer. In contrast to evocations of home where 'home' has inherent qualities, Cappello is relating her family's comfort and discomforts not to home *qua* home, but to the difficulties of 'making home' as part of the wider struggle to fit in. Being at home, then, is not merely conditional upon *finding* 'home' somewhere out there and slipping into its comforting fold, but is already constrained by wider social injunctions and definitions of 'home' and family. In other words, Cappello situates her family's dysfunction within the wider context of US fantasies of the Italian family, which is primarily defined in terms of gender roles – the sacrificial mother, the patriarchal macho father. 'Making home', in this context, is inextricably linked to 'making family'. By finding her queerness within the 'unresolved area of desire/lack' (1998: 181), Cappello speaks of a 'home-as-fantasy' that she and her kin not only desire, but *already inhabit*. Home and family are already fantasized, even when we are 'in it'.

Cappello relocates the movement between familiarity and estrangement firmly *within* the home. This stands in stark contrast to Sinfield's subcultures, Schimel's 'cultural homelands', or Corrin's 'real' home, all of which are grounded in the model of home-as-familiarity. In *Night Bloom*, home is not sentimentalized: it is a place of disjunction, of unbelonging, of struggles for assimilation/integration, thus a space that *already* harbours desires for hominess. Nor is 'home' fetishized. The familial home is a space that is always in construction, not only in the imagination, but in the embodied material and affective labour of women and men: the hard work (and despair) of daily maintenance of the family and the home, the emotional work of mediating between quarrelling kin, and so on. Rather than concealing the social, material and emotional conditions that determine the existence of 'home', Cappello never loses sight of them.

Her memoirs are a moving and powerful account of the legacies of the psychological 'disjunction' produced by failing to 'fit in'. Legacies of the marks that immigration, poverty and assimilation have left on herself and her family: legacies of suffering, of cold shivering bodies in badly heated apartments, of deaths, of worrying about the legal authorities, of fears of the striking hand or longings for the caressing one. It is about how she and her forebears found in the arts of gardening and of writing, lessons of desire, creativity and loss. How the delights of a blossoming orange tree co-exist with 'empty pockets' and the struggle to sustain a family (1998: 37).

To be sure, this 'home' is a product of her own memories, and as such, is part of fitting her childhood within her present adult self. But if *Night Bloom* may be read as a narrative of origin, one where Cappello revisits the past to situate her present queerness, she nonetheless resists the moralizing tendencies of origin narratives by the constant reminder of the material and historical conditions that produced her Italian-American family as 'queer'. In questioning the very ideas of Italianness and queerness, she conjures up a 'home' woven through her own reading of the diasporic memories that came her way through her forebears' written or spoken words, or in their silent art of gardening.

By emphasizing the predicament of the immigrant family, however, Cappello's version raises questions about the extent to which all childhood homes are potentially 'queerable' in this way. Is there something about the diasporic home itself that makes this possible? To paraphrase Eng and Hom (1998: 1), is there always something curiously queer – something curiously divergent, contradictory or anomalous – that arises from the experience of migration? I would not want to deny that the experience of migration comes with different experiences of 'home', potentially offering insights that allow us to think of 'home' differently. Such experiences, however, must be acknowledged in their specificity, for the danger is, as Ahmed (2000) has argued, to construct 'migrant ontologies' when migration is elevated as a form of being-in-the-world that is necessarily transgressive, or at least one that is necessarily 'other'. In contrast to Capone, Cappello is careful to identify the very specific living conditions and experiences of her family, which cannot be explained through ethnicity as such, nor through migration as such. At the same time, her questioning opens onto the wider socio-historical and discursive contexts that allow us to consider the ways in which ideas of 'home' are deeply embedded with ideas of family, gender roles and compulsory heterosexuality, which in turn are defined in terms of ethnic difference.

But another question arises about what counts as queer, here. Is Cappello's Italian diasporic family 'queer' simply on the basis of an inversion of US heteronormativity? Is 'queer' simply a shorthand for 'difference' or 'divergence'? We can read Cappello's move as one from the narrower anti-heteronormative definition of 'queer' to the wider anti-normative one. The term 'queer' is expanded, in this latter case, to define itself 'against the normal rather than [merely] the heterosexual' (Warner in Eng 1997: 50n35). But Cappello is not simply reducing queer to a metaphor for divergence, as she is insisting on her family's pains, struggles and sacrifices to survive against *both* the US and the Italian norms of 'family life'. By weaving a fabric of queerness beyond sexuality, Cappello is pointing to the necessary intersections of different forms of power, and the necessary recognition that oppression takes different forms. This bears important theoretical implications. Cappello's analysis of the simultaneous sexualization of ethnic norms and ethnicization of gender norms illuminates the limits of sexuality as an exclusive category of analysis. More to the point, with respect to this chapter's immediate concerns, the usefulness of Cappello's account resides in the invocation of a queer and diasporic assumption of the domestic that denaturalizes any claim on 'home' as the inevitable function of a universalized, decontextualized notion of *the* heterosexual (Eng 1997: 35). In doing so, Cappello denaturalizes any claims on the loss of home as the necessary consequence of 'coming out' and leaving home. 'Becoming queer', here, is not engendered in the movement away from home. It emerges, rather, from the very fabric of a queer family home.

'Homing Desires' and Motions of Attachment

The queer narratives of migration discussed here undeniably reveal the enduring affiliations of many queer migrants to 'home', or what Avtar Brah (1996: 180) would call 'homing desires' which, as stated earlier, are desires to feel at home in the context of migration. Connected to homing desires is the work of physically or symbolically (re)constituting spaces which provide some kind of ontological security in the location of residence, which is not the same as the location of 'origin'. Avtar Brah's definition of homing desires is decidedly cast in migration and defined against the physical return to an originary home(land). Here the homing desire is produced through migration. But homing desire also refers to a longing to belong, and as such, it suggests that 'home' is constituted by the *desire* for a 'home', rather than surfacing from an already constituted home, 'there' or 'here'. In this sense, home is produced through the movement of desire.

It is easy to read memories of homes as the longing for what *was* and no longer *is*, and the longing for home – homing desire as movement toward home – as a result of this loss. When 'leaving home' is the condition of possibility for finding a 'real' home, moving home establishes a clear distinction between the initial site of estrangement – home as not-home – and home as a new site of possibility. The emphasis here is on the future, on creating home as a space of safety and comfort, which is determined by the refusal of the childhood home. It is *through* this refusal that the childhood home acquires a definitional status. Ossified into a particular kind of immoveable heterosexuality, the childhood home becomes the origin not of queerness, but of the protracted quest for home, the endless suspension that Sinfield talks about. Homing desire as move-ment toward a new home also serves to reinstate the boundaries of 'home' and 'fix' it as an unchanging and incontestably desirable space, reinforcing the idea of home as familiarity, comfort and seamless belonging (Ahmed 2000). In this respect, 'homing desires' are constituted though *both* movement and attachment (Fortier 2000).

But 'homing desire' is not only about leaving the originary home behind, fixing it into a distant past, and seeking hominess elsewhere. It can also be part of returning 'home' to re-member it differently. In contrast to the first 'double life' model, where homes are isolated in the past and in the future, the second model of translation (Cant 1997) reassesses and reprocesses childhood life, bridging the gap between 'there' and 'here'. Re-membering the childhood home at once empties it of any definitional and absolute status; it is a space of belonging that proceeds from remem-brances of beginnings that *attach* 'home' to places (the hometown in Scotland; the house, garden and neighbourhood in Philadelphia), faces and bodies (the mother in the Isle of Man; the other outsiders in a Scottish town) and emotions (feeling at home in a network of dispersed friends; feeling the loneliness and fear of the immigrant).

Leaving home or returning home are about moving *between* homes. In both cases, homing desires are determined by an initial movement away from the childhood home. In contrast, Cappello relocates homing desires firmly within her childhood home. She reminds us that home is not simply a *sense* of place, but that it is also a material space, a lived space, inhabited by people who work to keep the roof over their heads, or to keep their family warm, safe and sane. In this sense, homing desires do not occur in the movement *toward* an endlessly deferred space, but they also emerge *within* the very spaces of inhabitance called home.

Cappello's memoirs themselves (as those in Cant's anthology) could be seen *as* homing desires – that is, that the very act of writing memoirs of her life might be motivated by a homing desire: a desire to revisit the childhood home and to create a sense of place for herself. In this sense, homing desires are deeply entwined with re-membering the childhood home. And re-membering that home combines forces of movement and attachment at once; it is about *motions of attachment*. It is lived in motions: the motions of journeying between homes, the motions of hailing ghosts from the past, the motions of leaving or staying put, of 'moving on' or 'going back', the motions of cutting or adding, the motions of continual reprocessing of what home is/was/might have been. But 'home' is also re-membered by attaching it, even momentarily, to a place where we strive to *make* home and to bodies and relationships that touch us, or have touched us, in a meaningful way. Re-membering home, then, is the physical and emotional work of creating 'home', and about the encounter with homing desires already *within* the home (Ahmed 2000), and not only outside of it. Motions of attachment are constitutive 'affective building blocks' (Hage 1997) of 'home'. Indeed, as Gassan Hage suggests, part and parcel of homey feelings are the aspirations for feelings of security, familiarity, and so on. Motions of attachments are about fostering *intima-tions* of imagined homey experiences from the past or projected into the future – a taste or smell from 'home cooking', an image, photograph, a new mug, a new chair – but which are imagined 'from the standpoint of the present' (Hage 1997: 107).

Thus the childhood home is more effectively rethought not by refusing 'home' and leaving it behind – which merely reinstates the authority of the heteronormative model of 'home' – but, rather, by conceiving it as a contingent product of historical circumstances and discursive formations – of class, religion, ethnicity, nation – that individuals negotiate in the process of creating home. In this sense, home is never fully achieved, never fully arrived-at, even when we are in it.

To suggest that encountering queerness in the familial 'home' should be the cause of leaving home simply reinstates home as inherently 'not-queer'. In contrast, I am arguing that it is more productive to remove the sentimental and fetishist cloak that wraps the ideal of home and that conceals the wider discursive injunctions and processes through which it is continuously produced. Reassessing the ideal of home-as-familiarity is about excavating the assumptions about 'home' and questioning the actions undertaken in the name of 'hominess' – home is not a necessary space of comfort, and it is not only constituted through relations between subjects who negotiate wider injunctions to 'fit in', but also whose posi-tions within the home are not necessarily equal. At a time when the heterosexualized model of home as familiarity – home as sameness – remains the preferred model for ideals of community and nation (for example in Britain), it is imperative that we rethink the model of home if we are to productively reassess what it means to be 'at home', and that 'home' is a contingent space of attachment that is not definitional or singular. Not only can home be a space of multiple forms of inhabitance – queer and others – but belonging can also be lived through attachments to multiple 'homes'. To be sure, motions of attachment are embedded within relations of power, within differential movements of subjects who do not share equal entitlements to claim a space as 'home'. The redefinition of home as 'queer', or more broadly of home as a space of differences rather than home-as-sameness might be one step toward engaging with histories of differentiation, suffering, inequality, exclusions and struggles that can constitute collective 'resources for the peaceful acknowledgement of otherness' (Gilroy 2002).

Acknowledgements

Many thanks to Claudia Castañeda and Mimi Sheller, whose editorial suggestions on earlier drafts of this chapter were extremely useful. Thanks to Jennie Germann Molz whose comments revitalized my enthusiasm at a time when it was waning, and to Anu Koivunen for her attention to important details that I would have otherwise missed.

Notes

1. While I am fully aware of the debates around the term 'queer' itself, I use 'queer', here, as a shorthand for 'lesbian and gay' and a range of non-heteronormative practices and desires that may be at the basis of the formation of individual identifications with a wider cultural or political platform of collective 'identity'. The writers discussed here use 'queer' or 'lesbian and gay' in these terms, except for Mary Cappello.
2. Some social theorists have examined the historical construction of home and the 'modern domestic ideal'. See Allen and Crow 1989 and Forty 1986.
3. Personal correspondence (first italics mine).
4. It is worth noting that the majority of the selected texts share one common feature: they connect queer migrations to 'diaspora'. In an article published elsewhere, I consider how these texts make different claims about the diasporic character of queer migrations, namely with respect to their different evocations of 'home'. See Fortier 2001.
5. For a fuller discussion of this notion of 'queer diaspora', see Fortier 2002.

6. This is highly reminiscent of the prototypical immigration narrative, where immigrants are perceived to move *from* one culture *into* another, thus assuming 'cultures' to be neatly bounded and separately located within distinct territories (Fortier 2000: 19). Sinfield's 'subculture' constitutes a timespace that is distinct and separate from the '(hetero-sexual) culture of our childhood', and puts an end to the sense of loss; it brings an end to migration. 'Home' is the antidote to migration. See Fortier 2001.

7. I am not suggesting that queer spaces are not 'sites of emergence' for many lesbians and gay men, as they may constitute safe spaces against a variety of threatening forces. In addition, going to the gay bar or moving within a lesbian subculture may solve, even if momen-tarily, the ontological problem about belonging to the 'lesbian and gay' culture in a heterosexist, homophobic world. In this respect, evocations of home are embedded in the struggles to create and maintain spaces of belonging and comfort in the face of adversity without (or within) the lesbian and gay 'community'. For further considerations on the relationship between sexuality, space, safety and home, see the website of the *Violence, Sexuality and Space Research Project*, Manchester University, http://les1.man.ac.uk/sociology/vssrp/home.htm (accessed 31.01.01).

8. I am informed, here, by Sara Ahmed's own definition of fetishism, which she draws primarily from Marx but also from Freud. See Ahmed 2000: 182n2.

9. See Fortier 2000 for a fuller discussion of re-membering.

10. For a more detailed discussion of the (dis)connections of homo-sexuality and ethnicity, see Fortier 1999.

References

Ahmed, S. (2000), *Strange Encounters: Embodied Others in Post-coloniality*, London and New York: Routledge.

Allan, G. and Crow, G. (eds) (1989), *Home and Family: Creating the Domestic Space*, Basingstoke: Macmillan.

Bergson, H. (1993 [1939]), *Matière et mémoire*, Paris: Presses Universi-taires de France.

Brah, A. (1996), *Cartographies of Diaspora. Contesting Identities*, London and New York: Routledge.

Brown, M.P. (2000), *Closet Space: Geographies of Metaphor from the Body to the Globe*, London and New York: Routledge.

Cant, B. (ed.) (1997), *Invented Identities? Lesbians and Gays Talk About Migration*, London: Cassell.

—— (1997), 'Introduction', in B. Cant (ed.), *Invented Identities? Lesbians and Gays Talk About Migration*, London: Cassell.

Capone, G. (1996), 'A Divided Life: Being a Lesbian in an Italian American Family', in A.J. Tamburri (ed.), *Fuori: Essays by Italian/American Lesbians and Gays*, West Lafayette, IN: Bordighera.

Cappello, M. (1996), 'Nothing to Confess: a Lesbian in Italian America', in A.J. Tamburri (ed.), *Fuori: Essays by Italian/American Lesbians and Gays*, West Lafayette: Bordighera.

—— (1998), *Night Bloom: An Italian-American Life*, Boston: Beacon.

Chambers, I. (1990), *Border Dialogues: Journeys in Postmodernity*, London: Routledge.

Clifford, J. (1994), 'Diasporas', *Cultural Anthropology*, 9(3): 302–38.

Clitheroe, J. (1997), 'Jean Clitheroe', in B. Cant (ed.), *Invented Identities? Lesbians and Gays Talk About Migration*, London: Cassell.

Corrin, C. (1997), 'Chris Corrin', in B. Cant (ed.), *Invented Identities? Lesbians and Gays Talk About Migration*, London: Cassell.

Eng, D. (1997), 'Out Here and Over There: Queerness and Diaspora in Asian American Studies', *Social Text*, 15(3–4): 31–52.

—— and Hom, A.Y. (1998), 'Introduction. Q & A: Notes on a Queer Asian America', in D.L. Eng and A.Y. Hom (eds), *Q&A: Queer in Asian America*, Philadelphia: Temple University Press.

Espin, O. (1996), 'The Immigrant Experience in Lesbian Studies', in: B. Zimmerman and T. McNaron (eds), *The New Lesbian Studies. Into the Twenty-First Century*, New York: Feminist Press.

Fortier, A.-M. (1999), 'Outside/In? Notes on Sexuality, Ethnicity and the Dialectics of Identification', http://www.comp.lancs.ac.uk/sociology/soc028af.html

—— (2000), *Migrant Belongings: Memory, Space, Identity*, Oxford and New York: Berg.

—— (2001), '"Coming Home": Queer Migrations and Multiple Evocations of Home', *European Journal of Cultural Studies*, 4(4): 405–24.

—— (2002), 'Queer Diasporas', in D. Richardson and S. Seidman (eds), *Handbook of Lesbian and Gay Studies*, London: Sage.

Forty, A. (1986), *Objects of Desire: Design and Society, 1750–1980*, London: Thames & Hudson.

Gilroy, P. (1993), *The Black Atlantic: Modernity and Double Consciousness*, London: Verso.

—— (2000), *Between Camps: Nations, Cultures and the Allure of Race*, London: Penguin.

——— (2003), '"Where ignorant armies clash by night": Homogeneous community and the planetary aspect', *International Journal of Cultural Studies*, 6(3): 261–276.

Hage, G. (1997), 'At Home in the Entrails of the West: Multiculturalism, Ethnic Food and Migrant Home-building', in H. Grace, G. Hage, L. Johnson, J. Langsworth and M. Symonds, *Home/World: Space, Community and Marginality in Sydney's West*, Sydney: Pluto.

James, A. (1998), 'Imaging Children "At Home", "In the Family" and "at School": Movement Between the Spatial and the Temporal Markers of Childhood Identity in Britain', in N. Rapport and A. Dawson (eds), *Migrants of Identity. Perceptions of Home in a World of Movement*, Oxford: Berg.

Khan, A. (1996), 'Homeland, Motherland: Authenticity, Legitimacy, and Ideologies of Place among Muslims in Trinidad', in P. van der Veer (ed.), *Nation and Migration: The Politics of Space in the South Asian Diaspora*, Philadelphia: University of Pennsylvania Press.

Monett, P. (1992), *Halfway Home*, New York: Avon.

Pittsberg, S. (1997), 'Spike Pittsberg', in B. Cant (ed.), *Invented Identities? Lesbians and Gays Talk About Migration*, London: Cassell.

Plummer, K. (1995), *Telling Sexual Stories: Power, Change and Social Worlds*, London and New York: Routledge.

Preston, J. (1991), *Hometowns: Gay Men Write about Where they Belong*, New York: Dutton.

Probyn, E. (1996), *Outside Belongings*, New York and London: Routledge.

Quick, A. (2001), 'Response to Nick Kaye', presented at the symposium *Locating Memory, Photographic Acts*, Institute for Cultural Research, Lancaster University, 10–11 May.

Rapport, N. and Dawson, A. (eds) (1998), *Migrants of Identity: Perceptions of Home in a World of Movement*, Oxford: Berg.

Rushdie, S. (1991), *Imaginary Homelands*, New York: Vikas.

Schimel, L. (1997), 'Diaspora, Sweet Diaspora: Queer Culture to Post-Zionist Jewish Identity', in C. Queen and L. Schimel (eds), *PoMoSexuals: Challenging Assumptions About Gender and Sexuality*, San Francisco: Cleiss Press.

Shakespeare, T. (1997), 'Tom Shakespeare', in B. Cant (ed.), *Invented Identities? Lesbians and Gays Talk About Migration*, London: Cassell.

Sinfield, A. (2000), 'Diaspora and Hybridity. Queer Identity and the Ethnicity Model', in N. Mirzoeff (ed.) *Diaspora and Visual Culture: Representing African and Jews*, London: Routledge.

–6–

Nostalgia, Desire, Diaspora: South Asian Sexualities in Motion
Gayatri Gopinath

In *Funny Boy*, Sri Lankan-Canadian writer Shyam Selvadurai's 1994 novel in six stories, the upper-middle class Sri Lankan Tamil narrator traces the seven years of his childhood and adolescence that preceded the Tamil-Sinhalese riots in 1983, and his family's subsequent migration to Canada. This experience of migration is the grounds upon which the narrative unfolds; the novel is structured in terms of remembrance, with the narrator Arjie recalling a 'remembered innocence of childhood . . . now colored in the hues of a twilight sky' (Selvadurai 1994: 5). Such a phrase, coming early on in the novel, seems to signal that the text can be comfortably contained within a conventional genre of exile literature, one that evokes from the vantage point of exile an idyllic, coherent, pre-exilic past shattered by war and dislocation. Similarly, the novel's parallel narrative of Arjie's sexual awakening initially locates the text within an established genre of 'coming-out' stories, where the protagonist grows into an awareness of his 'true' homosexual identity. Yet while *Funny Boy* references the familiar narratives of exile and 'coming out', it reworks the conventions of these genres as well as the very notions of exile and sexual subjectivity. In this chapter I will read Selvadurai's novel alongside two other South Asian[1] diasporic narratives of sexuality – Indian-Canadian filmmaker Deepa Mehta's 1996 film *Fire* and a scene from the popular 1993 Hindi film *Hum Aapke Hain Koun* – in order to interrogate our understandings of nostalgia, 'home' and desire in a transnational frame.

Non-Heteronormative Sexuality and the Nation

In the past decade there has emerged an important body of feminist criticism that examines the complicity of nationalist discourses with gender hierarchies and demonstrates how the figure of the woman in nationalist discourse acts as a primary marker of an essential, inviolable communal identity or tradition.[2] Anne McClintock and others have argued that a gender critique of nationalism reveals the ways in which the nation is construed in terms of familial and domestic metaphors, where 'the woman' is enshrined as both the symbolic centre and boundary marker of the nation as 'home' and 'family' (1995: 354). Deniz Kandiyoti, following Benedict Anderson, further explicates this conflation of 'woman', 'home', 'family' and 'nation' by pointing out that 'nationalism describes its object using either the vocabulary of kinship (motherland, *patria*) or home (*heimat*) in order to denote something to which one is "naturally" tied . . . The association of women with the private domain reinforces the merging of the nation/community with the selfless mother/devout wife' (1994: 382). The nation (as many critics have asserted) is a nostalgic construction, one that evokes an archaic past and authentic communal identity in order to assert and legitimize its project of modernization.[3] Women's bodies, then, become crucial to nationalist discourse in that they serve not only as the site of biological reproduction of national collectivities (Anthias and Yuval Davis 1989: 7), but as the very embodiment of this nostalgically evoked communal past and tradition.

If recent work on gender and nationalism has enabled us to see the ways in which women become emblematic of the concept of 'home' as nation, as feminized domestic space and as a site of pure and sacred spirituality (Grewal 1996: 7), much less attention has been paid to the production and deployment of non-heteronormative or 'queer'[4] sexuality within colonial, anti-colonial nationalist and contemporary nationalist discourses. Given the increasing recognition that sexuality historically secures the grounds for the production of gendered colonial and bourgeois nationalist subjects,[5] it is somewhat surprising that some recent attempts to consider the imbrication of discourses of nationalism and women's sexuality still presume the heterosexuality of the female subject.[6] By failing to examine the existence and workings of alterior sexualities within dominant nationalisms, such analyses leave intact hegemonic constructions of the nation as essentially heterosexual. Whereas 'the woman' carries a powerful symbolic freight in the constitution of the nation, a non-heteronormative subject necessarily has a very different relation to the constructions of 'home' and 'family' upon which nationalism depends. Within the familial and domestic space of the nation as imagined community, non-heteronormative sexuality is either criminalized,[7] or disavowed and elided; it is seen both as a threat to national integrity and as perpetually outside the boundaries of nation, home and family.[8] As M.

Jacqui Alexander states in her discussion of the 1991 Sexual Offenses and Domestic Violence Act in the Bahamas:

> The nation has always been conceived in heterosexuality, since biology and reproduction are at the heart of its impulse. The citizenship machinery is also located here, in the sense that the prerequisites of good citizenship and loyalty to the nation are simultaneously sexualized and hierarchized into a class of good, loyal, reproducing heterosexual citizens, and a subordinated, marginalized class of non-citizens (1997: 84).

Alexander's comment is instructive because it makes explicit the fact that the nation demands heterosexuality as a prerequisite of 'good citizenship', since it depends on the family as a reproductive unit through which the stability of gender roles and hierarchies is preserved. Heterosexuality, in other words, is fundamental to the way in which the nation imagines itself. Alexander goes on to elaborate upon the interplay of nation and nostalgia as understood by other critics by noting that the archaic past produced within nationalism is one of 'sexual 'purity' . . . imagined within a geography (and a home) that only heterosexuals inhabit' (1997: 85). If women under nationalism, as I noted earlier, are figured as 'inherently atavistic – the conservative repository of the national archaic' (McClintock 1995: 359), non-heteronormative subjects, conversely, are written out of national memory entirely. Thus within a nationalist logic where women embody the past, and that past is figured as heterosexual, the non-heterosexual female in particular is multiply excluded from the terms of national belonging and 'good citizenship'.

It is true that, as Alexander points out, the charge of sexual 'impurity' or 'perversion' is not solely levelled against lesbians and gay men, but also extends to all those who cannot be located within the strict confines of middle-class heteronormativity: prostitutes, those who are HIV-infected, working-class and single women, for instance (Alexander 1997: 97). 'Perversion', then, may most clearly mark the figure of the homosexual but is certainly not contained by or exclusive to it. Nevertheless, it is worth specifying the different forms of violence and disciplinary mechanisms that mark the various bodies within this 'marginalized class of non-citizens', as each subject position engenders its own highly particular forms of resistance to, and at times accommodation with, nationalist logic. This chapter, then, is a small part of a much larger project that begins the work of identifying the ways in which those who occupy one 'perverse' subject position – a 'queer South Asian diasporic subjectivity' – reimagine and reconstitute their particular fraught relation to multiple national sites, and as such demand a rethinking of the very notions of 'home' and nostalgia.[9] My contention here is that a consideration of a 'queer diasporic subject' prompts a different understanding of the mechanisms by which national belonging is internalized in the constitution of 'modern' national subjects. More specifically, I want to point to some of the ways in which 'queer diasporic subjects' – especially those who are women – negotiate their elision from national memory, as well as their function as both threat to home/family/nation and as perennially outside the confines of these entities. I stress queer female subjectivity in the diaspora because dominant diasporic articulations of community and identity intersect with patriarchal nationalist logic in its figuring of 'woman' as bearer and guardian of communal tradition.[10]

Queer Sexuality and the Diaspora

As Anannya Bhattacharjee has shown in her work on domestic violence within Indian immigrant communities in the United States, immigrant women are positioned by an immigrant male bourgeoisie as repositories of an essential 'Indianness'. Thus any form of transgression on the part of women may result in their literal and symbolic exclusion from the multiple 'homes' which they as immigrant women inhabit: the patriarchal, heterosexual household, the extended 'family' made up of an immigrant community, and the national spaces of both India and the United States (see Bhattacharjee 1997, 1992). Within the patriarchal logic of an Indian immigrant bourgeoisie, then, a 'non-heterosexual Indian woman' occupies a space of impossibility in that she is not only excluded from these various 'home' spaces, but quite literally simply cannot be imagined.

The impossibility of imagining such a subject within dominant diasporic and nationalist logics has been made all too apparent by the ongoing battle in New York City between the South Asian Lesbian and Gay Association (SALGA) and a group of Indian immigrant businessmen known as the Federation of Indian Associations (FIA), over SALGA's inclusion in the FIA-sponsored annual India Day Parade. The parade – which ostensibly celebrates India's independence day – makes explicit the ways in which an Indian immigrant male bourgeoisie (embodied by the FIA) reconstitutes anti-colonial and contemporary nationalist discourses of communal belonging by interpellating 'India' as Hindu, patriarchal, middle-class and free of homosexuals. In 1995, the FIA denied both SALGA and Sakhi for South Asian Women (an anti-domestic violence women's group) the right to march in the parade on the grounds that both groups were, in essence, 'anti-national'.[11] In 1996, however, the FIA allowed Sakhi to participate while continuing to deny SALGA the right to march. The FIA, as self-styled arbiter of communal and national belonging, thus deemed it appropriate for women to march as 'Indian women', even perhaps as 'feminist Indian women', but could not envision women marching as 'Indian queers' or 'Indian lesbians'; clearly the probability that there may indeed exist 'lesbians' within Sakhi was not allowed for by the FIA (nor apparently by Sakhi itself, who agreed to participate despite the ban on SALGA).

I mention the controversy surrounding the India Day Parade here because it highlights how hegemonic nationalist discourses, reproduced in the diaspora, position 'woman' and 'lesbian' as mutually exclusive categories to be disciplined in different ways. Within patriarchal diasporic logic, the 'lesbian' can only exist outside the 'home' as household, community and nation of origin, whereas the 'woman' can only exist within it. Indeed the 'lesbian' is seen as 'foreign', as a product of 'being too long in the West', and therefore is annexed to the 'host' nation where she may be further elided – particularly if undocumented – as a non-white immigrant within both a mainstream (white) lesbian and gay movement and the larger body of the nation state.

Given the illegibility and unrepresentability of a non-heteronormative (female) subject within patriarchal and heterosexual configurations of both nation and diaspora, the project of locating a 'queer South Asian diasporic subject' – and a queer female subject in particular – may begin to challenge the dominance of such configurations. To this end, I want to suggest here some reading strategies by which to render queer subjects intelligible and to mark the presence of what Alexander terms an 'insurgent sexuality' that works within and against hegemonic nationalist and diasporic logic. Indeed the representations of non-heteronormative desire within the three texts that I consider here call for an alternative set of reading practices, a 'queer diasporic' reading that juxtaposes wildly disparate texts and that traces the cross-pollination between the various sites of non-normative desires that emerge within them. On the one hand, such a reading renders intelligible the particularities of same-sex desiring relations within spaces of homosociality and presumed heterosexuality, and on the other hand, it deliberately wrenches particular scenes and moments out of context and extends them further than they would want to go. It would exploit the tension in the texts between the staging of female homoerotic desire as simply a supplement to a totalizing heterosexuality and the potentiality that they raise for a different logic and organization of female homoerotic desire. A 'queer diasporic' reading and viewing practice conceptualizes a viewing public as located within multiple diasporic sites, and the text itself as accruing multiple, sometimes contradictory meanings within these various locations. In other words, I place these texts within a framework of a 'queer South Asian diaspora', one which allows us to conceive of both the text and the viewer in motion; scenes and moments in popular culture which in their 'originary' locations simply reiterate conventional nationalist and gender ideologies may, in a South Asian diasporic context, become the very foundation of queer culture. Furthermore, queer diasporic readings within such a framework, as I hope to demonstrate, allow us to read non-heteronormative arrangements within rigidly heterosexual structures as well as the ways in which queer articulations of desire and pleasure both draw from and infiltrate popular culture. While queer reading practices alone cannot prevent the violences of heteronormativity, they do intervene in formulations of 'home' and diaspora that – in their elision and disavowal of the particularities of queer subjectivities – inevitably reproduce the heteronormative family as central to national identity.

Pigs Can't Fly

This framework of 'a queer South Asian diaspora' produces linkages between the various representations of queer desire and cultural practices among South Asians in migrancy. Such a framework enables us to consider formations of queer desire and pleasure in radically particular sites, as well as in the context of movement and migration. Reading these texts as both constituting and constituted by a queer South Asian diaspora also resituates the conventions by which homosexuality has traditionally been encoded in an Anglo-American context. Queer sexualities as articulated by the texts I consider here reference familiar tropes and signifiers of Anglo-American homosexuality – such as the coming-out narrative and its attendant markers secrecy and disclosure, as well as gender inversion and cross-dressing – while investing them with radically different and distinct significations. It is through a particular deployment of South Asian popular culture that this defamiliarization of conventional markers of homosexuality takes place, and that alternative strategies through which to signify non-heteronormative desire are subsequently produced. These alternative strategies suggest a mode of reading and 'seeing' same-sex eroticism that challenges modern epistemologies of visibility, revelation and sexual subjectivity. Indeed, the notion of a queer South Asian diaspora can be seen as a conceptual apparatus that poses a critique of modernity and its various narratives of progress and development.[12] A queer South

Asian diasporic geography of desire and pleasure stages this critique on multiple levels: it rewrites colonial constructions of Asian sexualities as anterior, pre-modern and in need of Western political development – constructions that are recirculated by contemporary gay and lesbian transnational politics[13] – while simultaneously interrogating different South Asian nationalist narratives that imagine and consolidate the nation in terms of organic heterosexuality.

'Pigs Can't Fly', the first story in Selvadurai's novel *Funny Boy*, lays out the complex system of prohibition, punishment and compulsion that governs and structures gender differentiation. The story tells of the childhood game 'Bride-Bride' that Arjie and his girl cousins play in the house of their grandparents, and which entails an elaborate performance of a marriage ceremony. For Arjie, dressing up as the bride – complete with shimmering white sari, flowers and jewellery – is a way of accessing a particular mode of hyperbolic femininity embodied both by his mother and by the popular Sri Lankan female film stars of the day. The pleasure Arjie takes in this activity causes intense embarrassment and consternation on the part of the adults, who decree that henceforth Arjie is to play with the boys. Arjie's eventual traumatic banishment from the world of the girls and his forced entry into proper gender identification is figured in terms of geography and spacialization, of leaving one carefully inscribed space of gender play and entering one of gender conformity: Arjie is compelled to leave the inner section of the compound inhabited by the girls and enter the outer area where the boys congregate. Similarly, Arjie is barred from watching his mother dress in her room, which throughout his childhood has been the site of his most intense spectatorial pleasure.[14]

The game itself, brilliantly titled 'Bride-Bride' (not Bride-Groom), offers a reconfiguration of the contractual obligations of heterosexuality and gender conformity. Arjie installs himself in the most coveted role – that of bride – and makes it abundantly clear that the part of groom occupies the lowest rung of the game's hierarchy. Indeed, the game is predicated on the apparent non-performativity of masculinity,[15] as opposed to the hyperbolic feminine performance of Arjie as bride. The game's title then references both the unimportance of the groom and the pleasure derived from Arjie's performance of hyper-femininity, as well as the potentiality of a female same-sex eroticism that dispenses with the groom altogether. Arjie thus sutures himself into the scene of marriage, radically displacing it from the scene of heterosexuality and calling into question the very logic and authority of heteronormativity. 'Pigs Can't Fly', then, encodes gender differentiation within multiple narratives, not all of which are necessarily pathologizing. While Arjie's father reads Arjie's cross-gender identification as unnatural and perverse, his mother is unable to come up with a viable explanation for the logic of gender conformity. When pushed to explain by Arjie why he can no longer watch her dress or play with the girls, she resorts to a childhood nursery rhyme, stating, 'Because the sky is so high and pigs can't fly, that's why' (Selvadurai 1994:19). Her answer attempts to grant to the fixity of gender roles the status of universally recognized natural law and to root it in 'common sense'; however, such an explanation fails to satisfy Arjie, and his mother seems equally unconvinced by it but unable to imagine an alternative 'order of things'. Thus gender conformity and non-conformity are narrativized through competing discourses in the story, where the rhetoric of nonconformity as perversion is undercut by Arjie's mother making apparent the non-sensical nature of gender codification, as well as by the antinormative performance of gender in 'Bride-Bride'.

Arjie's sexual encounters with a Sinhalese classmate, Shehan, and his realization that such homoerotic sex has pushed him outside the purview of 'family' as he has known it, can initially be read within the narrative tradition of the coming-out story. Such narratives can be characterized as journeys toward an essential wholeness, toward the discovery of a true gay identity through a teleological process of individuation that is granted representative status. Indeed, the novel's title, *Funny Boy*, can be read as a reference to Edmund White's 1982 narrative of gay coming of age in the 1950s, *A Boy's Own Story*.[16] However, unlike White's text, where sexuality is privileged as the singular site of radical difference and the narrator's sole claim to alterity, sexuality in *Funny Boy* is not one but many discourses – such as those of ethnic identity and forced migration – all of which speak to multiple displacements and exiles. For instance, gender inversion in 'Pigs Can't Fly' is not so much a primary marker of Arjie's latent homosexuality, a childhood signifier of adult homosexuality as charted along a linear narrative of sexual development that ends with a fully realized 'gay' subject. Rather, cross-gender identification in the story takes on numerous, complex valences given the novel's engagement with questions of loss and memory in the context of diasporic displacement.

It is from the vantage point of 'a new home ... in Canada' that the narrator remembers the intense pleasure derived from the ritual of becoming 'like the goddesses of the Sinhalese and Tamil cinema, larger than life' (Selvadurai 1994: 5), and of watching his mother dress. Thus the narrator's evocation of these remembered instances of cross-gender identificatory practices and pleasures becomes a means by which to negotiate the loss of 'home' as a fantasized site of geographic rootedness, belonging and gender and erotic play. Indeed if 'home,' as Dorinne Kondo states, is for 'peoples in diaspora' that which 'we cannot not want',[17] home for a queer diasporic subject becomes not only that which 'we cannot not want' but also that which we cannot and could never have. Home in the queer fantasy of the past is the space of violent (familial and national) disowning. Cross-gender identification – through the game of Bride-Bride and in his mother's dressing room – allows Arjie to momentarily lay claim to domestic space and its gendered arrangements. The remembrance of such moments, then, mediates the multiple alienations of the queer diasporic subject from 'home' as familial, domestic and national space. Sri Lankan popular culture – the images of 'the Malini Fonsekas and the Geeta Kumarasinghes' – acts as the vehicle through which 'home' is conjured into being, mourned and reimagined.

Cross-Gender Identification and Queer Diasporic Memory

The various meanings that the novel ascribes to Arjie's cross-dressing echoes anthropologist Martin Manalansan's depiction of the uses of drag within contemporary gay Filipino communities in New York City. Manalansan finds that for diasporic Filipino gay men, drag is inextricably intertwined with nostalgia, in that it evokes 'the image and memory of the Filipino homeland while at the same time acknowledging being settled in a 'new home' here in the U.S.' (Manalansan 1997). Similarly, the narrator's memory of cross-dressing in *Funny Boy* negotiates multiple cultural and geographic sites, while suggesting the uses of nostalgia for queer diasporic subjects. Indeed, Arjie's performance of what we can term 'queer femininity' radically reconfigures hegemonic nationalist and diasporic logic which depends on the figure of the 'woman' as a stable signifier of 'tradition'. Within a queer diasporic imaginary, the 'lost homeland' is represented not by the pure and self-sacrificing wife and mother, but rather by a queer boy in a sari.

The project of reterritorializing national space, and the uses of drag in such a project, are explicitly articulated within South Asian queer activism and popular culture in various diasporic sites. At the 1995 India Day Parade, for instance, where SALGA was literally positioned at the sidelines of the official spectacle of national reconstitution, one cross-dressed SALGA member held up a banner that read, 'Long Live Queer India'. The banner, alongside the SALGA member's gender presentation, interpellates not a utopic future space of national belonging but rather an already existing queer diasporic space of insurgent sexualities and gender identities. In another example of queer diasporic popular cultural reconfigurations of the nation, a SALGA flyer for a party celebrating the publication of

Selvadurai's novel depicts a sari-clad figure exclaiming, 'Shyam was right! I look better in Mummy ki sari!' On the one hand, the flyer makes apparent the ways in which popular cultural practices (parties and drag performances) and literary texts like *Funny Boy* inform and produce each other, and as such call into existence a 'queer South Asian diaspora'. The flyer also replaces the woman-in-sari that typically stands in for 'India' with a gay male/transgendered performance of queer femininity that references and remembers non-heteronormative childhoods in other national sites.[18]

The novel's final section makes all the more evident the ways in which 'home' is reconfigured in queer diasporic memory. Here Arjie has sex with Shehan for the last time before leaving with his family for Canada after the 1983 riots. The smell of Shehan's body lingering on his clothes becomes 'a final memento', not only of a remembered scene of homo-erotic desire but of Sri Lanka, of 'home' itself. The text thus 'queers' the space of Sri Lanka as 'home' by disrupting the logic of nationalism that consolidates 'the nation' through normative hierarchical sexual and gender arrangements; these arrangements coalesce around the privatized, bourgeois domestic space of 'home' as a site of sanitized heterosexuality. The mapping of homoeroticism onto the national space of 'Sri Lanka' also reverses the standard notion of a 'gay' subject having to leave a 'third-world' site of gender and sexual oppression in order to 'come out' into the more liberated West. As such, it disorganizes the conventional coming-out narrative that 'begins with an unliberated, "prepolitical" homosexual practice and that culminates in a liberated, "out," politicised, "modern" "gay" subjectivity' (Manalansan 1997: 3).

This moment in the narrative encapsulates the text's deployment of what I would call a generative or enabling nostalgia and homesickness, where the 'home' that is evoked signifies multiply: as both national space and domestic space, it is the site of homoerotic desire and cross-gender identification and pleasure, of intense gender conformity and horrific violence, as well as of multiple leave-takings and exiles. The text thus also complicates the axes of a conventional exilic novel with fixed points of origin and departure. Instead the stories detail the layered crises and multiple losses, the leave-takings and exiles that occur within the site of 'home' itself.

Female Homosociality, Queer Femininity

Arjie's game of Bride-Bride references not only a particular mode of hyperbolic femininity and cross-gender identificatory pleasure, but also suggests the possibility of a female homoeroticism located within the home and that works through the absence and irrelevance of the groom. Since the moments of cross-dressing that I have thus far discussed tend to privilege a gay male diasporic subject, I want to detach Arjie's perform-ance of queer femininity from a narrative of queer boyhood and instead use it to locate a queer female subject within multiple 'home' spaces. For a staging of the game of Bride-Bride within a female homosocial context, then, we can turn to the recent independent film *Fire*, by Indian-Canadian filmmaker Deepa Mehta. *Fire* depicts the relationship between literally two brides, that is, two sisters-in-law in the North Indian urban home of a middle-class extended family. Mehta quickly establishes the familiar familial violences and compulsions that underlie this space of home: both women (ironically named Radha and Sita)[19] do most of the labour for the family business while their husbands alternately abuse or ignore them, which eventually precipitates their turning to each other for sex and emotional sustenance.

The film renders explicit the female homoerotic desire hinted at in Arjie's game of Bride-Bride by producing a complicated relay between female homosociality and female homoerotic practices. In one scene, for instance, Sita massages Radha's feet at a family picnic, transforming a daily female homosocial activity into an intensely homoerotic one while the other members of the family unwittingly look on. The slide from female homosociality into female homoeroticism in this scene, as well as in another where Radha rubs oil into Sita's hair, serves to locate female same-sex desire and pleasure firmly within the confines of the home and 'the domestic', rather than as that which safely occurs 'elsewhere'.[20] This emergence of female homoeroticism at the interstices of heterosexuality interrupts, as Geeta Patel phrases it, the 'apparently necessary slide from marriage into heterosexuality,' and denaturalizes the linkages between heterosexuality and the domestic (1997: 7). This articulation of female same-sex desire within the space of the domestic directly confronts and disrupts contemporary nationalist constructions of the bourgeois Hindu home as the reservoir of essential national cultural values, embodied in the figure of the Hindu woman as chaste, demure and self-sacrificing.[21]

The erotic interplay between Radha and Sita furthermore speaks to a specific modality of South Asian femininity through which – in a middle-class context – lesbian desire is articulated within sites of extreme hetero-normativity. The trope of dressing and undressing that threads through *Funny Boy* marks *Fire* as well: in the absence of their husbands, the two women indulge in not only dressing each other but dressing for each other, donning heavy silk saris, make-up and gold jewellery in a performance of the hyperbolic femininity that Selvadurai's narrator also references. Their eroticization of a particular aesthetic of Indian femininity brings to mind the problematic sketched out by Kaushalya Bannerji in the South Asian lesbian and gay anthology, *Lotus of Another Color* (1993: 59–64). Bannerji remarks upon her alienation from a white lesbian aesthetic of androgyny, given her 'fondness for bright colors, long hair, jewelry' – bodily signs that have multiple meanings for her as an Indian-Canadian woman but read simply as markers of a transparent 'femme' identity within a white lesbian context. Bannerji's presentation of a South Asian femininity elicits fetishistic responses from white lesbians, whereas for her, this particular aesthetic is a means of negotiating and reconciling categories of both ethnic and sexual identity. Similarly, the two protagonists in *Fire* derive pleasure from a particular, middle-class version of South Asian (and specifically North Indian) femininity that sometimes slips into an equally class-marked articulation of female homoerotic desire.[22]

Clearly, then, the 'mythic mannish lesbian' (to use Esther Newton's (1989) term) that haunts Euro-American discourses of twentieth-century lesbian sexuality is not the dominant modality through which female same-sex desire can be read here; rather, within the context of the middle-class home in the film, it is Radha and Sita's performance of queer femininity that emerges as the dominant mode or aesthetic through which female same-sex desire is rendered intelligible. As such, the film suggests an alternative trajectory of representing female homoeroticism in a South Asian context – one that is at odds with conventional Euro-American 'lesbian' histories that chart a developmental narrative from a nineteenth-century model of asexual 'romantic friendship' between bourgeois women in privatized, domestic, gender-segregated spaces to a contemporary modern, autonomous, 'lesbian' identity, sexuality and community.[23] The film's depiction of the ways in which this privatized, seemingly sanitized 'domestic' space[24] can simultaneously function as a site of intense female homerotic pleasure and practices calls into question a narrative of 'lesbian' sexuality as needing to emerge from a private, domestic sphere into a public, visible, 'lesbian' subjectivity. *Fire*, then, like *Funny Boy*, refuses to subscribe to the notion that the proper manifestation of same-sex eroticism is within a 'politics of visibility' in the public sphere. Rather, it suggests that what constitutes 'lesbian' desire in a South Asian context may both look and function differently than it does within Euro-American social and historical formations, and draw from alternative modes of masculinity and femininity. In other words, the film makes explicit the ways in which not all female same-sex desire culminates in an autonomous 'lesbianism', and not all 'lesbianism' is at odds with domestic marital arrangements.

The film in a sense references this problematic of visuality and identity in its opening scene, which recurs throughout the film. The scene is that of Radha's dreamscape: a wide open field of yellow flowers, where Radha's mother exhorts a young Radha to 'see the ocean' lying at the limits of the landlocked field. This exhortation to 'see' differently, to 'see' without literally seeing, speaks to the need for a particular strategy of reading sexuality outside dominant configurations of visibility, desire and identity. I am not asserting here that the film depicts an authentic, autonomous or indigenous form of lesbian desire; rather, it suggests an alternative mode of reading and 'seeing' non-normative erotic and gender configurations as they erupt within sites of extreme heteronormativity. The film thus enacts the critique articulated by Manalansan of transnational gay and lesbian globalizing discourse, which in its privileging of Western definitions of same-sex sexual practices 'risks duplicating an imperial gaze in relation to nonwestern nonmetropolitan sexual practices and collectivities' (1997: 6).

Insofar as the two women come together due to the failures of their respective marriages, however, *Fire* recentres heterosexuality by relying on a conventional framing of 'lesbian' desire as the result of failed heteronormative arrangements. Yet one particular scene in the film hints at an alternative organization of female same-sex desire, and perhaps exceeds the film's narrative framing of 'lesbian' desire as simply an auxiliary to heterosexuality. In it, Sita (dressed in a suit with her hair slicked back) and Radha (as a Hindi film heroine) engage in a playful lip-synching duet that both inhabits and ironizes the genre of popular Hindi film songs. Whereas Radha's fantasy space is that of the field that gives way to the ocean, this evocation of popular Hindi film becomes Sita's fantasized site of erotic and gender play. This scene of cross-gender identification stands apart from an earlier scene of playful cross-dressing, where Sita discards her sari and dons her husband's jeans and smokes his cigarettes as a way of temporarily laying claim to male authority, freedom and privilege. In the later scene, cross-dressing is not a means by which to claim male privilege but rather functions as an articulation of same-sex desire; echoing *Funny Boy*, the film suggests that if one mode by which to make lust between women intelligible is through the representation of hyperbolic femininity, another is through the appropriation of popular culture and its particular gender dynamics.

Family Values, Female Homoeroticism

We can read this scene in *Fire* as referencing a strikingly similar female cross-dressing scene in the immensely popular 1993 mainstream Hindi film *Hum Aapke Hain Koun*. This sequence takes place during a women-only celebration of an upcoming marriage, around which the film's entire plot revolves. Into this space of female homosociality enters a woman cross-dressed as the film's male hero, in an identical white suit, who proceeds to dance suggestively with the heroine (played by Madhuri Dixit) and with various other women in the room. What follows is an elaborate dance sequence where the cross-dressed woman and Dixit engage in a teasing, sexualized exchange that parodies the trappings of conventional middle-class Hindu family arrangements (that is, marriage, heterosexuality, domesticity and motherhood). Halfway through the song, however, order is apparently restored as the cross-dressed interloper is chased out of the room by the 'real' hero (Salman Khan). The cross-dressed woman disappears from both the scene and indeed the entire film, and Salman Khan proceeds to claim his rightful place opposite Dixit. What meanings, then, can we ascribe to these instances in both *Fire* and *Hum Aapke* of an explicitly gendered erotics between women? Clearly, neither scene is purely transgressive of conventional gender and sexual hier-archies: in *Fire*, the gendered erotic interplay of the two women can be seen as simply an articulation of their desire for each in the absence of 'real' men, while in *Hum Aapke* the cross-dressed woman seems merely to hold the place of the 'real' hero until he can make his entrance, and indeed to hold in place the hierarchical gendered relations in the scene.[25] Indeed, the film can afford such a transparent rendering of female-female desire precisely because it remains so thoroughly convinced of the hegem-onic power of its own heterosexuality.

However the fact that gender reversal in *Hum Aapke* occurs with a space of female homosociality renders the implied homoeroticism of the scene explicit to both the characters and the film's audience, and as such makes it eminently available for a queer diasporic viewership. For a 'queer South Asian viewing subject', the scene foregrounds the ways in which South Asian popular culture acts as a repository of queer desiring rela-tions; it also marks the simultaneous illegibility of those relations to a heterosexual viewing public and their legibility in a queer South Asian diasporic context.[26]

It is critical to note that upon *Hum Aapke*'s release, the popular press attributed its tremendous and sustained popularity to its return to 'family values', a phrase which apparently referred to the film's rejection of the sex and violence formulas of other popular Hindi movies. However, this phrase speaks more to the ways in which the film works within Hindu nationalist discourses of the nation by articulating a desire for a nostalgic 'return' to an impossible ideal, that of supposedly 'traditional' Hindu family and kinship arrangements that are staunchly middle-class and heterosexual. The incursion of female homerotic desire into this ultra-conventional Hindu marriage plot – both suggested and contained by the scene between Dixit and her cross-dressed partner – threatens the presumed seamlessness of both familial and nationalist narratives by calling into question the functionality and imperviousness of heterosexual bonds.

Pigs with Wings

The nostalgia evoked by *Hum Aapke* is quite unlike the longing in *Funny Boy* for a space of 'home' that is permanently and already ruptured, rent by colliding and colluding discourses around class, sexuality and ethnic identity. *Funny Boy* lays claim to both the space of 'home' and the nation by making both the site of non-heteronormative desire and pleasure in a nostalgic diasporic imaginary. Such a move disrupts nationalist logic by forestalling any notion of queer or non-heteronormative desire as insufficiently authentic. *Funny Boy* thus refuses to subsume sexuality within a larger narrative of ethnic, class or national identity, or to subsume these other conflicting trajectories within an overarching narrative of 'gay' sexuality. Within *Funny Boy* as well as in *Fire* and *Hum Aapke*, sexuality functions not as an autonomous narrative, but instead as enmeshed and immersed within multiple discourses. Clearly none of these texts allows for a purely redemptive recuperation of same-sex desire, conscribed and implicated as it is within class, religious and gender hierarchies. Indeed, it is precisely in the friction between these various competing discourses that queer pleasure and desire emerge. In both *Fire* and *Hum Aapke*, for instance, female homoerotic pleasure is generated and produced by the very prohibitions around class, religion and gender that govern and discipline the behaviour of middle-class women.

Throughout this chapter, I have attempted to gesture toward the ways in which nation and diaspora are refigured within a queer diasporic imaginary. Nostalgia as deployed by queer diasporic subjects is a means by which to imagine oneself within those spaces from which one is perpetually excluded or denied existence. If the nation is 'the modern Janus', a figure which at once gazes at a primordial, ideal past while facing a modern future (McClintock 1995: 358), a queer diaspora instead recognizes the past as a site of intense violence as well as pleasure; it acknowledges the spaces of impossibility within the nation and their translation within the diaspora into new logics of affiliation. The logic of 'pigs can't fly' becomes transformed, in the diaspora, into the alternative queer diasporic logic that allows for two brides in bed together, a marriage without a groom, pigs with wings. In other words, a queer diasporic logic displaces heteronormativity from the realm of natural law and instead launches its critique of hegemonic constructions of both nation and diaspora from the vantage point of an 'impossible' subject.

Notes

1. I use the term 'South Asian' throughout this article to reference a particular diasporic political formation that locates itself outside the national boundaries of any one national site (such as Bangladesh, Bhutan, India, Nepal, Pakistan or Sri Lanka). However I am also aware of the regional hierarchies that may be resurrected within the term. For a cogent explication of the oppositional uses and limits of the term 'South Asian' among activists in the United States, see Anannya Bhattacharjee 1997: 309.
2. A few examples of such work include Partha Chatterjee 1993, Anne McClintock 1995, Floya Anthias and Nira Yuval 1989, and Deniz Kandiyoti 1994.
3. See for instance Tom Nairn 1981, Homi K. Bhabha 1991, Benedict Anderson 1991 and Kandiyoti 1994.
4. I use the term 'queer' throughout this article to suggest a range of non-heteronormative sexual practices and desires that may not necessarily coalesce around categories of identity.
5. For an exemplary study of heterosexuality and colonialism, see Mrinalini Sinha 1995.
6. For one recent instance of this particular blindspot in feminist critiques of nationalism, see *Embodied Violence* (Jayawardena and Malathi de Alwis 1996).
7. In India, for instance, Section 377 of the Indian Penal Code bans same-sex sexual relations as 'unnatural offences'. The law was initially instituted under British colonial rule in the 1830s, which makes explicit the complicity of colonial and anti-colonial nationalist framings of sexuality.

8. See M. Jacqui Alexander's important essay, 'Erotic Autonomy as a Politics of Decolonization: An Anatomy of State Practice in the Bahamas Tourist Economy' (1997).

9. For work that begins to trace the contours of queer South Asian subjectivity, see for instance Patel forthcoming, Gopinath 1997 and Ratti 1993.

10. For further discussion of how diasporic articulations of community and identity both replicate and challenge the masculinist logic of conventional nationalisms, see Gopinath 1995.

11. The official grounds for denying Sakhi and SALGA the right to march was ostensibly the fact that both groups called themselves not 'Indian' but 'South Asian'; the possibility of Pakistanis, Bangladeshis or Sri Lankans marching in an 'Indian' parade was apparently too much of an affront to FIA members.

12. The imbrication of narratives of 'progress', 'modernity' and 'visibility' is made obvious in what Alexander terms 'prevalent metropolitan impulses that explain the absence of visible lesbian and gay movements [in non-Western locations] as a defect in political consciousness and maturity, using evidence of publicly organized lesbian and gay movements in the U.S. . . . as evidence of their orginary status (in the West) and superior political maturity' (Alexander 1997: 69).

13. See Martin Manalansan 1997 for an important interrogation of contemporary gay transnational politics.

14. In its depiction of the 'inner' as a female site, but also a site of gender play and reversal, the story refigures in interesting ways anti-colonial nationalist framings of space that posit the 'inner' as a space of essential spirituality and tradition, embodied by 'woman', as opposed to the 'outer' male sphere of progress, materiality and modernity. For an analysis of the creation of 'inner' and 'outer' spheres in anti-colonial nationalist discourse, see Chatterjee 1989.

15. See Judith Halberstam, *Drag Kings: Queer Masculinity in Focus* (1998) for a discussion of masculine non-performativity in the context of female 'drag king' performances.

16. See Edmund White's (1982) novel.

17. Dorinne Kondo suggests this formulation of 'home' in her essay on Asian American negotiations of community and identity (1996: 97).

18. However, the flyer's use of Hindi (rather than Tamil or Sinhala) even when referencing a Sri Lankan text points to the ways in which (North) Indian hegemony within South Asia may be replicated within queer South Asian spaces in the diaspora. 19 In Hindu mythology,

Sita proves her chastity to her husband Ram by immersing herself in fire, and as such embodies the ideals of womanly virtue and self-sacrifice. Radha, similarly, is the devoted consort of the god Krishna, who is famous for his womanizing. The irony in the film's naming of the two female protagonists lies in their refusal to inhabit these overdetermined roles of woman as devoted, chaste and self-denying.

20. I have further explored this particular relation between female homo-eroticism and female homosociality in a South Asian context in a discussion of Ismat Chughtai's short story 'The Quilt'. See Gopinath 1997.

21. See Chatterjee 1989 for an analysis of the ways in which anti-colonial nationalism used the figure of the woman as a bearer of inviolate tradition in order to imagine the independent nation.

22. Outside the confines of the middle-class North Indian home depicted in *Fire*, female homoerotic desire may manifest itself in forms other than that of hyperbolic or queer femininity. As Geeta Patel has noted in her discussion of the controversy around the 1987 'marriage' of two policewomen in central India, the police barracks in which the two women lived constituted a site of complicated and explicitly gendered erotic relations between women. See Patel, 14–22.

23. See Newton 1989 for a critique of nineteenth-century 'romantic friendships' as proto-lesbian/feminist relationships.

24. Clearly, a Euro-American bourgeois space of 'home' is not akin to the domestic space represented in *Fire*, given that the latter is marked by a history of British colonialism, anti-colonial nationalism and con-temporary Indian (and Hindu) nationalist politics.

25. *Hum Aapke*'s brief interlude of gender reversal and implied female homoeroticism seems to locate the film within Chris Straayar's definition of the 'temporary transvestite film', those which 'offer spectators a momentary, vicarious trespassing of society's accepted boundaries for gender and sexual behavior. Yet one can relax con-fidently in the orderly [heterosexual] demarcations reconstituted by the films' endings' (Straayar 1996: 44).

26. These scenes of cross-dressing and gender reversal can also be read as gesturing toward the gendered arrangements of female same-sex desire that Patel details, and that shadow the middle-class domestic locations of both *Fire* and *Hum Aapke*.

References

Alexander, M.J. (1997), 'Erotic Autonomy as a Politics of Decolonization: An Anatomy of State Practice, in the Bahamas Tourist Economy,' in M.J. Alexander and C.T. Mohanty (eds), *Feminist Genealogies, Colonial Legacies, Democratic Futures*, New York: Routledge.

Anderson, B. (1991), *Imagined Communities*, London: Verso.

Anthias, F. and Yuval Davis, N. (eds) (1989), *Women-Nation-State*, London: Women's Press.

Bannerji, K. (1993), 'No Apologies', in R. Ratti (ed.), *A Lotus of Another Color: An Unfolding of the South Asian Gay and Lesbian Experience*, Boston: Alyson.

Bhabha, H. (ed.) (1991), *Nation and Narration*, New York: Routledge.

Bhattacharjee, A. (1992), 'The Habit of Ex-Nomination: Nation Woman, and the Indian Immigrant Bourgeoisie,' *Public Culture*, 5(1): 19–46.

—— (1997), 'The Public/Private Mirage: Mapping Homes and Undom-esticating Violence Work in the South Asian Immigrant Community', in M. Jacqui Alexander and Chandra T. Mohanty (eds), *Feminist Genealogies, Colonial Legacies, Democratic Futures*, New York: Routledge.

Chatterjee, P. (1989), 'The Nationalist Resolution to the Woman's Question', in K. Sangari and S.Vaid (eds), *Recasting Women: Essays in Colonial History*, New Delhi: Kali for Women.

—— (1993), *The Nation and its Fragments*, Princeton: Princeton University Press.

Gopinath, G. (1995), '"Bombay, U.K., Yuba City": Bhangra Music and the Engendering of Diaspora', *Diaspora*, 4(3): 303–22.

—— (1997), 'Homo-Economics: Queer Sexualities in a Transnational Frame', in Rosemary M. George (ed.), *Burning Down the House: Recycling Domesticity*, New York: Westview/Harper Collins.

Grewal, I. (1996), *Home and Harem: Nation, Gender, Empire and the Cultures of Travel*, Durham, NC and London: Duke University Press.

Halberstam, J. (1998), *Drag Kings: Queer Masculinity in Focus*, New York: Serpent's Tail.

Jayawardena, K. and de Alwis, M. (eds) (1996), *Embodied Violence: Communalising Women's Sexuality in South Asia*, New Delhi: Kali for Women.

Kandiyoti, D. (1994), 'Identity and its Discontents: Women and the Nation', in P. Williams and L. Chrisman (eds), *Colonial Discourse and Post-Colonial Theory*, New York: Columbia University Press.

Kondo, D. (1996), 'The Narrative Production of "Home", Community and Political Identity in Asian American Theater', in S. Lavie and T. Swedenburg (eds), *Displacement, Diaspora and Geographies of Identity*, Durham, NC: Duke University Press.

McClintock, A. (1995), *Imperial Leather: Race, Gender and Sexuality in the Colonial Context*, New York: Routledge.

Manalansan, M. (1997), 'Under the Shadows of Stonewall: Gay Transnational Politics and the Diasporic Dilemma', in Lisa Lowe and David Lloyd (eds), *Worlds Aligned: Politics of Culture in the Shadow of Capital*, Durham, NC: Duke University Press.

—— (1997), 'Diasporic Deviants/Divas: How Filipino Gay Transmigrants "Play With the World"', in C. Patton and B. Sanchez-Eppler (eds), *Homosexuality in Motion: Gay Diasporas and Queer Peregrinations*, Durham, NC: Duke University Press.

Nairn, T. (1981), *The Break-up of Britain: Crisis and Neo-Nationalism*, London: Verso.

Newton, E. (1989), 'The Mythic Mannish Lesbian: Radclyffe Hall and the New Woman', in Martin Duberman et al. (eds), *Hidden from History: Reclaiming the Gay and Lesbian Past*, New York: Meridian.

Patel, G. (1997), 'Housewives Run Amok: Lesbians in Marital Fixes', *Unpublished manuscript*.

Ratti, R. (ed.) (1993), *A Lotus of Another Color: An Unfolding of the South Asian Gay and Lesbian Experience*, Boston: Alyson.

Selvadurai, S. (1994), Funny Boy, Toronto: McClelland and Stewart.

Sinha, M. (1995), *Colonial Masculinity: The 'Manly Englishman' and the 'Effeminate Bengali' in the Late Nineteenth Century*, Manchester: Manchester University Press.

Straayar, C. (1996), *Deviant Eyes, Deviant Bodies: Sexual Reorientations in Film and Video*, New York: Columbia University Press.

White, E. (1982), *A Boy's Own Story*, New York: Dutton.

–7–

Global Modernities and the Gendered Epic of the 'Irish Empire'

Breda Gray

A television series on the Irish world-wide entitled *The Irish Empire* was produced in 1999 for RTE (Ireland), the BBC (Britain) and SBS (Australia).[1] The website for the series locates it in relation to the controversial use of the trope of 'Empire' as follows:

> Ireland is *a tiny country* that has never sought world domination, yet *has established Irishness and Irish power bases and communities* from Chicago to Vladivostok, from Australia to Argentina. This is no physical empire, but an empire of the imagination, a virtual empire, whose followers outnumber the native population by over fifteen to one. From a home population today of just 5 million, some 70 million people around the world call themselves Irish, or claim Irish descent (emphasis added).

This empire of the imagination relies on assumptions of a relatively benign past in which the Irish did not, like the British and other empires, seek domination, but as a result of high levels of emigration made their presence felt in some parts of the world. Emigration occupies a contradictory position in Irish cultural memory as something to be forgotten and remembered depending on socio-political context. However, like many other emigrant nations in the 1990s (e.g. India, Mexico, El Salvador and Haiti), the Republic of Ireland was reclaiming its diaspora as a means of refiguring the national as global.

The increasing significance of the mass media in the reproduction of memory (Appadurai 1996) has been accompanied by a proliferation of documentaries as forms of 'infotainment' which bring histories and memories together to form new *lieux de mémoire* (Nora 1994).[2] The business of the documentary is to record memories, but also to take on the responsibility of remembering. The *Irish Empire* series combines historical accounts with personal memories in ways that challenge the structure of memory and relations between past, present and future. This chapter examines the work done by memory and history in this series on Ireland and Irish culture as global.

The web introduction to the series identifies it as a timely intervention in the analysis of Irish identity.

> Never before has interest in Ireland and things Irish been so widespread. Aside from the arrival of the 'Celtic Tiger' economy, *the Irish have acquired a new world status* from business entrepreneurs, internationally known politicians, to oceans of writers; the musical Riverdance has established the story of the Famine and migration well beyond the shores of academia; and the export of the Irish pub from Paris to Singapore is a marketing triumph in itself. (emphasis added)

Music, dance, stories of Famine and migration, but also practices of business and marketing are just some of the technologies of memory that produce the 'new world status' of 'the Irish'. Ireland and Irish culture are cast within 'new geographies of imperialism' (Jacobs 1996: 163) that are structured by neo-liberal and free-market practices as well as new paths of cultural flows and intermixing (Hardt and Negri 2000). As one reviewer noted, 'in its own way, this multinational cultural product tells us as much about Ireland in 1999 as it does about the history of Irish emigration . . . [by] telling a story of economic success, cultural fluidity and techno-logical empowerment' (Linehan 1999: 6). Another reviewer pointed to the provocative use of the term 'Empire', which he saw as bucking conven-tional nationalist notions of Ireland as 'victim of an empire' (Holt 1999: 5). The Empire in this series might be seen, then, as a trope for Ireland as a global nation and one that unsettles nationalist 'victim of empire' narratives. But that would be to reduce the complexity of the series to one uncomplicated agenda.

Given Ireland's history of resistance to British colonialism as well as the country's ambivalent and 'collaborative' relationships to the British Empire,[3] it is not obvious how the idea of 'Empire' might work in this series. The series offers an opportunity to consider new questions about the relationships between memory and constructions of an Irish global 'ethnoscape' via the trope of Empire. This chapter takes up this oppor-tunity by addressing the following questions relating to Empire and memory. How does the trope of Empire which takes us into complicated narratives of past and present, help to locate the 'tiny country' of Ireland at the beginning of the twenty-first century? In what ways does this trope stage encounters between colonialism, postcolonialism and global capital-ism? What work is done by history, memory and imagination in the constitution of an Irish diasporic Empire in this series? And, how do the multiple narratives of Irish women's migrancy presented in this series work to produce Irish specificity?

The *Irish Empire* series consists of five fifty-minute programmes which are structured by the following five themes: the dispersal of Irish migrants, the Irish 'at work' around the world, women in the diaspora, religious differences and, finally, the 'homeland' and return. It was first screened by RTE in Ireland in November/December 1999, by BBC2 in Spring 2001 and by the SBS network in Australia, also in Spring 2001. The ratings for the series in Ireland were very high and relatively high in Britain given the off-peak slot on BBC.[4] This chapter takes the first and third programmes of the series as its focus for discussion – the first because it frames the series, and the third because it is dedicated to women in the diaspora and, as I argue below, because it constitutes gender as defining Irish cultural difference. The chapter is divided into two interconnected parts based on each of these programmes and examines the workings of the trope of Empire through the focus in the series on diasporization as the site where memories circulate and reimaginings of the national takes place.

The Global Scattering

To discuss the first programme, I focus on three clips from the programme as illustrative bases for discussion. These clips help to frame the series and are suggestive of themes that permeate all of the programmes.

Programme One – 'The Scattering' – Clip 1. *The first programme opens with the series theme tune and images of a patterned sky at sunset before cutting to a 'talking head' 'masked interview'[5] sequence beginning with critic Fintan O'Toole: 'There are few parallels anywhere in the world for the extent of the exodus from Ireland which has not happened in the same way anywhere else . . . There is a kind of tragic aspect to Irish history and the history of people leaving in large numbers, but the question is for whom is it tragic, for the people themselves in many cases it led to an improvement in their lives . . .'. Alongside blurred images of a beach scene with a young man and woman moving towards each other and embracing, the female voice over informs the viewer that 'There are 70 million people of Irish descent scattered around the world. They have helped to shape the United States, Canada, Britain and Australia, but they are also citizens of an invisible realm, an Empire, not of kings and armies, but of memory and imagination'. The voice over continues (alongside a close up image of the couple separating from one another and then panning out to capture them moving in opposite directions along the beach) 'They form a rich mosaic of achievement and survival, of silent shame and flagrant sentimentality, often their extraordinary story has floated away over the horizon of romance'. This sequence ends with an image of a ship at sea. The camera cuts to a close up of historian Donald Akenson at his desk. He asserts that 'Emigration has always been looked at as the once and forever tragedy. It has been etched so deeply, so unthinkingly, that it's going to be part of Irish traditional memory long after emigration has ceased to exist, and is anything except taking a Concorde flight to New York to trade stocks'.*

The camera then cuts to close-up images of the underside of a Boeing 737 against the background sound of air traffic communications. These images pan out to a full Aer Lingus aeroplane, then to the Dublin airport building, the large sign DUBLIN above the building, then to a baggage trolley leaving a plane, to a number of Ryanair planes slowly moving around near the airport building. As the camera moves away, the earnest voice over intervenes again: 'In the globalised electronic market place of today, Irish emigrants no longer travel from a remote and backward place to gleaming cities beyond their wildest imaginings. But they have continued to travel the world, making connections, leaving traces, helping by their presence to make the world a smaller place'. Towards the end of the voice over, the camera cuts to the air traffic control tower in the sunset, and finally, to the satellite aerials turning against the sky at dusk.

'The Scattering' – Clip 2. The camera cuts from images of an Irish airport, to landscape images of sea and land in Newfoundland. The background music mellows and the viewer is informed of the advent of Irish migration to Newfoundland with the herring fishing trade in the late 1500s. Images of waves rolling on the beach and a pony standing on the grassy edge of the Atlantic are followed by views of the laneway between the home of an Irish-Newfoundland man and the sea. The voice over sets the scene: 'In Newfoundland, the look of the land and the sound of the people's accents are eerily like Ireland. The Irish influence is so strong that the place sometimes seems like a part of the old country that floated across the Atlantic'. The Newfoundland man's memory of his Irish ancestry is scanty and he reminds the viewer of this by his constant invitation to the inter-

viewer to confirm or otherwise the stories that have been passed down to him. He begins: 'In the late seventeen hundreds, old Bat McGrath, he came from Ireland, Tipperary, I think. Well I don't know exactly . . . The old fellows used to be talking. Every Sunday something would come up about the old times, the way it started . . .'. His accent is strong so subtitles accompany his contributions to the programme. He goes on 'Perhaps I'm saying the wrong thing, but you feel like you lean a bit towards them (Irish people) . . . which I think is good. ' The camera cuts to a picture of Jesus with photographs of children in the frame. He continues, 'for one thing, they're friendlier'. The camera cuts back to a portrait image, 'Now you take them from England, now they're not friendly. But the Irish people, if you meet an Irishman he's friendly . . . The old fellows would tell you what they knew about it. They'd talk about the time of the Famine, the Potato Famine they used to call it. That's the reason a lot of people left Ireland and went to the States . . . Potato Famine they used to call it. Whether it happened or not, I don't know, but I often heard them say it did. Did you ever hear of it?' Towards the end of this section of the programme, the camera lingers on his wrinkled hands holding a packet of Players cigarettes, then cuts to the cigarette lighter on the kitchen table and pans out to close with an image of this elderly man in profile, sitting at his kitchen table gazing out the window towards the coastal landscape beyond.

The first programme establishes that Irish emigration is unique in the world and has been remembered primarily as a tragedy. This tragedy is romantically imaged at the beginning of the programme by the embracing and separation of the couple on the beach. There is a mapping of heterosexual desire onto a patriotic desire for national families and through them, the reproduction of the nation (Sommer 1991). The embrace can be read as a nationalizing embrace, a metaphor for the return of all emigrants and, thereby, for the consolidation of a nation that can grow and reproduce itself. This romantic narrative of Irish migration as traumatic gives poignancy and significance to the Irish diaspora as a source of memory and cultural resources for re-imaginings of the national. The voice-over then turns the trauma of separation and loss through migration in Ireland into gains for the United States, Britain, Canada and Australia. Success and tragedy coexist in this Empire of 'memory and imagination'. However, Akenson's contribution, which ends this sequence, points to the tenacity of the motif of loss, noting that even as the nature of migration itself changes, the memory of Irish migration as tragic will endure pre-cisely because it has become a habit of Irish collective memory.

Yet, this habit of memory is out of step with a late twentieth-century Ireland that is visually represented in this programme as a location of airports and motorways. These 'non-places of modernity' or 'sites of pure mobility' (Urry 2000: 39/63) construct contemporary Irish belonging in 'scapes of movement' and 'conduits of travel' (Urry 2000: 74). Images of the state-sponsored Aer Lingus planes and the planes of the market-oriented company Ryanair incorporate past and present, the nation and global market, and signify diverse styles and practices of mobility. The 'obsession' with the past, long associated with Irish people, is effaced in images of spaces that facilitate speedier mobility so that those on the move do not have time to look back. This contemporary Ireland, 'no longer a remote and backward place', is contrasted with rural Newfoundland, which could be a bit of 'the old country' because the landscape 'looks familiar' and a stereotypically Irish accent and 'way of life' are preserved there.

Irish memory in this programme is extended across time and space in the body and cultural memories of a descendant of Irish migrants to Newfoundland. For this man, the self as memory is achieved by his location of himself within larger narratives of Ireland and its diaspora (Antze and Lambek). The stories he heard on Sundays about 'the old times' and 'the way it started' help him to make sense of his own belonging in Newfoundland. His 'leanings toward' the Irish are accounted for by stereotypical comparisons between Irish and English people and his questioning of the story of the Famine points to its mythical status in diaspora culture. His 'lived' memory is of an Irish-Newfoundland culture that is separated by six or more generations from the migrant generation. So his identification with Irishness is mediated by layers of memory, myth and imaginings.[6]

The 'untouched' landscape of Newfoundland is reminiscent of the spaces in the West and other parts of Ireland that 'were opened up by a combination of hunger, eviction and emigration' during and after the Great Famine (Brewster and Crossman 1999: 56). The traditional west-of-Ireland cottage, empty landscape and associated memories of emigration and loss are uncannily simulated in the space and memory of Newfound-land Irish migrant culture and place. In this sequence, memory is inscribed in the landscape, the material culture, the accent and gestures of this contributor as well as by the photographs of family and images that adorn his mantelpiece. These sites of 'Irish' memory in Newfoundland deterri-torialize Irish belonging while simultaneously anchoring it again in a place and in practices that are seen as preserving 'traditional' and recognizable aspects of Irish identity.[7] This man's embodied memory presents a recognizable past to those in Ireland whose global Irish belongings are mediated by a global and national media culture characterized by a standardized Hiberno-English, an infrastructure of mobility and the visual styles of the metropolitan centre.[8]

Two contradictory assumptions underpin constructions of migration. The first is that migrants embrace the modern world leaving those 'at home' behind and the second is that migrants are trapped in time warp holding on to the cultural practices associated with when they left and long superseded in the homeland. Both positions construct migration as movement between distinct spaces, which are temporally marked as more or less modern. Both assumptions circulate in this programme, but in ways that trouble the here/there, modern/traditional dichotomies and linear narratives of the national. The juxtaposition of 'traditional' Irish culture in the diaspora and global modernity in Ireland seems to reverse assumptions of migration as a modernizing activity and to reinforce the assumption that the 'old ways' are clung to in the diaspora as those 'at home' move on. But the memory work that Newfoundland does for Ireland and vice versa undoes the location of modernity in one place and tradition in the other. Constructions of Irish modernity in this series rely on globally scattered versions of Irish tradition. At the same time as the producers of the series seek out Irish memory in the diaspora through this contributor, he invites the interviewer to confirm whether or not the Famine happened. This sequence stages an exchange of memories and emphasizes the circulation of stories of Irishness which cannot be incorporated into a linear national or migration narrative. The viewer is made conscious that this man's memory is crucial to constructions of Irishness in Ireland, while Ireland has a mythical status in his mind. Irish identity is constructed as trans-temporal, trans-spatial and reliant on diverse narratives of cultural belonging. As the temporalities associated with nations become more indeterminate because nations are less spatially determined and increasingly marked by mobilities, cultural belongings are constituted in more diffuse ways. A synchronous diversity is produced in this programme through the repetition, multiplicity and multi-locatedness of memory. The coexistence of diverse and even irreconcilable versions of Irishness is achieved through diasporization and is central to constructions of Irish global modernity.

> Programme 1. Clip 3. *About halfway through this programme the voice over states that 'Ironically, the Irish spread their influence by riding on the backs of two aggressively imperial forces, America and Britain'. This is followed by a sequence in which Donald Akenson, speaking from his desk, backs up this interpretation of Irish migration. Alongside black and white footage of the Indian army standing to attention and then marching, he suggests that 'If you wanted to map the Irish Diaspora at any point . . . you would find that the Irish very cannily moved on to the opportunities that these two Empires provided. Now, when I've said that, I've opened* **a terrible potential wound** *(emphasis added), because the Irish nationalist mentality has pretty much said we always have been anti-imperialist. That's true, but . . . as England and as America were . . . taking over entire continents, were wiping out indigenous cultures, amongst the most willing foot soldiers were millions of Irish people. Once you're part of an imperialist machine, you are part of that whole imperialist world that reshaped the world in about a hundred-year period'.*

In this clip, the mapping of Irish migration onto the map of Empire[9] challenges postcolonial nationalist strategies that identify migration with tragedy. Irish migration as exile and tragedy was taken up by the new state in the south as a means of masking its inability to stem out-migration following independence (Miller 1990). However, by the 1990s, there were a collection of individuals in the media and 'official Ireland' who celebrated secular, liberal and post-national versions of the nation and diaspora above postcolonial nationalist narratives (see McCarthy 2000; Kearney 1997; and Smyth and Cairns 2000). Akenson's contribution to this programme, by introducing a narrative of agency, relative privilege and collaboration with Empire, challenges 'the wounded attachment' (Brown 1995) to nation produced by the nationalist narrative of emigration as postcolonial 'exile'. This mode of attachment, which produces the 'flagrant sentimentality' identified with the diaspora at the beginning of the first programme, is opened up for question. Yet, the 'wound' and sentimentality are central to the reproduction of certain forms of 'otherness' in the twentieth century and circulate as important resources within global consumer culture. The resistance, creativity and anti-imperialism associated with the sign 'Irish' lend these characteristics to products identified as Irish. The narrative of romantic tragedy has become a habit of memory that renders the sign 'Irish' familiar in the global marketplace. Irish cultural responses to colonialism which include the taking up of the position of the 'other' and sentimentalism become positive resources in a multicultural present in which spaces of consumerism seek out diversity and signs of otherness (Jacobs 1996). The colonial other of the past becomes the 'exotic' within the parameters of consumer culture (Forsdick 2001: 14). Such exoticism goes with the grain of globalization, corporate multiculturalism and changing configurations of self and other (ibid.: 19). But this is not the whole story. The trope of Empire operates in the series both to signal the shifting parameters of signs of Irishness within global consumer culture and also, through the interventions of Akenson, to highlight the other side of Ireland's relationship to British colonialism. Ireland's contested past is represented paradoxically through perceptions of migration as a national tragedy or 'wound' but also in relation to the spreading of Irish influence and community around the world by 'riding on the backs' of the British and US Empires. Neither story is lost in this programme, which poses memory and history in tension.

It is the doubleness of Ireland's subject and object status in relation to the British and US Empires which produces the tensions that help to keep memory alive. The dynamics of history are still contested in Ireland and in the diaspora breathing new life everyday into memory and narratives of what Irishness means. The multiplicity of voices represented in the programme constructs a cosmopolitan multicultural Irish diasporic identity. Histories and memories are posed together as different styles and narratives of the past that circulate in and structure the present. Questions of past and current power relations are signalled, but are ultimately elided in the liberal celebration of diversity and contestation that marks this first programme of the series. In the following section, I suggest that the emphasis on 'living memory' and 'personal memory' in the programme dedicated to women in the diaspora suggests a much more uneasy negotiation of national attachment and belonging in a diasporic, transnational and multi-cultural world. The programme on women and the diaspora foregrounds the impact of migration on 'the imaginative resources of lived, local experiences' (Appadurai 1996: 52).

'A World Apart'?

In the third programme, entitled 'A World Apart', the voice-over asserts that 'unlike other European migrations the Irish exodus has been predominantly female'.[10] This programme is structured around the diverse personal memories of nine Irish migrant women of different generations, class and geographical locations. Contrasting modes of Irish migrant femininity convey the complexity of socio-political, economic and cultural relations in the diaspora. The trope of Empire permeates the narratives not least through the contrasting traces and practices of the British and US Empires in their multi-located narratives. These narratives are testimony to the ambivalent positioning of Irish migrants by the racialized legacies of the British Empire. For example, in one narrative Mexican farm workers and in another a black Zimbabwean man provide mute backdrops against which Irish women who look 'white' are constructed as heroic through motifs of resistance, survival, hard work and 'civilizing' the frontier. Louise O'Connor is a fifth-generation Irish American whose ancestors were Irish colonists in Mexico and whose family now owns and runs a large ranch in Texas. Her grandmother recorded the family history from county Wexford to the frontier and now Louise is recording Texas ranching history. Following images of her interviewing a Mexican worker about his memories of the farm, she notes that her women ancestors 'brought culture and civilisation in here' and that 'as they were fighting the wilderness they were building civilisation'.

Liz McClelland is introduced by an image of her sitting with a black stone sculptor who is telling her the significance of his design. She left Ireland in the 1960s for southern Rhodesia, as it was then known, where she married and settled. Her narrative emphasizes her adjustment to 'the bush' and her protest against the treatment of the black majority via a letter to the newspaper. The voice-over asserts that 'her voice of objection was shunned by her white peers' and Liz notes that she received one response suggesting that she should 'go back to your Irish bog where you so obviously belong'. Liz McClelland's narrative points to her double positioning as privileged and subordinated. She looks 'white' but is recognized as 'Irish' and so is easily reidentified with the 'uncivilized' 'bog' from whence she came. The modes of femininity represented in all of these narratives are made to speak for wider Irish culture via motifs of survival, hard work, double positioning and family (Ware 1992).

Another key motif in this programme is that of cultural discontinuity which emerges most powerfully in the accounts of Irish women in England. For example, Fran Hegarty is introduced via her work as a performance artist walking in a bright pink Victorian bustled dress across a train platform in Britain. Her art, she tells the viewer, is influenced by her negotiation of Irish identity in Britain. She migrated as a child with her family from County Donegal to Glasgow. Her contribution to the programme ends with a tone of regret. Despite her attempts to impart Irish culture to her son, the negative stereotypes of Irish identity in Thatcher's

Britain mean that this could not be an aspirational identification for him, and she notes that this 'made him very different from me culturally'. The maintenance of cultural continuity is foregrounded in this programme via intergenerational practices of memory, including the writing of memoirs or family histories, visits to Ireland and Catholic educational practices. However, questions of cultural continuity are perhaps most urgently addressed in relation to cultural transmission within the diasporic family. Family as an achievement and an important site of the gendered Irish self in migration is most powerfully articulated by Mary Williams's story, which is the focus of the remainder of this section. I will argue that her narrative becomes an exemplary narrative of Irish migrancy in this programme but also points to the limitations of celebrations of the dia- spora as a sign of diversity and tenacious cultural transmission. To make Mary's narrative emblematic of Irish national migration, her origins in the contested space of Northern Ireland are elided in this programme.

Programme 3. Clip 1: *Mary Williams left Ireland initially for the US in the 1940s and begins her story against black and white images of New York in that period. In a sequence of images that cut back and forth between clips from 1940s US advertisements to portrait images of Mary as she tells her story, Mary accounts for her leav- ing: 'I was 17 when I emigrated, I went to America, the reason why I went there, or why I wanted to go, we hadn't many opportunities in Northern Ireland, no opportunity really. We were out on the farms and my brothers were there and whatever was to be given was to be given to them, we weren't to get anything. I had a wanderlust anyway. It was like a dream to go. I wanted to find out about the people that we heard so much about, the millionaires. That was a problem as to how to get into their homes and that's where I wanted to be, to see how they lived, what they looked like, what did they eat? What did they wear? Where did they go for entertainment? That's what I wanted to know, also they paid very very well. I got a job as chambermaid/waitress in one of those big houses on 5th Avenue. The thing is, I didn't know how to wait on a table, not the kind of table they had there. The cook taught me how to do it . . . there were rows of cutlery . . . and finger bowls and silver everywhere . . .*

Much of the feminist literature on Irish women's migration to the US focuses on the remaking of the feminine self as autonomous, independent and future oriented (Diner 1983; Nolan 1989; O'Carroll 1990). However, Mary's account of her first migration to the United States emphasizes the gendered conditions of her leaving, noting that the girls in the family 'weren't to get anything'. Her narrative locates her as an observer of wealthy American lifestyles rather than aspiring to inhabit this lifestyle for herself or her potential children. New York is a spectacle, a site of wonder, observation and adventure. Her account suggests less a journey in self-fulfilment or advancement than one motivated by a kind of anthropological curiosity. New York is a site of participant observation, not one of personal progress, freedom or the discovery of an authentic self. Migrating to New York is like a 'dream', not of liberation, but of a lifestyle so removed from her 'reality' that it cannot hold out promise of liberation or personal autonomy, enabling only a relationship of voyeurism to her surroundings.

Programme 3. Clip 2: *Mary's story continues in a later excerpt when she talks about her commitment to sending remittances to her family in Ireland. 'My mother was a widow and there were five others younger than me. So we needed the money and the reason that it was important was that we needed to stabilize the old farm at home so we could keep it running'.*

Programme 3. Clip 3: *Later in the programme, the voice over sets the scene for Mary Williams' return to live in Ireland noting that 'By tradition, these women were supposed to return with their faith and morals intact, their dowries saved to a faithful welcome home. But that welcome was often mixed with envy and suspicion'. Mary then describes her experience of return. 'When I did come back, I felt that I wasn't being treated quite the same. I had different clothes on, clothes that weren't being used at home. For instance, I had nylon see through blouses and they were all the rage in America, but they weren't the rage at home and I was treated very differently. I couldn't sort of be myself at all there. I remember my brother, when I was going to a dance, when I was wearing one of those things, and he suddenly decided he wasn't going and I said "why?" And he said, "I can't go with you dressed like that". And that was only part of it, there was a lot more really'.*

In clip two, Mary constructs her migration and the work she did in New York in terms of supporting her mother and siblings as well as keeping the farm in Ireland viable. She includes herself in the familial 'we' that needed to keep the farm running. Although remittances can help to 'maintain a stake in the home' (Olwig 1999: 459), until the middle of the twentieth century at least, they also helped to prop up the patriarchal system that contributed to Irish women leaving in the first place (Neville, 1995: 209).

If Mary's leaving was motivated by a lack of economic prospects in Ireland as a woman and a curiosity about the spectacle of wealth in New York, her return is marked by the pressure to conform to particular notions of Irish femininity. Grace Neville notes that returned women were criticized for 'no longer knowing their "proper"/subservient place having learnt different manners and risen "above their station" in the United States' (1995: 211). Resentments about migration and the potential it offered to women in particular were projected onto the bodies and sexual practices of these women (ibid.). Mary's original exclusion through migration as a response to restricted opportunities for women in Ireland is repeated when Mary's choice of clothes sexualize and suggest a relationship of enjoyment to her gendered body and mark her as an outsider. It is on her return, rather than on arrival in the United States, that Mary identifies an 'authentic' self that she cannot or is prevented from occupying in Ireland. Becoming an Irish woman emerges as a more explicit project, not via a developmental narrative of liberation in the United States, but through the negotiation of her Irish feminine and migrant self in her family in Ireland (Luibheid 1999). The next sequence reintroduces Mary as 'the returned Yank' drawing attention to the ways in which she is denationalised by exceeding the codes of Irish femininity on her return.

Programme 3. Clip 4: *Voice over – 'London 1953, Mary Williams "the returned Yank" now left Ireland for good. She and hundreds of young Irish women were recruited to be part of their [London Transport's] "virgin" team of clippies'. A sequence of black and white images of London buses and conductors in the 1950s and women in 1950s fashions, is followed by an image of Mary standing beside a red double-decker London bus in the London Transport Museum. As the camera zooms in for a close- up image of Mary, her narrative continues with memories of her work with other Irish women on the buses, meeting her Irish husband and their difficulties finding accommodation because they were Irish in 1950s London. This excerpt closes with her assertion that '. . . one of the most important things to me was to get a family and to give them the opportunities that I didn't have, or that I didn't think I had anyway'.*

Mary's second migration from Ireland is as part of a cohort of Irish women who meet the gendered labour-force needs of London Transport in the 1950s. The use of the term 'virgin' clippies acknowledges London Transport's initiative to employ young women bus conductors and sexualizes the women's initiation into this work. It is the smart uniform, the make-up, her comradery with other Irish women and the hard work that emerge as Mary's strongest memories of this job. Her memories of getting married and setting up home in London are structured by a narrative of discrimination with regard to housing, the need to 'stick together' with other Irish migrants and the loneliness of bringing up a family while her husband worked in construction alongside other Irish men. This part of the narrative ends with an assertion of her investment in family as a site of identification, a 'source of the self' and a project insofar as she might facilitate a better future for her children. It is through family that Mary finds a space for herself and that she legitimates her presence in England (McKenna, 2001). The final clip of Mary's story ends the programme.

> Programme 3. Clip 5. *A close up image of Mary sitting on the top deck of a London bus heralds the end of her story which is related in an emotional tone of voice. 'I think my children have lost quite a bit of their Irishness, they're more British than Irish and they're not fully understanding what it is that motivated us in the first instance. We're behind and they're now part of here. At times, it makes me feel pretty lonely and sometimes, (pause) I think it wasn't worth it, to lose my own family at home and then to lose a family here as well'.*

This clip resonates with the imaging of the national tragedy of migration by a couple embracing and then separating at the beginning of the first programme. National attachment is restaged in Mary's account through the private negotiation of familial loss which repeats the 'wounded attachment' of the postcolonial national narrative. The wound, a sign of injustice, provides a basis for justice claims, repeated in different sites, but in Mary's account, through the trope of the divided family. The wounded mother citizen reproduces a familiar national sentimentality, a familial story that is deemed to exemplify the subordination of the nation (Berlant 2000). In the final clip, the viewer is forced into sentimentalized empathy at Mary's loss and her liminality. Sentimentality is returned as a rhetorical means by which the pain (mapped onto collective national pain), rather than the gendered politics of migration, is advanced (ibid.). Mary's narrative reanimates identification with the wound of migration as national tragedy that Akenson signals in the first programme.

Mary's narrative of a familial self gestures toward idioms for narrating diasporic collective identity. Yet, her narrative stages a breakdown of familial and national chronotopic[11] conventions when narrating diaspora. The two locations of England and Ireland do not come into a unified narrative except insofar as Mary narrates herself as 'in between' and as a postcolonial subject in England. Her crisis, having lost two families, can be read as standing in for the contemporary crisis of the nation state, as multi-located/temporal Irish lives and cultural products can no longer be tied to any one 'place' of belonging. But it is also produced by the power dynamics of this particular geo-political site of diaspora. For all the fluidity and diversities of Irish culture celebrated in the first programme in the series, second-generation 'difference' in England cannot easily be incorporated within a narrative of diasporic Irishness. The narratives of Irish women in Rhodesia (Zimbabwe), South Africa and the United States articulate a multi-located and multi-temporal Irishness structured by relations between here *and* there, memories of leavings, journeys, arrivals and encounters. However, Mary's narrative and those of some of the other women can be read as the failure of the promise of cultural belonging in diaspora to deliver on continuity and bi-local attachment in England at least. Any identification with Britishness or Englishness suggests a potential Irish subject lost to British/English culture. The multiple implications of past and present Irish/British intercultural contact are not readily available as cultural resources for diasporic Irishness in the 1990s.

The chronotope of the heteronormative family suggests genealogy and continuity, but how is memory carried forward in a diaspora that is transnational and multicultural? How are the conditions of migration to be remembered in diaspora? By making Mary's narrative an emblematic one, this programme frames 'normative femininity and reproduction' as hard-wired into the 'work of expressive femaleness' so that 'gender praxis becomes established as a ground of [Irish national and diasporic] solidarity' (Berlant 2000: 44).[12] The emotionality of the sequence and the assumed intensity of this emotionality when kinship is invoked produces a reidentification with loss and tragedy as markers of the Irish diaspora. The failure of the patriotic desire to reproduce an Irish family in the diaspora becomes another form of national 'wound' or loss. Ironically, this narrative restages the motif of migration as national tragedy and through affect makes memory and endurance central practices and signs of Irishness in the diaspora. At the same time, genealogical lineage and kinship, identified as central to the Irish Empire in this series, produce the most profound gaps and discontinuities and, perhaps, the most unsettling moments of responsiveness for viewers of the series. Such moments, as well as re-enchanting the national, can be seen as opening up the conditions of possibility for a new 'politics of becoming' in diaspora and in relation to the global as the viewer struggles to make sense of these women's personal memories and the assumptions that structure them.

Conclusion

Emigration has been the object of contradictory wishes for forgetfulness and memory in Irish culture. Like many other emigrant nations at the beginning of the twenty-first century, Ireland is claiming its diaspora as a means of transnationalizing the meaning of nationhood and refiguring the national as global. The growing imbrication of the national and the global in ways that involve a renegotiation of the legacies of Empire alongside the production of new imperial practices of global consumer capitalism lie at the heart of the *Irish Empire* series. In the first programme of the series, the trope of Empire enables a holding-together of nationalist memory of the colonial 'wound', historical accounts of collaboration with Empire, the cultural flows that mark neo-liberal free-market practices, and narratives of Irishness in the diaspora. These related but discrepant sites of Irishness represent a synchronic diversity that invigorates the sign 'Irish' and suggests a new temporality and spatiality of global Irish modernity. In the third programme, the contradictory positioning of migrant Irish women in relation to Empire depending on their geo-political destination is identified via a range of modes of Irish migrant femininity. These femininities come to represent Irish cultural difference via motifs of survival, hard work, 'the Irish family' and ambiguous relationships to looking 'white'. Mary Williams's narrative reveals the patriotic desire for a consolidation of the diasporic nation by reproducing Irish families in the diaspora. The potential of the national/family romance to bolster the 'Irish Empire' of memory and imagination, not least through motifs of loss and separation, is identified, but so too is the instability of the family as a site of cultural transmission and reproduction of cultural belonging. Nonetheless, the family continues to symbolize patriotic desire and solidarity at the beginning of the twenty-first century. This is perhaps most obviously so in President Mary McAleese's use of the trope of the 'global Irish family'.

We owe a debt of gratitude too, to those who left this island . . . It was our emigrants who globalised the name of Ireland. They brought our culture with them, refreshed and enriched it with the new energy it absorbed from the varied cultures into which it was transplanted . . . They gave us that *huge multicultural Irish family* now proudly celebrated and acknowledged in the new Article Two of the Constitution.[13] (President's Address to the Joint Houses of the Oireachtas, 16 December 1999)

The globalizing of Ireland by emigrants puts the homeland in debt to the diaspora because, by transporting Irish culture and by their modes of adaptation and survival in new countries, Irish migrants and their descendants have enriched and re-energized it. It is through the diaspora, then, that the Irish in Ireland both come to see Ireland as globalized and are reassured about Irish cultural survival because 'they' (emigrants and descendants) bring 'our' (non-emigrants) culture to other parts of the world and give 'us' ('at home') 'a huge multicultural Irish family'. In her speeches, the president locates ideas of the global in the private through concepts of kin and genealogy (Strathern 1992). Irishness can operate transnationally and interculturally through the symbolic projection of Irish identity as kinship. The tensions produced in the disjunctures of national, diasporic and global codes of belonging are negotiated via the trope of the 'global family'. The global Irish family holds out a promise of continuity and recognition, yet, as Mary Williams's narrative suggests, the most poignant sites of non-recognition are also within the family. By migrating she lost the recognition of her family in Ireland and cannot recognize anything Irish in the identities of her children.

Ireland as a global nation operates transnationally and interculturally through the circulation of signs of Irishness in consumer products such as the Irish pub or Riverdance. Although not universally familiar or recognizable, some signs of Irishness resonate globally because the work of diasporizing Irish culture has been going on for two centuries and more. This domestication of Irishness through relative familiarity is made possible by an assumed access to cultural difference through consumption and by the reification of Irish culture into 'exchangeable aesthetic objects' (Huggan 2001: 19). Yet, this series, by telling the story of Irish collaboration in Empire, resists total domestication and keeps the tensions between memory, popular culture and history alive. Also the narratives of migrant women identify some of the unassimilable differences within the Irish Empire of memory and imagination. The disjunctures of the national, diasporic and global produce uncertainty with regard to transgenerational memory transmission (Binde 2001). This uncertainty is gestured toward via the controversial use of the trope of Empire and the many tensions between memory, history and lived experiences of diaspora that this trope evokes in the series. Questions of transmission shift the focus from the past to the future and away from the presentness of global consumer culture toward a temporality of expectation and promise. The many practices and technologies of memory that this series addresses position the viewer within discrepant temporal and spatial parameters and locate questions of Irish belongings past, present and future on both familiar and unfamiliar grounds. Perhaps, most importantly, new questions of belonging and cultural transmission are posed which open up new expectations and promises.

Notes

1. The co-ordinating producer was London-based Richard Cogan and executive producers were James Mitchell (Little Bird) Dublin, André Singer (Café Productions) and Chris Hilton (Hilton & Cordell). The script consultant for the series was writer and commentator Fintan O'Toole. Dublin-based Alan Gilsenan directed Programmes 1 and 5; Dearbhla Walsh, also Dublin based, directed Programme 3 on women in the diaspora; and Australia-based David Roberts directed programmes 2 and 4. The three main academic advisors were Piaras MacÉinri, the Irish Centre for Migration Studies, National University of Ireland, Cork; Paddy Fitzgerald of Queen's University, Belfast and Centre for Migration Studies Omagh; and Patrick O'Sullivan, Bradford University, England. I had a minor advisory input on the programme on women in the diaspora.
2. At the 2002 Cannes film festival more documentaries were shown than ever before (Cousins 2002).
3. Irish migrants and their descendants in the British Empire, according to Donald Akenson, contributed to imperialism not least through the displacement and destruction of indigenous cultures (Akenson 2000). The school systems of Ontario, British Columbia and parts of the Canadian prairies, he suggests, were modelled directly on those of Ireland. The Catholic Church fought to influence this national school system segregating Catholic and Protestant children and instating Irish ideas within these institutions (ibid.). Sheridan Gilley argues that nineteenth-century Irish migrants created an international Catholic

church in the British Empire and North America, which he characterized as a true Irish Empire beyond the seas (1984). If imperialism is
seen as a political and economic event that operates through a range
of cultural processes (Jacobs 1996), then the activities of the Irish
Catholic Church have been part of wider European practices of Empire.
These questions and ideas frame many of the 'talking heads' contributions to the Irish Empire series.

4. The RTE slot was mid-week at 10 p.m. (post prime-time). Documentaries usually get lower than average ratings, yet the *Irish Empire* got
31 per cent audience share. The average for a very popular entertainment show such as the Irish *Who wants to be a Millionaire?* is about
55 per cent and 35 per cent for drama is considered good, so this rating
for a documentary is high. The rating on BBC2 was just over 6 percent,
which represents a good viewership when compared with a general
average for all programmes on BBC2, including primetime, of 11 per
cent.

5. In 'masked interviews' the documentary maker is neither seen nor
heard in the final cut although he or she has instigated the response.

6. As late as 1828 there were probably more Catholic Irish in Newfoundland than in any other part of North America. It is because they lived
in isolated coves and harbours around 6,000 miles of coastline that so
many folkways have been maintained (O'Hara 1991). O'Hara argues
that today they take their politics from Canada but spiritually and
culturally remain Irish because they see it as the old folks' background
and therefore theirs too.

7. Around the time that this series was screened in Ireland in late 1999,
the unavailability of Irish workers in the tourist industry led Galway
Chamber of Commerce to recruit Newfoundland labour because their
accents would provide an 'authentic' Irish experience for tourists.
Newfoundland workers were called on to provide an 'authentic' Irish
experience 'at home'. The unemployment rate in Newfoundland was
running at 17 per cent at the time. In the event, most of these workers
found it difficult to adjust to largely seasonal work in Ireland and
returned to Newfoundland.

8. The use of subtitles to translate this contributor's Newfoundland accent
locates his accent as non-standard English and a use of the language
that does not travel/translate easily.

9. This programme also locates earlier periods of Irish migration in the
contexts of European Empires. In the early modern era the Irish migrated
to continental Europe as priests, scholars and military personnel at a
time when religion was an internationalizing force (O'Connor 2001).

Catholicism served as a marker of 'civil connectedness for the Irish with the greater European sphere as they forged alliances with their coreligionists in Spain and France in the fight against English occupation and in the name of the Counter Reformation' (Murphy 1999). This history located Ireland at the time in 'greater European political and military framework' (ibid.).

10. Between 1800 and 1922, about four million Irish women left Ireland (Nolan 1989).

11. The chronotope is that particular space-time continuum/figure in which the action/memories of the narrative are construed (Bakhtin 1981).

12. In 1994, about half the Irish lesbians and gay men who were 'out' were living outside of Ireland (Rose 1994: 31), yet lesbian migrations which potentially undermine heterosexual genealogies of diaspora are not included in the programme.

13. Article 2 of the amended Irish constitution: 'It is the entitlement and birthright of every person born in the island of Ireland, which includes its islands and seas, to be part of the Irish nation. That is also the entitlement of all persons otherwise qualified in accordance with law to be citizens of Ireland. Furthermore, the Irish nation cherishes its special affinity with people of Irish ancestry living abroad who share its cultural identity and heritage'.

References

Akenson, D.H. (1993), *The Irish Diaspora: A Primer*, Belfast: Institute of Irish Studies.

—— (2000), 'No Petty People Pakeha History and the Historiography of the Irish Diaspora', in Lyndon Fraser (ed.), *A Distant Shore: Irish Migration & New Zealand Settlement*, Dunedin: University of Otago Press.

Antze, P. and Lambek, M. (1996), 'Introduction', in P. Antze and M. Lambek (eds), *Tense Past. Cultural Essays in Trauma and Memory*, New York: Routledge.

Appadurai, A. (1996), *Modernity at Large: Cultural Dimensions of Globalization*, Minneapolis: University of Minnesota Press.

Bakhtin, M. (1981), *The Dialogic Imagination*, Austin: University of Texas Press.

Berlant, L. (2000), 'The Subject of True Feeling: Pain, Privacy and Politics', in S. Ahmed, J. Kilby, C. Lury, M. McNeil and B. Skeggs (eds), *Transformations: Thinking Through Feminism*, London: Routledge.

Binde, J. (2001), 'Toward an Ethics of the Future', in Arjun Appadurai (ed.), *Globalization*, Durham, NC: Duke University Press.

Brewster, S. and Crossman, V. (1999), 'Re-writing the Famine: Witnessing in Crisis', in V. Crossman, S. Brewster, F. Becket and D. Alderson (eds), *Ireland in Proximity: History, Gender, Space*, London: Routledge.

Brown, W. (1995), 'Wounded Attachments', in J. Rajchman (ed.), *The Identity in Question*, New York: Routledge.

Cousins, M. (2002), 'Imagining reality', *Prospect* (June): 34–8.

Diner, H. (1983), *Erin's Daughters in America*, Baltimore: Johns Hopkins University Press.

Forsdick, Charles (2001), 'Travelling Concepts: Postcolonial Approaches to Exoticism', *Paragraph*, 24(3): 12–29.

Gilley, S. (1984), 'The Roman Catholic Church and the Nineteenth-Century Irish Diaspora', *Journal of Ecclesiastical History*, 35(2): 188–207.

Hardt, M. and Negri, A. (2000), *Empire*, Cambridge, MA: Harvard University Press.

Hawkins, G. (2001), 'The Ethics of Television', *International Journal of Cultural Studies*, 4(4): 412–26.

Holt, E. (1999), 'TV Review', *Irish Times* 11 December: 5.

Huggan, G. (2001), *The Post-Colonial Exotic: Marketing the Margins*, London: Routledge.

Huyssen, A. (2001), 'Present Pasts: Media, Politics, Amnesia', in A. Appadurai (ed.), *Globalization*, Durham, NC: Duke University Press.

Jacobs, J.M. (1996), *Edge of Empire: Postcolonialism and the City*, London: Routledge.

Kearney, R. (1997), *Postnationalist Ireland: Politics, Culture, Philosophy*, London: Routledge.

Linehan, H. (1999), 'Mapping the Irish Empire', *Irish Times*, 14 December: 6.

Liubheid, E. (1999), 'Queer Circuits: The Construction of Lesbian and Gay Identities through Emigration', in R. Lentin (ed.), *Emerging Irish Identities*, Dublin: Ethnic and Racial Studies, Department of Sociology, Trinity College.

Lury, C. (1998), *Prosthetic Culture: Photography, Memory and Identity*, London: Routledge.

Maier, C.S. (1992), 'A Surfeit of Memory? Reflections on History, Melancholy, and Denial', *History and Memory*, 5 (Winter): 136–51.

McCarthy, C. (2000), *Modernisation, Crisis and Culture in Ireland, 1969–1992*, Dublin: Four Courts Press.

Miller, K.A. (1990), 'Emigration, Capitalism and Ideology in Post-famine Ireland', in R. Kearny (ed.), *Migrations: The Irish at Home and Abroad*, Dublin: Wolfhound.

Murphy, A. (1999), *But the Irish Sea Betwixt Us: Ireland, Colonialism and Renaissance Literature*, Kentucky: University of Kentucky Press.

Neville, G. (1995), 'Dark Lady of the Archives: Towards an Analysis of Women and Emigration to North America in Irish folklore', in M. O'Dowd and S. Wichert (eds), *Chattel, Servant or Citizen*, Belfast: Institute of Irish Studies.

Nolan, J. (1989), *Ourselves Alone: Women's Emigration From Ireland, 1885–1920*, Lexington: Kentucky University Press.

Nora, P. (1994), 'Between Memory and History: Les Lieux de Mémoire', in G. Fabre and R. O'Meally (eds), *History and Memory in African-American Culture*, Oxford: Oxford University Press.

O'Carroll, I. (1990), *Models for Movers: Irish Women's Emigration to America*, Dublin: Attic Press.

O'Connor, T. (2001), *The Irish in Europe 1580–1815*, Dublin: Four Courts Press.

O'Hara, A. (1991), 'The Irish in Newfoundland', in Galway Labour History Group (ed.), *The Emigrant Experience*, Galway: Galway Labour History Group.

Olwig, K.F. (1999), 'Caribbean Place Identity: From Family Land to Region and Beyond', *Identities*, 5(4): 435–67.

Rose, K. (1994), *Diverse Communities: The Evolution of Lesbian and Gay Politics*, Cork: Cork University Press.

Smyth, J, and Cairns, D. (2000), 'Dividing Loyalties: Local Identities in a Global Economy', in M. Peillon and E. Slater, (eds), *Memories of the Present: A Sociological Chronicle, 1997-1998*, Dublin: Institute of Public Administration.

Sommer, Doris (1991), *Foundational Fictions: The National Romances of Latin America*, Berkeley: University of California Press.

Strathern, M. (1992), *After Nature: English Kinship in the Late Twentieth Century*, Cambridge: Cambridge University Press.

Suleiman, S.R. (2002), 'History, Memory and Moral Judgement in Documentary Film: On Marcel Ophul's *Hotel Terminus: The Life and Times of Klaus Barbie*', *Critical Inquiry*, 28(2): 509–41.

Urry, J. (2000), *Sociology Beyond Societies: Mobilities for the Twenty-first Century*, London: Routledge.

Ware, V. (1992), *Beyond the Pale: White Women, Racism and History*, London: Verso.

Young, R.J.C. (1995), *Colonial Desire: Hybridity in Theory, Culture and Race*, London and New York: Routledge.

–8–

'They're Family!': Cultural Geographies of Relatedness in Popular Genealogy
Catherine Nash

Geography and Genealogy

The idea of being connected to a place because an ancestor was born and lived there is familiar, ordinary, unremarkable. Yet, it also depends upon particular modes of imagining kinship and particular ways of framing the relationship between identity, culture and geography. In this chapter I want to undo the obviousness of the ways in which relationships to places and people are imagined in popular genealogy, and explore its relationship to ideas of 'race', ethnicity, inheritance, property and belonging. The sort of genealogy in question has its own specific geography, with origins in European models of descent, and dispersed locations as it has travelled with European settlers to New Zealand, Australia, Canada and the United States. My interest is in the genealogical work of third-, fourth- and sometimes later-generation descendants of Irish migrants doing their family trees. These are stretched-out diagrams which chart ancestry back in time, map the migrations of their ancestors from Europe, and figure their own imaginative connections with 'ancestral homes'. For those who can afford it, these family trees also shape genealogical research itineraries. The search for roots sets people off on trips to local, regional and national archives and on transatlantic and long-haul journeys to find distant relatives and significant places. My focus in this chapter is on the genealogical work of tracing an Irish ancestral connection and the cultural geographies of identity and relatedness reproduced, enacted and reworked in the practice of genealogy.

In one way, this settler genealogy of old-world ancestry reflects a nostalgia for an imagined time when place, identity, culture and ancestry coincided. Where you lived was where your ancestors had lived and there was no dissonance between cultural identity and location. This is the ideal of bounded places, deep roots and shared culture that characterizes the modern notion of the nation. National genealogies are potent models of belonging that naturalize the nation as sealed, exclusive and culturally uniform through the entwined metaphors of the family, the body and the arborescent: family trees, roots and branches, blood and soil (Featherstone 1995: 142–3; Gilroy 2000; Malki 1992). Yet, though prompted at least in part by the appeal of ethnically distinct places (Gupta and Ferguson 1992: 10) these popular genealogies are also products of transnational flows of images, information and people, in the past and in the present. As cultural theorists search for alternatives to the exclusive language of pure, rooted and primordial cultures and 'races' assigned to politically differentiated spaces, thousands of personal genealogical projects map out complicated geographies of migration, origins and belonging, sometimes reproducing, sometimes subverting the language of cultural purity, fundamentalism and essentialism. Tracing the dynamics of identity and belonging within the practice of genealogy involves considering different spatial imaginations of culture and location – local, national, transnational, global, diasporic – and different ways of imagining human relatedness.

This discussion of popular settler genealogies brings together cultural geography's attention to what sorts of connection to place matter to people, and anthropology's interest in which connections between people 'carry particular weight socially, materially, affectively' (Carsten 2000: 1). In particular, I draw on new kinship studies which explore the ways in which ideas of kinship have been put to use in the past and are recon-figured in the present through a reformulated focus on 'cultures of related-ness' in new sites and contexts (Carsten 2000; Franklin and McKinnon 2001). As part of a reflexive critique of anthropology's analytic categories, feminist anthropologists have challenged the naturalization of kinship as a universal feature of human societies. The term 'cultures of relatedness' is used to convey 'a move away from a pregiven analytical opposition between the biological and the social' (Carsten 2000: 4), an opposition that underpinned the notion of kinship as the social meaning of the 'natural fact' of sexual reproduction and naturalized specific models of gender, reproduction and the family. It points to an expanded sense of human relatedness 'beyond what kinship has traditionally been used to represent, and the project of re-imagining what kinship can connect through unfam-iliar uses of genealogy' (Franklin and McKinnon 2001: 7) as the idioms of kinship – descent, paternity, maternity, inheritance – are deployed, for example to construct relationships between commodities and between consumers and brands (Franklin et al. 2000: 68–74). Here I want to put the theoretical tools of new kinship studies to work to address a practice which at first suggests a much narrower version of relatedness – popular genealogy with its the multiple sources and methods that characterize the work of doing a family tree: registers of birth, marriages, baptism, deaths, family stories, photographs, memorabilia, memories, graveyard inscriptions, on-line records, obituaries. 'Genealogy' signals both the family tree as a figure for a specific mode of kinship reckoning through linear bilateral descent, and the cultures of relatedness that are figured, produced and performed in the practice of genealogy.

My interest in particular is in how notions of property and inheritance shape ideas of personhood, ethnicity and relatedness within popular genealogy. As a device that historically ordered the transfer of property, genealogy continues to be characterized by the language of ownership, possession and inheritance whether spoken about in terms of bodily substance (genes or blood) or memory, culture, heritage or genealogical information itself. At the same time, national identities are conventionally expressed in terms of the shared possession of a culture and heritage within a bounded territory. Ethnicities, whether they coincide with, are contained within or override nation state borders, are similarly constructed through ideas of collective ownership of shared culture heritage and especially shared ancestry. Having a genealogical connection to a place and the cultural forms associated with it is a routine guarantor of the right to say 'that is my culture'. In the political struggles of indigenous people it is also a way of saying 'this is our land'. The symbolic dimensions of ideas of bodily inheritance and imaginative possession within popular genealogy that I foreground in this discussion of 'Irish roots' are always shadowed by the historical and continued nexus of ancestry, 'race', nation and gender. Notions of physical inheritance in human reproduction and racialized and gendered ideas of embodiment are entwined with the material transfer of wealth and hierarchies of power. What, then, are the relationships between personal identities shaped by ideas of bodily and cultural inheritance and the possession of genealogical knowledge in this specific cultural practice, and collective cultural property and ownership? This consideration of genealogy's conventional and novel forms of relatedness means keeping in tension the personal and intimate meanings of ancestry and descent and the social and political implications of fashioning cultural identities through genealogy.

In this chapter I focus on different cultural geographies of genealogical relatedness, exploring how the plural meanings of kinship and diverse place-based identities intersect and are mutually shaped. I begin by seeing what genealogy means and does in relation to the cultural politics of ethnicity and cultural identity, focusing especially on the United States. The chapter then moves with genealogical tourists to Ireland and explores

Family Ties

the experience of being in Ireland and meeting relatives, where the
certainties of blood and soil meet the ordinary awkwardness as well as
rewards of archives and reunions. The final section considers the dispersed
geographies of relatedness produced through the practice of genealogy
that both depend on and displace the significance of blood relations.[1]

Being of Irish Descent

Genealogy involves ideas of cultural and biological inheritance, personal
identity, shared heritage, blood and belonging. But the significance of
having Irish ancestry varies in different genealogical projects and across
a spectrum of approaches to ancestry and ethnicity. In North America,
Australia and New Zealand, searching for Irish roots can be one of several
ways of identifying strongly and often exclusively with Ireland and Irish
cultural traditions and asserting an Irish ethnicity, and is often prompted
by the positive connotations of Irishness in these contexts as well as the
influence of parents and grandparents who pass on traditions, stories of
Ireland and an interest in Irish music, dancing or history. Alternatively,
Irish descent can be valued as one strand within entangled ancestral charts
of diverse origins and intersecting ethnicities. In both cases ancestry is
routinely viewed as a meaningful, legitimate, valuable and natural source
of personal and collective identity: 'Without my ancestors I would not be
here today. It makes me who I am'. But what appears natural has a history
and geography. Genealogy both is shaped by and supports the ways in
which cultural difference, 'race' and ethnicity feature in discourses of the
nation state.

In the United States the 'ethnic revival' of the 1960s exerted a profound
challenge to the model of national assimilation, already been eroded by
the persistent discrimination on ethnic and racial grounds highlighted in
the civil-rights movement (King 2000: 264). This revival historically
occurred primarily among working-class and lower middle-class Americans whose families had migrated to the United States from Southern and
Central Europe earlier in the twentieth century, and reflected their antagon-
ism to black political militancy and affirmative action and their own
economic vulnerability and marginality (Colburn and Pozzetta, 1994).
Today, however, the idea of ethnicity is now prevalent among middle-class
Americans who can afford time for a genealogy that is personally symbolic but politically significant (King 2000: 263). The continued challenge
to the ethos of assimilation is cross-cut by racialized ideas of belonging
and difference which mean that the celebration of ethnic distinctiveness

among white Americans coincides with widespread hostility toward positive discrimination and alarm about immigration. Mary Waters (1990) has argued that for Americans with European ancestry, ethnicity is a significant but voluntary aspect of personal identity that provides a sense of distinctiveness and collective identity without compromising ideals of choice and freedom. It is this apparently benign but depoliticized version of cultural difference that David Lloyd has criticised as a 'sentimentalising and fetishising desire' of Irish-Americans 'to establish their genealogy in the old country'. This he argues, 'has been augmented recently by the successes of liberal multiculturalism that has left many white Americans, whose roots are by now twisted and entangled in the soil of several European lands, seeking the cultural distinctiveness that they have learned to see as the "privilege" of ethnic minorities' (Lloyd 1999: 102). What genealogy means and does for the politics of 'race' and ethnicity in this context depends on the ways in which individuals locate themselves in relation to the positive associations of ethnic distinctiveness, the specific characteristics attributed to particular ethnicities, discourses of genetic inheritance, their personal experiences of ethnic traditions in families or community groups and, for the majority of Americans of European descent, their own mixed ancestries.

In family histories which are seldom characterized by marriage within only one ethnic group, and in a genealogical tradition in which kinship and ethnicity can be reckoned through paternal and maternal descent, doing genealogy involves choices about which line or lines to follow and which ancestors matter. Often these choices are managed through ideas of a biological inheritance via blood and genes or a cultural inheritance passed on from generation to generation. Culture is biologized via genealogy, and genealogy marks difference. Yet computing ethnicity via biology does not necessarily mean valuing all biological inheritance equally. The social and the biological are flexible criteria for defining kin (Edwards and Strathern 2000). Biology makes identity, but need not hinder ethnic choices:

We are talking about the blood and guts and the molecules that make up the human body. I feel and believe I am more Irish than anything. My father was 3/4 Irish, 1/4 Scotch/American Indian/German, I believe. My mother was 100% British (brother and sister born in UK the rest of the family in Canada). (email response from woman living in Canada, for whom 'being a Canadian means nothing', August 2000)

My nationality is American . . . but my cultural identity is definitely Irish . . . my father's family is 100% Irish, my mother's family is 100% Polish, but

my identity is totally with Ireland . . . [Ireland] is my true homeland . . . Ireland
is my heart, my hope, my heritage. (email response from the United States,
August 2000)

The discourse of identity in genealogy is often of a biologically determined and biologically inherited ethnicity, but the practices of identification involve choices which sometimes simply override a convoluted
mathematics of ethnic fractions. Though the model of the Irish diaspora
is meant to emphasize a global community composed of different versions
of Irishness as identification with Ireland intersects with other identifications (Irish American, Irish Australian and so on), a focus on Irish roots
can result in other sources of identity via ancestry being overlooked,
ignored or dismissed as insignificant. Having Irish ancestry, even in an
ethnically mixed family tree, simply means being Irish.

Having Irish roots can also be one strand within a white European
American ethnicity. This emerging collective ethnic identity that encom-
passes diverse European ancestries is characterized, Richard Alba (1990)
argues, by a shared sense of belonging to a history of European immigration, hard work, sacrifice, individual effort, upward social mobility and
nation-building. In one respect this is a highly privatized ethnic identity
but it is also socially useful as family histories serve as cultural capital
among affluent and educated white Americans. Yet, genealogy is also a
way of tracing a personal family narrative within a dominant account of
Euro-American history that can be mobilized in times of conflict over
resources or in response to the challenges of non-European groups, in
ways that shape the experiences of recent immigrants from Asia, the
Caribbean, and Central and South America. The commemoration of Irish
migrant experience can therefore be part of a reactionary appeal to European heritage. Respondents to my query about the reasons for an interest
in Irish roots sometimes hinted at and sometimes made explicit their
anxieties about the cultural composition of the United States or Canada.
For some people the value of their Irish roots is that they are *white
European* roots.

But the whiteness of Irishness is a historical achievement. Indeed, the
history of the construction of ideas of difference between 'the English' and
'the Irish', or between 'the Irish' and 'Anglo-Saxon' Americans, is one in
which the 'semantics of race' (Goldberg 1992) slip between 'race' as
culture, nation and language. Though the Victorian representation of Irish
people as simian and savage is the most well-known example of their
colonial racialization (Curtis 1997; Mac Laughlin 1999), the construction
of the categories of Celtic and Anglo-Saxon by nineteenth-century

philologists and ethnologists was part of the wider racial categorization of European and non-European people (Morash 1997). These categories served both colonial and Irish nationalist discourses of difference (Cairns and Richards 1988). Yet, as labour historians have shown, Irish immigrants to the United States in the mid-nineteenth century, whose whiteness was sharply in question, struggled to join the English as white (Ignatiev 1995; Roediger 1991: 140–3, 1994: 181–98). In doing so they both challenged anti-Celtic Anglo-Saxon supremacy and helped naturalize a model of white American citizenship. In competing for wage labour and seeking political citizenship, Irish American men – for these were gendered arenas[2] (Marston, 1990) – used their newly-achieved whiteness to maintain a status above the 'not-yet-white' Southern and Central European immigrants of the early twentieth century, and above Asian Americans, African Americans and Native Americans, in the nation's racial hierarchy (Barrett and Roediger 1997).

Now, however, the whiteness of Irishness is taken for granted and the turn to Irish roots, for some at least, can be a reaction to fears of the erosion of a white and European heritage.

> western European people are heading toward minority status in this country within the next couple decades. I'd like to leave a written record of my bit on western European ancestors (email response, American woman of Irish descent, August 2000)

Ireland appeals as a place far from the trouble of 'loose immigration laws' and demanding 'minorities' in Canada where Irish and Scottish cultural traditions 'represent multiculturalism at its finest' (email response, Canadian woman, August 2000). This is a multiculturalism confined to the varieties of European ethnicity. One visitor to the National Library in Dublin from Boston talked at length about the significance of her Irish connections, and praised Native Americans 'holding on to their traditions', but was irritated by Spanish-speaking migrants refusing to 'assimilate' and speak English, and refused to accept that schoolchildren who for her were simply 'black' could describe their ethnic identities as Haitian or Jamaican. Here arguments about the cultural distinctiveness and autonomy of indigenous people are crudely appropriated to support the significance of Irish ancestry as a source of identity. The celebration of ethnicity is limited to those within a white European American ethnicity to which others must assimilate. Furthermore, racist assumptions that blackness determines identity are used to suggest that ethnic identifications that are not also white are fanciful fictions. It is the marking of Irishness as white that means that 'African' ancestries in predominantly European genealogies are often overlooked, and identification with Irish ancestry among African American genealogies has to be asserted against the assumption that blackness subsumes other ethnic identities. The construction of whiteness as a racial category is elided within a discourse of ethnic fluidity, while 'blackness' is fixed by 'race'. Those who enjoy the privileges of the assumed Irishness-as-whiteness can fail to acknowledge the legitimacy of other self-definitions. Futhermore, the celebration of ancestral emigrants as nation-builders in the New World and the commemoration of the trauma of leaving Ireland does not necessarily lead to an understanding of the experience of more recent migrants. Even when parallels are made, the argument that recent migrants are experiencing the same struggles as earlier waves of migrants and like them will ultimately prosper can be used to suggest that support for minority groups is unnecessary (Waters 1990).

Yet genealogy is not necessarily tied to political conservatism and cultural defensiveness. Nor does it always foster ideas of simple ancestral roots or pure cultural categories. The empirical imperative of genealogy can create family trees which reflect family connections across ethnic groups. The work of tracing ancestry back from the present can direct attention to recent generations that frequently feature several ethnicities. The factual presence of difference within the family tree can make the process of choosing an ethnicity more overt and self-conscious. Gene-alogical results do not always confirm an identity that had previously been assumed, and the connection with Ireland can become more distant and less stable than imagined. The ideal of a fixed point of origin is frustrated by the potentially infinite nature of the family tree, and when the 'Irish' connection becomes one stage within a longer history of migration. Though genealogy seems to offer a simple and single answer to origins, as family trees grow backwards in time they can fail to satisfy the desire to define identity through 'where I am from'. Genealogy, I was told, can dispel ideas of cultural purity.

> One thing that I have learned is that we are all one people, a distinct pure line is not a reality. There was such migration, cross-breeding, raiding plundering, such purity is impossible. (email response from man living in United States, August 2000)

Others come to a wider understanding of culture as dynamic and fluid:

> I think that one of the ideas I have received from my research is that culture is not as fixed or stable as most of us believe. I think that this is an important idea

because it means that we don't have to be so protective of our culture if we see it as evolving. I would hope that this idea gives groups who hate [the] permission to see things differently. (email response from a woman in the United States, August 2000)

This anti-racist genealogy can also be articulated through a kind of multiculturalism of biologically inherited cultural types that are transmitted without change. Sometimes these cultural traits are manifest in their pure form in one person, who is 'typically German' for example; sometimes these ethnically marked traits are combined in one individual. For some, national diversity is mirrored in their mix of personal physical or character traits that are understood to derive from a diversity of distinctive 'ethnic ancestries', in the sense of 'getting' particular traits from particular roots – Irish, French, German, English, Polish, Greek and so on.

It makes me appreciate the diversity of our nation. My father is Irish, small, laughing, quick-tempered. My mother's brother is German, tall big-boned, brilliant . . . Doing family history work has helped me to understand the many facets of myself and from where they probably came . . . I am proud to have gleaned so much richness from my diverse ancestors. (email response, 'My cultural identity is German, Irish, French, English, and American Indian. My nationality is American', August 2000)

This understanding of personal identity reckoned via genealogical fractions and conventional national or ethnic characteristics suggests the pleasures of a pick-and-mix personal multiculturalism and the security of deterministic notions of biological ethnic inheritance. Genealogy can be harnessed to a version of biological inheritance centred on traits that are marked as recognizably ethnic, at the same time as it is deployed within a discourse of shared humanity and non-hierarchical difference:

I feel a connection to all people of the world now. We are mostly all immigrants in one way or another and we need to celebrate our differences and encourage our sameness (decency, mercy, understanding) (email response, Canadian woman with Anglo and Ulster-Scots roots, August 2000)

Though this clearly challenges ideas of racial hierarchies and antagonistic difference the idea of shared connections with 'all people of the world' rests on an assumed system of equivalence, where there is no dominant group, and no system of differentiation between the different conditions of migration. As Ien Ang points out, the notion that 'we are all migrants'

– 187 –

suggests that 'we' are all travellers in the same universe, 'the only difference residing in the different itineraries undertaken' (2000: 24).

The political implications of genealogical imaginations of ancestry and
ethnicity are clearly complex and often contradictory, and can't be decided
upon by a blanket critique of roots. Within genealogical discourses,
culture can appear to be a set of characteristics that are transmitted
unchanged through generations along with bodily substance. Its language
is one of transmission and inheritance rather than of process and production. Yet culture in the sense of collective heritage can also be figured as
vulnerable to cultural dilution or corruption. Hence the defensive turn to
genealogy. But genealogical research can also be a practice that points to
culture as a fluid and continuous making of meaning that challenges fixed,
essentialized and exclusive versions of culture as property. Critical
genealogies that explore the relationships between family history and
wider structures of power and patterns of inequality stand out because of
their relative rarity, but they do suggest ways of harnessing the appeal of
roots for politically progressive accounts of nationhood and culture.
Genealogy is not necessarily a reliable index of investment in ethnicity
since it can be both an intense performance of ethnicity and a pleasurable
but emotionally detached numerical exercise. The significance of genealogy lies in its contribution or challenge to the ways in which culture,
'race' and nation are imagined through ideas of purity and racialized
categories of 'white' and 'black'. The refiguring of nation through genealogy inevitably impacts upon the ways in which new immigrants to the
United States of the 1990s 'are being categorized, learning race and
experiencing racism' (Roediger, 2002: 495). Genealogy can be harnessed
to support racialized and racist versions of nationhood and ethnicity but
it can also serve as a way of reimagining the fixity of belonging, culture
and inheritance in postcolonial contexts.

Being in Ireland

Travelling to Ireland to trace Irish connections or to visit the place which
ancestors left brings different genealogical and geographical imaginations
together. Returning to the places ancestors left behind or travelling in
search of the information that will pinpoint those places – a county,
barony, diocese, parish, village, townland or even a farm or cottage – is a
process of imaginative repossession. Standing on the land that ancestors
knew produces a sense of genealogical connection that is sometimes
explained through physical inheritance and blood, sometimes as an

inexpressible sense of spiritual affinity, and often experienced bodily in 'shivers down the spine' and 'goosebumps'. Despite what may have changed, the experience of the topography, the shape of a hill, the sight of the horizon is often imagined as a shared physical experience that links ancestors to their descendants across time and difference. The visit to Ireland is a pilgrimage and mission in honour of ancestors who could never go back. It is sometimes a ceremony enacted with gestures and objects that symbolically reconnect them to their home – soil from a grandfather's grave in the United States scattered on the land he knew in Ireland, or a grandmother's prayer book buried in an Irish graveyard.

For the descendants of Famine and post-Famine migrants this return is frequently framed by discourses of colonial dispossession, forced exile and the trauma of displacement. Personal genealogies that trace the journeys of poor evicted tenants from cottage to tenement can illustrate these processes but they can also be complicated as colonial histories of conflict and dispossession are entangled with family histories of conflict over land. As one professional genealogist in Dublin explained

> You don't have to go back very far and in families who have something to leave or something to inherit . . . you have major rows going on for years because so and so got something who shouldn't have got it. And then you have farms that have been inherited and someone comes back and upsets the whole system. It is a recurring theme. (interview, Dublin, 1998)

Genealogy can reveal the intersections of colonialism and capitalism. Tracing connections between those who left and those who remained foregrounds issues of class that have been downplayed in nationalist histories of colonial injustice and national unity. The return of migrants' descendants can result in new concerns about material repossession for the descendants of those who remained, many of whom benefited from the migration of the poorest strata of the rural population and became the rural middle class. Desires for imaginative repossession of Ireland can create anxieties about claims to material repossession of property and land.

These issues of cultural and physical property extend to the ownership and control of genealogical information. Ireland features in the discourses of Irish roots not just as a land of rolling green fields and cottages but as a source of data, as a place of authenticity and ancestral origins and of more or less accessible and intensely desired genealogical sources. Though many researching their ancestry want to know much more than names and dates of births, baptisms, marriages and deaths, these are the 'gems' of genealogical information that allow family trees to grow, help locate key places and structure the narratives of family life and migration. Despite the amount of material available on-line and in national archives overseas, the Genealogical Office, National Archives and National Library in Dublin, the Public Record Office of Northern Ireland in Belfast and county-based genealogical and heritage centres are key sites in this imaginative geography of Ireland. These places are both sources of genealogical information and points of mediated or restricted access to original documents and their promise of verifiable genealogical information. The common dissatisfaction with the quality and cost of information from heritage centres and the frustration of restricted access to diocesan and parish records – certain Catholic bishops in particular refuse to grant access to them – means that the intense desire for genealogical connection and the imaginative investment in Ireland has to be reconciled with difficulties of getting data. Love of Ireland has to withstand bureaucratic or ecclesiastical blocks to information. For some this problem of restricted access to knowledge seems to imply that their research and their genealogical connection to Ireland is insignificant.

> The most frustrating aspects have been from the Irish Cultural Centres. The raw data is there, but no one is looking at it through my eyes, how devastating it is to find a clue, and then to be told that that area of County Cork has not been put on computer, and that it will be another 10 years before the data is online. Also, while I have had some very good experiences with people helping me from Mallow Heritage Centre, the small parishes that I have contacted do not have any one there to look things up and copy them and send them off to you. And in some instances, don't see what the big deal is, and don't do a thorough search. This is my own family they are looking for, and it is like a religious experience for me – I would expect them to take the time to look thoroughly for me. (email response, Canadian woman with Irish cultural identity, August 2000)

The practical process of researching Irish ancestry within genealogical archives again involves these questions of imaginative possession, cultural ownership and claims to membership in the collective heritage called Irish. While many experiences of seeking information in Irish archives and through professional genealogists are undoubtedly rewarding, these concerns about mediated and sometimes blocked access to genealogical data reveal something of what is at stake when intense identifications with Ireland are tested in the process of genealogical research.

As well as archives and record offices, people in Ireland that share ancestral connections within the visitor's family tree are key sources of family history and genealogical information. Meeting distant relatives in

Ireland is as significant to the genealogical experience as finding the location and being in the place ancestors left behind. As genealogy has become more popular, the case of people in Ireland being contacted as possible relations is increasingly familiar. This can be a hugely confirming experience when the visitor is welcomed as part of a family and the sense that they are linked since they collectively share what belongs to them personally – in this case dead relatives – is reciprocated (Edwards and Strathern 2000). Years of research and the significance of genealogical relatedness make these meetings highly charged. Yet these encounters are often experienced through feelings of difference as well as connection. They can be laced with anxiety on both sides. A woman whose parents decided to emigrate to the United States with their children in the 1950s rather than watch them leave as young adults, expressed her concern about how she would appear to her relatives in Ireland, acutely aware of the question of cultural difference: 'I would love to see them. I worry about being considered a "Yank" since I know how my parents felt about such people.' The different attitudes to Irish culture – history, music, dancing, language, mythology – that can surface in these encounters intersect with the ordinary awkwardness of different priorities and amounts of time and money. As one professional genealogist in Dublin explained

'You can have a visitor going down to a farm. They are on holidays but the people on the farm aren't on holidays so you can have that kind of tension you know . . . You see it depends on what kind of situation you are coming to, what is the relationship first of all, in the house or the cottage or whatever, questions of money. Do they come back to see their cousins but stay in hotels? (Interview, Dublin, August 1998)

One significant way in which visitors become aware of cultural differ-ence is in attitudes to ancestry itself. The frustration of the woman who felt her quest for genealogical information was hindered by the heritage centres was compounded by the apparent disinterest of possible distant relations in Ireland in 'sharing their family ancestry':

they do not have any interest in sharing their family ancestry, and were actually rude about the interest in their family and country. I know this is an isolated case, but for those of us thirsting to know more about our Irish heritage, every bit of information is like a new gold nugget. I would think that it would be in the best interest of all Irish people to share their beautiful history and ancestry. We are not trying to take over their country, or to Americanize it in any way. We only have a right to find out where we came from, and finding information easily available would do much to increase the tourism and good will of

Ireland. (email response, Canadian woman with Irish cultural identity, August 2000)

Even in happier contacts many visitors are surprised that their deep interest in genealogy and family history is not shared by the relatives they meet. Popular genealogy is grounded in a sense that relationships between people based on blood and marriage matter, and that within an understanding of kinship as a reciprocal system of affinities, rights and duties, these connections should matter as much to all those who are related. The curious lack of interest among these newly discovered family in Ireland confounds these expectations and reveals genealogy to be a personal practice with no guarantee of reciprocation. The resistance of some families to genealogical inquiries can make some visitors feel that their interests appear acquisitive rather than part of a natural process of exchange. In other cases the lack of interest among relatives in Ireland suggests to visitors that genealogy is simply an unnecessary project for those already rooted by residence and unbroken ancestry.

> I suppose we spend time trying to assess who we are, and where we come from, in order to pass it on to the succeeding generations . . . One of the things that amazed me was that so many of the Irishmen in Ireland don't seem to much care to learn about their 'ancestry'. Perhaps, it's because they know that their 'kin' have lived in the surrounding countryside for centuries. They know their past stories through storytelling and music. We, here in the U.S. are newcomers to this land. Our ties are back in the old country, and we wish to find them. (email response, American woman with Irish roots, August 2000)

The experience of visiting Ireland can illustrate the different geographies of Irish identities as constrasting versions of Irishness become apparent in these genealogical encounters.

These different degrees of interest means that sometimes these relationships are sustained – photographs and letters continue to travel back and forth – and sometimes they aren't. A newly found family may welcome visitors to Ireland but not respond to subsequent letters or emails. This works both ways. Relatives that help are sometimes only temporarily valued as sources of information. Establishing meaningful connections with the country through relationships with living distant relatives is central to many people's processes of genealogical identification with Ireland. But rushed trips around the country can mean that sustained encounters are sacrificed for the sake of getting back to the archives. Though being in the ancestral place is often talked about as a sacred moment of return, this is not always matched by what professional or amateur genealogists in Ireland feel to be an appropriate and sustained engagement with that place. One genealogist explained her irritation with an apparently superficial and impatient approach to genealogy and ancestral geography:

> I am a very placid person but when I find myself suddenly getting [*laughs*] cross it is when you find people, they want the whole thing, like mathematic, there and then and they can't . . . when you really want them to walk the land, you know, where they came from, get yourself into that . . . But they are people in a hurry. You need to be open, be interested. Not on the highway all the time. Not the person who is going to do three hundred miles in one day and then more the following day. (Interview, Dublin, August 1998)

The complex combinations of senses of cultural connection and differ-ence that are experienced by those who travel to Ireland in search of Irish roots and relatives both enact and test the model of diasporic Ireland (see Breda Gray in Chapter 7 of this volume). The celebration of an inclusive diversity within the Irish diaspora translates into personal experience of managing social and cultural difference across genealogical connections. Often visitors' intense investment in Irishness meets casual disinterest as well as generous openness. In these emotionally charged meetings with newly found relatives, recognizing what is not shared despite shared ancestry can be a challenging part of the process of exploring the mean-ings of belonging, identity and Irish ancestry. Unreciprocated interests in genealogy or different perspectives on Irish history temper the joys of being in Ireland.[3] Visitors' interests in genealogy are sometimes natural-ized by a notion that knowledge of ancestors is a universal need and right (as in 'we' all 'have' a genealogy), that genealogy itself charts pre-existing bonds of bodily and affective connection, and the extension and deepening of these connections by the ready exchange of information follows naturally from their existence. When this is deliberately or unknowingly thwarted by official or family record keepers these assumptions of ethnic and family affinity and reciprocity are painfully revealed and put in question. Though the conventional reckoning of kinship in this form of genealogy privileges blood relations, as a practice genealogy is also a process of creating family bonds that are not automatically secured by blood. Genealogy can generate new and unexpected forms of relatedness and new geographies of genealogical kinship.

Making Genealogical Relations

The appeal of genealogy is its ability to both embody and individualize the past. Famous events or significant processes of historical change can be understood and personalized through the stories of ancestors who were present, involved and affected by them. These can be heroic acts but are also often stories of ordinary survival and struggle that enliven narratives of social inequality and social change – constant movement in search of work, high rates of infant mortality and women dying in childbirth. However, the genealogical impulse to gather more and more information in an ever-growing family tree can also reduce past lives to genealogical data. Ancestors are sometimes talked of as hiding from their present-day descendants, or imagined as wilfully not leaving clues or trails for those trying to 'track them down'. Contemporary interest in genealogy is projected backwards. As one genealogical detective wondered: 'Didn't they think someone one day would want to find them?' For some at least, this intense interest in cataloguing the past suggests that contemporary lives should also be recorded for genealogical posterity. Lives of the dead and the living are converted into files of connected data.

Yet the translation of lives into family trees, and family stories into printed histories, is also a matter of complex forms of genealogical relatedness in which the significance of biological connection is simultaneously central, challenged and displaced. Genealogy is often a memorial to past relatives, sometimes distant ones whose move from Ireland is a 'pivotal event' in the family history, sometimes more close – a parent or grandparent – whose ageing or death prompts an interest in finding out about the family's past, or figures as bequest to future generations as the birth of children or grandchildren poses questions about what story of the family past should be passed on. The labour of this research – with its demands of time, money and emotion – is often figured as a more or less appreciated gift to immediate and future family, a way of making sense of family traditions and individual experiences, and of forging family bonds between generations in the face of concerns about the fragility of close family networks and the decline of 'family values'. Though genealogy is driven by the significance of family relations, many people explained their work as a response to the apparent insignificance of blood and family among their own relatives and in Western society more generally. At the same time, interest in the family history within families can be a source of shared pleasure, but also one of possessiveness if genealogical information – stories, documents, dates, letters, photographs – is not adequately reciprocated or is monopolized by one person, or when one member's role as custodian of family history is challenged by another's genealogical research. Genealogy's discourses of possessive individualism and maps of relationality (Strathern 1995) can produce tensions over the ownership of shared histories of family relationships. Though shared ancestry potentially creates infinite networks of relatives in bilateral kinship systems, proprietorial attitudes to genealogical knowledge can effectively 'cut the network' (Strathern 1996).

As genealogy mediates and is mediated by existing family relationships it is also a practice through which new forms of relatedness are forged, sometimes with very distant relations or with people of no blood relation but bonded through a shared interest in genealogy. Genealogy clearly prioritizes relationships between those who, living or dead, are related through blood. Yet, doing genealogy can also create forms of relatedness that do not necessarily depend on the closeness or even the existence of biological connection. The social relationships that develop may start from a shared interest in a shared surname, in Irish roots in general or in a specific place in Ireland, but they are relationships shaped by a shared interest in ancestry and a shared experience of doing genealogy.

> I believe genealogists are so helpful and supportive of each other because they have an understanding of the trials and frustrations involved and the possible importance of one little clue or piece of information. I have never come across anyone who was not positive, even if they couldn't help much. There is a real sense of community amongst amateur researchers who are selfless in their attitude to other researchers. (email response, 'Australian [woman] of Anglo-Irish descent, August 2000)

Other forms of relatedness result from meeting 'on-line cousins' or 'virtual relatives'. This contact via email and the internet is a routine part of genealogy, as people respond to information or enquiries posted on personal or organizational websites and to a range of general and specialist email discussion lists. Several email lists exist for Ireland in general, for particular sorts of diasporic communities and for each county in Ireland. Hundreds of surname groups exist. These internet sites and groups foster informal on-line networks that link individuals across the world who share interests in specific places or ancestries. This practice of linking family trees across the migrant geographies that have stretched them globally is also encouraged by commercial providers of genealogical software who sell packages, such as RootsWeb WorldConnect, that make it possible to convert personal family trees to on-line archives that can be searched for genealogical connections. The global reach of internet projects to archive the recent genealogy of humanity parallel and sometimes overlap with human genome mapping projects. Both reduce the complexity of human life to code (Haraway 1997: 245–6). Yet, converting the lives of dead relatives to data can mean that new sorts of relationships with living relations can develop as this data is mobilized as a gift, shared inheritance or personal possession. These internet sites and networks create new opportunities for personal on-line relationships. As one respondent put it:

> As I meet distant cousins over the internet from all over the world – we immediately bond, it seems – we really do begin to feel like 'real cousins'. I have become very close to some. We have even begun to arrange to meet. Always seems like we have known one another forever. It seems to be a very 'natural' kind of feeling. (email response, 'American [woman] with Scots-Irish ancestry', August 2000).

The emails that travel back and forth between people in Ireland and other places, and between other places but about Ireland, in response to shared interest in a surname or a particular place – Ireland in general or a specific county, town, parish, village or townland – sometimes lead to connected family trees or more often to a sense of commonality and affinity through shared interests and the exchange of gifts of genealogical and geographical information. Someone in Australia sends someone of no relation in Canada pictures of a certain place in Ireland, or as one man helping with his wife's research explained

> In an effort to start tracing her ancestors through this line, I subscribed to the Donegal message board at rootsweb and posted a brief message giving the birthdates of John and Jane and the name and birthdate of each child, all of whom were born in Donegal. Within 24 hours, I had a response from a gentleman in NZ who had marriage records for Donegal going back to the 1600s. He identified that John and Jane were married in 1815 in a C of I church in the parish of Killee. And then, 24 hours later, another message arrived from a woman in Australia who was able to find the parents of both Jane and John from the birth dates of our John and Jane and each of their children. So in just 48 hours with the help of some dedicated volunteer searchers from halfway around the world, we were able to push that family back another generation. (email response, Canadian man with ancestral connections to Ulster, August 2000)

The degree of cooperation and sense of community is emphasized by the fact that this culture of relatedness is not based on the 'natural' bonds of blood relationships: 'We have never had a rebuff or unpleasant response from anyone, even those who turned out to be unrelated to us':

All have been unfailingly helpful and kind. I, in return, share information and give help whenever I can. None of these people shared my surname, but all were willing to help, and even though I will probably never see any of them in person, I feel their friendship is genuine. (email response, 'My nationality is American. Father's family: his mother was Ulster Scot, his father English, with one gm of Dutch ancestry. Mother's family: her father was German, her mother English and Norwegian.' August 2000)

In these genealogical networks Ireland is one node in a complex geography of genealogical connections that do not depend on conventional notions of consanguinity. On county-based email lists, members living in Ireland frequently help solve mysteries about the micro-geographies of place names and administrative boundaries. Other networks link people far apart though a shared interest in a specific place in Ireland. They can include distant relations in Ireland and other places or simply people willing to share knowledge about sources and exchange genealogical stories. Many of the strongest expressions of connection with people were about the value and meaning of these on-line relationships. As one woman explained:

I have met many, many people over the internet in regards to the surnames I'm researching. There's a kinship with these people that no one else can experience. They're family! (email response, US American woman, August 2000)

These expressions of 'unnatural' family-like relationships developing with conventionally unrelated people challenge and, at the same time, figure the contrast between the biological and the social that is central to Western discourses of relatedness.

Yet, as in conventional families, these on-line relationships are strained when the gifts of genealogical knowledge are not reciprocated or trust is violated when family trees and written histories based on shared information are published as if they were produced and possessed by one individual as genealogical progenitor of the family tree. Other tensions arise when overseas researchers feel that their depth of commitment or degree of knowledge, or the validity of their identification with Ireland, are challenged when list members from Ireland correct genealogical or historical misinformation on-line. The question of the degree of genealogical and geographical closeness to Ireland and the significance of being born and living in Ireland can disturb the harmony of these extended families of genealogical kin as well as being the basis of their connection. Those who celebrate the significance of their ancestors being Irish born,

bred and thoroughly rooted can inadvertently undermine their own quali-
fications as Irish since, being descendants of Irish migrants (and often
other ethnicities), they fail to meet their own criteria of 'true' belonging
in Ireland.

These new genealogical maps of relatedness chart networks of connection that are shaped by shared interests in genealogical and geographical
roots but at the same time challenge the significance of consanguinity
and simple geographies of identity. They are both about significant
points of origin and stretched-out networks of relatedness in which
blood both matters and doesn't matter. This is a complex geography of
relatedness that at once prioritizes and overrides biological relatedness.[4]
Though genealogy privileges blood relations, genealogical networks
constitute forms of kinship based on shared interests and mutual support.
Non-blood based social networks are based on shared interest in blood
relations.

Conclusion

Genealogy's cultures of relatedness depend upon and rework ideas of
inheritance, property and possession. My foregrounding of ideas of
inheritance and property has not been to simply reiterate genealogy's own
genealogy as a device for managing the legitimate transfer of property and
status. Notions of personal and collective possession of people, the past,
attributes, knowledge, culture, heritage or place are threaded though the
discourse of popular genealogy and closely tied to senses of identity and
belonging. The possession of ancestral connections, ideally confirmed
through genealogical research, are often mobilized to support and naturalize a desire to say 'this is my culture' and 'this is my home'. Yet, journeys
to repossess Ireland imaginatively can create anxieties for visitors about
access to and possession of genealogical data and, by implication, their
cultural belonging in Ireland and the legitimacy of claims to be Irish
through Irish migrant ancestry. Since settler genealogies that look to the
old world implicitly idealize a relationship between identity, place and
culture based on the long, undisturbed ancestral residence, ancestral
connection alone becomes an unstable guarantee of the legitimacy of
settler descendants' claims to cultural ownership of the 'homeland'. For
those researching what are now distant Irish roots, the sense of the difference between those whose ancestors left and those whose ancestors stayed
creates a troubled sense of cultural loss, disconnection and difference.
Their uneasy identification with Ireland and Irishness is upset by any

suggestions that their claims to Irishness and Irish culture are not equally valid.

Though sharing ancestry implies that in some sense relatives discovered through genealogical research belong to each other, the meeting of distant relatives can undermine the significance of biological relatedness, especially when the most striking cultural difference is the value that is accorded to shared ancestry itself. In these encounters the potentially limitless nature of the family tree meets the self-limiting practices of kinship which determine who among an infinite number of possible relatives really are 'family' (Edwards and Strathern 2000). The character of these encounters is shaped by where families in Ireland draw the line across geographical and genealogical distance. Yet, despite the madly extendable nature of genealogical charts and databases, these maps of ancestry are themselves already limited by choices about what sorts of ancestral connection matter. These choices can be the result of personal affection toward particular family members and the appeal of certain family stories or wider histories. As a mode of articulating and exploring subjectivity and ethnicity, genealogy offers a compelling language of inherited identity shaped by the transfer of genes, blood or culture. Yet popular genealogy is often characterized by a mixed discourse of determination and choice. It can be a calculus of ethnic fractions or a source of 'true' identity.

At the same time, genealogical data can be mobilized as a gift or shared possession in ways that generate new forms of relatedness. Genealogy is thus not simply descriptive but generative of kinship connections. Using the idiom of kinship and the family to describe relationships to people who share an interest in ancestry but are not related in the conventional sense suggests that new forms of relatedness are realized through the practice of genealogy. In this sense, the significance accorded to blood relations shape relationships between people of no conventional genealogical connection. These new modes of genealogical relatedness are often global networks of relationships that electronically criss-cross the geographies of European settler societies. Like blood and biological relatedness in genealogy's new cultures of relatedness, Ireland is both central to this imaginative geography and decentred by transnational genealogical networks. At the same time, local places in Ireland are now having to be shared with people worldwide who identify these places as ancestral homes. In Northern Ireland, this overseas genealogical interest intersects with local disputes about cultural ownership and belonging and with efforts to reimagine local places as sites of shared rather than antagonistic histories. The continued significance of these places among descendants of emigrants is used to encourage a sense of shared ownership that has implications for local disputes about cultural property and territory. The flows of culture and capital mobilized by popular immigrant genealogies do not simply support old divisions and antagonisms.

Genealogy's transnational networks can link different political geographies of belonging in other ways. Tracing the political implications of ideas of roots as they travel with genealogical tourists and via the internet scrambles the simple opposition between the supposedly politically progressive ideas of rootlessness and the supposedly regressive idea of roots. The popularity of Irish genealogy, for example, cannot be understood in isolation from the political implications of the revival of white European ethnicities in the United States. Yet at the same time, ideas of the Irish diaspora as an extended national genealogy are being mobilized in attempts to rethink questions of culture and identity in Ireland (Nash 2002; see Breda Gray in Chapter 7 of this volume). Those white European Americans troubled by shifting patterns of culture and ethnicity in the United States look to an imagined Ireland of whiteness and untroubled ethnic purity, while ideas of multi- or interculturalism, ethnic diversity and cultural pluralism are being explored as productive alternatives to the model of two antagonistic 'traditions' in Northern Ireland and as ways of challenging exclusive versions of Irishness that fuel discrimination toward travellers and racism toward ethnic minorities, refugees and asylum seekers (Longley and Kiberd 2001; Rontin, 1999). The imaginative geographies of Ireland that travel with roots tourists may be impervious to these shifts but there are always possibilities that they can be disrupted. As relationships based on shared cultural and biogenetic inheritance are charted in family trees, and as new forms of relatedness are produced through genealogy in action, the different versions of Ireland that meet in genealogy can aggravate anxieties as to whom Ireland imaginatively belongs to, and as to who belongs in Ireland. The reckoning of cultural location and kinship – what sorts of connection to places and between people matter – through genealogy can produce unsettling as well as predictable results.

Acknowledgements

I am grateful to the editors for inviting me to present this research in the Uprootings/Regroundings seminar series and for the thoughtful comments of Anne-Marie Fortier and Mimi Sheller on this chapter, to Miles Ogborn, my reader, and to all those who contributed to the research.

Notes

1. This research was conducted through observation and interviews with professional genealogists, research staff and visitors to Ireland in the newly opened Genealogy Centre in the National Library of Ireland in Dublin, in the National Archives in Dublin, in the Public Record Office of Northern Ireland in Belfast, and as a delegate on the annual residential genealogical conference and study tour organized by the Ulster Historical Foundation in Belfast, over the summers of 1998 and 1999. In August 2000 I posted a set of questions about the meaning, practice and experience of genealogy to Irish and county-based email discussion lists. In drawing on the interview material and the 167 email replies to my email posting, I have changed or omitted the names of people and places to maintain the anonymity of the respondents and wherever possible identified them by their own description of their ethnicity or nationality.
2. The intersection of gender, 'race' and Irishness has been explored also in research on the racial location of Irish people in Britain which, for Irish women especially, results in both racialized exclusion and invisibility within an undifferentiated category of whiteness (Hickman and Walter 1995; Walter 1995, 2001).
3. Though visitors can find their perspectives on Irish history challenged by their own genealogies and by the attitudes they encounter in Ireland, their genealogical research can also direct attention to those lives overlooked in the conventional narratives of Irish nationhood. I discuss the implications of genealogy for approaches to Irish history in more depth elsewhere (Nash 2002).
4. What is less certain is whether this new geography of relatedness overrides racialized categories of difference, or the extent to which this is a transnational relatedness based on the shared significance of white European ancestry and narratives of white migration, struggle and achievement.

References

Alba, R.D. (1990), *Ethnic Identity: The Transformation of White America*, New Haven and London: Yale University Press.

Ang, I. (2000), *On Not Speaking Chinese*, London and New York: Routledge.

Barrett, J.R. and Roediger, D. (1997), 'Inbetween Peoples: Race, Nationality and the "New Immigrant" Working Class', *Journal of American Ethnic History*, 16: 3–44.

Cairns, D. and Richards, S. (1988), *Writing Ireland: Colonialism, Nationalism and Culture*, Manchester: Manchester University Press.

Carsten, J. (2000), 'Introduction: Cultures of Relatedness', in C. Carsten (ed.), *Cultures of Relatedness: New Approaches to the Study of Kinship*, Cambridge: Cambridge University Press.

Colburn, D.R. and Pozzetta, G.E. (1994), 'Race, Ethnicity and the Evolution of Political Legitimacy', in D. Farber (ed.), *The Sixties: From Memory to History*, Chapel Hill and London: University of North Carolina Press.

Curtis, L.P. (1997), *Apes and Angels: The Irishman in Victorian Caricature*, Washington and London: Smithsonian Institution Press (rev. ed.).

Edwards, J. and Strathern, M. (2000), 'Including Our Own' in C. Carsten (ed.), *Cultures of Relatedness: New Approaches to the Study of Kinship*, Cambridge: Cambridge University Press.

Featherstone, M. (1995), *Undoing Culture: Globalization, Postmodernism and Identity*, London: Sage.

Franklin, S. and McKinnon, S. (2001), 'Relative Values: Reconfiguring Kinship Studies', in S. Franklin and S. McKinnon (eds), *Relative Values: Reconfiguring Kinship Studies*, Berkeley, Durham, NC and London: Duke University Press.

——, Lury, C. and Stacey, J. (2000), *Global Nature, Global Culture*, London: Sage.

Gilroy, P. (2000), *Between Camps: Nations, Cultures and the Allure of Race*, London: Penguin.

Goldberg, D.T. (1992), 'The Semantics of Race', *Ethnic and Racial Studies*, 15: 543–69.

Gupta, A. and Ferguson, J. (1992), 'Beyond "Culture": Space, Identity and the Politics of Difference', *Cultural Anthropology*, 7: 6–23.

Haraway, D. (1997), *Modest-Witness@SecondMillennium.FemaleMan©-MeetsOncoMouse™*, London and New York, Routledge.

Hickman, M. and Walter, M. (1995), 'Deconstructing Whiteness: Irish Women in Britain', *Feminist Review*, 50: 5–19.

Ignatiev, N. (1995), *How the Irish Became White*, London and New York: Routledge.

King, D. (2000), *Making Americans: Immigration, Race and the Origins of the Diverse Democracy*, Cambridge, MA and London: Harvard University Press.

Lloyd, D. (1999), *Ireland After History*, Cork: Cork University Press.

Longley, E. and Kiberd, D. (2001), *Multi-culturalism: the View from the Two Irelands*, Cork: Cork University Press.

Mac Laughlin, J. (1999), '"Pestilence on their backs, famine in their stomachs": the Racial Construction of Irishness and the Irish in Victorian Britain', in C. Graham and R. Kirkland (eds), *Ireland and Cultural Theory: The Mechanics of Authenticity*, London: Macmillan.

Malki, L. (1992), 'National Geographic: The Rooting of Peoples and the Territorialization of National Identity among Scholars and Refugees', *Cultural Anthropology*, 7: 24–44.

Marston, S. (1990), 'Who are "the People"?: Gender, Citizenship and the Making of the American Nation', *Environment and Planning D: Society and Space*, 20: 449–58.

Morash, C. (1997), 'Celticism: Between Race and Culture', *Irish Review*, 20: 29–36 and 44–5.

Nash, C. (2002), 'Genealogical Identities', *Environment and Planning D: Society and Space*, 20: 27–52.

Roediger, D. (1991), *The Wages of Whiteness: Race and the Making of the American Working Class*, London: Verso.

—— (1994), *Towards the Abolition of Whiteness: Essays on Race; Politics and Working Class History*, London: Verso.

—— (2002), 'Reflections on "Whiteness and Ethnicity in the History of 'White Ethnics' in the United States"', in P. Essed and D.T. Goldberg (eds), *Race Critical Theories*, Maldon, MA and Oxford: Blackwell.

Rontin, L. (ed.) (1999), *The Expanding Nation: Towards a Multi-Ethnic Ireland*, Dublin: Trinity College.

Strathern, M. (1992), *After Nature: English Kinship in the late Twentieth Century*, Cambridge: Cambridge University Press.

—— (1995), 'Nostalgia and the New Genetics', in D. Battaglia (ed.), *Rhetorics of Self-Making*, Berkeley, Los Angeles, and London: University of California Press.

—— (1996), 'Cutting the Network', *Journal of the Royal Anthropological Institute* (N.S.), 2: 517–35.

Walter, B. (1995), 'Irishness, Gender, and Place', *Environment and Planning D: Society and Space*, 13: 35–50.

—— (2001), *Outsiders Inside: Whiteness, Place and Irish Women*, London and New York: Routledge.

Waters, M.C. (1990), *Ethnic Options: Choosing Identities in America*, Berkeley, Los Angeles, and Oxford: University of California Press.

Part III
Trans/nations and Border Crossings

Part III
International Benefit Sharing

9

Transporting the Subject: Technologies of Mobility and Location in an Era of Globalization

Caren Kaplan

Travel Plans

'You have ruined our vacation', my students tease at the close of a course on the cultural studies of gender and travel. Since inflicting guilt and eliminating pleasure are not the goals of the course, I remind them that critique is not necessarily a form of rejection. Critique of what one loves and knows best is what we learn to do in feminist studies, where so many of us begin our work by looking at the family. Feminists critique the family by deconstructing it, historicizing its structures and practices, analysing its normalizing operations in specific contexts, and even re-envisioning or reworking it, but few of us reject our own families. So it is with an activity as complex and pervasive as travel. Moderns value mobility, especially leisure travel, and many of us take travelling for granted. But if travel is central to modernity, then the critique of travel must be a fundamental priority in contemporary critical practices. In this critical approach to deconstructing something that one engages deeply and cares about, the term 'travel' signifies the multiple aspects of an expanded field including transportation and communication technologies, divisions of labour, and representational practices. Travel in this expanded sense leads to a theoretical practice, to theorizing subjects and meaning in relation to the varied histories of the circulations of people, goods and ideas.

The relation between theory and travel is embedded in etymology. One of the older definitions of *theory* stemming from Greek antiquity refers to a 'body of *theors* sent by a state to perform some religious rite or duty'. These sacred envoys, while described as a 'solemn legation', apparently were also marked by their splendid dress and sumptuous mode of travel. What is most interesting, given more recent developments, is that the state-sponsored *theor* is also referred to as a 'spectator', as 'one who travels in order to see things'. This history spurs James Clifford to describe theory as a 'product of displacement, comparison, a certain distance' (Clifford 1989: 177). That is, theorizing requires the authenticating activity of travel, moving to see things as a witness and an observer. Also linked to the allusion to the dress and appearance of the *theor* is the archaic sense of theory as a 'sight' or 'spectacle,' tying the term even more firmly to another, 'theatre'. Looking and being looked at in turn may signal a performative dimension of knowledge formation that expands this inter-disciplinary definition of travel even further. Certainly this emphasis on the empowering properties of the visual, so integral to modern notions of subject formation and perspective since the European Enlightenment, resonates in the classical terms for travel and theory.

But if theory can be defined as a kind of travelling, travel can be defined as a manifestation of pain or work. Etymologically, *travel* is linked to *travail* or 'labour, toil, suffering, trouble'. Thus, in addition to the more commonplace meaning of taking a journey, *travel* evokes hard labour (including childbirth) and difficulty. This aspect of both travel and theory bears further examination: the labour of theorizing, the troubling of subjects of theory, or the work of travel and theory. Following this vein of etymological musing, Clifford defines travel as 'a range of practices for situating the self in a space or spaces grown too large, a form of both exploration and discipline' (Clifford 1989: 177). Edward Said also investi-gates the work of theory, its travel or travail, in his discussion of secular criticism and the production of knowledge. In his essay, 'Traveling Theory,' Said argues that the circulation of ideas and theories is an 'enabl-ing condition of intellectual activity' in modernity (Said 1983: 226). But the work of travelling theory is complex and not always easily accom-plished. The successful transportation of theory or ideas, he argues, requires four stages:

> First, there is a point of origin, or what seems like one, a set of initial circum-stances in which the idea came to birth or entered discourse. Second, there is a distance transversed, a passage through the pressure of various contexts as the idea moves from an earlier point to another time and place where it will come into a new prominence. Third, there is a set of conditions – call them conditions of acceptance or, as an inevitable part of acceptance, resistances – which then confronts the transplanted theory or idea, making possible its introduction or toleration, however alien it might appear to be. Fourth, the now full (or partly) accommodated (or incorporated) idea is to some extent trans-formed by its new uses, its new position in a new time and space (Said 1983: 226–7).

In this account of travel, there are references to birth, distance, resistance, incorporation and transformation. I am most interested in Said's situating of theory, in the stress on location in his description of travel. Both Said and Clifford emphasize the locational imperatives of any notion of travel. As Clifford writes in an essay that can be read as a companion piece to Said's, '. . . like any act of travel, theory begins and ends somewhere' (Clifford 1989: 177). To theorize, to critically engage or to know, one 'leaves home' (ibid.). The condition of estrangement or distance from a 'point of origin' or field, discipline, national or cultural context and so on has been identified as a foundational structure in modernist thought, and there is always more to be said about this complex articulation. But following Said's modernist and Clifford's postmodernist interventions into the production of theory and the work of the critic, I would like to focus on the imbrication of location in the discourse of travel. The trajectory of knowledge and ideas as they 'begin and end somewhere' speaks to a vital aspect of subject formation in modernity. In the current moment in metropolitan life, when so much of the world appears to be linked by global media, transnational finance and culture, and other manifestations of contemporary mobility and speed, how do we understand 'points of origin' and the 'where' of 'somewhere'? How do we theorize the locatedness of travel in an era of globalization?

Location is as difficult to take for granted as travel without an investigation of rhetorical and material histories. How subjects move or do not move tells us much about what counts as human, as culture and as knowledge. In particular, how do globalized information technologies, with their incumbent machinery and heavily freighted divisions of labour, come to be characterized as transitory and light, as playful practices of subjectivity that enable users to slip the moorings of location and materiality? Cyberspace may appear to be the ultimate vacation from the Puritan work ethic and from grounded industries of liberal modernity, but a closer look reveals location and materiality in the mobility and disembodied discursive practices of new information technologies. Yet, as technologies of transportation and communication become more and more disembodied, more and more displaced from corporeality and more and more a practice of mind or a simulation, the unified subject of the European Enlightenment is less and less a requirement. Whether or not we believe such a creature exists or ever existed, the shift in the paradigm of the subject is significant enough to warrant theorization.

Cyberphilia

June 21st 1995. If a date is needed for the start of the New Nomadic Age, this is as good as any. Late that afternoon, at Hakodate in Japan, Flight No. ANA857 was stalled on the local airport runway. The reason – a hijack. In the following 16 hours, twelve phone calls from passengers using their mobile phones told police that the hijacker was aged 22–30, that he wore sunglasses, jeans and white sneakers, that he was on the upper floor of the aircraft and that he appeared to be lightly armed. Acting on this information, police stormed the plane and arrested the hijacker without ill effects except that a stewardess was slightly injured and one of the passengers, pop singer Tokiko Kato, complained of being 'worn out and wanting to sleep' . . . There could be no better example of the power of one of the early tools of the New Nomadic Age – the mobile telephone – to alter events. The phone is just the start of it. Over the next decade technology will deliver to us a range of tools that will give us all the facilities of our homes and offices – in our pockets. (Makimoto and Manners 1997: 1–2)

At the turn of the twenty-first century, the rhetoric of cyberspace and information technologies relies heavily on the hyperbole of unlimited power through disembodied mobility. Whether we read theorizations of new cityscapes published by university presses or advertisements in magazines for wireless internet connections, references to boundless space, unfettered mobility and speedy transfers abound. In this heady environment, the promise of new technologies is couched in terms of ever-increasing powers of transformation and transport – of information, business, and self – and the benefits of surveillance and tracking. More and more in this context, the concept of a person or of human beings appears to depend on the attenuated possibilities of cyberspace. If the heavy, immovable facts of embodied existence can be ameliorated or discharged through the creation of new identities on the internet, for example, or through new collective personas or communities, then what or who counts as a person becomes transformed. The self is believed to have expanded capacities as soon as it is released from the fixed location of the body, built environment or nation. But the self is always somewhere, always located in some sense in some place, and cannot be totally unhoused. New technologies appear to promise ever-increasing degrees of disembodiment or detachment, yet they are as embedded in material relations as any other practices. They require hard industries as well as light ones; in addition to the bright and mobile world of designers and users, human hands build the machines in factories that are located in specific places regulated by particular political and economic practices. Thus, in the production of the machinery and materials of cyberspace, another form of mobility can be discerned, that of labour in this moment of globalization. Determined by exigency, diasporas and markets, this mobility is more strictly bounded than the apparent *jouissance* of cyberspace. But an understanding of the history of concepts and metaphors of displacement in modernity brings these diverse mobilities into relation with one another. They cannot be reduced to the same thing but they can be linked through representational legacies and political pasts and futures.

The rhetoric of cyberspace proposes a kind of travel that expands upon a long history of metaphors of displacement. The emancipation of ideas promised by flows across borders and boundaries is a Western Enlightenment dream – no boundaries for the mind of the subject. In this structuring fantasy, the body may be imprisoned or constrained, but through print media or communication technologies ideas can move where bodies cannot or achieve mobility in ways that are denied to bodies. Or, driven out of a homeland, pursuing personal safety or economic stability, the exiled or immigrant body brings its ideas and theories with it. Which bodies? Under what conditions? In Western modernity, universalized displacement is so structurally foundational for the unified subject that any examination of the material differences and uneven social relations that create and depend on distinctions is discouraged or mystified (Kaplan 1996). From the democratic spatialization of the public sphere to the interiorized consciousness of the bounded individual subject, Western modernity since the Enlightenment tends to privilege mobility of one kind or another. If differences between mobilities matter, the stakes in one kind or another can be summoned into and out of view as a matter of political convenience. Most Enlightenment political philosophies and social structures share the tendency to celebrate mobility, oscillating among democratic, imperialist and fascist notions of expansion and movement in various historical moments. Technologies emerge from this context and not the other way around. That is, the rhetoric of explanation and definition connected to most information and communication technologies is drawn from the same pool of metaphors generated in and through Western modernity.

These circulations and expansions appear to be economically, politically and intellectually beneficial, giving rise to innovation and new kinds of identities and communities. However, the movements can be viewed also as discrete, always uneven and infused with power relations of tremendous complexity. Thus, contemporary power relations require fixed locations and mobile circulations – both aspects are a crucial dynamic in capitalist cultures across the span of modernity. Perhaps this tension between mobility and location in the promise of the Enlightenment prompted Theodor Adorno's mid-twentieth-century aphorism: 'Dwelling, in the proper sense, is now impossible' (Adorno 1974: 38). Certainly, Adorno was deploring the horrors of war and his own refugee experience. But the bittersweet pathos of displacement's enabling powers for the artist, the energizing jolt that influxes of new populations bring to the economies and cultures of the metropoles, and the emergence of postcolonial aesthetics and cultural practices can be traced throughout the social theories of the Frankfurt School as well as in the work of Raymond Williams, for example (Williams 1989). The intense contradictions of late capitalism, especially notable in the modernist frictions between old and new, have given rise to impossibilities of all sorts; wonderful, horrifying, frustrating and worrisome. This postmodern condition, so famously celebrated and lamented by legions of critics and social commentators, can be seen as, if anything, the return of Enlightenment's contradictions writ larger and more powerfully thanks to globalized practices such as media, communications and transnational finance and business (Lyotard 1979; Harvey 1989). The oscillation and tension between the liberating promise of mobility and the security of fixed location is one of modernity's most enduring and complex oppositional binaries.

The value placed on mobility in representations of subjectivity in cyberspace or new technologies is not new, then, but can be seen to be the full articulation of something old: travel. Travel proceeds from some point in space and time, endures across a span of places, and results in an arrival or a return to a fixed site. More specifically, following the concept of the voyage of the Athenian *theor*, foundational to Western culture is the idea that travel produces the self, makes the subject through spectatorship and comparison with otherness. Thus, in this ideology of subjectivity, distance is the best perspective on and route toward knowledge of self and others. Self-knowledge, standpoint, then, requires a point of origin, a location that constitutes the subject as a viewer and a world of objects that can be viewed or surveyed (Gombrich 1956; Curry 1998).

Since the European Renaissance, the viewer's eye has been construed to be central to perception. This Cartesian visual scenario should not be oversimplified or generalized since it incorporates numerous versions and counter-versions that subvert or complicate the distancing gaze or 'scopic regime' of Enlightenment perspective (Jay 1988; Poole 1997). But it is reasonable to argue that sight is a privileged sense in the discourse of subjectivity and knowledge in Western modernity, providing significant metaphors for and influences on the design and implementation of technologies. The desire to visualize the invisible, to peer into otherwise occluded spaces of interiority or outer space, links exploration, expansion and sight to the constitution of science and medicine in the modern period (Cartwright 1995). The invention and use of the microscope, magnifying lenses and other devices generated metaphors of internal or local exploration that resonated with the activities of economic and political expansion in the world at large, activities that required new technologies of mapping, navigation and surveying.

The current moment is no less concerned with visuality and technologies generated by modern scopic regimes. As Barbara Maria Stafford has written, communication technologies organize information in increasingly disembodied forms: 'We communicate with images of people, with "artificial persons," existing as bites, bytes, and bits of optical and aural messages. Flesh and blood, or tactility, recede in the presence of mediated encounters' (Stafford 1993: 26). Similarly, Donna Haraway has argued that the 'perverse capacity' of Western Enlightenment vision distances 'the knowing subject from everybody and everything in the interests of unfettered power' (Haraway 1991: 188). Haraway warns that new technologies are without apparent limit, extending the worst tendencies of Enlightenment subjectivity – the rending of subject and object in the name of power:

> (T)he eye of any ordinary primate like us can be endlessly enhanced by sonography systems, magnetic resonance imaging, artificial intelligence-linked graphic manipulation systems, scanning electron microscopes, computer-aided tomography scanners, color enhancement techniques, satellite surveillance systems, home and office VDTs, cameras for every purpose from filming the mucous membrane lining the gut cavity of a marine worm living in the vent gases on a fault between continental plates to mapping a planetary hemisphere elsewhere in the solar system (Haraway 1991: 189).

This descriptive explanation evokes the crowded and speedy vision of technoscience in advanced capitalism and, in particular, the normalized micro-miniaturization of science and surveillance in metropolitan daily life. Haraway charges that such a scopic regime begets 'unregulated gluttony; all perspective gives way to infinitely mobile vision'. She calls for a reconfigured socialist feminist praxis of objectivity to discipline vision and make manifest its situated materiality : 'Feminist objectivity is about limited location and situated knowledge, not about transcendence and splitting of subject and object' (Haraway 1991: 189–90).

The argument for 'situated knowledge' as a new form of looking and knowing theorizes embodied spaces as ideal communities whose members generate collaborative identities through learning 'how to see faithfully from another's point of view', even, as Haraway puts it, 'when the other is our own machine' (ibid.). Who are these truly different others in our world who will teach us their standpoint? Does metropolitan Western culture still produce truly different others who must be cast out in order to be reclaimed? Do the romantic narratives of banishment and rescue still serve the same epistemological function? To see faithfully 'from another's point of view', however, suggests something authentic and real, utterly distinct, that can be lovingly and attentively learned. In this regard, it is difficult not to think of Mary Shelley's scientist and his monster, engaged in their tragic Hegelian dialectic. If the other is always required for our making, then we must have a clear sense, first of all, that we are a discrete entity that is empowered to this extent and, second, that we can visualize and thus know the monster. That is, to continue the allusion, can Dr Frankenstein and the creature acknowledge their kinship and shared culture through anything else besides horrified recognition and enraged rejection?

The pleasures of the possibility of this new relation beyond identification and rejection, figured as between plural subjects or subjects who are situated and embodied, are argued for in N. Katherine Hayles's study of the technoculture of 'posthumans'. Careful to distinguish herself from the glib 'techno-ecstasies' of much of the discourse surrounding cyberspace, Hayles proposes an ironic use of the 'ambiguities of the plural' that leads toward a posthuman collectivity: '. . . an "I" transformed into the "we" of autonomous agents operating together to make a self' (Hayles 1999: 6). The performative dimension of this conceptualization of we echoes Haraway's concern with the excesses of fantasies of dislocation and unlimited scopic powers:

> If my nightmare is a culture inhabited by posthumans who regard their bodies as fashion accessories rather than the ground of being, my dream is a version of the posthuman that embraces the possibilities of information technologies without being seduced by fantasies of unlimited power and disembodied immortality, that recognizes and celebrates finitude as a condition of human being, and that understands human life is embedded in a material world of great complexity, one on which we depend for our continued survival (Hayles 1999: 5).

Both Hayles and Haraway call for a reconsideration of embodiment as a way to counter the radical separation between knower and known, viewer and object. The detachment of body from pluralized situation results in commodification, individualism and alienation. Because of technologies of distance and disembodiment, subjects are tracked, identified, charted, tabulated, pictured and filed. In clusters of data recombining and sorting themselves endlessly in machines, subjects have an existence, a virtual reality, of which they are never fully aware (Poster 1996). Simply stating distaste for a life as a bundle of data is not very effective. Few modern subjects can exist without any interface with aspects of data as identity. The state does not recognize or take care of subjects who cannot be hailed in this systematic process. Yet computer-assisted technologies of surveillance, tracking and tracing of subjects have multiple facets. They not only imprison and oppress people but also provide them with consumer pleasures, prosthetic powers of imagination and subjectivity, as well as convenience and arenas of play. Do these contradictions augur hegemony or resistance?

Digital Transfers

In a piece published in *New Left Review* a few years ago, Julian Stallabrass takes a firm stand, claiming that cyberspace is nothing but 'hi-tech Hegelianism' (Stallabrass 1995: 8). Arguing that the nature of data has changed dramatically under digitalization, he points to the printed phone book as an example of an older format – a material object that is portable but also heavy and awkward, requiring an understanding of the logic of the numbers. But in cyberspace, he argues, information can be 'extracted from its material support and purified' so that it can 'be in many places at once, and sent at near the speed of light' (ibid.). Yet cyberspace never does away with representation because the only way to access or use the data is through 'a sensorial form' (ibid.). This tension between a desire for liberation from form and its recuperation in simulation haunts many of the discussions of cyberculture. As Stallabrass points out, there is always an unacknowledged or suppressed location in the midst of all this zippy mobility, primarily through the necessary assumption of visual form on the computer screen:

> The Hegelianism of the cyberphiles is not one of process, a form of becoming . . . Rather, it is a fixed state in which the end of history and the total realization of mind is finally achieved: in this way it is a fixed Platonic form. Yet data, which must be handled in the visual arena of cyberspace, like numbers on the stock market, has already been abstracted from the real world and made fungible. Its particularity has already been stripped away in its reduction to number. In cyberspace, where it is given an apprehensible form, this data must be constantly animated, as if in a movie. Given that the function of virtual representation is tied to movement, a fixed perfection like that of architecture

will certainly elude these forms. Yet even these clean, mobile cyberspace forms can never show the material suffering behind a row of financial figures, for this has been stripped away a long time ago in the very collection of data. When a form is restored to this data, the 'reality' it adopts is utterly cleansed of anything that cannot be exchanged (Stallabrass 1995: 9).

As Stallabrass argues, much of the discourse of mobility and displacement vis-à-vis the information technologies and cyberspace fixes and locates through the appearance of movement and flux. Yet in critiquing the romanticization of mobility, he reveals a deep yearning for a humanist representational practice. In asking how it might be possible to 'show' the 'material suffering behind a row of financial figures', he counters the dominant discourse, which evacuates the historical and material context from the things of this world, leaving behind static, alienated numbers, functions or pure lines of rationality.

Is there another approach? The telephone is an instructive example. Phone lines are still necessary for cyberspace – although wireless trans-missions seem to be about to replace them. Wireless telecommunication allows for seemingly infinite mobility. Yet, our gains in time, speed and mobility still leave open questions of context and embodiment. As Peter Hugill points out, telegraphic messages lack 'the expressive meaning inherent in human speech', and thus they are 'subject to misinterpretation' (Hugill 1999: 21). The problem of immediacy, recognition and embodied resonance is present throughout the history of modern communication technologies. But Carolyn Marvin's account of the cultural effects of electricity suggests that people used devices such as the telephone in ways that sutured time and space – such as the two women she describes who waltzed around a Western Union parlour in the late 1880s listening to the music of a hotel band through a telephone receiver (Marvin 1988: 211). Stephen Kern says that the telephone not only allowed people to speak across great distances, it also encouraged them to 'think about what others were feeling and to respond at once . . .' (Kern 1983: 69). For all the wonderful examples of crazy people calling dearly departed relatives on the phone or European aristocrats fighting vainly to keep the technology for their own spectacles and amusements, in its infancy the telephone, finally, recuperated the dominant culture's communities of friends and families versus strangers along with other codes and practices of power (Marvin 1988: 197). If telephones 'whet the appetite for visits', as Kern puts it, expanding lived spaces and intensifying experiences of both intimacy and separation, they also allowed men to 'take liberties' with the unseen but palpably 'present' female operators (Kern 1983: 215).

The shift in expectations and ideas about embodied corporeality, presence and power in relation to communication technologies such as the telephone give us a good sense of some of the questions we might extend to new information technologies. As Kenneth Lipartito says, the telephone made possible a highly successful 'techno-labor system' that segmented women into lower-paying, limited employment as operators (Lipartito 1994: 1091). Thus, historical examples remind us that embodiment does not always translate into transformative practices. Yet gendered embodiment in the matrix of mobility and location is accomplished in complex and uneven ways. For example, the tension between distance and home is worth considering in relation to the business of phone sex, a profession that employs a good number of women at the turn of this century. Here the contemporary emphasis on subjects as data finds its way into a debate about the relation between workers and clients, bodies across space and time, and the politics of location in sex work. In her description of her fieldwork with female phone-sex workers, Sandy Stone argues that the commercial transaction of the world's oldest profession over the phone involves a kind of data compression:

> Consciously or unconsciously, phone sex workers translate all the modalities of experience into audible forms . . . The sex workers took an extremely complex, highly detailed set of behaviors, translated them into a single sense modality, then further boiled them down to a series of highly compressed tokens. They then squirted those tokens down a voice-grade phone line. At the other end of the line the recipient of all this effort added boiling water, so to speak, and reconstituted the tokens into a fully detailed set of images and interactions in multiple sensory modes. (Stone 1995: 396)

On one level, we might argue that all commercial sex involves a kind of compression and tokenization, a playing-out of signs and emblems in a fashion similar to that described by Stone. What captures my attention in Stone's discussion is the way she describes the distinction between information and bodies:

> (W)hat was being sent back and forth over the wires wasn't just information, it was *bodies*. The majority of people assume erotics implies bodies; a body is part of the idea of erotic interaction and its concomitants, and the erotic sensibilities are mobilized and organized around the idea of a physical body that is the seat of the whole thing. The sex workers' descriptions were invariably and quite directly about physical bodies . . . (ibid).

Stone describes a form of travel – bodies compressed into data and transported via 'voice-grade phone line' to some kind of proximity and experience with other bodies elsewhere. But we could also say that the sex workers' *work* was about power and labour as well as diverse kinds of desire. We could also recognize that there might be more to corporeality than what can enter into the performance of this kind of communication – such as the sex worker's sneezing fit or hunger for lunch. Thus, the physical body at the heart of the communication remains a matter of representation. Stone bases a kind of resistance or progressive practice on this notion of a cyborgian mobility that can be corporeal in its eroticism and disembodied as an articulation of specific technologies, arguing that '. . . a disembodied subjectivity messes with *whereness*. In cyberspace you are everywhere and somewhere and nowhere, but almost never here in the positivist sense', disrupting the location technologies of the state, which struggle to maintain the appearance of the 'socially and legally constituted individual' in the face of continual slippage and flux (Stone 1995: 399).

The argument that positivist 'whereness' can be displaced to produce a subject who is 'many persons in many places simultaneously' (Stone 1995: 400) resonates with recent observations that territoriality is less and less viable or more and more fraught (Keith and Pile 1993; Gregory 1994; Pile and Thrift 1995; Duncan 1996). It speaks, as well, to a desire for a transformation of the more constraining and oppressive aspects of advanced capitalism. National governments use every locating and defining tool in their bag of tricks to preserve their sovereignty through the policing of borders and to limit benefits through the production of citizenship. The technology that promises so much to an inventive and progressive trans-gender theorist such as Stone also allows surveillance and exclusion. If financial data and corporate practices are less and less bounded by the nation, if subjects perform in increasingly multiple ways in cyberspace, how do we account for the multitudinous locating and tracking capacities of digital information technologies? Is there a critical practice in between Stone's desire for transported multiplicities of pleasure and Stallabrass's desire for a way to import the suffering of multitudes into the transfer of data? Stone and Stallabrass call for a recognition of their concerns through engineering, if you will. Both need to see and feel the fungible, legible and physical in such invisible transfers. Beyond the liberal constructs of the unified Enlightenment subject, Stone seeks pleasure and Stallabrass seeks justice.

Circuits

The deconstruction of the binary of mobility and location in the discourses
of communication and information technologies, especially in digital or
internet transactions and processes, animates the question of embodiment
in historically specific ways. Race matters in cyberspace as do all the other
identificatory epistemologies of the last several hundred years (Kolko et
al. 2000). The figure of the cyborg, a mix of flesh and machine, has been
discussed at great length by numerous commentators, and, although I do
not dwell on it in this essay, it is a vital player in these questions of the
boundaries and binaries of modernity (Haraway 1991; Gray 1995; Balsamo
1996; Bell and Kennedy 2000). The attachment of qualities and characteristics to a body is strained to the limit by data compression, wireless
transmissions, miniaturization and other techniques and attributes of new
technologies. The promise that the bulky devices of home and office will
be transformed into tools that can fit in our pockets, glibly prophesied by
Tsugio Makimoto and David Manners in their anecdote about the foiled
airplane hijacking, only underscores the cyborgian moment.

I remain sceptical, however, of the value of cyber-theorizing unless the
travail, the labour, of these travels can be articulated more carefully. For
example, I learn many things in Stone's smart and insightful essay, but I
do not learn how much the phone-sex workers get paid and whether it is
enough to live on. Posing questions about divisions of labour cannot be
left out of an inquiry into representational practices in information and
communication technologies. Even in Stallabrass's critique of the idealism
of Internet commentary, there is no discussion of the people who make the
devices that are used to achieve the dream of subjectivity (or to order plane
tickets or to look up a book in a distant library). Who suffers, who troubles,
who works these technologies of travel? To keep one's heart and mind,
corporeal or cyber, on the subject of poverty and misery in the contemporary moment requires a shift of a certain kind. Following Gayatri Spivak's
destabilization of radical chic in 'Can the Subaltern Speak?', we can no
longer simply summon resistance in the figure of the Other to suit our
critical needs (Spivak 1988). Politically progressive representation has
figured these Frankensteinian creatures in despair and suffering alone, for
example, picturing the victims of the global assembly-line as geared only
for production, their labour power usurped for the surplus value of the
transnational corporation. Recent scholarship on the new proletariat
sketches a somewhat different picture – a female worker, most likely, who
by gender, age and culture is marked for a specific kind of labour under

flexible accumulation, who sends money home but also spends her wages on consumer goods (Schein 1994; Kang 1997; Sen and Stivens 1998).

Whether it is the government, non-governmental organizations or well-meaning academics, everyone seems to have a view of the proper attitude toward and representational practice for the subject of poverty. At the turn of the nineteenth century, the Left labour unions sought to discipline the female shirtwaist factory workers because of their flamboyant style and love of fashion. They did not *look* like downtrodden victims of capitalism, although their wages were low enough. Nan Enstad has argued that working women in New York during this period were produced as subjects through consumption and that their identity and agency as political organizers and workers were hampered by the puritanism and masculinism of the socialist union leadership (Enstad 1998). Thus, subjects of labour history can be reconfigured in all manner of ways; the gendered politics of shopping and dress can challenge the methodologies of studying production and the origin of social change. In addition to gender and race politics in the United States, investigating the geopolitics of transnational divisions of labour can highlight the tensions between mobility and location, between consumption and production, and between resistance and hegemony for a more useful critical analysis of the workings of labor and technology, including their representation.

Transnational subjects are produced through location as well as mobility, certainly, as national economies dictate who moves to obtain work and who stays put. These subjects are not produced simply through the division between production and consumption. If there are new consumer subjects, new methodologies are required to understand them. Electronics workers or domestic workers in transit for work purposes do not have to be viewed as entirely separate from tourists or other kinds of travellers; a notion of travel as an expanded field in transnationality produces differently linked subjects. I am not arguing that the monied tourist is the same subject as the migrant worker or that the phone-sex worker is the same subject as the academic conference-goer. But a theorization of travel as a Foucauldian field with diverse points in tension with one another or even as a continuum with a point of origin and a discrete itinerary of sites, rather than the older binary format of 'this' versus 'that', may engender more plural subjects. Besides viewing the dispersal or disembodiment of the subject in cyberspace as reinforcing the discourse of mobility in modernity, are there other practices that generate flexible or multiple subjects allowing people to reveal the contradictory linkage of location and mobility?

For much of modernity, Western or metropolitan subjects have sought mobility as a panacea for the constraints on identity in capitalist cultures. Yet a concerted concern with location as the source of knowledge and identity has asserted itself in myriad ways. The paradox of standpoint – its Cartesian individualist and rationalist legacy along with its communitarian identity politics – propels theories of displacement and mobility. New information and communication technologies both continue and disturb this history. A deconstructive approach to cyberspace might articulate its divisions of labour and materiality, its travail in the sense of travel, along with its spectacles and pleasures. If theory travels, if knowledge remains linked to displacement, what comes to the fore when embodiment enters the circuit? The materiality of theory in an era of globalization may mean that subjects will travel to know in any number of ways.

Acknowledgements

I would like to thank the coordinators of the special topic issue of *PMLA*, from which this article is reprinted, especially Tony Kaes, for their interest in my work. In addition, my warmest thanks go to Tim Cresswell for his editorial and intellectual support as well as for his invitation to attend the Second Annual Colloquium of the Centre for the Study of Spaces in Modernity, at the University of Wales, 26–28 November 1999 where I presented an early version of this chapter. I have learned a great deal from the work of Ginette Verstraete, Jenny Terry, Bill Worthen and Mimi Nguyen. Their friendship and conversation resonate in this chapter (although I may not have managed to meet their erudition and depth of scholarly insight). As always, I owe thanks to Inderpal Grewal and Eric Smoodin for talking, reading and giving me suggestions about what to pack.

References

Adorno, T. (1974), *Minima Moralia: Reflections from a Damaged Life*, E.F.N. Jephcott (trans.), London: NLB.
Balsamo, A. (1996), *Technologies of the Gendered Body: Reading Cyborg Women*, Durham, NC: Duke University Press.
Bell, D. and Kennedy, B.M. (eds) (2000), *The Cybercultures Reader*, London: Routledge.

Cartwright, L. (1995), *Screening the Body: Tracing Medicine's Visual Culture*, Minneapolis: University of Minnesota Press.

Clifford, J. (1989), 'Notes on Theory and Travel', *Inscriptions,* 5: 177–88.

Curry, M.R. (1998), *Digital Places: Living With Geographic Information Technologies,* London: Routledge.

Duncan, N. (ed.) (1996), *Bodyspace: Destabilizing Geographies of Gender and Sexuality*, London: Routledge.

Enstad, N. (1998), 'Fashioning Political Identities: Cultural Studies and the Historical Construction of Political Subjects', *American Quarterly*, 50: 745–82.

Gombrich, E.H. (1956), *Art and Illusion: A Study in the Psychology of Pictorial Representation*, Princeton: Princeton University Press.

Gray, C.H. (ed.) (1995), *The Cyborg Handbook*, New York: Routledge.

Gregory, D. (1994), *Geographical Imaginations*, Cambridge: Blackwell.

Haraway, D. (1991), *Simians, Cyborgs, and Women: The Reinvention of Nature,* New York: Routledge.

Harvey, D. (1989), *The Condition of Postmodernity: An Enquiry into the Origins of Cultural Change*, Oxford: Blackwell.

Hayles, K.N. (1999), *How We Became Posthuman: Virtual Bodies in Cybernetics, Literature, and Informatics,* Chicago and London: University of Chicago Press.

Hugill, P.J. (1999), *Global Communications Since 1844: Geopolitics and Technology,* Baltimore: Johns Hopkins University Press.

Jay, M. (1988), *Force-Fields: Between Intellectual History and Cultural Critique*, New York: Routledge.

Kang, L.H. (1997), 'Si(gh)ting Asian/American Women as Transnational Labor', *positions: east asia cultures critique*, 5: 403–38.

Kaplan, C. (1996), *Questions of Travel: Postmodern Discourses of Displacement*, Durham, NC: Duke University Press.

Keith, M. and Pile, S. (eds) (1993), *Place and the Politics of Identity*, London: Routledge.

Kern, S. (1983), *The Culture of Time and Space, 1880–1918*, Cambridge, MA: Harvard University Press.

Kolko, B.E., Nakamura, L. and Rodman, G.B. (eds) (2000), *Race in Cyberspace*, New York: Routledge.

Lipartito, K. (1994), 'When Women Were Switches: Technology, Work, and Gender in the Telephone Industry, 1890–1920,' *The American Historical Review*, 90(4): 1074–1111.

Lyotard, J.F. (1979), *La condition postmoderne: rapport sur le savoir*, Paris: Editions de Minuit.

Makimoto, T. and Manners, D. (1997), *Digital Nomad*, Chichester: John Wiley & Sons.

Marvin, C. (1988), *When Old Technologies Were New: Thinking About Electric Communication in the Late Nineteenth Century*, Oxford: Oxford University Press.

Pile, S. and Thrift, N. (eds) (1995), *Mapping the Subject: Geographies of Cultural Transformation*, London: Routledge.

Poole, D. (1997), *Vision, Race, and Modernity: A Visual Economy of the Andean Image World*, Princeton: Princeton University Press.

Poster, M. (1996), 'Databases as Discourse: or, Electronic Interpellations,' in D. Lyon and E. Zureik (eds), *Computers, Surveillance, and Privacy*, Minneapolis: University of Minnesota Press.

Said, E.W. (1983), 'Traveling Theory', in idem, *The World, the Text, and the Critic*, Cambridge, MA: Harvard University Press.

Schein, L. (1994), 'The Consumption of Color and the Politics of White Skin in Post-Mao China', *Social Text*, 41: 141–64.

Sen, K. and Stivens, M. (eds) (1998), *Gender and Power in Affluent Asia*, London: Routledge.

Spivak, G.C. (1988), 'Can the Subaltern Speak?' in C. Nelson and L. Grossberg (eds), *Marxism and the Interpretation of Culture*, Urbana: University of Illinois Press.

Stafford, B.M. (1993), *Body Criticism: Imaging the Unseen in Enlightenment Art and Medicine*, Cambridge, MA: MIT Press.

Stallabrass, J. (1995), 'Empowering Technology: The Exploration of Cyberspace,' *New Left Review*, 211: 3–32.

Stone, S. (1995), 'Split Subjects, Not Atoms; or, How I Fell in Love With My Prosthesis', in C.H. Gray (ed.), *The Cyborg Handbook*, New York: Routledge.

Williams, R. (1989), *The Politics of Modernism: Against the New Conformists*, London: Verso.

10

Technological Frontiers and the Politics of Mobility in the European Union

Ginette Verstraete

Let me begin with a striking case study: the (temporary) joint venture between the Belgian harbour Zeebrugge and the American company DielectroKinetic Laboratories (DKL): 'The Science of Saving Lives'. The harbour used DKL's most important product, the LifeGuard, for the detection of stowaways in trailers for the greater part of 1999.[1] The LifeGuard is a gun-shaped remote sensing device that is supposed to work according to the principles of dielectrophoresis, better known as the principle of the compass:[2]

> When a compass needle points to the North Pole, it is reacting to the irregular magnetic field – also called a nonuniform magnetic field. In a nonuniform field, one part of the field is stronger than the other, and material without charge of its own is pulled toward the strongest part of the field, which physicists call the maximum spatial gradient position.[3]

The neutral material in this case is the $6000 to $15,000 LifeGuard. The nonuniform magnetic field to which it reacts like a compass is the ultra-low-frequency signals of a beating heart's electromagnetic field. The antenna of the gun is said to point to the electrical field surrounding a human heart up to 500 metres away, not only in the open, but also through concrete and steel walls, through earthen barriers, in moving vehicles, and under water. The LifeGuard, designed by American military engineers, was originally used for law enforcement (to scan buildings for the presence of criminals), for search and rescue (to detect persons in a sunken ship or in a house on fire) and for security (to detect unwanted visitors). The port of Zeebrugge began to use it in February 1999, faced by an 'uncontrollable' amount of refugees hiding in trailers and containers on their way to Britain.[4] Since US companies, especially Ford, and Vauxhall in Britain, were incurring damages to their goods because of the stowaways, the pressure on Zeebrugge to find more efficient ways of detecting them before departure was immense. After all, Zeebrugge was trying very hard to sell itself as *the* international place of transit in the car industry before Vlissingen (in the Netherlands) ran away with the prize. Thus, checks had to be made more thorough and less time-consuming. The port of Zeebrugge hired a Belgian private security firm who in turn rented one of the LifeGuards: 'the science of saving lives' became the science of removing them. Indeed, once the stowaways were detected, police officers would be called onto the scene to take them to the law-enforcement offices, from where the refugees were either sent to closed refugee centres or released on the streets with the order to leave the European Union's 'Schengen space' (see p. 228 in this volume) in five days.

The stakes were high, the money was big, and the marketing strategies developed accordingly. DKL redesigned its website immediately to accommodate this emerging market in the removal of illegal refugees. The security firm too placed the LifeGuard as a major attraction on its website and it sent its guards to the United States to be trained and to get, as the only firm in Europe, the certificate necessary to use the instrument and to train other future customers. Local and international newspapers and television crews were invited to attend the launching of this high-tech revolutionary device at Zeebrugge.[5]

But the biggest investment in this sophisticated detection of refugees came from the national authorities who used the images of stowaways huddled in trailers to reaffirm the necessity of erecting firm frontiers to discourage the Eastern European smugglers from making money out of the pitiful plight of these innocent victims 'from Kosovo' (it was around the time of NATO's war against Milosevic). Twisting the logic of the Fortress Europe and NATO mentality to their own advantage, authorities at a national level were quick to disclaim any responsibility for the situation and to proclaim more severe, preferably technologized, border controls. Cold War rhetoric was dug up again to legitimate and increase the expensive battle against the basic causes here: the Eastern European mafia. No word was ever said about the possible involvement of some Belgian truckers and transport companies. Above all, there was no word about the contradictory logic of a European Union investing massively in the very *national* border patrol that makes the *transnational* flow of money possible, an investment which makes the distinction between border maintenance and border crossing, legal and illegal capital, the local and the global very tenuous indeed.

So let us have a closer look at the contradictory logic that internally divides the European Union's 'Schengen space'. In what follows, I will analyse the EU's 'geopolitics of mobility'[6] as grounded in the concept of free movement through a European space without internal frontiers by subjects firmly located in national territory and identity, and in white property ownership. I will argue that this contradictory notion of unlimited mobility marked by the borders of the white capitalist nation state aims to serve a triple function: generalizing the national subject's position as European citizenship;[7] expanding national sovereignty to the external borders of the EU; and projecting the EU's national differences over the admission of migrants and refugees onto non-European 'others', onto people that cannot enter European space other than illegally, as criminals.[8] Problems emerge, however, when those illegal 'aliens' are so numerous within the EU that they can no longer be made invisible as the occasional criminal: instead they pose the question as to how various racial and ethnic bodies get structurally produced at the conjuncture between national and European space. In the face of these unwanted visitors, the (historical and spatial) limits of the European space-without-frontiers let themselves be felt. I will demonstrate how the incapacity of the nation states to tackle Europe's 'problems of migration' together, and to think in terms other than national sovereignty and national interest, reveals the extent to which the EU's post-industrial post-nationalism is still based on the old white nation state project, including its economic, ethnic and racial differences. In this current phase of transition from national to European space, we are confronted with the links and disjunctures between old national conflicts and nation-based divisions on the one hand and newly emergent forms of differentiation within the EU, but also between the EU and its multiple ethnic 'aliens', on the other.

My analysis of the multiple contradictions of Europe's freewheeling free-market citizenship – of Europe's common market as the fifteen nation states writ large – will show that its external and internal frontiers, the global and the local, are mutually constitutive and that therefore any emphasis on a homogeneous European mobile citizenship is going to be based on the massive erasure – on the massive production through negation – of local particularities of nationality, race and ethnicity, and on the removal of the groups of people marked by those particularities. Paraphrasing Liisa Malkki's critique of the Western objectification of refugees, one could speak in this context of the technological reproduction of stowaways (literally: stowed *away*) as local 'externality' or 'matter out of place' (Malkki 1992). In a space of unlimited mobility for a very limited group of people – Europe's propertied nationals – borders are abundant, the production and consumption of 'others' immense. What the example of Zeebrugge ultimately shows is that in this present moment of transfiguring the national into the transnational, the EU can only exist by way of a state-sanctioned traffic in illegal 'aliens' and their displacement through commodification. Let me explain.

Borderless Movement in Schengen Space

Ever since the Treaty of Rome (1957), which installed the European Economic Community, Europe has identified itself in terms of the 'four freedoms': free movement of goods, of people, of services and of capital. Basic to the idea of the European Community, held together by a common market, is the recognition that 'every citizen of the Union shall have the right to move and reside freely within the territory of the Member States' (Bainbridge 1998: 274). To that end, the Schengen Agreement was signed in 1985 and has applied throughout most of the European Union since 1995.[9] It implemented the gradual abolition of national border controls (which became common frontiers), and replaced them with limited passport and other document checks. It also installed closer cooperation between border police, the harmonization of taxes on imported and exported goods, and the abolition of duty-free goods.

The Schengen Agreement was meant to: minimize delays caused by traffic congestion and identity checks; stimulate the free and competitive flow of goods, money and people; create a common European market of a scale that would improve productivity, distribution and consumption; attract large foreign investments; and enable Europe to compete with the United States and East Asia. But it also had a strong ideological dimension: with the disappearance of state borders came the image, and hopefully experience, of a truly united European 'community'. The opening sentences of the Schengen Agreement leave little doubt as to its intention:

> The governments of [the signing countries, BeNeLux, France and Germany] . . . Aware that the increasingly closer union of the peoples of the Member States of the European Communities should be manifested through freedom to cross internal frontiers for all nationals of the Member States and in the free movement of goods and services.

> Anxious to affirm the solidarity between their peoples by removing the obstacles to free movement at the common frontiers between the States of the Benelux Economic Union, the Federal Republic of Germany and the French Republic, Considering the progress already achieved within the European Communities with a view to ensuring the free movement of persons, goods and services . . . have agreed as follows. (Select Committee 1989: 35)

To eliminate a history of paralysing conflicts of interests between the European Community's various nation states, to suppress the memory of a continent recently riven by two major wars, to transcend the old state divisions of this heterogeneous club and to smooth the passages toward a unified Europe, internal national differences were displaced and translated as the differences between Europe and its others. The disappearance of internal frontiers, it was argued, had to go hand in hand with the introduction of firm external frontiers to keep illegal immigrants, terrorists and drug-dealers out, and guarantee internal security and stability. With the free movement of goods and citizens in a European space without frontiers came the problem of how to detain those who, as non-EU citizens '*sans papiers*', posed a threat to this borderless territory. In other words, new frontiers had to be implemented to be able to distinguish between Europeans and non-Europeans, and between (authorized) travel and (unauthorized) migration. The freedom of mobility for some (citizens, tourists, business people) could only be made possible through the organized exclusion of others forced to move around as illegal 'aliens', migrants, or refugees. So with the production of a mobile citizenship in a Europe without (symbolic and literal) 'internal frontiers' came the tightening up of checks for immigrants and refugees at the 'external borders'. In the terms of the Schengen Agreement, external frontiers are points of entry for 'aliens' from non-Schengen countries: mostly airports, seaports and of course all the land frontiers in the most southern and eastern border countries – Spain, Italy, Greece and the old Eastern Germany – all of whom carry most of the burden of this agreement on the closing of the external frontiers.

The internal (domestic) frontiers (between European states) that disappeared in the travel of European citizens re-emerged as highly guarded external (international) frontiers (between EU and non-EU countries) in the movement of foreigners, especially immigrants and refugees. That is why a lot of European airports started to rebuild their infrastructures and divide them into domestic and international terminals: the domestic ones without checks, the international ones with at least two checkpoints – one for EU citizens with a smooth transit-regime, one for non-EU citizens with long queues. So rather than simply having disappeared – as the European rhetoric goes – borders have multiplied: permeable ones for some and durable ones for others. Alternatively, the same borders have accrued at least two meanings, two functions, two institutional settings according to the territory they demarcate: as a passage between two member states they are internal, as the border between EU and non-EU they are external. Similarly, borders differ enormously according to the people crossing them: for EU citizens (and for passengers who have embarked within the EU) they function as passageways; for non-Europeans with the right documents they are temporary check-points; for the people '*sans papiers*' they are points of return.

Not only have the Schengen countries built strong external barriers, but internal measures have also been taken to guarantee that only EU nationals (not EU residents) enjoy unlimited mobility.[10] Systematic controls at land frontiers have been displaced and relocated inland in the form of random spot-checks in the vicinity of the border on the one hand and arbitrary stop-and-search checks in the streets on the other. Both forms of control mostly consist of a quick *visual check* to see whether the traveller or pedestrian *looks* 'okay'. To give an example: I am occasionally stopped by – usually white male – police officers in search of drug dealers at the internal border I cross every day between my home in Belgium and my workplace in the Netherlands four miles down the road. Looking relatively clean and very white, I have never been asked to show any documents. My looks and the colour of my skin provide me with free mobility. The reverse is true as well: ethnic minorities in Brussels and Rotterdam are constantly being stopped and searched and asked for identification documents. Not only does this increase racial tensions, it also violates the basic human rights of the freedom of movement, the right to privacy, and the right to equal treatment. According to Alund, '[t]here is a growing interconnection between reinforced external barriers and internal constraints such as discrimination in the labour market, segregation in housing, political marginalisation and racism in everyday life' (Alund 1999: 148). Writing of the criminalization of illegal immigrants in the Netherlands, Engbersen and van der Leun comment:

> In practice, instead of targeting all undocumented immigrants, the immigration and local police target only those who cause inconvenience and display criminal behaviour. As a result of this selectivity, specific categories of undocumented immigrants rarely come into contact with the Immigration Police or local police departments . . . the daily police routine of arresting immigrants also plays a role . . . The police utilize informal rules and 'suspect typologies' to apprehend individuals and groups . . . These informal yet institutionalized rules lead inevitably to unequal probabilities of being apprehended by the police. It is less likely for undocumented Surinamese immigrants and immigrants from East and Middle Europe to be apprehended ('they will probably be legal') than for immigrants from Morocco, Algeria and other African countries. (Engbersen and van der Leun 1998: 208–9)

Of course, ethnic minority groups are not homogeneous: class, but also sexuality and gender, are important markers of difference. The association of migrant *women* with criminality, which Engbersen and van der Leun fail to discuss, often takes place within the context of the largely undocumented spheres of prostitution. As several critics have pointed out, the gradual closing of the European borders since the end of the 1980s has affected ethnic minority men and women differently (Anthias and Yuval-Davis 1992). In the words of Phizacklea:

> In the UK, for instance, despite formal sex equality in immigration law, the application of immigration rules is both sexist and racist. If a British Asian woman asks for permission for her non-British Asian husband to join her she is likely to be refused because it is very often claimed that the primary purpose for their marriage was to get him into Britain. If British Asian men or white British women seek permission to bring in their spouses their motives are far less likely to be questioned. (Phizacklea 1998: 30)

Women from non-EU countries are mostly allowed into Europe now only within the frame of family reunion, which makes them totally dependent on a male-regulated private sphere. In the same vein, women refugees who now flee to Europe because they are persecuted on the basis of gender and sexuality (through, for example, genital mutilation, forced marriages, rape or state-imposed population control) have less chance of being given asylum here because their cases are seen to belong to the private sphere, in which no state can interfere, while asylum is considered a right endowed in response to persecution within the – implicitly male – public sphere of war and politics (Bhabha 1999a). That the female body has for centuries been the site of state regulation in Western and non-Western countries is comfortably forgotten in these instances of judgement. Given this persistent association of migrant and refugee women with intimacy and family life, it is no wonder that the major illegal venues into Europe open to them also lie in these domains: domestic work and especially the sex industry. Put in an impossible situation, lots of women who have been denied access often turn to, or are forced to turn to, prostitution (see Brusse 1991). Once these women (increasingly from Eastern Europe and Africa) are caught in public spaces, 'deportation is likely to be the result for the worker as an illegal alien while the employer is likely to go free' (Phizacklea 1998: 31).

What this arbitrary but institutionalized implementation of immigration control proves is how much of Europe's external frontiers are embedded in, and productive of, domestic everyday racial practices (based on skin colour) and local gendered, sexual and class-based power. Geared to specific racial and gendered subjects, randomly selected in the vicinity of the border or in the street by individual, white, male officers, Europe's politics of mobility becomes very personal indeed, while its disembodied freely moving citizen turns out to be white and middle-class.

The countries that have signed the Schengen Agreement thus constitute an area of free circulation within Europe based on a geometry of borders that are invisible from an internal perspective – invisible to the white propertied subjects that are legitimated by those borders – but hard to miss when encountering them from the outside (when excluded by those borders), albeit that this relation between inside and outside frontier greatly depends on *where and by whom* in the EU it is implemented. The Schengen Agreement and all the provisions resulting from it are meant to create a borderless space surrounded by common external frontiers, a common passport and visa regime, a common procedure for the removal of illegal immigrants and overstayers and the common adoption of the Geneva Convention on refugees. Yet despite this fact, the way these regulations are interpreted varies from state to state, and from place to place. I have already mentioned that because of their geographical location within the EU, border ('marginal') countries such as Spain and the old Eastern Germany are made into buffer zones carrying all the responsibility for keeping Africans and Eastern Europeans respectively out. This explains their harsher migration regimes. Not only geographical location but also historical legacies (for example, a colonial past, the Cold War, previous migrations) and internal politics, such as the pressure exerted by the racist extreme right wing in Austria and Belgium, make the EU's external border a site of national (internal, racial, ethnic and economic) differentiation.[11] To accommodate these geographical, national and local differences, the External Frontiers Convention even explictly 'allows member states to retain exclusive control over the admission of third-country nationals for stays longer than three months' (Bainbridge 1998: 255). It is clear that the EU's external borders are the sites where the national and local differences are generously allowed to reappear, partly because they are the last symbolic strongholds of national sovereignty over territory, partly because it is in the political interest of the national governments (especially those that feel the breath of the extreme right down their necks), partly because it is in the state's economic interest: a lot of the European states live on the cheap labour of illegal immigrants particularly during the fruit-picking season.[12]

If it is in relation to the incoming outsider that the limits of a united Europe are systematically emerging, and if it is at the external frontiers that the internal divisions structurally recur, then I would argue that this is because borderlessness within the EU was from the beginning symbolically marked by white national identity and territory. What mediates the Union's 'four freedoms' of movement is the contradictory concept of a *European* space without internal borders, inhabited by a subject entitled to absolute mobility only insofar as he or she is firmly territorialized and identifiable as the *national* subject from a participating state. Mobility in Europe is without internal frontiers only to the extent that this limitless travel is firmly grounded in national territory and national identity. It is the nation state which grants or withholds the citizenship that allows the individual to go/live/work elsewhere in the EU, thereby relinquishing some of its powers over these citizens while extending its social divisions on a European scale. At the basis of Europe's politics of mobility lies an old-fashioned ethnic, racial, gendered and class-based struggle over sovereignty, resources and economic power.

To put this in other words: the national geopolitical conflicts within the Union have from the beginning been allowed to disappear only to the extent that they could reappear in another form, namely in relation to Europe's third-country nationals. Within the terms of the Schengen Agreement, the internal frontiers became the transitional sites where the old nation states relinquished part of their sovereignty and became 'member states' of a common European space at the outside borders of which the national sovereignty was reinstalled. Hence, according to the Schengen Agreement, each country has the right to decide autonomously on which refugees or asylum seekers to admit. The only thing that needs to be secured is a quick exchange of information – hence the installation of the Schengen Information System.[13] The Schengen Information System is a police database system that was installed to compensate for the abolition of identity controls at the common borders. Each participating state (not all Schengen countries participate in it) has control over its own national information system which is connected to a Central Schengen Information System through which passes all the (copied) information of the other national systems. The CSIS is meant to assist criminal-justice authorities, but also border police and customs officers checking the people and the goods crossing their countries' borders. The information provided concerns stolen vehicles or other objects (e.g. firearms, money) and persons missing, wanted for arrest or *denied entry into Schengen space*. Each national government decides how much information is provided in accordance with its own (privacy) laws. And although the data provided may vary considerably not only from state to state but also (within the Netherlands) from region to region, a report relating to a person usually complies with the standard identification procedures: name, age, place of birth and residence, sex, nationality and any particular visible and permanent physical feature, such as colour of eyes, hair and skin.

Needless to say, this surveillance technology largely extends, on a European scale, the kind of arbitrary race-based stop-and-search mechanisms that one finds in local city streets and which I discussed before. The system means that decisions by one member state can be followed by all other member states: if a request for asylum has been rejected by one country then this rejection will automatically apply to the whole Union. This is nothing less than national sovereignty making its reappearance on a European scale and vis-à-vis generalized others. By thus extending national borders to Europe's external frontiers, not only are the powers of the nation state increased, the internal national differences are also made invisible. Since the 'alien' rejected by one state is automatically denied access to the whole Union, and since he or she cannot enter other states to try again except illegally (with all the lack of legal protection, increasing vulnerability and risks of deportation involved), national differences over admission tend to disappear.[14] Is then Europe enabled to keep up the image of a homogeneous space without internal frontiers while decreasing the power of the individual asylum seeker?

Of course, none of Europe's external frontiers is totally impermeable to the outsider, at least not as long as foreign policy and matters of migration are a nation-based responsibility and the joint computerized information systems are ineffectively applied (see note 13): there is always an opening next door, so to speak. So if the influx of illegal migrants and refugees is the EU's greatest challenge nowadays, it is not so much because these outsiders are an economic or social threat to an already established internal stability as because they bear witness to the degree to which the Union's constitutive outsides are always already within: they are the nations' outsides. Here in the face of these unwanted visitors the solidity of the EU begins to crack not because of the inadequacy of its outside borders in and of themselves but because what was thought to be an external division between EU and non-EU clearly shows itself to be an internal one. Because, simply put, the member states are unwilling to cooperate in matters of migration for reasons other than their own national (economic) interest.[15] The 'uncontainable' influx of outsiders reminds us that in a European common market each nation wants its own illegal immigrants for internal political and economic reasons. And here I am thinking again of the increasing popularity of the extreme right wing wanting all foreigners (read: non-Western Europeans) out and of the manner in which all national economies profit from the cheap labour of illegal residents.

Corporate Citizenship: On Money and Migration

Given the fact that the EU's common market is based on the unlimited mobility of a cosmopolitan, preferably white and Western European but definitely economically powerful subject, it should not surprise us that the control of selective border crossing has become big business for several agencies often with conflicting interests.[16] In a space where the principle of freedom of movement is motivated by economic considerations it is difficult to dissociate the mechanisms of the market from immigration policies and border surveillance. One striking example of this close association between freewheeling capital and political border control is of course the Schengen Agreement's endorsement of the principle of 'carriers' liability' under which airlines and other commercial transport operators can be fined if their passengers are found on arrival not to have a right of entry. Countries that receive the first request for admission into the EU are responsible for the application. When the individual is denied access, these first countries of arrival must take care of their removal. For instance, if the third-country nationals who have been refused by Spain show up in another EU country such as France, then France has the right to ship them back to Spain. But if the 'aliens' arrive illegally by plane or truck, the transport companies are held responsible for their return and they may be fined up to US$5000 per immigrant found. Increasingly, the responsibility for the illegal entrance and transit of 'aliens' is becoming the burden of private enterprises, mostly air carriers who are begging to be assisted by border police and immigration officers to advise them who and what to watch out for. Judgements over asylum requests in Belgium are often made at Sabena desks in Kinshasa.

The reverse is true as well: not only is border control a burden for private enterprises, it can also be a gain. Lots of money is to be made in the implementation of strict borders, ranging from high-tech surveillance systems to the deployment of security guards to the deportation of illegal 'aliens' by commercial airlines. Furthermore, the harder the external border, the more attractive the unofficial routes circumventing it. Smuggling people in has become a lucrative business, and not only in the countries of departure. Since the possibility of people migrating legally has become minimal, several European truckers are getting rich through organized trafficking networks. Let me give an example that has recently brought home the hypocrisy of Europe's profitable migration policies in a gruesome way.

On Sunday 18 June 2000 a Mercedes truck from Rotterdam was heading for Bristol with a cargo of tomatoes. The Dutch trucker stopped at

Zeebrugge in Belgium and, unusually, paid cash for a ferry-crossing to Dover (most drivers have a seasonal pass). Once across the channel he was stopped by British customs officers at Dover who had been alerted to this 'suspicious' truck by the ferryliner's crew. The customs officials thought they would find an illegal traffic in drugs or cigarettes but instead:

> behind some pallets of tomatoes, they found dead bodies: 54 men and four women who had been on the final leg of a four-month journey from China. In total darkness and sweltering heat, after trying to open a small air vent that had been closed from the outside, pounding on the walls with their shoes and making cries for help that no one heard, all but two of the 60 would-be immigrants suffocated as they used up all the oxygen in the sealed container that became their tomb (McAllister 2000: 26).

The moral outcry that swept through the European media was immense, most of it targeting the inhumanity of 'these Chinese criminal networks'. Surprisingly soon after the calamity eight people were charged with illegal trafficking and manslaughter: a Chinese couple and six Dutchmen, including the driver who later confessed to having made the cross-channel tour with a truck full of people seven times before. He received about US$500 per stowaway. According to the Dutch police, the man's cross-channel route was only a small circuit in much larger Dutch-Turkish and Dutch-Iranian smuggling networks. Apparently the police had been following these criminal gangs for a while, but were waiting to intervene until enough information about the key figures had been gathered. As was suggested in the Belgian newspaper *De Morgen*, for the sake of data human lives had been sacrificed ('Nederlandse Bende' 2000: 8). In this respect, the criminal networks had begun to function as state-sanctioned information superhighways, while the fifty-eight bodies were the unfortunate nodes in this transgressive constellation of illegality and the law. We will return to this link between nation-state power and global (criminal) capital in a moment.

As for the migrants, most of them were reported to come from the rural province of Fujian in Southeast China and were believed to have made the trans-Siberian train ride to Moscow, from where they travelled into Eastern Europe by train, truck and horse-drawn carts and from there into Germany, the Netherlands and Belgium in the back of a lorry. The final destination should have been London, where they were most likely to be put to work in the businesses (restaurants, sweatshops, prostitution, domestic work, fruit industry) run by the gangs to whom they owed the money for the journey:

The journey to the West is called 'sneaking across the water'. It's made possible
by Fujianese guides known as 'snakeheads'. They are important figures in their
homeland. 'Everybody knows who the snakeheads are,' says Chen Mei Xing,
a Fujianese who slipped into England a few weeks ago. 'He's a businessman
with a very high status.' According to US authorities, snakeheads are also part
of Chinese gangs known as Triads or Tongs. They charge as much as $60,000
for a trip to the United States; half as much for Britain. Typically, a down
payment of 5 to 10 percent is made up front. A migrant who uses the snake-
head's services can spend years repaying the debt. The Fujianese who emigrate
see the fee as a smart investment. In the end Fujian benefits too. Fujianese
migrants pump large sums of money into the economy they left behind. City
officials in Changle (population: 600,000) estimate that locals who have gone
abroad put $100 million back into the city's economy each year in remittances
to their families and property investments back home (McGuire 2000: 19).

That the export of cheap labour is often condoned by the countries of
departure is not new. Poorer countries like the Philippines are famous for
sending out their citizens (mostly women as domestic servants, prostitutes
and mail-order brides) in return for a high-level investment in housing and
local industries. The southeast region of China too has a long history of
men migrating to the United States, Canada and lately also to Europe in
the hope of improving their (female) families' living conditions. The
salary of one month's indentured labour in London often equals that for
a whole year of work in China.[17] The globalized and regionalized political
economy that witnesses the rapid mobility of goods, services and finance
also relies on the circulation of cheap labour – including the sexual
division thereof – from poorer areas in need of remittances. That the maps
of inequality thereby produced do not solely run along the old state lines
(or West–East, South–North axes) should be clear by now. Europe's
current economic and migration policies, I have argued, are situated in the
transition from national to transnational space, while its illegal traffic in
labour proves to be to the advantage of various actors from both the
sending and receiving countries. A complex racial, gendered and class-
based cross-border division of power is seen to emerge from this one
highly publicized, example of human smuggling between China and
Britain alone. And we haven't even begun to mark out the much less
discussed but no less structural *sexual* violence involved in human trafficking. In a recent interview in *De Morgen*, Patsy Sørensen (representative of the Belgian Green Party in the European Parliament and Founding
Director of the first European shelter for prostitutes) stated that the illegal
traffic in women and child prostitutes has been big business in Europe for
many years, but that it has never received this kind of media attention, not

even when in 1987 seventeen women from the Dominican Republic were found dead in a container under similar circumstances (Sørensen 2000: 33).

What was particularly cynical about the heated debates following the deaths at Dover was the insistence on the part of officials from France, Belgium and the Netherlands that Europe's asylum policies should be separated from the operations by these 'criminal gangs'. One was in the field of migration and asylum, the other the shady area of crime which could only be fought by means of 'more Europe': meaning more police cooperation, more transfer of information, more surveillance. In Britain, where 'more Europe' has never been an option, the Home Secretary Jack Straw declared that if there was anything to be learned here, it concerned the extreme danger of these criminals: 'may it be a warning to all those who consider putting their lives in the hands of these gangs' ('EU' 2000: 5). To which he added that it should also be a lesson for Belgian colleagues, reluctant as they are to deport the illegal 'aliens' found on their territory back to their own country less for humanitarian than for financial reasons – it is cheaper to let them loose and hope they will move on, mostly to Britain, which is not yet a Schengen country.

If at the beginning of the week political voices in the EU condemned the traffic in illegal migrants en bloc, then by the time concrete measures were proposed four days later, government officials on European and national levels were accusing each other of thinking only in terms of their own interest. In Belgium alone the disagreements concentrated around the question of who was going to pay for the increase in surveillance technologies: the Ministry of Internal Affairs (head of the police forces but also responsible for migration), the Ministry of Finance (in charge of customs) or the private transport (shipping) companies? The latest proposal, officially aired as this chapter is written, serves as a good illustration of the way the mechanisms of the market are increasingly mediating nation-based surveillance practices. Following the profitable strategies in the harbours of Rotterdam and Calais, the Belgian Minister of Finance has finally agreed to place X-ray scanners in the harbours of Antwerp, Ostend and Zeebrugge in the hope of gaining a triple victory against the illegal traffic in drugs, cigarettes, and – a gift to the colleagues in Internal Affairs – stowaways. As it was pointed out with irony in *De Morgen*, the emplacement of container scanners may well cost 25 million euros, but the government will recuperate 10 million euros worth of evaded taxes on cigarettes alone (van Scharen 2000: 6). In the end, the business of catching stowaways will bring in big money for our National Treasury. Add to this the Belgian government's suggestion that the private shipping companies help to finance the detection technologies in exchange for a reduced fee when it comes to carriers' liability (see p. 235 of this volume), and the financial picture becomes very attractive indeed. There is a lot to be gained from illegal migration, and not only by the Snakeheads.

This, then, is the central paradox of a capitalist nation state wanting to extend its reach to the borders of a European common market. It must carefully organize, through all kinds of border practices, the free flow of capital and professionals way beyond its state (and even community) borders, but in its own interest – an interest it tries to recuperate by delegating the implementation of its territorial boundaries to transnational capital itself. In what follows I want to return to the case study mentioned at the beginning, to illustrate the nexus of nation state power, the European common market and global capital at one of Europe's external frontiers – the harbour of Zeebrugge – and to see how border maintenance and border crossing, the local and the global, but also legal and illegal transit, are mutually constitutive once the national border is of transnational economic interest. The questions I want to raise are the following. How much of Europe's common market is based on the reproduction and consumption of national borders and of the illegal bodies that emerge along with them?[18] To what extent is the economic exploitation of the border the site where the nation state imposes its (white propertied) standards of citizenship even as they are, in the end, spent and exhausted? How much does this capitalist form of national border control contribute to the dispersal of state power and how contestatory can this deterritorialization of national boundaries by capital be? In what way does the linkage of transnational capital and national border surveillance contribute to the global production of the illegal 'alien' as a highly lucrative site of investment on the one hand and of the European nation as a safe place for capital on the other, and what does this co-production of outside and inside, illegality and legality tell us about the heterogeneity – and destabilization – of the national border in a European space without national frontiers?

Tracing the Heart of the Matter in Zeebrugge

I began with the use made by the authorities in Zeebrugge of DKL's LifeGuard in 1999. As already explained, the LifeGuard is an expensive remote sensing device that purports to be able to locate the electromagnetic field around the beating heart of a stowaway. Working like a compass, the antenna of the gun-shaped tracking system points to the 'irregular magnetic field' caused by the movement of the illegal 'alien's' heart. The harbour began to use it when faced with the large number of refugees hiding in trailers and containers bound for Britain. Since its customers were incurring immense carriers' liability fines, the pressure on Zeebrugge to find more efficient ways of detecting them before departure was immense. The stakes were high, the money was big, and the marketing strategies were developed accordingly. As was illustrated above, DKL, the security firm hired by the harbour, the harbour itself, the media industry and the national authorities seized on this emerging market in the removal of stowaways to promote their indispensable role in it.

And the 'detected' refugees themselves? I realize that this chapter is sorely lacking in specificity concerning the identities and experiences of the refugees who recently arrived in Zeebrugge. Not all of them are males, and not all of them come from Bosnia, Kosovo, Albania and other Balkan regions. According to the officials that were interviewed during the various news reports that I gathered, a lot of the stowaways also come from Sri Lanka, Pakistan, Iran, Iraq, Afghanistan and China. I cannot pretend to be able to speak for any one refugee seeking shelter in the EU, but I would like to quote one passage from a moving collection of 'refugee voices' that seems particularly to the point here. It was written by an anonymous 54-year-old refugee from Bosnia, probably a Muslim woman, residing in Germany:

> None of us have legal papers. We came too late. They already had enough of us refugees. But we are the ones who stayed so long because we never wanted to come. We are the ones who came only after we lost family members, only after our houses and towns had become completely destroyed. I don't know what I would say if I met the man who wrote in the paper that we are mostly economic migrants. What does he know about my life? Should I show him the photos? No, he doesn't deserve to know me. (Mertus 1997: 123)

'*Sans papiers*', such people are often unidentifiable, unlocatable. Furthermore, as was clear from an interview with them on Belgian television, most of them don't want asylum, they don't even want to stay; they are merely 'in transit', on their way to Britain.[19] They are the mobile subjects par excellence, but as non-EU citizens at the mercy of domestic laws.[20] In Belgium they officially exist only as an obstacle to be detected, and removed, at the nation-state border in accordance with a private company's principle of dielectrophoresis: the polarized movement of a *neutral* body toward a *nonuniform* electrical field, in this case the low-frequency electrical signal of the 'alien's' beating heart. Once the 'alien' is thus translated – objectified – within the parameters of physical science, once he or she is reduced to the generic polar electrical field of a heartbeat, another mode of polarization comes into view, that of man versus animal. Eager to commercialize, DKL is proud to tell you that it can distinguish between the electrical signals of a breathing human being and that of an animal: 'The *LifeGuard*'s patented technology can distinguish between humans and any other animals' (DKL website). This forging of a link between 'aliens' and animals – a link that allows to minimally differentiate them – is a crucial step in the definition of the stowaway as an animal-like, dangerous non-citizen who needs to be detained at a 500-metre distance by a long-range gun aiming at the heart. An identification in terms of criminality is by now more than justified: 'After chasing a suspect into a 22,500 square foot warehouse containing manufacturing equipment, a California drug task force used the LifeGuard to detect the suspect's hiding place . . . In a Los Angeles County SWAT team hostage situation, the LifeGuard was used to locate the rooms in the house where hostages were being held by a suspect wanted for the attempted murder of a police officer' (ibid.).

It may be that the American military engineers who designed the LifeGuard were mainly thinking of targeting enemies and murderers, but DKL's (and the media's) recodification of Zeebrugge's border control, first in terms of the principle of the compass, then (by way of the human/animal binary) in terms of combating violence and terrorism, tells me a lot about the ideology at work here. What we are dealing with is a state-sanctioned violent reconfiguration of particular racial, ethnic immigrant bodies (of beating hearts), according to the logic of various key players in Europe's global economy, with the sole purpose of making both the stowaway and the safe harbour marketable in various places. Those global forces include: the science behind DKL; information technology – in its latest version the LifeGuard is plugged into a portable computer which translates the sensed movement via detection algorithms into digital signals displaying the amplitude of various shock waves on-screen while emitting a sound signal when the frequencies of a beating heart have been reached; DKL as a corporate firm with links to the major players in the global e-commerce; Belgian and American law-enforcement agencies; the car and shipping industries; and the national and international media industry.

Global networks are thus seen to produce a local-global nexus for the continuously reconfigured foreign body such that it becomes an interface between state and capital, as well as a lucrative passage between Belgium, the EU and the United States. Along the way, the stowaway is reproduced along a set of Western cultural relations – man versus animal, the law versus the criminal, technology versus humans, movement versus location – that situate him/her at once inside and outside the capitalist nation, inside and outside European territory. He or she is, in one and the same breath (pun intended), the target of the gun-shaped LifeGuard, of national security, of police officers, of Europe's external frontiers and of global capital investment. Thus, national borders are secured and tracked by means of transnational capitalist and technological networks, transgressing national territory the better to be able to lock onto the particular foreign body and displace it through commodification. In the process, the nation state becomes a safe place for the transportation of goods, Europe's external frontier an ideal site for more investment.

This example from Zeebrugge illustrates how in the current European space without frontiers, the old national borders are displaced *and reinscribed* via the local-global logic of a 'common market' dominated by transnational forces that capitalize on specific nation-based economic, racial, ethnic and gendered differences only to market, and in the process homogenize, those differences across nations and places. Europe's border practices, which purport to create a frontierless Schengen space of flows, are here seen to first produce local (nation-based) differences, which are then removed through commodification and reproduction on a European but also global scale.

Once again it has become clear how, in current European developments, internal and external frontiers, the local and the global, are co-constitutive and how nation-state formations play a crucial role in this. Rather than declaring the nation state extinct in an age of globalization, as so many social and political theorists are fond of doing, it is probably more correct to state that European (and non-European!) states are differentially embedded in complex cross-border networks of transnational capital, digital technology, (illegal) migration, and policy-making. That global technology has an important function in this reconfiguration of nation-state power is one more proof of the embeddedness of technology that Katherine Hayles (1999) and Donna Haraway (1997) have repeatedly insisted on. Rather than associating the global spreading of information (and other) technologies with disembodiment and universalization, these critics invite us to look for the power-structures involved as well as for the complex relations between standardized technologies and local experiences. In Haraway's words, we need to focus on how technologically 'consolidated identities [which in this context might include subject versus object, European versus "alien", culture versus nature] for some produce marginalised locations for others' within material-semiotic contexts that are racial and gender-based (1997: 38). Whereas Hayles and Haraway largely study the social-material relations making up the realm of science and technology (informatics, biotechnology, for example), Saskia Sassen extends the scope of the debate to the interaction between digital technology, transnational economy and nation-state power. She too wants to 'examine the underside of globalisation in order to show that the dominant line of theorisation with its emphasis on the hypermobility and liquidity of capital is a partial account; further, it is partial in a way that carries significant implications for questions of state and nonstate-centred regulatory capacities and, more generally, questions of governance and accountability in a global economy' (Sassen 1998: 196). Despite her ongoing interest in the persistent role of nation-state power in a global context, Sassen's work has so far mainly limited itself to the *transformation* of nation-based legal systems (for example, contracts) and modes of government. Eventually, Sassen too pleads for a radical reconception of sovereignty and accountability that goes far beyond the traditional nation state. She claims new openings for alternative power structures, ranging from emancipatory alliances between women and 'other non-state actors' (ibid.: 94) to – less optimistic – city-based service and market industries and strategic concentrations of infrastructure that form the conditions under which the hypermobility of capital and economy becomes possible.

As should be clear by now, this chapter has – much in the spirit of Jacqueline Bhabha – argued that it is much too soon to declare the nation state powerless in the face of globalizing and regionalizing economies. The national state and transnational capital have always been contradictory allies in the history of the (European) capitalist nation state, the one insisting on maintaining its legal borders, the other on transgressing and reinscribing them. Thus, the story of Zeebrugge is not only a tale about the unequal incorporation of the nation state's 'aliens' into the workings of global capital, it is also about the nation state's implication in a decentralized economy that thrives on the worldwide production and consumption of national borders and the illegal bodies that emerge along with them.

Counterstrategies in Europe's Fee-Space[21]

My analysis of the workings of the external frontier at Zeebrugge points to the contradictions inherent in Europe's production of a borderless world. In a space of unlimited mobility for a very limited group of people – white propertied nationals – borders are abundant, the production and consumption of 'others' immense. In this present phase of transition from national to European space, the EU can only exist by way of this state-sanctioned traffic in illegal 'aliens' and their displacement through commodification.

Not surprisingly then – and this is the other side of the coin – most illegal migrants do eventually arrive at their destination, at least as long as they play by the rules of the market and follow the routes of commodities and money. As the young man in the interview (see note 19) mockingly said upon his removal from a truck in Zeebrugge: 'I will try again tomorrow. Not necessarily here though. There are many other ways to get to Dover'. Upon which he and his youthful male companion walked away from the camera laughing. In an economy based on the removal of differences through objectification, 'aliens' get to travel like packages in trailers: without frontiers as long as they are paid for at the start. So the stowaway can laugh because he knows his illegality is marketable, in the end state-supported. It only takes him the contradictory logic of Europe's economy to enter the nation. Money is what loosens the conjunction of one nation and one state: money produces the hyphen in nation-state, the imprecise fit between nation and state, identity and territory, where ethnic, gendered and economic differences come to the surface on a European and global scale. The man laughs because he knows that this disjuncture, which multiplies as global capital flows into the common market, is his way into the Union. And together with him, there are thousands of others.

Notes

1. Part of the following discussion is based on an interview that I had with security personnel who used the LifeGuard in Zeebrugge. They preferred to remain anonymous. The critical interpretations of DKL are mine.
2. For pictures and descriptions of DKL's products, see its website at *http://www.dklabs.com/products.html*
3. DKL booklet, *Is Anyone Alive in There?*, p. 9. Copy handed to me by the security firm.
4. In public discussions of migration in Europe hardly anything is said about the millions of displaced in Africa (Congo, Uganda) and Asia (Afghanistan, Pakistan). Annie Phizacklea (1998: 22) speaks of more than 100 million: 'Over half of all these migrants are women, and 20 million of this 100 million are officially classified as refugees or

asylum seekers, 80 per cent of whom are women accompanied by dependent children'. The EU takes less than 10 per cent of the world's refugees.

5. See the survey of newspaper reports on DKL's website. The idea for this chapter came after I had seen an interview with DKL during a Belgian (Flemish) news report in February 1999. I was shocked to see a supposedly non-commercial state-sponsored TV channel make full-blown publicity for this gun-shaped detection device on its daily news.

6. The phrase 'geopolitics of mobility' is taken from Hyndman's (2000) book on the economies of power dominating the humanitarian spaces of refugee relief, riveted as these are by a discrepancy between the flows of refugees on the one hand and the circulation of financial aid and neocolonial means of managing migration on the other.

7. European citizenship is granted only to EU nationals, not to migrants who have resided in the EU for years. Accordingly, only citizens, not residents, can bring their family into the Union. See Jacqueline Bhabha's (1999b) wonderful analysis of the vulnerabilities involved in the marginal position of EU resident non-citizens in the era of Maastricht.

8. 'Europe's restrictive refugee policies have been criticised by UNHCR. In February 1999, the head of UNHCR, Sadako Ogata, bemoaned the fact that European policy on asylum issues was increasingly coming down to the "idea of controlling immigration and domestic security". However, measures taken by European countries to fight illegal immigration "equally affect immigrants and refugees, who are in need of protection"' (Amnesty International 1999: 9).

9. The Schengen Agreement has been signed and applied by the Netherlands, Luxemburg, France, Germany, Spain, Portugal, Italy, Austria, Greece, Finland and Sweden. Denmark signed with partial opt-out. Great Britain and Ireland have not yet signed. Norway and Iceland, not yet EU countries, also joined Schengen space.

10. It is important to note that the conditions under which one becomes a national citizen in the EU differs from country to country: in France, which is a 'civil' nation, nationality is determined by place of birth; in Germany, an 'ethnic' nation, it is determined by blood relation or descent. By focusing on the strategies of in- and exclusion at the nations' European borders, my chapter uncovers the ethnic dimensions of so-called 'civil' nation states.

11. That colonial history plays a role in Europe's migration policies is, for instance, clear from the fact that the High Level Working Group,

which has to formulate economic intervention strategies for the most 'urgent' countries of emigration, has put Sri Lanka (Britain's ex-colony) on top of its list (besides Iraq, Iran, Afghanistan and Morocco).

12. It is common knowledge that thousands of illegal workers are employed in the Spanish fruit industry during the summer. Even Belgium has its annual load of illegal Sikhs to pick strawberries and cherries in June and July but this year the government has decided to employ more than 1500 asylum seekers for the (paid) jobs. In *Die Zeit*, the migration expert Klaus Bade goes as far as saying that whole branches of Europe's industries would collapse were one to eliminate all illegal workers: a third of the French highways and car industry would never have existed without them, while Britain's construction and garment industries would disintegrate immediately (Böhm 2000: 14).

13. For more information on CSIS, including its random use and possible misuse, see the Netherlands Court of Audit reports ('Netherlands' 1996; 'Netherlands', n.d.). For a wonderful critique of the identification procedure of undocumented 'aliens' by means of digitalized fingerprinting ('Eurodac'), see van der Ploeg 1999.

14. For a good discussion of the way in which EC law can function to protect the rights of EU nationals but not of third-country nationals (who are entirely dependent on domestic law for protection), see Bhabha 1999b. While TCNs can appeal to the European Court of Human Rights in Strasburg, 'the scope of the Strasburg Court should not be overestimated. Through the doctrine of "the margin of appreciation" developed by the European Court of Human Rights, states are accorded considerable discretion and leeway, particularly in "sensitive" areas of decision making such as public security and immigration' (ibid.: 119). All this leaves non-EU citizens largely unrepresented, and hence unprotected, by European law.

15. The Intergovernmental Council of fifteen Heads of State needs a unanimous vote for something to become law. Each nation state has the right to a veto if its national interest is not met.

16. Robert Miles's detailed discussion of the political economy of migration control in Britain offers good examples of this conjuncture of money and migration (Miles 1999).

17. Roger Cohen comments: '"Europe," the old continent, persistent source of hordes of migrants to the New World, has become the Ersatz United States of modern asylum seekers. Where just 30,000 people applied for asylum in the U.S. last year, down from 127,000 in 1993, more than 365,000 did so in the European Union . . . The collapse of

the Soviet Union has opened up new land routes to Europe from Asia and turned once-closed cities like Moscow and Kiev into nodal points of migrant travel from Afghanistan and China' (Cohen 2000: 1).

18. According to Robert Miles (1999) the commodifying of migration control is an example of the state's incapacity to deal with these problems because of lack of resources and, hence, it is a clear symptom of the state's withdrawal. His article criticizes Britain's refusal to sign the Schengen Treaty and relinquish its sexist and racist borders which it is incapable of controlling anyway. Eventually Miles hopes that this incapacity will force Britain to join Schengen. Needless to say, I do not agree with his analysis of the commodified border as a sign of the weakening state's withdrawal in matters of migration control. If anything, it adds to the state's economic power. Nor do I consider Schengen an alternative to the nation's racist and sexist border control; rather, it is an extension of it.

19. VRT-program *Ter Zake*, 12 November 1999.

20. Only European citizens have access to protection by European law; see note 14.

21. I heard Saskia Sassen use the term 'fee-space' during a public lecture at the World InfoCon in Brussels.

References

Alund, A. (1999), 'Feminism, Multiculturalism, Essentialism', in N. Yuval-Davis and P. Werbner (eds), *Women, Citizenship and Difference,* London and New York: Zed.

Amnesty International (1999), 'Refugees from Afghanistan: The World's Largest Single Refugee Group', ASA 11/16/99, London.

Anthias, F. and Yuval-Davis, N. (1992), *Racialized Boundaries: Race, Nation, Gender, Colour and Class and the Anti-Racist Struggle,* London: Routledge.

Bainbridge, T. (1998), *The Penguin Companion to European Union,* London: Penguin.

Bhabha, J. (1999a), 'Embodied Rights: Gender Persecution, State Sovereignty and Refugees', in N. Yuval-Davis and P. Werbner (eds), *Women, Citizenship and Difference,* London and New York: Zed.

—— (1999b), 'Enforcing the Human Rights of Citizens and Non-Citizens in the Era of Maastricht: Some Reflections on the Importance of States', in B. Meyer and P. Geschiere (eds), *Globalization and Identity: Dialectics of Flow and Closure*, Oxford: Blackwell.

Böhm, A. (2000), 'Fleißig, Billig, Illegal', *Die Zeit*, 29 June: 14.

Brusse, L. (1991), *Survey on Prostitution, Migration and Traffic in Women: History and Current Situation,* EG/Prost (91) 2, Council of Europe, European Committee for Equality between Women and Men, Strasbourg.

Cohen, R. (2000), 'For Immigrants from the East, Europe Is Today's New World', *International Herald Tribune,* 3 July: 1.

DKL, Dielectrokinetic Laboratories, LLC, website http://www.dklabs.com/products.html (Accessed 15 September 1999).

Engbersen, G. and van der Leun, J. (1998), 'Illegality and Criminality: The Differential Opportunity Structure of Undocumented Immigrants', in K. Koser and H. Lutz (eds), *The New Migration in Europe: Social Constructions and Social Realities,* Basingstoke: Macmillan.

'EU: Hardere Aanpak van Mensensmokkel', *NRC Handelsblad,* 20 June: 5.

Haraway, D. (1997), *Modest_Witness@Second_Millennium. Female Man©_Meets_OncoMouse™: Feminism and Technoscience,* London and New York: Routledge.

Hayles, K. (1999), *How We Became Posthuman: Virtual Bodies in Cybernetics, Literature, and Informatics*, Chicago and London: University of Chicago Press.

Hyndman, J. (2000), *Managing Displacement: Refugees and the Politics of Humanitarianism,* London and Minneapolis: University of Minnesota Press.

Malkki, L. (1992), 'National Geographic: The Rooting of Peoples and the Territorialization of National Identity among Scholars and Refugees', *Cultural Anthropology*, 7: 24–44.

McAllister, J.F.O. (2000), 'Snaking toward Death', *Time*, 3 July: 26.

McGuire, S. (2000), 'The People Trade', *Newsweek*, 3 July: 19.

Mertus, J., Tesanovic, J. Metikos, H. and Boric, R. (1997), *The Suitcase: Refugee Voices from Bosnia and Croatia. With Contributions from Over Seventy-Five Refugees and Displaced People,* Berkeley: University of California Press.

Miles, R. (1999), 'Analysing the Political Economy of Migration: The Airport as an "Effective" Institution of Control', in A. Brah, M.J. Hickman and M. Mac an Ghaill (eds), *Global Futures: Migration, Environment and Globalization,* Basingstoke: Macmillan.

'Nederlandse Bende Smokkelde al sinds Vorig jaar Chinezen', *Morgen,* 8 July: 8.

Netherlands Court of Audit (1996), *National Schengen Information System* (May 1996), http://www.rekenkamer.nl/en/misc/schengen.htm (Accessed on 15 September 1999).

Netherlands Court of Audit (n.d.), *Report upon the National Schengen Information System in the Netherlands*, http://www.rekenkamer.nl/en/audits/schengsu.htm

Phizacklea, A. (1998), 'Migration and Globalization: A Feminist Perspective', in K. Koser and H. Lutz (eds), *The New Migration in Europe: Social Constructions and Social Realities*, Basingstoke: Macmillan.

Sassen, S. (1998), *Globalization and Its Discontents*, New York: New Press.

Select Committee on the European Communities (1989), *1992: Border Control of People*, House of Lords, London: Her Majesty's Stationery Office.

Sørensen, P. (2000), interview with Douglas De Coninck, 'Moest Ik Me Dan Opeens met Bomen Gaan Bezighouden?', *Morgen*, 15 July: 33.

van der Ploeg, I. (1999), 'The Illegal Body: "Eurodac" and the Politics of Biometric Identification', *Ethics and Information Technology*, 1: 295–302.

van Scharen, H. (2000), 'Containerscan Is Meer Fiscale dan Humanitaire Noodzaak', *Morgen*, 10 July: 6.

11

The Difference Borders Make: (Il)legality, Migration and Trafficking in Italy among Eastern European Women in Prostitution

Rutvica Andrijasevic

'Do not ask us why are we here, ask us rather how we got here.'[1]

Introduction

Migratory flows from 'eastern'[2] to 'western'[3] Europe have increased in the last twenty years, largely triggered by geopolitical and geoeconomic changes in the former 'Eastern block'. Commonly referred to as the 'new' migration, the involvement of women in this 'East–West' migration has increasingly become a subject of alarm in countries of western Europe, namely with respect to the 'trafficking'[4] of eastern European women for the purpose of prostitution. The governments of the European Union (EU) member states have predominantly associated trafficking with 'illegal' migration from 'third' countries and organized crime. In this respect, the implementation of the border-protection scheme has been endorsed as a pivotal measure: 'Better management of the Union's external border controls will help in the fight against terrorism, illegal immigration networks and the trafficking in human beings' (Presidency Conclusions Leaken European Council, No. 42).

Instead of adopting the general term 'human trafficking', my work makes use of the term 'trafficking in women' not only because the vast majority of trafficked people are women (Wijers and Lap-Chew 1997) but also because, as feminist scholars have shown, the words 'human' and 'woman' are not interchangeable. In fact, the expression 'human trafficking' performs a conceptual collapsing which overlooks the dissymmetry of gender relations and the specificity of migrant women's experiences. Moreover, the term trafficking, usually intended to signify transportation of persons by means of coercion or deception into exploitative and slavery-like conditions,[5] is often used in ways that collapse a large span of operations. These involve, first, the recruitment and transportation of women from their departure to the destination country, and secondly, the living and working conditions upon arrival. As Wijers and Lap-Chew demonstrate (1997), although a woman might find herself in slavery-like conditions (violence and/or threat of violence, confiscation of legal documents, no freedom of movement), as a consequence of being transported to a foreign country, she might also be recruited without coercion and may or may not find herself in forced-labour conditions.

My analysis makes a distinction between these operations, focusing on the recruitment and transportation phase of trafficking. This choice was prompted not only by the lack of studies that investigate this side of sex trafficking in women, but also by interviews with trafficked women in Italy that brought to the fore the interrelation between trafficking and increased control of geo-political borders. Instead of focusing explicitly on exploitative labour conditions, this approach proposes an analysis of the material and legal immigration apparatus which fosters the legal, economic and physical vulnerability of trafficked women. Italy presents a unique field of study on this topic, since it has become a destination country only relatively recently (late 1970s) and is transitioning from being a country of emigration to a country of immigration. Moreover, Italy has often been considered a locus of permeable borders that allows a reasonably easy flow of undocumented migration into the EU. As far as trafficking is concerned, it is together with Belgium the only EU state to include a specific clause in its immigration laws that allows for social protection and legalization of trafficking victims.

The primary focus of this chapter is on accounts by eastern European migrant women trafficked into Italy. By drawing on these accounts, I critically assess the conceptualization of trafficking in the fields of current political and mass-media discourses and reveal some of the intricate processes that constitute the conditions of possibility for trafficking. My study is based on fieldwork undertaken in Bologna[6] between October 1999 and February 2000, with a group of twenty-five migrant women who, having arrived in Italy through trafficking, have worked as street prostitutes under different degrees of confinement[7] and in conditions of economic exploitation by one or more third parties. The respondents were aged between 18 and 25, and originated from various eastern European non-EU candidate countries (Romania,[8] Ukraine, Moldova, Russia, Croatia and FR Yugoslavia). Among the larger group of twenty-five women I selected fifteen to conduct unstructured in-depth interviews. At the time of the interviews, none of the respondents still worked as street prostitutes and all were struggling with questions pertaining to their new life arrangements – such as whether to return home or stay in Italy.

Throughout the chapter, I cast the women's narratives against the backdrop of discourses and representations of women's trafficking found in the mass media,[9] as well as in religious (i.e. *Caritas*) and feminist sources. The Catholic organization *Caritas* is one of the most influential actors in developing projects against sex trafficking in Italy, while Moroli and Sibona, authors of *Schiave d'occidente: sulle rotte dei mercanti di donne*,[10] are leading figures of a feminist association *Differenza Donna* based in Rome. The *Caritas* association runs various shelters where a large number of women have been assisted. It is worth noting that the materials produced by the above-mentioned religious and feminist sources have had extensive influence on public opinion and policy-making in Italy, and have been largely distributed on the national scale. By looking at processes of representation and how meanings are produced and allocated in public discourse, my analysis sheds light on different – often overlooked – aspects of trafficking. I question the official representation of trafficking and map out some of its central elements that re/appear in different sources and converge with the EU political agenda, thus underpinning the view of trafficking in terms of irregular migration and women as victims deceived and coerced into prostitution. I shall discuss the way in which women's narratives challenge accepted notions of victimhood (discussed in the second section) by scrutinizing their accounts of border crossings and how they entered into prostitution in Italy. In the last section, I also discuss the criminalization of illegal immigration in light of the respondents' own accounts of their immigration procedures within the Italian legal apparatus.

But my findings also suggest that when the categories of irregular migration, border and crime are brought into focus, a gap between the interviewee's accounts of migration and the dominant rhetoric of trafficking becomes visible. This discrepancy, as my work points out, is an integral part of a larger landscape within which gendered politics of belonging in the new, enlarged Europe are being sanctioned. In this respect, I begin by tackling the issues of migration in relation to the formation of the 'new' Europe.[11] In doing so, I hope to bring to the fore the political and legal formation of the enlarged EU and of its borders, and to reveal the ways in which borders are created through material and juridical means of controlling the movement of people and, as such, create the conditions for the proliferation of trafficking. In this respect, the juridico-material formation of borders constitutes a crucial element to be considered in the analysis of the women's accounts of migration.

Mapping the New Borders of an Enlarged Europe

In recent years various newspapers throughout western Europe have increasingly featured migration in the following terms: 'Immigration crisis!' and 'Emergency immigration!'[12] As Dal Lago (1999) and Sassen (1999) point out, this approach tends to portray migration as a flood that endangers the stability, security and wealth of the western European states. The 'invasion syndrome' gained particular momentum in the post-1989 period when the Berlin Wall fell, Russia relaxed visa policies to facilitate the travel of its citizens, and countries of eastern Europe got involved in a series of economic and 'political revolutions' (Wolff 1994). In addition to the immigration policies, the invasion discourse is also present on the level of textual and visual representation best discernible in the press. In *La Repubblica*,[13] for example, photographs of arrivals and crossings stir up fears of invasion with images of masses of people, and encourage the idea of migration as a crisis in need of containment.

The narrative of migration as crisis is not limited to the mass media, but is found within leading European political circles as well. As early as the European Summit in Luxembourg in June 1991, John Major addressed the need to control the supposed crisis with the following words: 'We must not be wide open to all-comers just because Rome, Paris and London are more attractive than Bombay or Algiers' (Cohen in King 1993: 184). In addition to its reference to cultural and economic superiority of European capitals, the statement explicitly points to the need for greater control over European external borders. While some scholars refer to migration from eastern Europe as 'the invasion that has never occurred' (Simoncini 2000: 31) and others have indicated that Europe was hardly wide open in the years preceding the 1990s (Dal Lago 1999), the 1990s are nevertheless characterized by the intensification of regulatory agreements. The most incisive is the Schengen Treaty signed in 1985, which reveals the political intention of the signatory member states[14] to construct a culturally homogeneous and economically protected area. The Treaty abolished internal borders between its member states, allowing for the free circulation of goods, capital, services and their citizens, yet it simultaneously reinforced EU external borders and set out to harmonize immigration and asylum policies. Supported by claims that the strict immigration policies are of a preventive nature,[15] the Schengen treaty created what has been dubbed as 'fortress Europe' (see Verstraete in Chapter 10 of this volume).

While Simoncini (2000) questions the appropriateness of the phrase 'fortress Europe' and claims that the EU does not possess the material means to achieve the level of control which would produce an impenetrable border, I use this term to highlight the human costs that accompany strict policing of the borders. The phrase stresses that borders do not simply mark the edges of the supranational body conceptually, but can also take the form of a material barrier, such as a wire or a wall. To survey the borders, there are deployed technological devices such as coastal radar stations used by Italian and Spanish police forces to intercept the arrival of the boats, infrared cameras and the X-ray scanners deployed on the English coast[16] or carbon dioxide detectors used by the German border police in order to detect people hidden inside a cargo. These forms of intensified and often violent border enforcement bring with them a large number of migrant fatalities. United for Intercultural Action, a Dutch-based European network against nationalism, racism and fascism, has counted 2406 deaths of migrants that have resulted from border policing, detention and deportation policies and carrier sanctions.

What Balibar has called a 'double regime of the circulation of people' (Balibar in Simoncini 2000: 32) has transformed into multiple regimes of exclusion produced through the proliferation of border controls throughout the accession countries. The EU enlargement eastward is creating a new external EU border that will separate the future EU member states of central east Europe[17] from the non-members.[18] The EU candidates are required to apply Schengen-type border and visa regulations toward those countries not included in the EU enlargement. This 'domino effect' (Dietrich 2000: 123) is achieved through establishing the 'Safe Third Country' rule. Safe third countries such as Poland, for example, have introduced EU-like asylum regulations which enable Polish authorities to deport undocumented migrants from Polish territory to the detention camps in Ukraine and Belarus (FFM 1998: 6). The domino effect can be further noticed in the introduction of visa requirements for countries further east. For example, the Czech Republic included Ukraine, Russia and Belarus in their proposal for new visa policies (Bort 2000: 6). Additional measures include amendments to the aliens law and the strengthening (or introduction) of laws against human trafficking in accession countries. These operations shift the responsibility for border protection and anti-trafficking measures from the EU to EU candidates and turn the accession countries into a kind of 'buffer zone' or, as Andreas puts it, 'into the EU's new migration gatekeepers' (2000: 8).

The construction of 'new' borders[19] creates a hierarchy between the EU states and third countries, and hints at the new geography of power of the future enlarged Europe (Regulska 2001). By this I mean that EU external borders are relational spaces upon which is inscribed the materialization of power relations not only between the EU and accession countries but also a new division between the EU candidates and non-candidates, namely between politically 'stable' and 'unstable' eastern European countries. Borders are not simply static demarcations: the effects of new borders do not merely extend outward to sanction new partitions but also are the effects of a set of institutional practices and discourses that extend inward into 'the EU', defining some people and nations as 'belonging' and others as 'not-belonging'. A communication from the Commission of the European Communities to the European Parliament is quite explicit on the matter: 'The conclusion of the European Council [of Leaken in December 2001] reminds us that coherent, effective common management of the external borders of the member states of the Union will boost security and the citizen's sense of belonging to a shared area and destiny' (COM (2002) 233: 2).

Constructions of Victimhood

Within the discursive economy of illegal migration, the border becomes a site of crime. It is a locus where the law is broken and where the established order is violated by those trying to cross undocumented. In the press, the visual rendering of border-crossings are highly gendered. The following question springs from these observations: when the border becomes a metaphorical and material reality for marginalization that produces gender-differentiated layers of in/visibility, how are female migrants talked about? The prevalent absence of women from visual depictions of border-crossing comes with a discursive scenario where migrant women are figured not as protagonists but as characters endowed with little or no agency:[20] while male migrants are portrayed as central characters of border-crossings, migrant women tend to fall out of view and gain visibility when portrayed as war refugees and/or as victims of trafficking. Newspapers abound with accounts of young, naïve, innocent victims lured into prostitution by malevolent traffickers:

> We will call them Olga and Natasha. Their story equals the stories of many other girls from the East who came to Italy blinded by a work promise, and then forced into prostitution by a pimp, a man of no scruples. As soon as they got off the bus that brought them illegally from Moldova to Italy, they were taken over by Rimi, an Albanian.

This newspaper clip from *Il Resto del Carlino* (18 July 1999) portrays these women's story in terms of deception into illegal migration and prostitution. It also places their chronicles alongside numerous other stories of the same kind and, by doing so, suggests the presence of a vast volume of East–West Europe trafficking. *Topoi* of a collective deception and dispersal are also brought into play in an educational booklet for high school students, jointly produced by Brescia City municipalities in northern Italy and the local Caritas group: 'Many young women in precarious living situations and eager to gain freedom get attracted with false promises of social and economic gain, and accept an offer to come and work in the West . . . The numbers suggest hundreds of thousands, maybe a million young women dispersed all over the streets of Europe (2000: 4)'.

Such references to the magnitude of trafficking, and the emphasis on the deceptive and coercive nature of a contract between migrant women and third parties, are not characteristic exclusively of the press and religious sources. The tropes of 'waves' of trafficked women and of trafficked women as 'victims', are deployed by a number of feminist scholars too. While Koser and Lutz (1998: 3) stress the unavailability of reliable data on female migrants trafficked illegally for the purpose of prostitution, other scholars (Caldwell et al. 1999; Lazaridis 2001: 70) rely on questionable statistical data provided by governmental and non-governmental bodies where numbers diverge by hundreds of thousands.[21] The vagueness and ambiguity of these figures foster accounts of trafficking from eastern Europe that speak of it in terms of an 'explosive increase' (Molina and Janssen 1998: 16) that has reached 'epidemic proportions' (UN in Pickup 1998: 44). Such alarmist portrayals not only inflate the statistics to produce an imagery of invasion but, as I shall argue below, obscure the relationship between illegal migration and the juridico-material creation of borders on the one hand, while they deploy a particularly gendered image of migration on the other.

In their investigations of trafficking of eastern European women for prostitution, some feminist scholars who have approached the topic from the perspective of migration and globalization (Phizacklea 1996; Anthias and Lazaridis 2000; Kofman et al. 2000) associate trafficking with illegal migration and perpetrate the narrative of victimhood. Phizacklea, for example, writes that 'trafficked women are often deceived and coerced into illegal migration' (1998: 31), while Orsini-Jones and Gattullo, who have examined the issue of women's migration and trafficking in Italy and Bologna in particular, observe that migrant women 'are part of the very sad "slave trade" flourishing across Europe' (2000: 128). The work of these feminist scholars has been path-breaking in introducing the important element of gendered relations of power in the study of migration and in theorizing the globalization of labour from a gendered perspective. However, the emphasis on the exploitation of women's sexual labour in the destination countries in studies on trafficking and prostitution fail to investigate the ways in which borders and visa regimes affect trafficked women's lives. Have all trafficked women been coerced into migrating to Italy? In what way and with whom did they cross the border and reach their destination? Were women undocumented or did they possess passports and visas? If they were in possession of a visa, how did they obtain it?[22] How long was the visa valid for?

Coerced across the Borders . . .

In the respondents' accounts, having or not having a visa is linked to the way in which they crossed the border and to the length of that crossing. The difference between documented and undocumented border-crossing is most apparent in the narratives of respondents who were 'trafficked' to Italy twice: first on foot without a visa and a second time by bus with purchased tourist visas. When the respondents crossed the borders undocumented on foot, in a truck or by boat, descriptions of their first journey constitute one of the central elements of their narratives and include detailed descriptions of the events and actors involved. In her account, Oksana recalls the number and names of women and traffickers with whom she travelled, the weather conditions when they crossed the Slovenian-Italian border, the vegetation surrounding them and even the state of the ground they walked on. When those same respondents returned to Italy for the second time with a valid visa, they travelled by plane or bus, crossed the international borders quickly and smoothly, and did not tell much about the practicalities of their travel. The disparity between the descriptions of undocumented and documented forms of travel is grounded in the degree of danger or risk the respondents underwent during the undocumented travel: the fear of being caught by the border police, being sexually abused by the traffickers, contracting a disease or an illness during a prolonged travel, having little or no control over the terms of the travel and therefore being dependent on the traffickers.

Contrary to the idea that women are always forced or coerced by traffickers into illegal migration, some respondents tell of how they were only able to realize their plans to leave for Italy with the help of traffickers. A striking example comes from Liudmila, who went to hire an agency to buy her visa and organize the trip to Italy. Yet, due to the instability in the region caused by NATO's bombing of Serbia, the agency in Moldova was not able to carry out this otherwise routine operation.[23] After months of waiting for the situation to improve, Liudmila finally decided to contact a trafficker who brought her to Italy in four days upon the condition that she work in prostitution. To some respondents it took longer to reach Italy because the group with which they travelled was intercepted by the border police. The unsuccessful crossing resulted in deportation from Austria in Kateryna's case and prohibition of entry into Hungary in Larisa's case. A few weeks later each of the respondents embarked upon another crossing via a different route: Larisa arrived in Italy from Albania by boat and Kateryna crossed the Slovenian-Italian border on foot. Kateryna comments on her second journey: 'I was scared of being caught and sent back home. Because if they [the border police] would have caught me I would have had to do it all over again.' Many narratives are punctuated by remarks that reveal women's awareness of the necessity to cross the borders secretly, as reflected in Kateryna's remark: 'Some girls travel hidden in the back of a truck. They take sleeping pills in order not to do anything and not to eat at all. They take sleeping pills and sleep during the entire journey.'

Not all respondents arrived to Italy undocumented; traffickers provided some with necessary travel documents. Realizing that she will have to cross the border on foot because her traffickers were not in the first instance willing to spend money to buy her a visa, Snezana refused to leave until she successfully negotiated a visa and a bus ride to Italy. Another respondent, Tatiana, flew from Moscow to Rome with a tourist visa valid for 15 days that was bought for her by two Russian women working as prostitutes in Italy. Oksana and Ioanna (Olga and Natasha in the newspaper clipping mentioned on p. 256 of this volume) reached Italy in two days. As the newspaper reports, they travel to Italy by bus. However, they did not enter Italy undocumented but were in possession of short-term visas which they bought, through an agency, with the money borrowed from a third party. This money covered the costs of the visa, travel from Ukraine to Poland, a night in a hotel in Warsaw and a bus ticket to Bologna. Even though it is quite difficult, if not impossible, to travel undocumented with a regular international bus line across Europe, the newspaper article reports that two respondents were 'illegal'. This conflation of trafficking with undocumented migration sustains and strengthens the representation of trafficking as necessarily a form of illegal migration. It relies on a distinction between 'illegal' and 'legal' migration which is oversimplified: a number of respondents entered Italy with a valid visa, but became undocumented after having overstayed the length of the granted visa.

As the above examples indicate, it is extremely problematic to endorse a model which positions trafficking – as a form of illegal migration – in opposition to legally approved modes of migration: trafficking might have legal elements such as legally obtained visas while legal migratory processes might involve illegal components such as requests for high fees advanced by the agencies or even illegal payments asked for by Consulates. Moreover, within the Italian legal system that classifies migrants in terms of non-citizens (Dal Lago 1999), a category constructed on social and political removal, being illegal is a ground for detention and deportation. Hence, the fear of being caught by the police and returned to the point of departure enhances migrants' dependency on the third parties and contributes to their conditions of confinement.

... and Deceived into Trafficking?

Besides kidnapping, the Italian press offers meagre information regarding the various ways by which women and traffickers get into contact. One of the few examples I came across concerned two women who responded to a newspaper ad in Moldova placed by an agency promising earnings up to US$800 per week (*Il Resto del Carlino*, 17 October 1999). An examination of the respondents' life-stories discloses a more complex reality of trafficking systems. In the respondents' accounts, third parties involved in organizing the journey to Italy were many and carried out a number of different tasks. The respondents do not portray the initial contact with individual recruitment people or agencies as abusive. This does not mean that the respondents are naïve when it comes to the third parties' economic interests. Nevertheless, the respondents do not underestimate the importance of the third parties' involvement and often refer to them in a manner similar to that of Oksana's account: 'They help girls to find a job in a foreign country.' Some parts of the network through which women are offered employment and access to Italy, and for which they subsequently work, seem to be part of a larger criminal network. Other trafficking systems, on the contrary, cover a wide variety of people such as taxi drivers, housewives and restaurant owners who seem to supplement their income through 'passing the word'. If on the one hand trafficking is a 'multi-billion dollar industry' (Ram 2000: 1), on the other hand it also seems to be an integral part of the local and informal economies of some eastern European countries.

Interestingly enough, newspaper notices do not report on the nature of the advertised job, thereby perpetuating the idea that third parties inevitably deceive foreign women into prostitution. In contrast, Wijers and Lap-Chew (1997: 99) point out that the majority of women who migrate through trafficking know about the nature of the work but are often unaware of the conditions they will work under. My findings point in the same direction. Within the larger group of respondents, disparities of the modes of entry into trafficking surfaced between those women who were deceived about the type of labour they were expected to perform and those who were informed that they were expected to work as prostitutes. For the respondents from the former group, prostitution was not an option. In her story, Ivana recounts how, instead of working as a waitress in Switzerland as agreed with third parties, she was forced through the use of physical violence into leaving Croatia and then prostituting in Italy.

As for the latter group, the fact that the respondents were told that they were to work in prostitution did not imply that they were informed about the working and living situation upon arrival. A respondent who accepted her lover's offer to work in Italy as a prostitute, for instance, was not aware of the conditions she would be working in, such as long hours, a large number of clients and the constant control by a third party or by peers. Another respondent was told more precisely what she was expected to do. Oksana, who was about to return to Italy for the second time, asked her friend Ioanna if she would like to join her and described her previous experience of street prostitution. (See again the newspaper clipping on Olga and Natasha mentioned on p. 256 which tells the story of the same respondents with emphasis on deception.) Ioanna states that she arrived in Italy prepared: 'I came to Italy and I knew all about it – what to tell to the clients, what to do, where to go – I knew it all.' However, from the examination of the 'contract' between a third party and the respondent, it emerges that the respondent did not know that she would be required to surrender most of her earnings and prostitute under conditions of confinement which made it difficult to retract from the contract.

Even so, for this group, entering into a prostitution contract emerged as part of a bigger migratory project. At this point, I would like to reiterate that at the time of the interviews all of the respondents had already left prostitution. Given the fact that my evidence is limited to this specific category of migrant women, it is impossible for me to know whether interpreting prostitution – in its intersection with trafficking – as a migratory project is representative of the larger population of trafficked women or if it is specific for a group of subjects who have already left prostitution and construe their experience of trafficking in terms of a migratory project. Notwithstanding its interpretative limits, an investigation of entry into trafficking systems and prostitution from the perspective of the respondents' lives generates new insights into the complexity of trafficking.

Hence, entering the trafficking system and consenting to prostitute was merely a means to an end, as for Ana, who 'just' wanted to 'get to Italy', unconcerned about the details of her work in prostitution. For Ioanna, coming to Italy was linked to the lack of opportunities at home: 'I am twenty-three years old and now I am able to take care of things on my own. I came to Italy because there was no job for me back home. Initially I said no, but if there was no work then going to Italy was the last chance to find a job.' While Ioanna left the Ukraine planning to improve her and her family's situation, Kateryna left Romania in order to break away from her depressive state caused by humiliation in school and past violence at home: 'I wanted to start my life all over again in a place where no one knew me or things about me. I wanted to create a new image of myself.' For these women, migration to Italy for work in prostitution is part of a project designed to lead them out of poverty, lack of employment, lost self-esteem, family abuse, interrupted education and a general sense of life stagnation. Paradoxically, my data suggests that the EU borders, visa-regimes and restrictive immigration regulations that aim at suppressing trafficking and hampering the illegal movements of people work in favour of the third parties who organize trafficking, whether individuals and agencies, because they become a kind of supplementary migration system or even an alternative to the EU regulated migration. In fact, for a number of interviewees, entering Italy via trafficking systems was a means of travel and migration.

Setting the Crime Scene

Next to the exposé on victims, texts from the press, religious and feminist sources also put forward numerous portrayals of traffickers. For example, the authors of the joint City of Brescia and *Caritas* educational booklet present traffickers as follows: 'Smuggling in people and trafficking in arms, drugs, and cheap labour are all closely connected to the traffic of foreign girls. Due to an excellent and very close communication network, the criminal web spreads across all countries of eastern Europe. Its terminals are fashion, employment and travel agencies' (City of Brescia et al. 2000: 6). Using the image of an overarching criminal web, this booklet represents trafficking as all-encompassing and even perhaps unavoidable for women found at its 'terminals'. Another example comes from *Schiave d'occidente* mentioned earlier, where traffickers are portrayed as ferocious criminals who affirm their masculinity through physical abuse: 'There was no need of a valid reason to unleash Genti's rage.

A mere pretext, invented in that very moment, would do. Each time I returned from working [on the street], he greeted me with a good beating ... Of course, he also raped me in order to affirm his rights of ownership' (Moroli and Sibona 1999: 39). Throughout the book, the authors intervene in the text by combining their own views on trafficking with the direct quotes from women. This type of operating is best visible in the last sentence of the above quote where the point of view of the teenage character filters the authors' viewpoint of prostitution in terms of expression of male sexuality based on women's domination. This type of authorial manipulation of characters' perspectives produces a narrative which inscribes 'other' women as victims of violent men (usually from their own patriarchal culture).

In her reading of 'western feminism and third world prostitute' through the work of Wendy Brown, Doezema points out that 'the desire for the protection of injured identities leads to the collusion with, and intensification of disciplinary regimes of power' (2001: 33). Western feminist strategies, such as those in *Schiave d'occidente*, that aim at illustrating the horrendous 'reality' of trafficking by focusing exclusively on male violence and exploitation of women, re-enforce the idea of foreign women as powerless victims, and of foreign men as violent. Moreover, the authors do not question the role of the Italian state or immigration regulations as pivotal factors in sustaining migrants' social and political exclusion and their vulnerability to violence. Instead, they look to the authorities in the effort to combat and suppress trafficking.[24] In a similar manner, the authors of the *Migration Dossier 1999*, published by *Caritas*, assume the illegal and criminal nature of trafficking and put forth the measures to combat it through 'the creation of the special border-police, . . . and financial and technical support for the poorer countries in order to achieve better border control' (1999: 31).

The *topos* of violence is popular with the press too. Newspapers often highlight that migrant women who press charges against their traffickers are intimidated with threats of violence: traffickers threaten women's families in their home countries, or the women themselves. These women therefore face an enormous risk in returning home or reporting the crimes of which they have been victims. Article 18 of L. n. 40/1998 of the Italian Immigration Law is quite unique in that it allows persons trafficked to Italy, whose lives would be endangered if returned home, to stay in Italy and obtain a residence and a work permit on the condition that they agree to leave prostitution and participate in a social-protection programme. While I recognize the importance of legal measures that protect victims, I am wary of the ways in which Article 18 institutionalizes and essentializes the rhetoric of victimization. It requires that applicants leave prostitution, disqualifying in this way the possibility that for some women prostitution might be part of their migratory projects, and establishes a normative narrative of victimhood grounded in very particular forms and patterns of violence. For example, when the threat of violence upon returning home or the danger of traffickers' retaliation is not clearly discernible from a woman's story, immigration officials do not accept her claim to stay in Italy. In Natalya's case, for example, her request for a residence permit on the basis of Article 18 was rejected by the authorities, which rejection was justified as follows: 'Currently, there are no concrete dangers for the safety of the claimant, which would be caused by the claimant's attempt to escape organizations that exploit prostitution.'[25] In this way, the current legal conceptualization of trafficking not only disqualifies women's agency by establishing a normative narrative grounded in forced migration, coercion into prostitution and economic exploitation, but also penalizes those women who fall out of the established norm. By being refused access to Article 18, they are unable to legalize their status, and might be deported.

A respondent who told *La Repubblica*[26] that she cannot return home because of a dangerous situation awaiting her there gives another version of the story in the interview. She explains that mentioning the threat of violence was a strategy to be allowed to apply for a special residence permit for those people who were trafficked against their will and who are at risk of serious violence if returned to their country of origin. This strategy was suggested to Oksana by the foreign police officer responsible for her case. While there is no adequate space here to get into the ambiguous aspect of this police officer's position, I would like to stress that presenting oneself as a victim is indeed indispensable if an undocumented migrant woman is to use the legal immigration apparatus to her advantage and obtain the right to remain in Italy. I am not suggesting that episodes of violence do not occur. However, I am interested here in the rhetorical use of violence that creates a discursive space able to accommodate various narratives of violence. Although I have focused on women's experiences of migration as a way of countering dominant discourses and representations of trafficking, I am not arguing that women's narratives are not informed by established discourses, nor that they are necessarily in an oppositional relationship with them. However, at the same time, the topic of violence points to the complexity of the production of the victimhood narrative: its plot lends itself for manipulation because of its being already available within the mainstream discursive scenario on trafficking; but, simultaneously, its appropriation feeds into and further sustains the dominant rendering of trafficking in terms of crime and violence.

Conclusion

In this chapter I have mapped threads of the current official Italian discourse on trafficking of women from eastern Europe for work in prostitution. From the perspective of the actors partaking in this debate – the press, religious and feminist organizations – trafficking in women for prostitution is regarded as a form of coerced migration. Migrant women are portrayed as victims deceived into trafficking, and forced into illegality by the traffickers. Traffickers are represented mainly as 'foreign men' joined in organized criminal networks that stretch across the whole of eastern Europe. Tighter control over the external EU borders and stricter immigration laws are called upon as indispensable measures to rescue migrant women, apprehend the traffickers and combat trafficking.

In contrast, I suggest that the official re/presentation of trafficking is highly gendered and re/produces stereotypical narratives of femininity and masculinity. The narratives of victimization and criminality are a form of contemporary fiction that discloses the dissymmetry of power relations in the new Europe. I argue that in order to investigate trafficking in its contemporary European dimension, one needs to tackle the issues of migration in relation to the formation of the EU and its enlargement eastward. Viewed within this framework trafficking emerges as intrinsically linked to the interception of undocumented migration, the enforcement of border-regimes, and the tightening of immigration regulations. Rather than inviting stricter border control to prevent trafficking, the migrant women's narratives suggest that for them, making use of the trafficking networks became one of the few available means of informal labour migration. Given the gap between official discourses on sex trafficking, government policies and respondents' narratives, I argue that there is an urgent need of attention to the nuances of how trafficking is lived and negotiated on the one hand, and represented and institutionalized on the other. Trafficking as such is an inadequate category to account for the complexity of current social-political transformations in Europe and women's experiences of international migration.

As discussed in the third section (see pp. 256–58), a number of feminist scholars who have investigated trafficking from the perspective of migration and/or globalization fall short of addressing critically the convergence that some anti-trafficking campaigns and governments establish between trafficking, illegal migration and crime. Instead of remarking casually, as Lazaridis does, that the 'lightly protected borders' (2001: 92) facilitate trafficking of eastern European women into Greece, a politically and theoretically informed feminist scholarship should, in my view, bring to the fore the material terrain of the EU immigration regulations, and address the implications of strict Schengen border regime and visa policies on trafficking in women. Interrogating the effects of the border-regimes of the new Europe and its material and legal apparatus, and theorizing trafficking within the context of the EU enlargement, in particular the processes of recruitment into trafficking and cross-border travel, might help us to challenge our current understandings of trafficking, and of migrant women as duped into trafficking. Not to take issue with the notions of coercion and deception means to bolster trafficking as a criminal activity rather than a phenomenon predicated upon legal, political and economic inequalities. This reasoning would allow a move away from that perspective which sees the countries of eastern Europe as the main producers of crime and trafficking, and would reallocate the responsibility for persistence of trafficking onto the EU member states.

Acknowledgements

I would like to thank the Open Society Institute for its support of my doctoral research during the academic year 2001/2. I also wish to thank Anne-Marie Fortier and Claudia Castañeda for their extensive comments and incredibly laborious editorial work; Bridget Anderson, Sarah Bracke, Rosi Braidotti, Bettina Knaup and Joanna Regulska for their insightful suggestions on previous versions of this text; and finally, Elsa Antonioni, Elspeth Guild and Sandro Mezzadra for encouraging my work. A very special and warm thanks to Diana Anders, whose friendship and support made this result possible.

Notes

1. This is the phrase with which the respondents greeted me during one of our first meetings. All the quotes from the conversations and the interviews with respondents as well as the excerpts from newspaper, religious and feminist sources have been translated from Italian into English. The translations are my own.
2. I use the terms eastern and western Europe to indicate distinct geopolitical areas. I put them in inverted commas and do not capitalize the

terms in order not to perpetuate images of two static blocks. In the post-1989 era, and especially at the moment of the European Union (EU) enlargement, this conceptualization would be erroneous. From here on, west and east Europe will be used without inverted commas.

3. By 'western Europe' I mean the EU member states.
4. While people might be trafficked for purposes of domestic work, prostitution, entertainment industry, agriculture and construction work, this chapter is concerned exclusively with trafficking for prostitution. The inverted commas are used to indicate my criticism of the term 'trafficking', which I develop in the chapter. In order not to burden the chapter with too many inverted commas and repetitions, from this point onward trafficking for prostitution will appear simply as trafficking and without inverted commas.
5. I am paraphrasing the United Nations' *Protocol to Prevent, Suppress and Punish Trafficking in Persons* that constitutes an internationally agreed-upon definition of trafficking. The Protocol was adopted in November 2000 at the UN Convention Against Transnational Organized Crime.
6. For more than a decade, the city has housed several innovative projects on trafficking, such as *Moonlight* working as an outreach street project, and *Progetto Delta* aiming at social protection and/or voluntary repatriation of trafficking victims.
7. I borrow the term 'conditions of confinement' from O'Connell Davidson. With this term she intends 'conditions that prevent exit from prostitution through the use of physical restraint, physical violence or the threat thereof, or through the threat of other non-economic sanctions, such as imprisonment or deportation' (1998: 29).
8. Even though Romania is an EU candidate it is considered to be lagging behind the other candidates and until recently (January 2002) its citizens needed a visa to enter Schengen territory.
9. The newspaper clippings have been collected between 1998 and 2000 from *La Repubblica,* a national daily, and *Il Resto del Carlino*, a Bologna local daily newspaper. The clippings are relevant not only for their portrayal of trafficking in general, but also because they concern the very same women I had interviewed.
10. *Slaves to the West: Tracing the Routes of Traffickers of Women.*
11. By 'New Europe' I mean the post-1989 Europe influenced by the end of the Cold War, which entailed the restructuring of Eastern Europe and the former Soviet Union, and the integration of the EU and its enlargement eastward.

12. See among others *la Repubblica* (Italy), *El País* (Spain), *de Volksgrant* (The Netherlands), and *Der Spiegel* (Germany).
13. I examined *La Repubblica* during the years 1999 and 2000.
14. At the time of writing, the Schengen area is comprised of Austria, Belgium, Denmark, Finland, France, Germany, Greece, Iceland, Italy, Luxemburg, Netherlands, Norway, Portugal, Spain and Sweden.
15. In his work King (1993) criticizes these claims and shows that in 1990, according to Eurostat Demographic Statistics, the total amount of third-country aliens in 12 countries of the EU did not exceed 2.5 per cent. A similar argument is found in Bort (2000) concerning the link between cross-border crime and undocumented migration. Bort shows that the initiatives to prevent cross-border crime in the border regions between Schengen and accession countries have little to do with a 'real' amount of crime perpetrated by the citizens of the accession countries.
16. Europeans became acquainted with those technologies in 2000 when 58 Chinese people were found dead in a Dutch truck after it had reached England at Dover.
17. Czech Republic, Estonia, Hungary, Latvia, Lithuania, Poland, Slovak Republic and Slovenia. Bulgaria and Romania are considered pre-accession countries, and their entry into the EU should take place in 2007.
18. Albania, Croatia, Bosnia and Herzegovina, Federative Republic of Yugoslavia, Former Yugoslav Republic of Macedonia, Moldova, Russia and Ukraine.
19. 'New' indicates that the character and function of these borders are new, whereas their geographical locations are not.
20. Biemann has made similar observations concerning the Mexican-US border (2000).
21. The International Organization for Migration (IOM) estimates that 700,000 women and children are trafficked per year across the globe while United Nations (UN) sources oscillate between two million (IMADR in McDonald et al. 2000: 1) and four million people (Ram 2000: 2). As far as trafficking in women from eastern Europe into the EU is concerned, some EU sources report 500,000 women (ibid.) while others estimate between 200,000 and 500,000, a number that rounds up the presence of women from eastern Europe as well as Latin America, Africa and Asia (Molina and Janssen 1998: 16).
22. In some countries one cannot find an Italian embassy. For example, citizens of Ukraine needed to go to Budapest (Hungary) to present a visa request.

23. The respondents report that an agency charges between US$360 and US$500, depending on the country of departure, for a visa and a bus ticket to Italy. By way of comparison, those informants who worked as school teachers or secretaries in Moldova or Ukraine earned between US$20 and US$30 per month.
24. It is no coincidence, perhaps, that Arlacchi, the Director General of the UN Programme of Drug Control and Crime Prevention, provides the preface to *Schiave d'occidente*.
25. P.p. n. 3349/96–21 R.G. P.M. dated 26 November 1998. The Italian Immigration Law has recently been revised since the Government found it to be too permissive. A new clause, which considers illegal entry into Italy a criminal offence, was introduced. Accordingly, if an illegal person re-enters Italy after deportation, he or she could be punished with six months to one year of prison. If the same person enters illegally for the third time, imprisonment will vary between one and four years.
26. The exact date of the article is withheld for the safety of the informant.

References

Andreas, P. (2000), 'Introduction: The Wall after the Wall', in P. Andreas and T. Snyder (eds), *The Wall Around the West. State Borders and Immigration Controls in North America and Europe*, New York: Rowman & Littlefield.

Anthias, F. and Lazaridis, G. (2000), 'Introduction: Women on the Move in Southern Europe', in F. Anthias and G. Lazaridis (eds), *Gender and Migration in Southern Europe*, Oxford: Berg.

Biemann, U. (2000), 'Performing the Border: Gender, Transnational Bodies and Technology', in *been there and back to nowhere: Gender in Transnational Spaces*, Berlin: b_books.

Bort, E. (2000), *Illegal Migration and Cross-Border Crime: Challenges at the Eastern Frontier of the European Union*, EUI Working Paper RSC 2000/9.

Caldwell, G., Galster, S., Kanics, J. and Steinzor, J. (1999), 'Capitalizing on Global Economies: The Role of Russian Mafia in Trafficking in Women for Forced Prostitution', in P. Williams (ed.), *Illegal Immigration and Commercial Sex*, London and Portland: Frank Cass.

Caritas (1999), *Immigrazione. Dossier statistico 1999*, Rome.

City of Brescia, Centro Caritas Darfo and Coordinamento Imp-Sex Brescia (2000), *Stop! Fermiamo il traffico*, Brescia.

Commission of the European Communities COM(2002) 233, 7.5.2002. Communication from the Commission to the Council and the European Parliament, *Towards Integrated Management of the External Borders of the Member States of the European Union*, Brussels.

Dal Lago, A. (1999), *Non-persone. L'esclusione dei migranti in una società globale,* Milan: Feltrinelli.

Dietrich, H. (2000), 'Regime di controllo delle frontiere e nuove migrazioni nell'Europa di Schengen. Il caso tedesco', in S. Mezzadra and A. Petrillo (eds), *I confini della Globalizzazione*, Rome: Manifesto libri.

Doezema, J. (2001), 'Ouch! Western Feminists' "Wounded Attachments" to the "Third World Prostitute"', *Feminist Review*, 67: 16–38.

FFM (1998), 'Living Near the Border: The Involvement of Border Population into what Can Be Called the German Border-Regime at the German Polish Border', *MoneyNations@access Magazine*, 6–11.

King, M. (1993), 'The Impact of Western European Border Policies on the Control of "Refugees" in Eastern and Central Europe', *New Community*, 19(2): 183–99.

Kofman, E., Phizaklea, A., Raghuram, P. and Sales, R. (2000), *Gender and International Migration in Europe*, London and New York: Routledge.

Koser, K. and Lutz, H. (1998), *The New Migration in Europe: Social Constructions and Social Realities*, Basingstoke: Macmillan.

Lazaridis, G. (2001), 'Trafficking and Prostitution: The Growing Exploitation of Migrant Women in Greece', *The European Journal of Women's Studies*, 8(1), 67–102.

McDonald, L., Moore, B. and Timoshkina, T. (2000), *Migrant Sex Workers from Eastern Europe and the Former Soviet Union: The Canadian Case*, Ottawa: Status of Women Canada.

Molina, F.P. and Janssen, M.-L. (1998), *I Never Thought This would Happen to Me: Prostitution and Traffic in Latin American Women in the Netherlands*, Amsterdam Foundation Esperanza.

Moroli, E. and Sibona, R. (1999), *Schiave d'occidente. Sulle rotte dei mercanti di donne*, Milan: Mursia.

O'Connell Davidson, J. (1998), *Prostitution, Power and Freedom*, Ann Arbor: University of Michigan Press.

Orsini-Jones, M. and Gatullo, F. (2000), 'Migrant Women in Italy: National Trends and Local Perspectives', in F. Anthias and G. Lazaridis (eds), *Gender and Migration in Southern Europe*, Oxford: Berg.

Phizacklea, A. (1996), 'Women, Migration and the State', in S. Rai and G. Lievesley (eds), *Women and the State: International Perspectives*, London: Taylor & Francis.

—— (1998), 'Migration and Globalisation', in K. Koser and H. Lutz (eds) *The New Migration in Europe: Social Constructions and Social Realities*, Basingstoke: Macmillan.

Pickup, F. (1998), 'More Word but no Action? Forced Migration and Trafficking in Women', *Gender and Development*, 6(1): 44–51.

Presidency Conclusions Leaken European Council, 14 and 15 December 2001, Conclusion No. 42.

Ram, M. (2000), 'Putting an End to the Trafficking of Women in the NIS and CEE', IREX Policy Paper, http://www.irex.org.

Regulska, J. (2001), 'Gendered Integration of Europe: New Boundaries of Exclusion', in H.M. Nickel and G. Jahnert (eds), *Gender in Transition in Eastern and Central Europe*, Berlin: Trafo Verlag.

Sassen, S. (1999), *Guests and Aliens*, New York: New Press.

Simoncini A. (2000), 'Migranti, frontiere, spazi di confine. I lavoratori migranti nell'ordine salariale', *altreragioni*, 29–45.

UNITED. http://www.united.non-profit.nl.

Wijers, M. and Lap-Chew, L. (1997), *Trafficking in Women, Forced Labour and Slavery-like Practices in Marriage, Domestic Labour and Prostitution,* Utrecht: STV.

Wolff, L. (1994), *Inventing Eastern Europe: The Map of Civilization on the Mind of the Enlightenment*, Stanford: Stanford University Press.

–12–

Creolization in Discourses of Global Culture

Mimi Sheller

In recent narratives of 'global culture' the concept of creolization has been adopted as a convenient way to describe general processes of transnational cultural mixture and hybridization. What is now called 'the creolisation paradigm' (Howes 1996) is employed to describe the ways in which cultural consumers throughout the world creatively adapt 'global' commodities, brands, and ideas to 'local' contexts. Mike Featherstone, for example, speaks of creolization in global culture as a process of mixture, incorporation and syncretism (Featherstone 1995). 'We all' are experiencing creolization (Hannerz 1996) due to the increasingly rapid and extensive interchange of capital, information, people and cultural objects between far-flung parts of the world (Robertson 1992; Beck 2000; Urry 2000). 'Throughout contemporary Euro-American criticism from the late '70s to the present,' notes Caren Kaplan, 'a universalized concept of creolization or hybridity has come to reflect a postmodern turn in cultural criticism' (Kaplan 1996: 129). Yet seldom is it asked what the effects are of appropriating a concept, moving it to the 'centre' as a 'global' referent and (as I shall argue in this chapter) gutting it of its political edge and theoretical complexity.

The US and British proponents of 'global' creolization usually borrow the idea from the work (often unacknowledged) of Caribbean and Caribbean diaspora theorists. In contrast to this universalization of *créolité* as a reputedly new global condition, I want to ask about what gets left behind (and what gets taken) when Caribbean theories – and theorists – migrate to new homes (cf. Said 1983; Clifford and Dhareshwar 1989). This chapter offers a located historical account of the meaning of creolization within Caribbean culture and theory, tracing how a theoretical term developed in the Caribbean in contexts of transatlantic slavery and colonialism was 'uprooted' and 'regrounded' in the quite different context of metropolitan self-theory.[1] Related concepts, such as Cuban theorist Fernando Ortiz's 'transculturation', have also taken on far wider resonance (Pratt 1992), with a suggestion that 'in postcolonial times, one of the attractions of this concept may be that it is in itself an example of counterflow, from periphery to center' (Hannerz 2000: 14). What are the dynamics of such 'counterflows' and what part do they play in the reconfiguration and redeployment of metropolitan culture? How has the concept of creolization moved from the periphery to the centre, for whom, and with what political effects? Do deracinated theoretical terms differ from more located political usages, such as those that understand 'creolising practices' as counter-appropriations of 'master-codes of the dominant culture' (Mercer 1988; Aravamudan 1999)? And what grounds for resistance are lost in making creolization shorthand for cultural hybridization and the fluidity of 'global' identities?

In considering these questions of theoretical piracy I begin by tracing the formation of the Caribbean and its diaspora(s) as sites of mobility and transmigration, touching upon the origins of the term 'creole' and its connotations of what I call an achieved indigeneity. I link the origins of the concept of creolization to concrete and specific histories of Caribbean displacement, migration and transnationalism. Most importantly, I consider how the concept of *créolité,* or creoleness, unravels the distinction between home (as origin) and migration (as movement away from home). Next I trace the Caribbean elaboration of the theoretical term 'creolization', and show how it has a specific genealogy stemming from the African diasporic experience of violent uprooting and regrounding in the New World. Here I describe how the political commitments associated with theories of creolization shifted from a national project linked to decolonization in the 1960s–1970s (for example in the work of Kamau Brathwaite and Rex Nettleford), to a postcolonial and post-national project grounded in the Caribbean diaspora in the 1980s–1990s (for example Stuart Hall, Paul Gilroy, Edouard Glissant).

Finally I turn to the ways in which recent theorists of global culture have appropriated the concept to describe the Western metropolitan experience of globalization as one of becoming more creolized. Here I suggest that the language of universality and 'we-ness' used by these theorists to describe this 'new' global condition with which 'we all' are now said to be living belies a specifically located (Western, metropolitan, privileged) position of those using the concept in this way. Current forms of postmodern hybridity, envisioned as a disavowal of roots in favour of dwelling in a fluid state of 'liquid modernity' (Bauman 2000), are in fact exercises of power through which metropolitan theorists establish an unmarked but privileged position of locational invisibility which they then identify as 'global'.[2] The sanitized version of cultural synergy with which we are left erases the specific itineraries of migration, resistance, and conflict out of which both 'creole cultures' and Caribbean theories of creolization emerged.

Caribbean Migrations Home: Achieving Indigeneity in Mobility

The Caribbean has long been at the forefront of processes of migration and cultural mixture at a global scale. These include not only the colonial empire-spanning systems of enslavement and indentured servitude, but also more recent transnational flows of trade and investment, migration and displacement, and intermixture of ethnic, linguistic and cultural groups. Cuban-American literary theorist Antonio Benítez-Rojo describes the Caribbean as a 'meta-archipelago' in which there was 'an extraordinary collision of races and cultures' in processes of 'syncretism, acculturation, transculturation, assimilation, deculturation, indigenization, creolization, cultural *mestizaje*, cultural *cimarronaje*, cultural miscegenation, cultural resistance, etc.' (Benítez-Rojo 1996: 37). His typical excess of descriptive terms hints at the definitive complexity of 'Caribbean culture', if there is any such singular entity. For some influential anthropologists creolization[3] is that which defines the Caribbean as a region (Mintz and Price 1985: 6), and its creole cultures are said to have become 'a paradigm for modern syncretic cultures' (Clifford 1988). Thus a brief overview of Caribbean migration, creole genesis and transnationalism can help us to explain how and why 'creoleness' has come to define the essence of the Caribbean.

Caribbean migration studies suggest that the 'essence of Caribbean life has always been movement' and that 'movement is a significant and conscious reflection of identity in the Caribbean' (Duval 2002: 261, 263; Thomas-Hope 1992; Lewis 1990: *xiii*). The region is described as more 'deeply and continuously affected' by migration than any other region of the world (Foner 1998: 47).[4] Its migration histories include not only the itineraries of indentured, enslaved and free people from Africa, Europe and Asia, but also the intra-Caribbean labour migrations of the nineteenth century and the out-migrations, 'remigrations' and return migrations of the twentieth. Some of the Leeward islands are even described as having 'migration cultures' based on 'trans-island communities' in which migration has been crucial to patterns of survival since the post-slavery period (Richardson 1983; Thomas-Hope 1995). Out of these many migrations emerged what anthropologists in the 1950s defined as 'creole societies' (a debated term to which I return below).

The term 'creole' is itself unstable, having been continually adapted by different groups over time within the Caribbean and increasingly beyond the Caribbean context.[5] It is thought to have an African origin, which entered Portuguese in the early period of the Atlantic slave trade (Allen 2002: 49–50). In Spanish the term *criollo* was used from the sixteenth century to refer to people of Iberian descent born in the Americas, as well as locally born and bred 'livestock and slaves' as distinguished from imports of European stock or 'salt-water' slaves.[6] As Carolyn Allen points out in an important reading of diverse definitions and historical usage of the term, its core features include '[a] movement away from origin and the difficulty of reconstructing a path back to the source(s) suggested in the [uncertain] etymology of the term . . . [and] [w]ith the historical experience of colonialism which gave rise to its use, the primacy of cross-cultural encounter and the location of Creoleness at its intersection' (2002: 56–7). As a 'movement away from origin' and an intersection for colonial encounters, creoleness is about both displacement and the generation of new modes of dwelling with difference. Out of this, Allen notes, comes a process of modification 'involving rejection, adaptation, accommodation, imitation, invention', ending eventually in a dynamic new 'type' which is recognized as 'belonging to the locale' but continuing to interact with new influences (ibid). As Raphael Confiant and Patrick Chamoiseau express it in *Élogé de la créolité*, 'Neither Europeans, nor Africans, nor Asians, we proclaim ourselves Creoles' (Shepherd and Richards 2002: xiii).

In general, then, the term carries the connotation of what could be called an achieved indigeneity – a new claim of belonging to a locale, but a belonging grounded in movement, difference and transformation rather than stasis or permanence. Becoming 'Creole' is a process of achieving indigeneity[7] through the migration and recombination of diverse elements that have been loosed from previous attachments and have reattached themselves to a new place of belonging. That is to say, it refers to a process of being uprooted from one place and re-grounded in another such that one's place of arrival becomes a kind of reinvented home. It implies the displacement (yet not total loss) of a previous home/culture and the claiming of a new place of belonging. It also carries the connotation of a mobility and mixture of peoples, cultures, languages and cuisines, but in a way which specifically privileges subaltern agency against the power of a colonizing 'centre'. Being 'creole' destabilizes the very notion of home by showing the constitutive mobilities that always already inform dwelling (cf. Ahmed 2000; Fortier, Chapter 5 in this volume). Creolization could thus be described as the repeated genesis of newly negotiated homes-in-migration in ongoing processes of 're-homing'.[8]

There is also another way in which the Caribbean experience complicates theories of home and migration, due to the significant degree of 'remigrations' and returns. Caribbean 'migration streams' are in fact constituted by swirls and eddies such that migration is not a one-way trip, but a way of life. Many migrants engage in return visits to their birthplaces or send their children to spend summers with family in the Caribbean, or to be educated there. Increasing numbers are returning to island homelands, especially in retirement (Gmelch 1992; Duval 2002). Duval argues that Caribbean patterns of return migration require a more dynamic theorization of home, and of the links between visiting and returning. The 'fluid and dynamic nature of [Caribbean] migration experiences', he argues, cannot 'be compartmentalised into a dichotomy of return [versus] settlement' (Duval 2002: 263). Thus, Caribbean Creole cultures are described as 'profoundly diverse and mobile' (Vergès 2001: 170).

For many living in North America or Europe the Caribbean remains a kind of home, even as new belongings are claimed. Indeed the maintenance of ties to the Caribbean and the politicization of a pan-Caribbean (and in some cases pan-African) identity in the diaspora became the original prototype for theories of 'transmigration' and 'transnationalism' (Georges 1990; Schiller et al. 1992; Basch et al. 1994). As Elsa Chaney puts it, 'Caribbean life in New York City is the product of the continuous circular movements of people, cash, material goods, culture and lifestyles, and ideas to and from New York City and the islands and mainland territories of the English- and Spanish-speaking Caribbean and, in recent times, the island of Haiti' (Chaney 1987: 3). Constance Sutton refers to the economic and cultural 'Caribbeanization of New York City', which she describes as 'the Caribbean cross-roads of the world' and 'the largest Caribbean city in the world' (Sutton 1987: 19). These locations have been made into new Caribbean homes, and moving between these homes has become a Caribbean mode of dwelling in 'transmigration' between more than one home.

Caribbean experiences of transmigration(s) have thus contributed to the destabilization of nations as imagined homogeneous communities and of migration as a linear movement from one nation state to another. The migration of West Indians to Britain, Antilleans to France, or Surinamers to the Netherlands was imagined both as a home-coming and a home-leaving, a re-making of what was already understood as home in an imagined elsewhere and a remembering of a home left behind. While the arrival of Caribbean migrants in Europe and North America in the post-Second World War period was initially perceived through models of ethnic 'assimilation' and racial 'integration' (Rex and Mason 1986), these migrations became the catalyst for fracturing such homogenizing models of national belonging. Theorists of Caribbean origin played a key role in the theorization of both the supra-national identities linked to pan-Africanism and to 'outer-national' formations such as the 'Black Atlantic' (Hall 1990; Gilroy 1993), both of which call into question any simplistic conjunction of home, 'race' and nation. They insist that the descendants of Africa have ties and attachments that extend outside the borders of the European and North American states where they have 'settled'. They also point toward other modes of South-South, or intra-Caribbean connection, which are overlooked by metrocentric theorists of migration.[9] As Françoise Vergès argues, 'Creole cosmopolitanism emerged then as a response to colonial racism and as an expression of a translocal sensibility' (Vergès 2001: 172).

In all of these ways, Caribbean cultures are cultures-on-the-move, which are already creole and in turn are said to have 'creolized' the metropolis. Having begun as collisions of diverse cultures that became indigenized as 'creole', they went on to spill across the Atlantic world spreading their influence into the 'global cities' that became key Caribbean cross-roads. However it is not only populations and popular cultures that cross international boundaries, but also more complex theoretical formations. It has gone largely unrecognized that the key theoretical terms for describing contemporary global culture have also travelled. The Caribbean has contributed a special terminology to theories of inhabitance and cultural transformation based on the concept of creolization, first as it was elaborated within the Caribbean, then as it migrated with Caribbean diasporic theorists into the mainstream of cultural studies of contemporary Western societies. The national and transnational formations sketched above are crucial to understanding how Caribbean theory is located within global discourses, and how it moves across them. In tracing these moves, I hope to bring greater attention to bear on questions of roots, origins, grounds and locations, asking more explicitly how each of these come to be shifted, rearticulated or made invisible within various theoretical projects. My key concerns are first to highlight how theories of creolization are inflected by the particular locations and specific political conditions in which they arise, and secondly, to show how metropolitan global theory pirates peripheral theory for the reproduction of its own discourses of power.[10]

Grounding Creolization in Caribbean Culture

Creolization is an ambiguous word with many different and even incommensurable meanings within its Caribbean context and beyond (Shepherd and Richards 2002). I focus here on the usage in which creolization refers to the active agency of subalterns in situations of colonial cultural conflict. It exists within a constellation of terms invented by earlier generations of Caribbean intellectuals to craft powerful tools for political critique of colonialism and imperialism, for example 'transculturation' (Ortiz 1947; cf. Spitta 1997), 'inter/culturation' (Brathwaite 1974), 'transversality' (Glissant 1981). I will first consider those theorists who used the concept of creolization in the context of the national independence movements of the 1960s and early 1970s. I then turn to such Caribbean diaspora theorists as Stuart Hall and Paul Gilroy who in the 1980s have re-worked the concept of creolization into a tool capable of challenging nationalist projects, forging a more supple theory of non-essentialist identity formation and transnational belonging.

The historian and poet Kamau Brathwaite, from Barbados, was one of the most significant early theorists of creolization.[11] His work was part of the post-independence nation-building projects of the 1960s, which 'developed partly in response to the legacy of racist thought that had helped to shape the written history of the region' (Richards 2001: 10). Brathwaite's historical analysis of 'creole society' in Jamaica can be situated as a postcolonial response to the cultural anthropology of the Caribbean in the mid-twentieth century, which was deeply influenced by the 'plural society' thesis (Shepherd and Richards 2002: *xii–xiii*). This dominant view of the Caribbean posited that there were separate cultural strands within each Caribbean society, a lack of any indigenous local culture, and only the broken remnants of African cultures (Smith 1965). In contrast, some anthropologists argued that there were African 'survivals' across the New World, which informed Caribbean cultural formations (Herskovits 1964). Others suggested furthermore that there was a uniquely creole cultural formation that drew on both European and African elements, but was distinctive to the New World plantation societies (Mintz and Price 1992 [1976]).

Claims to Creole identity in the postcolonial period signal an intellectual 'turn away from the "mother country" and an embryonic national consciousness which would develop into the anti-colonial movement towards self-possession and definition' (Allen 2002: 53). Brathwaite accordingly argued that 'African cultural norms had played a decisive role in the formation of the culture of the local population in the Anglophone

Caribbean and that this culture was not merely a poor imitation of Europe's but a new "Creole" culture' (Richards 2001: 10; Brathwaite 1971). He understood creole culture as a complex and dynamic relation between the culture(s) of the European colonizers and of the enslaved African peoples, and he defined creolization as a dual process of

> ac/culturation, which is the yoking (by force and example, deriving from power/prestige) of one culture to another (in this case the enslaved/African to the European); and inter/culturation, which is an unplanned, unstructured but osmotic relationship proceeding from this yoke. The creolisation which results (and it is a process not a product) becomes the tentative cultural norm of the society. (Brathwaite 1974: 6, cited in Shepherd and Richards 2002: *xii*).

Thus he theorized that the colonial relation was not simply one of domination, but of constant and dynamic cultural collision and 'osmosis'. Through decolonization the Caribbean could be reconstituted not as a failing outpost of European empires, but as a self-invented world where older cultures were being constantly cleaved amid new relations of power. His elaboration of the concept of inter/culturation and his understanding of the African contributions to Caribbean culture were influential on later ideas of 'transculturation' (Pratt 1992) and 'hybridity' (Bhabha 1994) in postcolonial literary theory (Shepherd and Richards 2002). For Homi Bhabha (1994), for example, the hybridity of language, with its Bakhtinian heteroglossia, draws attention to the ever-present potential for subversion and destabilization of colonial authority.

Insofar as creolization refers specifically to the process by which the descendants of enslaved Africans forged a new Caribbean culture, the use of the theoretical term in the 1970s retained a sense of dynamic critique and strategic rearticulation. Rex Nettleford in 1978 wrote that the 'two-pronged phenomenon of decolonisation and creolisation (or indigenisation) represents that awesome process actualised in simultaneous acts of negating and affirming, demolishing and constructing, rejecting and reshaping' (Nettleford 1978: 181). It 'refers to the agonising process of renewal and growth that marks the new order of men and women who came originally from different Old World cultures (whether European, African, Levantine or Oriental) and met in conflict or otherwise on foreign soil . . . The operative word here is "conflict"' (Nettleford 1978: 2). Creolization, then, was not simply about moving and mixing elements, but was more precisely about processes of cultural 'regrounding' following experiences of uprooting, or what Vergès refers to as 'cultures of survival' (Vergès 2001: 170).[12]

As Nigel Bolland argues and Richard Burton seconds, the more recent 'portrayal of creolization as a "blending" process, a mixing of cultures that occurs without reference to structural contradictions and social conflicts' is insufficient. This reduction 'obfuscates the tension and conflict that existed, and still exists, between the Africans and Europeans who were the bearers of these traditions' (Bolland 1992: 64; Burton 1997: 6). Creolization, they insist, is 'a process of *contention*', one deeply embedded in the history of enslavement, racial terror and subaltern survival in the Caribbean. This contentious process of intellectual nativization or indigenization played a crucial part in nationalist movements during the period of decolonization and independence in the former British West Indies and elsewhere in the Caribbean (Retamar 1989; Bolland 1992; Allen 2002). Moreover, 'the emergence of an indigenous historical tradition in the English-speaking Caribbean and the challenge posed by 'local' historians such as Kamau Brathwaite to the British imperial historical tradition has been described as the 'Creolization of West Indian history' (Shepherd and Richards 2002: *xii*; see Higman 1999). The impact of this important decolonizing gesture remains invisible when the work done by Caribbean theorists is not cited in later works that appropriate the term without reference to the Caribbean.[13]

The work done by Brathwaite and others can be situated in a long tradition in the Caribbean of intellectuals consciously identifying with the oppressed, a practice which the Guyanese radical Walter Rodney referred to as 'groundings' (Rodney 1969; cf. Campbell 1987). Caribbean theories of creolization are grounded in a grass-roots politics of the subaltern, carrying with it responsibilities of remembrance and solidarity with the most oppressed groups in society. Responsibility toward the 'grass-roots' and the subaltern, I suggest, is crucial to the Caribbean theorization of creolization, but has been lost in the subsequent metropolitan appropriation of the concept. By maintaining a sense of the *groundings* of the concept of creolization in Caribbean history, Caribbean theorists have been able to keep in play the tension between its dual meanings, locating it at the intersection of a system of cultural domination and a politics of subaltern resistance.

Before moving on to the appropriation of the concept of creolization in global theory, however, I want to draw attention to an intermediate step in the migration of this theoretical term from a regional context to global ubiquity. It was only in the 1980s that theorists across the wider Caribbean diaspora began to extend usage of the concept of creolization and to free it of its nationalist or nativist connotations (though still keeping its decolonizing politics). Caribbean diaspora theorists located in Europe and

North America transformed it into what Paul Gilroy calls an 'outer-national' project (Gilroy 1993). Unlike later metropolitan theorists, however, Caribbean diaspora theorists kept track of the roots of the concept in slavery and African-Caribbean cultures of resistance. They are acutely aware that postcolonial migrations have been tightly controlled by the power of borders and passports, visas and quotas, and the highly limited forms of hospitality or welcome accorded to them on arrival in their destinations. This enabled them to understand creolization as *a conflictual process of re-homing or re-grounding, rather than simply a playful uprooting and re-mixing of dislocated cultures.*

Gilroy's influential work on the Black Atlantic brought the concept of creolization to a far wider audience, beyond the relatively small field of Caribbean studies. He argues that the 'theorisation of creolisation, métissage, mestizaje, and hybridity' is a difficult yet productive way 'of naming the processes of cultural mutation and restless (dis)continuity that exceed racial discourse and avoid capture by its agents' (Gilroy 1993: 2). Against 'ethnic absolutism' and nostalgic nationalisms of all kinds (including African, and presumably Caribbean) he holds onto the possibilities offered by 'the untidy workings of diaspora identities . . . [and their] creolized, syncretized, hybridized, and chronically impure cultural forms' (Gilroy 2000: 129). His political project is to free the theory of creolization from its nationalist connotations by applying it to the diasporic experience. The Caribbean plays a part in his descriptions of the Black Atlantic as a 'routing' of black cultures via the Americas and a 're-rooting' of these cultures (especially musical) by Caribbean migrants in Europe. Yet apart from several citations of C.L.R. James, and despite his own Caribbean diasporic connections, it is not always made evident that his work is indebted to Caribbean theoretical antecedents; his approach is, however, deeply grounded in the histories of slavery, colonialism and migration, by which the creole cultures of the Caribbean and its diaspora were formed.

Gilroy's work helped to spread these concepts throughout cultural studies, though he is not alone. Edouard Glissant, of Martinique, published an essay entitled 'Créolization du Monde' in 1998 in which he argued that the continuous processes of cultural fusion and re-differentiation at work in creolization are analagous to the cultural *métissage* associated with contemporary globalization (Glissant 1998; Medea 2002: 127). For Glissant, 'Creolization produces identities that are not rooted but grow as rhizomes (Glissant borrows Deleuze and Guattari's notion) and which do not seek to delimit a territory on which to express themselves' (Vergès 2001: 179). Kobena Mercer also suggested that 'across a whole range of cultural forms there is a "syncretic" dynamic which critically appropriates elements from the master-codes of the dominant culture and "creolises" them, disarticulating given signs and re-articulating their symbolic meaning' (Mercer 1988: 57). The value of such anti-nationalist cultural projects, according to Stuart Hall, is in their capacity to address questions of 'hybridity, syncretism, of cultural undecidability and the complexities of diasporic identification which interrupt any "return" to ethnically closed and "centred" original histories' (Hall 1996: 250). By re-grounding cultural signs, meanings and symbols, they resist the power of the colonizing centre and throw confusion into any nostalgic longing for a 'pure' origin or 'uncontaminated' cultures among which differences are clear.

Hall himself has been extremely influential as a prime voice both of the Caribbean (Jamaican) diaspora and of Cultural Studies in Britain. He observes that Caribbean culture negotiates a 'doubleness' that is simultaneously grounded by continuity with the past (the cultural, linguistic, musical and culinary traces and bodily practices of Africa) yet always ruptured by difference and discontinuity, arising from the historical traumas of displacement, dismemberment and transportation. Creolization cannot simply be about 'localizing' the global, since it rightly disturbs this dichotomy by suggesting that the most local, even intimate, aspects of Caribbean culture (such as the home itself, the deportment of the body, the styles of music and dance) always already carry traces of the 'global'. It is rather 'a response to crisis and extreme upheaval, which operates upon a series of linguistic, psychological and ontological levels' (Thomas 2000: 11). In the following section I want to pursue this politics of grounded theory by considering how theories of creolization have been consumed by theorists of 'global culture' working in Europe and the United States in the 1990s.

Appropriations of Creolization in Global Culture

The explosive, politically engaged and conflictual mode of conceptualizing creolization in the nationalist period of the 1970s was transformed, I have argued, into a more general Black Atlantic theory of cultural resistance by Caribbean diasporic theorists working in metropolitan academic institutions in the 1980s. By the 1990s, however, the concept was increasingly being used to refer to *any* encounter and mixing of dislocated cultures, divorced from any connection to the legacies of transatlantic slavery and without citation of the Caribbean theorists who developed the concept. While there have been clear gains – theoretically and politically – in the postcolonial move to destabilize the borders and boundaries of nation states and cultures, the slippage of theoretical terms from the periphery to the centre has had some unintended consequences. As theories (and theorists) become mobile and *un*grounded, are they at risk of being consumed within mainstream culture stripped of their oppositional meanings?

As the concept of creolization began to be pried loose from its specific grounding in the Caribbean and taken up in a more general sense in the theorization of the cultural fluidity of postmodernity and globalization, its meaning changed. Although Caribbean diaspora theorists initiated this movement, others carried it in new directions. In a 1987 article entitled 'The World in Creolization' the anthropologist Ulf Hannerz argued for a new macro-anthropology of culture that would encompass both the 'Third World' and 'metropolitan' culture. Recognizing the cosmopolitan connections of all 'local' cultures and drawing on creole linguistics, he defines creole cultures as 'those which draw in some way on two or more historical sources, often originally widely different. They have had some time to develop and [to] integrate, and to become elaborate and pervasive'. Note that there is no mention of colonization or conflict here. The 'complexity and fluidity' of the world system, he concludes, suggests that '[in] the end, it seems, we are all being creolized' (Hannerz 1987: 552, 557). The concept of creolization became what he called a 'root metaphor' and 'keyword' in much of his subsequent work (Hannerz 1989, 1996, 2000), used as a device to free anthropological description from ideas of cultural integration within homogenous communities. As he puts it:

> here we are now, with hybridity, collage, mélange, hotchpotch, montage, synergy, bricolage, creolization, *mestizaje*, mongrelization, syncretism, trans-culturation, third cultures and what have you; some terms used perhaps only in passing as summary metaphors, others with claims to more analytical status, and others again with more regional or thematic strongholds. (Hannerz 2000: 13)

Hannerz prefers the term creolization as being more precise and restricted than the others, yet his loose conjunction of all of these terms, without citations, tends to blur their meanings. Moreover, in theorizing the new 'global' condition he erases both the *earlier* Caribbean experience of creolization and the Caribbean theorists who worked on the concept in a context that was *already* 'global' long before the late twentieth-century declarations of globalization being upon 'us' only now.

Having claimed that 'we are all being creolized', Hannerz also admits that 'some cultures are more creole than others' (ibid.: 14). He suggests that 'a creolist view is particularly applicable to processes of cultural confluence within a more or less open continuum of diversity, stretched out along a structure of center-periphery relationships which may well extend transnationally, and which is characterized also by inequality in power, prestige and material resource terms' (ibid.: 14). Yet, given such inequalities, nowhere does he consider on whose terms 'we' are 'with creolization' only *now*. Others (especially in the Caribbean) have long been creole, yet are excluded from these recent accounts of the emergence of transnational global modernity. As Hall dryly observes, 'The notion that only the multi-cultural cities of the First World are "diaspora-ised" is a fantasy which can only be sustained by those who have never lived in the hybridised spaces of a Third World, so-called "colonial" city' (Hall 1996: 250). So 'their' peripheral creolization is not like 'ours' in the centre, for whom becoming creole functions as a safe way of getting closer to other cultures ('confluence' rather than conflict), taking in a little bit of differ-ence (cf. hooks 1992; Ahmed 2000: 123; Stacey 2000; Sheller 2003). Hannerz's temporal understanding of globalization as something happen-ing only now forecloses, moreover, the possibility that 'we' (in the West) might *already be creole* due to what Brathwaite called the unintended 'inter/culturations' of the colonial period.

The influential US anthropologist James Clifford also claimed that 'We are all Caribbeans now in our urban archipelagos . . . hybrid and heteroglot' (Clifford 1992). His claim to the Caribbeanness of 'us all' also raises a number of thorny questions. What happens to the specificity of Caribbean cultural identity if the whole cosmopolis is said to be Caribbean? If creolization has its origins in Caribbean cultures of resistance, in the survival of enslavement and colonial plantation systems, and in move-ments of decolonization, in what sense can postmodern metropolitan culture possibly share in its dynamic? Clifford at least cites the Caribbean sources from which his ideas originate. He adopted Aimé Césaire as a 'forerunner of postmodern hybridity', according to Kaplan, by focusing on his use of language, in particular its 'radical indeterminacy' and 'resistance to easy translation', which 'constitutes a "Caribbean" practice of pastiche' (Kaplan 1996: 128–9; see Clifford 1988). In his 1990 essay on 'Traveling Cultures' Clifford mentions some Caribbean paragons of the analysis of travel and displacement, including C.L.R. James, V.S. Naipaul, Edouard Glissant, Alejandro Carpentier, Paulette Nardal, and Jamaica Kincaid. He further mentions the work of Paul Gilroy and Stuart Hall, refers to the transnationality of migrants to the United States from Haiti, Puerto Rico and the Dominican Republic, and alludes to the 'Caribbeani-zation' of New York City as part of his own biography (Clifford 1997).

Faced with the rise of 'the South', Clifford observes that the movements that matter most now are those of postcolonial intellectuals, who,
he says (again citing C.L.R. James),

> move theories in and out of discrepant contexts, addressing different audiences,
> working their different 'borderlands'. Theirs is not a condition of exile, of
> critical 'distance', but rather a place of *betweenness*, a hybridity composed of
> distinct, historically-connected postcolonial spaces . . . Theory is always
> written from some 'where', and that 'where' is less a place than *itineraries*:
> different, concrete histories of dwelling, immigration, exile, migration. (Clifford
> 1988: 184–5)

I agree that it is precisely the concrete histories of Caribbean theorizations
of creolization that need to be foregrounded. It is crucial that we attend to
where, when, and for what purposes Caribbean theorists first developed
the concept of creolization, and then moved it along their own itineraries
of diasporic travel. They are not so much 'working borderlands' as
reworking borders by finding multiple ways of moving through and
dwelling among them. Creolization as a theory of uprooting/regrounding
allows for a dwelling in migration predicated upon the imaging of 'routes'
not simply away from home, but also towards homes, and the imagining
of 'roots' not simply as origins but also as claims to belonging.

In sum, creolization has transmogrified from a politically engaged term
used by Caribbean theorists located in the Caribbean in the 1970s, to one
used by Caribbean diaspora theorists located outside of the Caribbean in
the 1980s, and finally to non-Caribbean 'global' theorists in the 1990s.
Along the way its meaning has been watered down. As suggested above,
creolization in the Caribbean context referred not only to mobility and
mixture, but also to conflict, trauma, rupture and the violence of uprooting. Different dwelling places have called for different theoretical articulations of the term, but it is the memory of the roots of the concept in the
conditions created by transatlantic slavery that informs any meaningful
politics of theory in this case. In contrast, current usage in 'global' theories
(not located in the Caribbean) has little to say about the negating, demolishing and rejecting to which Nettleford alludes. When the concept is used
in a more general sense, with little attention to structural inequalities, it is
reduced to a bland kind of cultural mixing in which 'we' – the urban,
hybrid, heteroglot – all share. This failure to recognize the more critical
and political implications of the term as used by Caribbean theorists leaves
the current 'creolization paradigm' with little to contribute to an operative
theory of conflict and unequal power relations.

Conclusion

The appropriation of creolization as a universal signifier of border-transcending cultural confluence and a tame term for multicultural mixture divorces it from questions of power, resistance and survival (cf. Puri, 2003). Hegemonic creolization has become a mode of 'becoming (the) other', erasing the transformative cultural agency not only of the Creole subaltern subject but also of the Caribbean theorists who disappear from current citations. I have argued that the concept of creolization shifted grounds as differently located theorists utilized it for different kinds of projects. As a term that was already quite fluid and malleable it has been easily pirated by theorists of global culture, who have (perhaps inadvertently) emptied it of its oppositional political meaning. In appropriating the metaphor of creolization within sites of contemporary metrocentric theory, the specificity of its Caribbean historical, political, cultural and economic roots has been erased. This erasure has significant implications for the reproduction of unequal power relations between those who are 'at home' in the West and those who are in some way uprooted. A generic and dislocated notion of creolization denies the very rootedness that has enabled Caribbean 'creole' cultures to recreate homes away from home in the face of colonial dislocation and racial terror. Such global theory is oblivious to (or purposefully disavowing of) the relevance of (post)-colonial positioning, and is thus incapable of locating any grounding for a subaltern decolonizing politics.

In retracing the migrations of this theoretical concept out of the Caribbean I hope to have contributed to a renewed interest in the Caribbean not merely as an object of study, but also as a place from which important postcolonial theories of home, migration and mobility have originated. If we pay greater attention not to mobility in general but to specific practices of cultural travel and transportation, border crossing and return, symbolic visas and restrictions on movement, we can remember the structural parameters of uprootings and regroundings in different times and places. If some borders are dissolving in the 'world in creolization', it should not go without saying that others are being kept in place. It matters who is speaking, where they have come from, where they are going and who has stayed put in order to enable their movements (cf. Ahmed 2000 and Kaplan, this volume). In returning to the Caribbean roots of the concept of creolization and tracing its specific social and political itineraries, we might recover the political meanings and subaltern agency that have been barred entry by the free-floating gatekeepers of 'global' culture.

Acknowledgements

An earlier version of this chapter was presented as a paper at the conference 'Rethinking Caribbean Culture', June 2001, at the University of the West Indies, Cave Hill, Barbados, whose participants I thank for their comments. I also want to thank all of the co-editors of this volume for their comments. Research for this chapter was supported in part by the Arts and Humanities Research Board.

Notes

1. This chapter arises out of a larger project exploring the ways in which the Caribbean has been consumed in Europe and North America (Sheller 2003).
2. The gesture toward rootlessness brings with it unacknowledged locational privileges much in the way that critical race theorists have argued 'whiteness' operates as an unmarked yet dominant position in racial discourses (Dyer 1997; Frankenberg 1993).
3. The focus here will be on the concept of creolization alone, rather than on the full panoply of possible terms, in order to avoid conflation and the loss of historically specific usage.
4. Between 1950 and 1980, 'about 4 million persons left the Caribbean to establish permanent residence elsewhere . . . [representing] 5 to 10 percent of the total population of nearly every Caribbean society, a higher proportion [of migrants] than for any other world area' (Chaney 1987: 8–9; Castles and Miller 1998).
5. For debates on the origins and meanings of the term 'creole' see Shepherd and Richards 2002; Balutansky and Sourieau 1998; Mintz and Price 1992 [1976].
6. The conflation of human and animal not only is typical of the dehumanization of enslaved people, but also hints at the conceptual entanglements of notions of biological, cultural and 'racial' hybridization (cf. Young 1995).
7. The conflictual relation between creole and indigenous cultures in the Caribbean is beyond the scope of this chapter (see for example Hulme 2000; and Moreton-Robinson in Chapter 1 of this volume, on the indigenous relation to place in Australia).

8. Fortier (Chapter 5 in this volume) inspired the idea of 'homing' as a verb.
9. Prevalent studies of migration from the periphery to the metropolitan centre have been at the expense of the equally important movement of people between different Caribbean locations. Such migrations produce distinctive kinds of local cultural interchange and hybridization, which are ignored in 'global' theories (Puri, forthcoming).
10. My analysis is informed by efforts to articulate a feminist postcolonial 'politics of location' (for example Frankenberg and Mani 1993; Alexander and Mohanty 1997).
11. Brathwaite spent time living in England, Ghana, Jamaica and the United States, where he currently holds a chair in poetry at New York University.
12. Nettleford was a founder of and has long been artistic director of the Jamaican National Dance Theatre Company, which exemplifies the effort to establish an indigenous, decolonized and *national* creative arts. More recently he has served as Vice-Chancellor of the University of the West Indies.
13. It is worth noting that creolization theories enact a particular kind of *masculine* nationalist politics, which forecloses certain other questions of gender and 'race'. Significant work remains to be done on the sexual/racial politics of (de)colonization in which women's bodies are the grounds upon which claims to 'mixed' identities have been staked, in both nationalist and post-nationalist versions. For some starting points in the investigation of nationalisms and sexualities in the Caribbean see Kutzinski 1993; Alexander 1997; Mohammed 1998; and Findlay 1999.

References

Ahmed, S. (2000), *Strange Encounters: Embodied Others in Post-coloniality*, London and New York: Routledge.
Alexander, M.J. (1997), 'Erotic Autonomy as a Politics of Decolonization: An Anatomy of Feminist and State Practices in the Bahamas Tourist Economy', in M.J. Alexander and C.T. Mohanty (eds), *Feminist Genealogies, Colonial Legacies, Democratic Futures*, London and New York: Routledge.
Alexander, M.J. and Mohanty, C.T. (1997), *Feminist Genealogies, Colonial Legacies, Democratic Futures*, London and New York: Routledge.

Allen, C. (2002), 'Creole: The Problem of Definition', in V. Shepherd and G. Richards (eds), *Questioning Creole: Creolization Discourses in Caribbean Culture*, Kingston: Ian Randle, London: James Currey.

Aravamudan, S. (1999), *Tropicopolitans: Colonialism and Agency, 1688–1804*, Durham, NC: Duke University Press.

Balutansky, K. and Sourieau, M.A. (eds) (1998), *Caribbean Creolization: Reflections on the Cultural Dynamics of Language, Literature and Identity*, Gainesville: University Press of Florida and Kingston: University of the West Indies Press.

Basch, L., Glick Schiller, N. and Szanton Blanc, C. (1994), *Nations Unbound: Transnational Projects, Postcolonial Predicaments, and Deterritorialized Nation-States*, Amsterdam: Gordon and Breach.

Bauman, Z. (2000), *Liquid Modernity*, Cambridge: Polity.

Beck, U. (2000), *What is Globalization?* London: Polity.

Benítez-Rojo, A. (1996), *The Repeating Island: The Caribbean and the Postmodern Perspective*, trans. J. Maraniss, Durham, NC and London: Duke University Press [*La isla que se repite. El Caribe y la perspectiva postmoderna*, Ediciones del Norte, 1989].

Bhabha, H. (1994), *The Location of Culture*, London and New York: Routledge.

Bolland, N. (1992), 'Creolization and Creole Societies: A Cultural Nationalist View of Caribbean Social History', in A. Hennessey (ed.), *Intellectuals in the Twentieth-Century Caribbean*, Vol. I, London: Macmillan.

Brathwaite, E.K. (1971), *The Development of Creole Society in Jamaica 1770–1820*, Oxford: Clarendon Press.

—— (1974), *Contradictory Omens: Cultural Diversity and Integration in the Caribbean*, Mona, Jamaica: Savacou.

Burton, R. (1997), *Afro-Creole: Power, Opposition and Play in the Caribbean*, Ithaca and London: Cornell University Press.

Campbell, H. (1987), *Rasta and Resistance: From Marcus Garvey to Walter Rodney*, Trenton: Africa World Press.

Castles, S. and Miller, M. (1998), *The Age of Migration: International Population Movement in the Modern World*, 2nd edn, Basingstoke, Hanover: Macmillan.

Chamberlain, M. (ed.) (1998), *Caribbean Migration: Globalised Identities*, London: Routledge.

Chaney, E. (1987), 'The Context of Caribbean Migration', in C. Sutton and E. Chaney (eds), *Caribbean Life in New York City: Sociocultural Dimensions*, New York: Center for Migration Studies of New York.

Clifford, J. (1988), 'A Politics of Neologism: Aimé Césaire', in J. Clifford,

The Predicament Of Culture: Twentieth-Century Ethnography, Literature and Art, Cambridge, MA: Harvard University Press.

—— (1989), 'Notes on Theory and Travel', in J. Clifford and V. Dhareshwar (eds), 'Traveling Theory, Traveling Theorists', *Inscriptions*, 5: 177–88.

—— (1992), 'Travelling Cultures' in L. Grossberg et al. (eds), *Cultural Studies*, New York and London: Routledge.

—— (1997), *Routes: Travel and Translation in the Late Twentieth Century*, Cambridge, MA: Harvard University Press.

Clifford, J. and Dhareshwar, V. (eds) (1989), *Traveling Theory, Traveling Theorists, Inscriptions*, 5, Santa Cruz: Group for the Critical Study of Colonial Discourse and the Center for Cultural Studies.

Duval, D. (2002), 'The Return Visit-Return Migration Connection', in C. Hall and A. Williams (eds), *Tourism and Migration*, Dordrecht, Boston, London: Kluwer Academic.

Dyer, R. (1997), *White*, London and New York: Routledge.

Featherstone, M. (1995), *Undoing Culture: Globalization, Postmodernism and Identity*, London: Sage.

Findlay, E.S. (1999), *Imposing Decency: The Politics of Sexuality and Race in Puerto Rico, 1870–1920*, Durham, NC and London: Duke University Press.

Foner, N. (1998), 'Towards a Comparative Perspective on Caribbean Migration', in M. Chamberlain (ed.), *Caribbean Migration: Globalised Identities*, London: Routledge.

Frankenberg, R. (1993), *White Women, Race Matters: The Social Construction of Whiteness*, Minneapolis: University of Minnesota Press.

—— and Mani, L. (1993), 'Crosscurrents, Crosstalk: Race, "Postcoloniality" and the Politics of Location', *Cultural Studies*, 7(2).

Georges, E. (1990), *The Making of a Transnational Community: Migration, Development and Cultural Change in the Dominican Republic*, New York: Columbia University Press.

Gilroy, P. (1993), *The Black Atlantic: Modernity and Double Consciousness*, London: Verso.

—— (2000), *Between Camps: Nations, Cultures and the Allure of Race*, London: Penguin.

Glissant, E. (1981), *Le Discours Antillais*, Paris: Editions du Seuil [English translation: J.M. Dash, (ed.), *Caribbean Discourse*, Charlottesville: University of Virginia Press, 1992].

—— (1998), 'Créolization du Monde', in J.C. Ruano-Borbalon (ed.), *L'Identité: L'Individu, le Groupe, la Société*, Auxerre: Sciences Humaines Editions.

Gmelch, G. (1992), *Double Passage: The Lives of Caribbean Migrants Abroad and Back Home*, Ann Arbor: University of Michigan Press.

Hall, S. (1990), 'Cultural Identity and Diaspora', in J. Rutherford (ed.), *Identity: Community, Culture, Difference*, London: Lawrence & Wishart.

—— (1996), 'When was "The Post-Colonial"? Thinking at the Limit', in I. Chambers and L. Curti (eds), *The Post-Colonial Question*, London and New York: Routledge.

Hannerz, U. (1987), 'The world in creolization', *Africa*, 57(4): 546–59.

—— (1989), 'Culture between Center and Periphery: Toward a Macro-anthropology', *Ethnos*, 54(3/4): 200–16.

—— (1996), *Transnational Connections: Culture, People, Places*, London: Routledge.

—— (2000), 'Flows, Boundaries and Hybrids: Keywords in Transnational Anthropology', in A. Rogers (ed.), *Transnational Communities Programme Working Paper Series*, WPTC-2K-02.

Herskovits, M. (1964), *The Myth of the Negro Past*, New York: Octagon.

Higman, B. (1999), *Writing West Indian Histories*, London and Basingstoke: Macmillan.

hooks, b. (1992), 'Eating the Other', in b. hooks, *Black Looks: Race and Representation*, London: Turnaround.

Howes, D. (ed.) (1996), *Cross-cultural Consumption: Global Markets, Local Realities*, London and New York: Routledge.

Hulme, P. (2000), *Remnants of Conquest: The Island Carib and their Visitors, 1877–1998*, Oxford and New York: Oxford University Press.

Kaplan, C. (1996), 'Traveling Theorists: Cosmopolitan Diasporas', in C. Kaplan, *Questions of Travel: Postmodern Discourses of Displacement*, Durham, NC: Duke University Press.

Kutzinski, V. (1993), *Sugar's Secrets: Race and the Erotics of Cuban Nationalism*, Charlottesville: University of Virginia Press.

Lewis, G. (1990) 'Forward', in R. Palmer (ed.), *In Search of a Better Life: Perspectives on Migration from the Caribbean*, New York: Praegen.

Massey, D. (1999), 'Imagining Globalization: Power-geometries of Time-Space' in A. Brah, M. Hickman and M. Mac an Ghaill (eds) *Global Futures: Migration, Environment and Globalization*, Basingstoke and London: Macmillan.

Medea, L. (2002) 'Creolisation and Globalisation in a Neo-Colonial Context: the Case of Reunion', *Social Identities*, 8(1): 125–41.

Mercer, K. (1988), 'Diaspora Culture and the Dialogic Imagination: The Aesthetics of Black Independent Film in Britain', in M. Cham and C. Andrade-Watkins (eds), *Blackframes: Critical Perspectives on Black Independent Cinema*, Cambridge, MA: MIT Press.

Mintz, S. and Price, R. (1992 [1976]), *The Birth of African-American Culture: An Anthropological Perspective*, Boston: Beacon.

Mintz, S. and Price, S. (1985), *Caribbean Contours*, Baltimore and London: Johns Hopkins University Press.

Mohammed, P. (1998), 'Towards Indigenous Feminist Theorizing in the Caribbean', in 'Rethinking Caribbean Difference' issue of *Feminist Review*, 59: 6–33.

Nettleford, R. (1978), *Caribbean Cultural Identity: The Case of Jamaica, An Essay in Cultural Dynamics*, Kingston: Institute of Jamaica.

Ortiz, F. (1947), *Cuban Counterpoint: Tobacco and Sugar*, trans. Harriet de Onis, New York: A.A. Knopf [*Contrapunteo Cubano del tabaco y el azucar*, La Habana: J. Montero, 1940].

Pessar, P. (1997), 'New approaches to Caribbean migration and return', in P. Pessar (ed.), *Caribbean Circuits: New Directions in the Study of Caribbean Migration*, New York: Center for Migration Studies.

Pratt, M. (1992), *Imperial Eyes: Travel Writing and Transculturation*, London and New York: Routledge.

Puri, S. (2003), *The Caribbean Postcolonial: Post/Nationalism, Social Equality and Cultural Hybridity*, London and New York: Palgrave/St Martin's.

—— (ed.) (forthcoming), *Marginal Migrations: The Circulation of Cultures Within the Caribbean*, London and Oxford: Macmillan.

Retamar, R. (1989), *Caliban and Other Essays*, trans. Edward Baker, Minneapolis: University of Minnesota Press.

Rex, J. and Mason, D. (1986), *Theories of Race and Ethnic Relations*, Cambridge: Cambridge University Press.

Richards, G. (2001), 'Kamau Brathwaite and the Creolization of History in the Anglophone Caribbean', unpublished paper.

Richardson, B. (1983), *Caribbean Migrants: Environment and Human Survival on St. Kitts and Nevis*, Knoxville: University of Tennessee Press.

Robertson, R. (1992), *Globalization: Social Theory and Global Culture*, London: Sage.

Rodney, W. (1969), *The Groundings with my Brothers*, London: Bogle-L'Ouverture.

Said, E. (1983), 'Traveling Theory', in idem., *The World, the Text and the Critic*, Cambridge, MA: Harvard University Press.

Schiller, N.G., Basch, L., and Blanc-Szanton, C. (eds) (1992), *Towards a Transnational Perspective on Migration: Race, Class, Ethnicity and Nationalism Reconsidered*, New York: New York Academy of Sciences (Annals, 645).

Sheller, M. (2003) *Consuming the Caribbean: From Arawaks to Zombies*, London and New York: Routledge.

Shepherd, V. and Richards, G. (2002), *Questioning Creole: Creolization Discourses in Caribbean Culture*, Kingston: Ian Randle, London: James Currey.

Smith, M.G. (1965), *The Plural Society in the British West Indies*, Berkeley: University of California Press.

Spitta, S. (1997), 'Transculturation, the Caribbean, and the Cuban-American Imaginary', in F. Aparicio and S. Chávez-Silverman (eds), *Tropicalizations: Transcultural Representations of Latinidad*, Hanover, NH and London: University Press of New England.

Stacey, J. (2000), 'The Global Within', in Franklin, S., Lury, C. and Stacey, J. (eds), *Global Nature/Global Culture*, London: Sage.

Sutton, C. (1987), 'The Caribbeanization of New York City and the Emergence of a Transnational Socio-cultural System', in C. Sutton and E. Chaney (eds), *Caribbean Life in New York City: Sociocultural Dimensions*, New York: The Center for Migration Studies of New York.

Thomas, H. (2000), *Romanticism and Slave Narratives: Transnational Testimonies*, Cambridge and New York: Cambridge University Press.

Thomas-Hope, E. (1992) *Explanation in Caribbean Migration*, London: Macmillan.

—— (1995), 'Island Systems and the Paradox of Freedom: Migration in the Post-Emancipation Leeward Islands', in K. Fog Olwig (ed.), *Small Islands, Large Questions: Society, Culture and Resistance in the Post-Emancipation Caribbean*, London: Frank Cass.

Urry, J. (2000), *Sociology Beyond Societies: Mobilities for the Twenty-first Century*, London: Routledge.

Vergès, F. (2001), 'Vertigo and Emancipation, Creole Cosmopolitanism and Cultural Politics', *Theory, Culture & Society* 18(2–3): 169–83.

Young, R. (1995), *Colonial Desire: Hybridity in Theory, Culture and Race*, London and New York: Routledge.

Index

Abu Shayib, Suhair, 83
Adorno, Theodor, 212
Aer Lingus, 162
Ahmed, Sara, 61, 117, 128
 Strange Encounters, 100–1
Akenson, Donald, 159, 161, 164, 165,
 171
Alba, Richard, 184
Alexander, M.J., 6, 50, 51, 138, 141
alienation, 64
 from homeland, 11
'aliens', illegal
 see migration
Allen, Carolyn, 275–8
Allen, Peter, 24
Alund, A., 230
Anderson, Benedict, 138
Andreas, P., 255
androgyny, 149
Ang, Ien, 187–8
animism, 47
anthropology, 180–1
 cultural, 279
Antoni, Janine, 73
Anzaldúa, Gloria, 4–5, 51
assimilation, 45, 51, 53, 182–3, 185, 278
Attorney General of the Isle of Man v
 Mylchreest (1879), 35
Australia, 44–5
 British migrants, 23–6, 29
 dispossession, 23–5, 26, 27, 30
 immigrants
  assimilation, 45
  post-war, 49, 53
 Indigenous people, 11, 23–7, 28–31
  ancestral beings, 31–2
  belonging, 25, 27, 31–2
  land rights, 30, 31–3, 35–6
  'primitive', 42
  spirituality, 34

state policies, 33
 women's life histories, 33–5
non-white migrants, 26–8
postcolonial, 24, 30, 49
'postcolonizing', 30–1
settlers, 29, 30–1, 42, 46
white Australians, 11, 23–4, 27–8, 30,
 48

Bannerji, Kaushalya
 Lotus of Another Color, 149
belonging, 1, 3, 4, 12–13
 communities and, 14, 91–4, 96–9, 103,
  106
 Indigenous, 25, 27, 31–2
 Irish, 162, 171
 model of, 104
 national, 139, 140
 non-belonging, 85
 racialized, 24, 25
 reimagining of, 107
Benítez-Rojo, Antonio, 275
Bergson, H., 123
Bhabha, Homi, 29, 280
Bhabha, Jacqueline, 243
Bhattacharjee, Anannya, 140
blackness
 Irish ancestry and, 185–6
black women
 family life and, 8–9
bodies
 absent, 72, 74–5, 81, 83
 as data, 218
 female, 91–4
  communities and, 94–100, 101
  in Western art, 68
 physical residue, 72
 place and, 61
 see also Hatoum, Mona; Rabah, Khalil
Bolland, Nigel, 281

Index

Brah, Avtar, 101, 115–17, 129–31
Brathwaite, Kamau, 279, 281, 283–4
Brazil
  shanty towns, 102–3
Brescia City municipalities, 257, 262
British Empire, 24, 25, 29
  Ireland and, 158, 164–5, 166
British migrants
  Australia, 23–6, 29
Brown, Wendy, 263
Buckley, Sandra, 44
Burton, Richard, 281

Chaplin, Charlie, 83
Cant, Bob
  Invented Identities? Lesbians and Gays Talk About Migration, 120–1, 121, 123, 124
capital, 2
  accumulation of, 25
capitalism, 212
  technoscience and, 213
Capone, Giovanna (Janet), 125
Cappello, Mary, 130–1
  Night Bloom, 125–9
Caribbean
  creolization and, 273, 278–83
  cultural identity, 285
  diaspora, 281–3
  independence movements 278–83
  migration, 275–8
  theorists, 278–83
Caritas, 253, 257, 262
  Migration Dossier 1999, 263
carriers' liability, 235, 239, 240
Cartesian vision, 212
Cassandra, 53
centre-periphery relationship
  creolization and, 283–5
Césaire, Aimé, 285
Chambers, Iain, 29
Chamoiseau, Patrick
  see Confiant, Raphael, and Chamoiseau, Patrick
Chaney, Elsa, 277
Chicano/a culture, 4–5, 51
Chinese transnational subjects, 4
citizenship
  American, 185

European, 227, 233
gendered, 96
homosexuality and, 139
mobile, 229
civil-rights movement, 182
Clifford, James, 208, 209
  'Traveling Cultures', 285
Clitheroe, Jean, 122
Cockburn, Cynthia, 103, 105
colonization, 15, 23–4
  histories of, 7
  narrative of, 28
  see also British Empire; Empire
'coming out', 12, 13, 115–17, 119, 129
  narrative, 137, 144, 146
communication technologies, 209, 213, 217
  see also telephone
communities, 4, 12, 184
  belonging and, 14, 91–4, 96–9, 103, 106
  conflict and, 91–4
  imagined, 99, 101, 104
  scattered, 63
Confiant, Raphael, and Chamoiseau, Patrick
  Élogé de la créolité, 276
Corrin, Chris, 121–2
cosmopolitanism
  mobility and, 4
'creole' cultures, 275–6
creolization, 15
  appropriation of, 274, 283–7
  Caribbean culture and, 278–80
  conflict and, 280–3
  diaspora and 281–3
  global culture and, 273–5, 283–6
  independence movements and, 279–83
  the metropolis and, 278
  theorization of, 278–83, 286, 287
cribs
  in Palestinian art, 72–5, 83
cross-dressing, 145, 147, 149, 150
cross-gender identification, 144–6, 149
cultural
  mixing, 283–6
  purity, 186–7
customary law, 24–5
cyberphilia, 210–15

Index

cyberspace, 209, 210, 216, 218
  'hi-tech Hegelianism', 215
  race and, 219
  rhetoric of, 211
cyborg, 219
Czech Republic, visa policies, 255

Darwish, Mahmoud, 59, 84
decolonization
  histories of, 7
  see also Caribbean independence
    movements
Deleuze, Gilles, and Guattari, F.
  'What is a Minor Literature?', 43–4
De Morgan, 236, 237, 238
deportation, 231, 259, 260
Derrida, Jacques
  writing and speech, 42
diaspora, 7–8, 28, 145
  Caribbean, 281–3
  Irish, 13, 157–9, 161, 163, 184
  cultural belonging, 171
  language and, 52
  queers and, 117–18, 120–1, 125, 128
Dielectrokinetic Laboratories (DKL),
  225–6, 239–43
difference
  cultural, 183, 191–2
Differenza Donna, 253
digital transfers, 215–18
Dir Yasin massacre, 66, 68, 70
'Dis-Orientalism', 63
displacement, 6, 61, 211
  forced, 101–2
dispossession, 11
  in Australia, 23–5, 26, 27, 30
Doezema, J., 263
double consciousness, 120
double-life model, 120
drag
  see cross-dressing
Duval, D., 277

electricity
  cultural effects of, 216
embodiment, 12, 32, 214, 219
  communication technologies and, 217
  gendered, 217
  of home and migration, 11

see also Palestinian artists
Empire, 24, 25
  Ireland and, 166
    collaboration, 164–5
  Irish, 158–9
Engbersen, B., 230–1
Eng, David, 115–17, 119, 128
Enlightenment, 211, 212
Enstad, Nan, 220
essentialism, 32
ethnicity
  assimilation and, 185
  conflict and, 103, 105
  genealogy and, 181–8
  homosexuality and, 125–6, 129
  minorities, 230–1
  'ethnic revival', 182
European
  citizenship, 227, 233
European Economic Community, 228
European Renaissance, 212
European Summit, 254
European Union
  asylum policies, 238
  border controls, 4–5, 226, 228–31,
    233–4, 239–43, 251, 255–6
  private enterprise and, 235, 238
  see also LifeGuard
  borderlessness, 14–15, 232–3
  enlargement, 255–6
  external borders, 232–4, 254–6
  migration and, 184, 227
  migration policies, 235, 237, 254, 255
  see also Shengen Agreement
exile, 11, 61, 63, 137
External Frontiers Convention, 232

family, 12, 13
  dislocated, 71
  histories, 183, 184, 194–5
  patronymic
    loss of, 45
  trees, 13, 105, 179, 181, 194, 196
    ethnicity and, 186
  values, 150–1
  see also home
Fanon, Frantz, 45, 60, 85
  Black Skin, White Masks, 79
Featherstone, Mike, 273

Index

Federation of Indian Associations (FIA),
140–1
feminism, 3
  transnational, 6
feminists
  black, 8
  geographers, 5
  theorists, 7, 52–3, 91–4
Filipino communities, 145
Fire, 137, 147, 148–9, 150, 151
Ford, 225–6
'Fortress Europe', 226, 254
Foucault, Michel, 95, 96
  power and, 93–4, 97, 99–100
  'What is Enlightenment, 93
Frankfurt School, 212
Freud, Sigmund
  cultural marginality, 45
  'The Uncanny', 47, 48

Gallery Anadiel, 81, 87n17
Gattull, F., 257
Gelder, Ken, and Jane Jacobs
  *Uncanny Australia, Sacredness and
    Identity in a Postcolonial Nation*,
    29–30
gender, 5, 6, 83, 98, 99, 143–4, 146
gendered
  relations of power, 257
Genealogical Office, 190
'genealogical tourism', 13–14
genealogy, 12, 13–14
  culture and, 188
  female, 104–6
  geography and, 179–82
  inheritance and, 181, 183, 187, 189
  people as resource, 191–3
  political implications, 188
  race and, 182–8
  relationships and, 194–8
  return of descendants, 188–93
  technology and, 195–8
geography
  genealogy and, 179–82
Gilroy, Paul, 122–3, 279, 282
Giroux, Henry, 53
Glissant, Edouard
  'Créolization du Monde', 282
globalization, 2, 3, 14, 15, 184, 212, 242–3

creolization and, 273–5, 283–4
migration and, 257
of Ireland, 163, 173
Gold Rush, The, 83
Grace, Patricia
  Baby No-Eyes, 49–50
grafting, 78
Gray, Breda, 107
Guattari, G.
  see Deleuze, Gilles, and Guattari, F.
Guttman, Freda
  Cassandra: An Opera in Four Acts, 44

Hage, Gassan, 131
Hall, Stuart, 28, 279, 282–4
Hannerz, Ulf
  'The World in Creolization', 283–5
Haraway, Donna, 213, 214, 242–3
Hatoum, Mona, 61, 83, 85–6
  biography, 62–4
  Changing Parts, 64–6, 65
  Corps étranger, 68–70, 69
  Entrails Carpet, 68
  First Step, 73–5
  Incommunicado, 72, 73
  Jardin Public, 72
  Marrow, 73, 75
  Measures of Distance, 70–2
  Silence, 73, 74
  Socle du Monde, 68
  The Negotiating Table, 66, 67
  Under Siege, 64–6
Hayles, N. Katherine, 214, 242–3
Hegarty, Fran, 166–7
Hegelianism, 215
heterosexuality, 13
  home and, 115–16, 129–31
  the nation and, 138–9, 161
history
  memory and, 157–8, 165
Hoffman, Eva, 9, 46
  'The Sandman', 47
Hogue, Cavan, 25–6
Hom, A.Y., 128
home, 1, 9, 10–15, 66, 116
  arrival, 118–19
  belonging and, 1, 12–13
  childhood and, 120–4
  diaspora and, 7–8, 144–5

Index

Index

Makimoto, Tsugio, 219
Malkki, Liisa, 227
Malouf, David
  Remembering Babylon, 42–3, 53
Manalansan, Martin, 145, 149
Manners, D., 219
Mansour, Sliman, 61, 85–6
  Hagar, 59, 60
  Heart, 60, 61
Manzoni, Piero, 68
Marlatt, Daphne, 52
Marvin, Carolyn, 216
massacres
  in refugee camps, 66, 68
maternal body, 70–2
  denial of, 104, 105
McAleese, Mary, 172–3
McClelland, Liz, 166
McClintock, Anne, 138
McNeil, Kent, 35
medical gaze, 68–70
medicine, 81
Mehta, Deepa, 137, 147
memory, 9–10, 47, 163
  history and, 157–8, 165
  home and, 123–4, 128
  Irish, 162
  mass media and, 157
  migration and, 137
  personal, 165
memory work, 163
Mercer, Kobena, 283
migration, 1–3, 10–15, 61, 229
  a modernizing activity, 163
  as crisis, 254
  as homecoming, 119
  Caribbean, 275–8
  constructions of, 163
  diaspora and, 7–8
  fatalities, 236–7, 238, 255
  feminism and, 3–7
  illegal, 14, 231, 234, 254, 256
    marketable, 244
  memory and, 137
  postcolonial theory and, 28–31
  queer, 8, 12–13
    home and, 117–20, 124, 128, 129–32
    narratives of, 115–17, 118, 122
  removal and, 14, 33, 235, 240, 241

route, 236–7
women, 100–1
  see also prostitution
  see also Australia; Irish migration
mobility, 1, 2, 7, 14
  cyberphilia, 210–15
  displacement and, 216
  identity and, 221
  in Europe, 233
  location and, 212, 219, 220
  of labour, 211
modernity, 211, 212
Mohanty, C.T., 6
Molz, Jennie Germann, 116
Monette, Paul
  Half-Way Home, 118
Morgan, Sally
  My Place, 34
Morokvasic, Mirjana, 97, 98
Moroli, E. and Sigona, R.
  *Schiave d'occidente: sulle rotte dei
    mercanti di donne*, 253
Morris, Barry, 34–5
mother-daughter relationship, 70, 71, 105,
  121–2
mothering
  discourse of, 102–3
motions of attachment, 130–2
movement
  differentiated histories, 7
  see migration; mobility
multiculturalism, 185
  in Australia, 26, 28
  personal, 187

Nannup, Alice
  When the Pelican Laughs, 34
nation, the
  nostalgia and, 138, 139
  sexuality and, 137–40
National Archives, 190
nationalism
  gender and, 138
  heterosexuality and, 146
  Indian, 13
nationalist
  discourse, 98–9, 150
  women and, 137–8
  narratives, 143

Index

Index

racial
  practices, 231–2
  tension, 230
Racial Discrimination Act (1975), 35
racialization
  of Irish, 184–5
Rank, Otto, 84
rape, 97–8
Read, Peter
  Belongings: Australians, Place and Aboriginal Ownership, 26–7
refugee camps, 101
  massacres in, 66, 68
refugee centres, 226
refugees, 27–8, 226–7, 229, 233, 234
  collection of stories, 240
  women, 231
religion, 81
removal of migrants, 14, 33, 235, 240, 241
repression, 47
resistance, 93–4
Rodney, Walter, 282
Rodriguez, Richard
  memoirs, 51–2
Rogoff, Irit, 84–5
rootedness, 61
RootsWeb WorldConnect, 195
Ryanair, 162

Sabra refugee camp, 66, 68
'Safe Third Country' rule, 255
Said, Edward, 63–4, 66
  'Traveling Theory', 208–9
Sakhi for South Asian Women, 140–1
Sassen, Saskia, 243, 254
Saussurian
  parole and *langue*, 46
Schengen Agreement, 228, 229, 232–3, 254
  'carriers' liability, 235, 239, 240
Schengen Information System, 233–4
'Schengen space', 226
Scheper-Hughes, Nancy
  Death Without Weeping, 102–3
Schiave d'occidente: sulle rotte dei mercanti di donne, 262–3
Schimel, Lawrence, 119, 120
science and medicine, 213
secret (*heimlich*), 47

self, the, 46, 79, 80, 210
self-knowledge, 212
Selvadruai, Shyam
  Funny Boy, 137, 145–6, 151
  'Pigs Can't Fly', 143–4
settler societies
  Australia, 29, 30–1, 42
sex industry, 231
sexuality, 71
  the nation and, 137–40
  see also queer sexuality
Sexual Offenses and Domestic Violence Act
  Bahamas, 139
sexual violence, 94, 237
sex workers, 217, 218, 231, 257–8
Shakespeare, Tom, 122
Shapira, Sarit, 84–5
Shatila refugee camp, 66, 68
Shelley, Mary, 214
sight, 47, 212
Sigona, R.
  see Moroli, E. and Sigona, R.
Simoncini, A., 254–5
Sinfield, Alan, 117–19, 120, 123
'situated knowledge', 213–14
'slave trade', 257
smuggling networks, 236–7
  see also trafficking
social reproduction, 25–6
  see also women, reproductive work
Sørensen, Patsy, 237
South Asian femininity, 147–8
South Asian Lesbian and Gay Association (SALGA), 140–1, 145–6
South Asian popular culture, 142, 145
speech
  stammer, 44
Spivak, Gayatri Chakravorti, 43, 44
  'Can the Subaltern Speak?', 219
spot-checks, 230
Stafford, Barbara Maria, 213
Stallabrass, Julian, 215–16, 218
stammer, 42–3, 44, 53
stammering pedagogy, 53
stereotypes, 71, 79
Stone, Sandy, 217–18, 219
stop-and-search checks, 230
  race-based, 234
stowaways

Index

detection of, 225–6
removal of, 240, 241
see also LifeGuard
Straw, Jack, 238
stutter
see stammer
subaltern, 44, 279, 281
subject formation, 209
subjectivity, 33–4, 45, 46, 212
surveillance, 210
science and, 213
technology, 215, 218, 233–4, 238
Sutton, Constance, 277

Tamil-Sinhalese riots, 137
technologies, 214
communication, 209, 213, 217
genealogy and, 195–8
labour and, 220
limitless, 213
material relations and, 210–11
mobility and, 211, 212
surveillance, 215, 218, 233–4, 238
transport, 209, 210
visuality and, 213
technoscience, 213
telephone, 216–17
Terra Nullius, 24, 25, 35
tracking, 210
see also surveillance
traditional society, 71
trafficking, 14, 235–6, 251–2
as illegal migration, 259–60
portrayals of traffickers, 262–4
systems, 260–2
to Italy, 252–3
see also prostitution
transculturation, 273–4, 280
transformation, 210
transmigration, 277
transnationalism, 2, 3–5, 6, 14, 277, 283–4
transportation technologies, 209, 210
travel, 209, 211, 220
labour and, 219
subjectivity and, 212
theory and, 207–9
undocumented, 258–9
see also migration; mobility
Treaty of Rome, 228

'two-mindedness', 120

uncanny (*unheimlich*), 47, 48–9
unconscious, the, 48
United for Intercultural Action, 255
United States
companies, 225–6
Empire, 164–5, 166
Irish immigrants and, 182
Mexico and, 51

Van Gogh, Vincent, 81
Vauxhall, 225–6
violence
sexual, 94, 237
traffickers and, 263–4
visuality
technology and, 213

Walker, Michelle Boulous, 104–5
Ward, Glenyse
Wandering Girl, 34
Waters, Mary, 182–3
Weil, Simone, 76–7
white Australia policy, 25–6
White, Edmund
A Boy's Own Story, 144
whiteness, 29, 38n3
the Irish and, 184–7
white sovereignty, 28
Wijers, M., 251, 260–1
Williams, Mary, 167–72
Williams, Raymond, 212
wireless telecommunication, 216
women
alliances, 103–4
disembowelled, 66, 68
employment and, 217, 220
exploitation, 263
positioning of, 91, 104
power and, 94–6, 97
refugees, 231
reproductive work, 96–7, 101–7
see also prostitution
writing
land and, 48
stammer, 44

Zeebrugge
LifeGuard and, 225–6, 227, 239–43